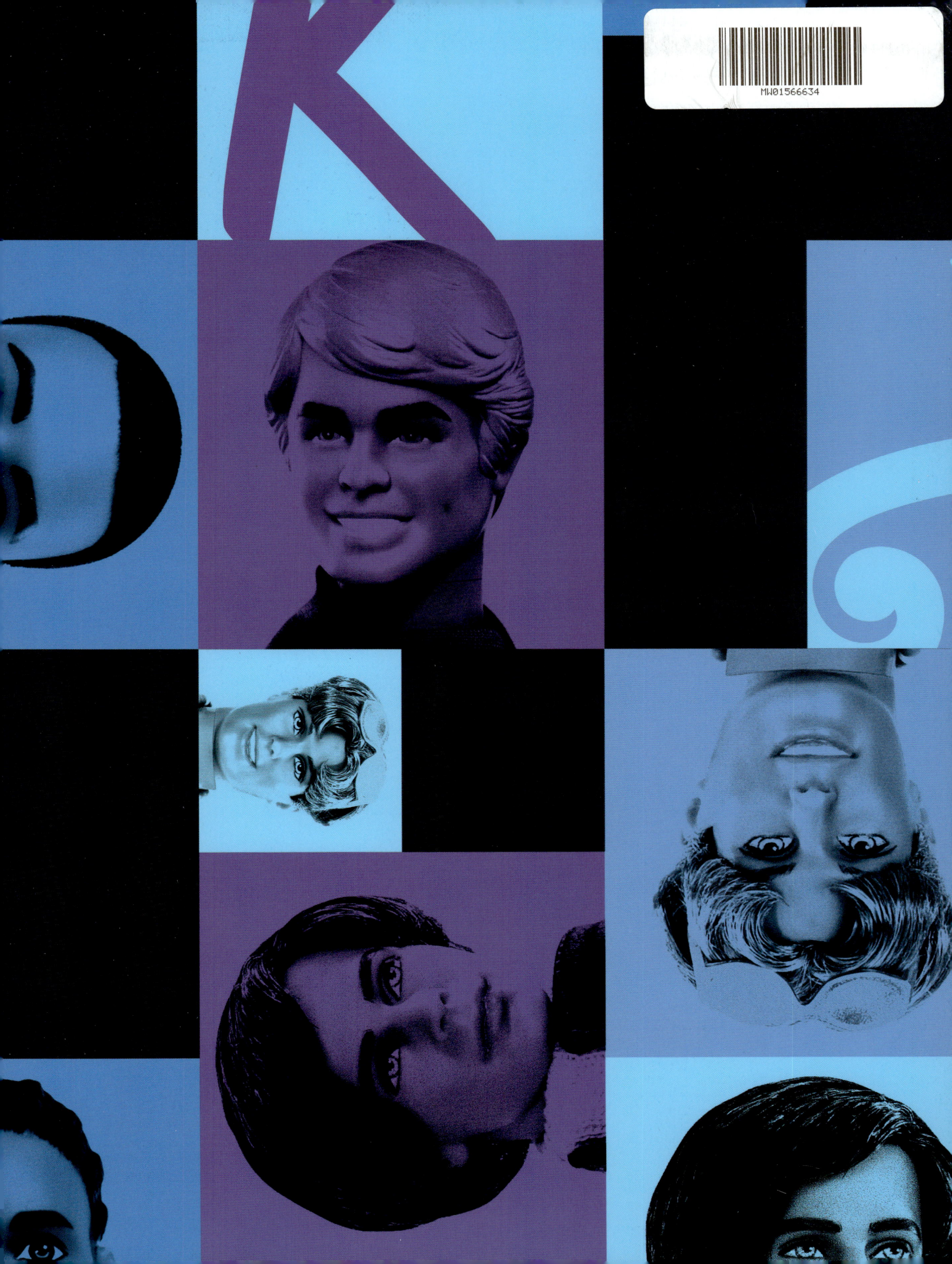

Massimiliano Capella

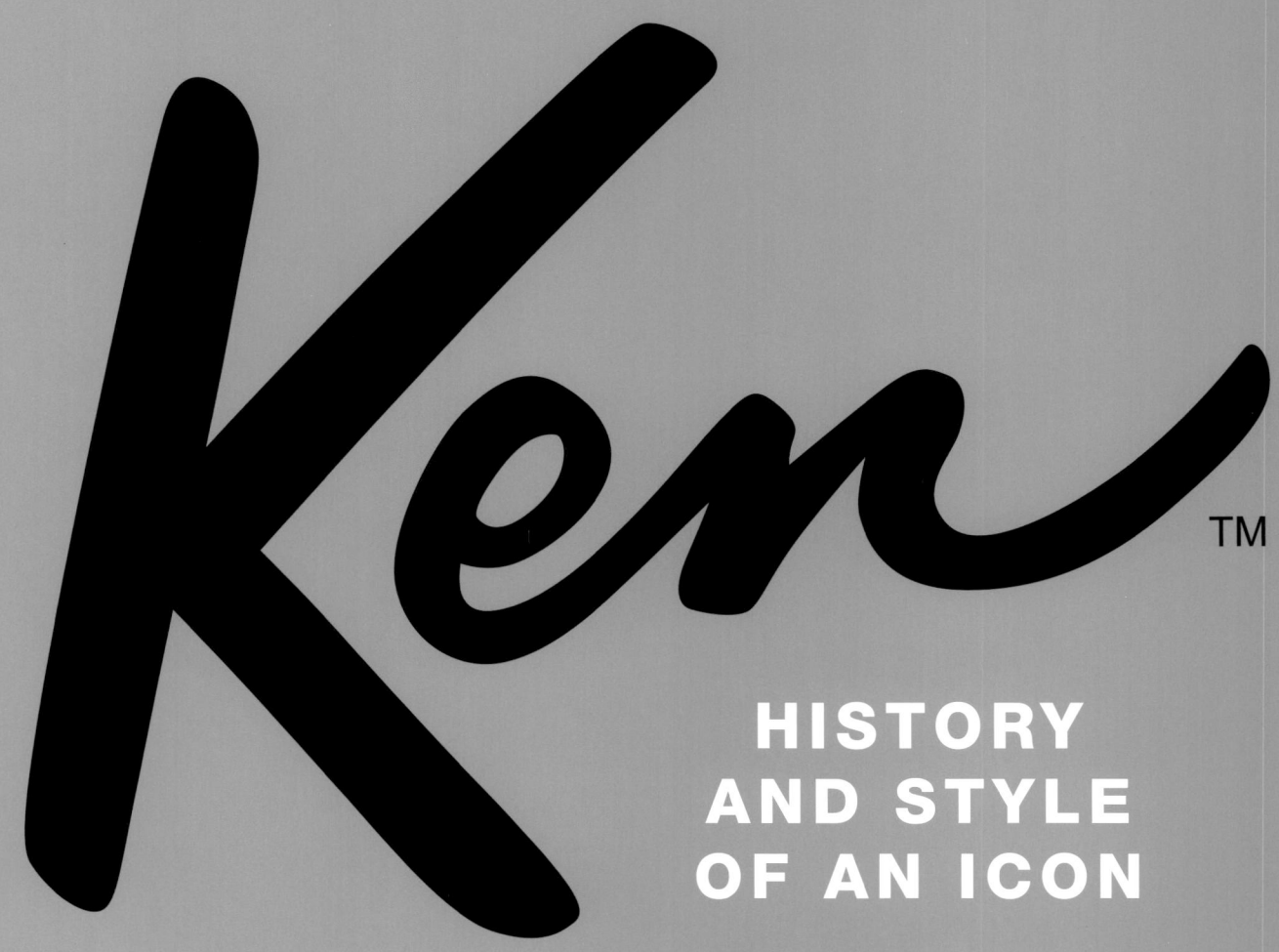

Ken™

HISTORY AND STYLE OF AN ICON

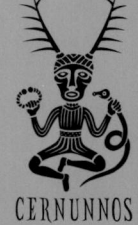

CERNUNNOS

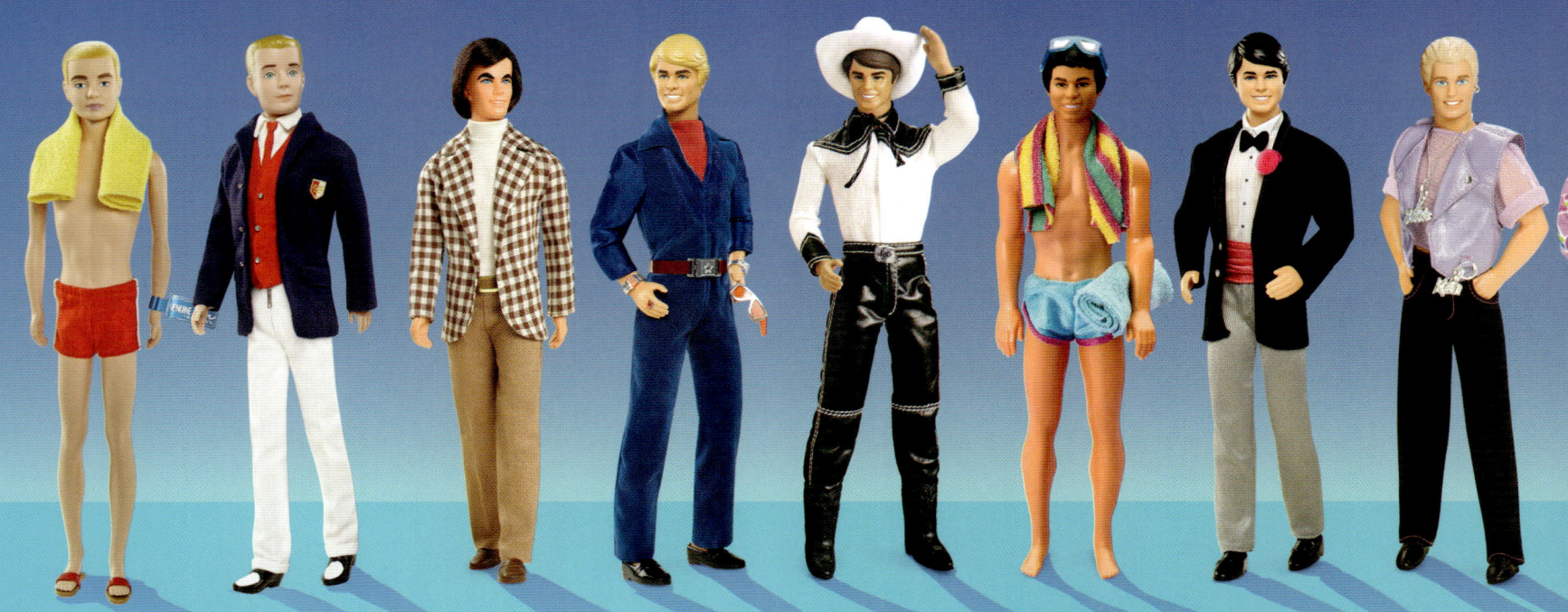

The evolution of Ken from the 1960s to today, from Barbie's friend to global icon.

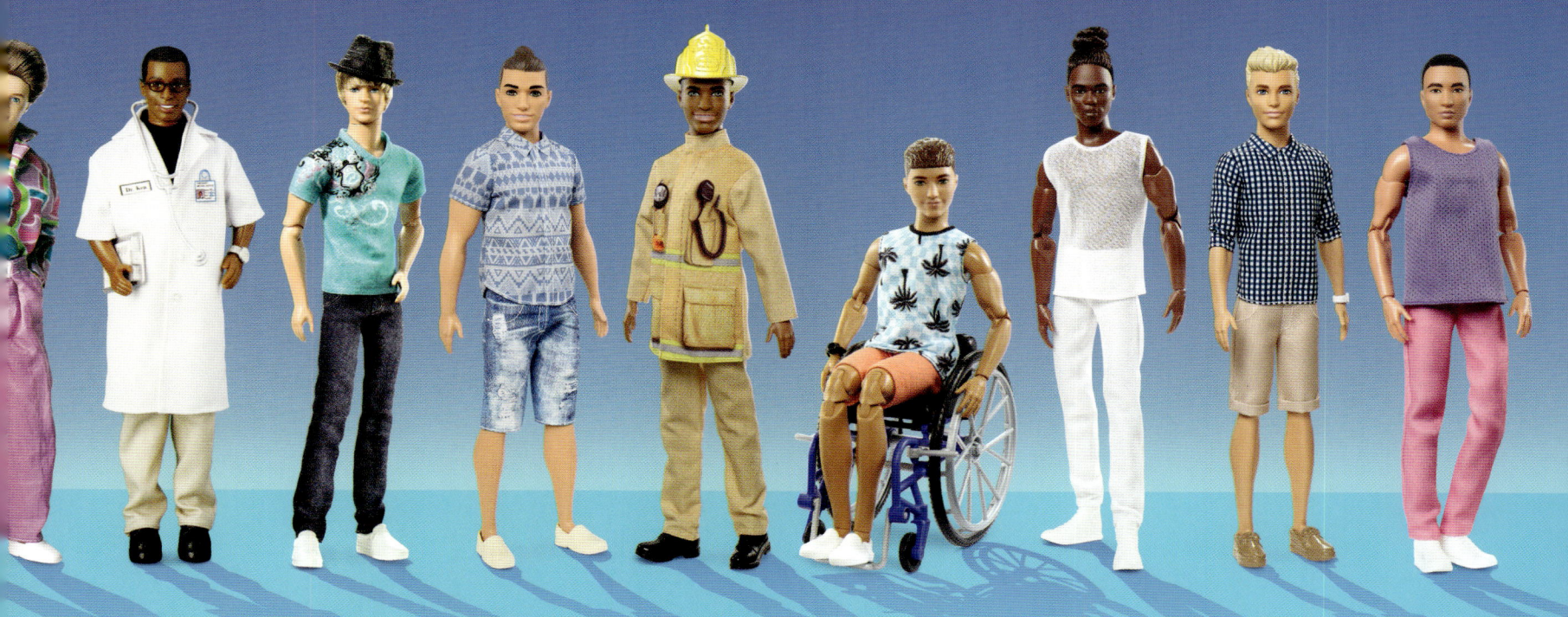

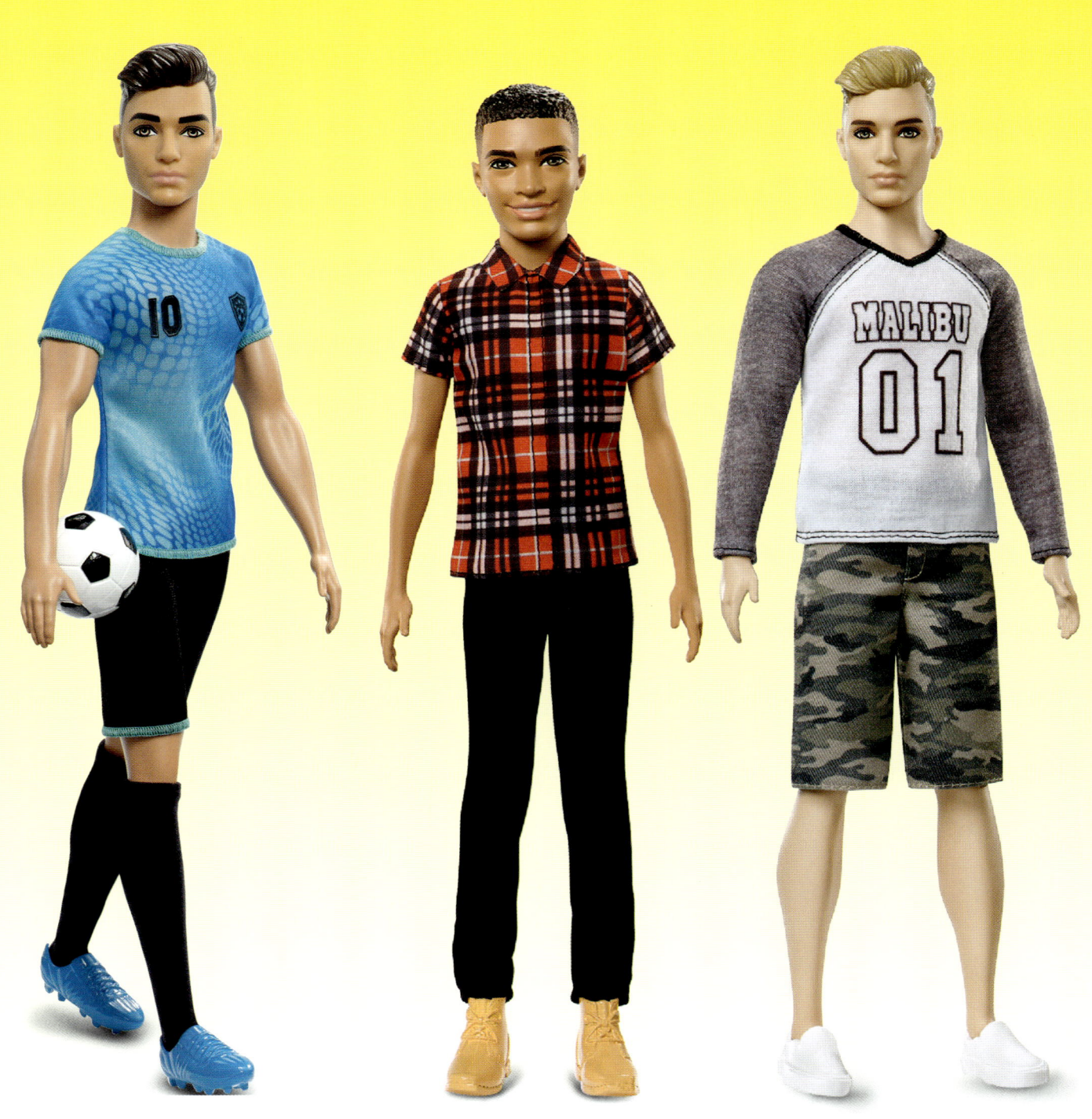

Ken and his most recent evolution from 2017 to 2023.

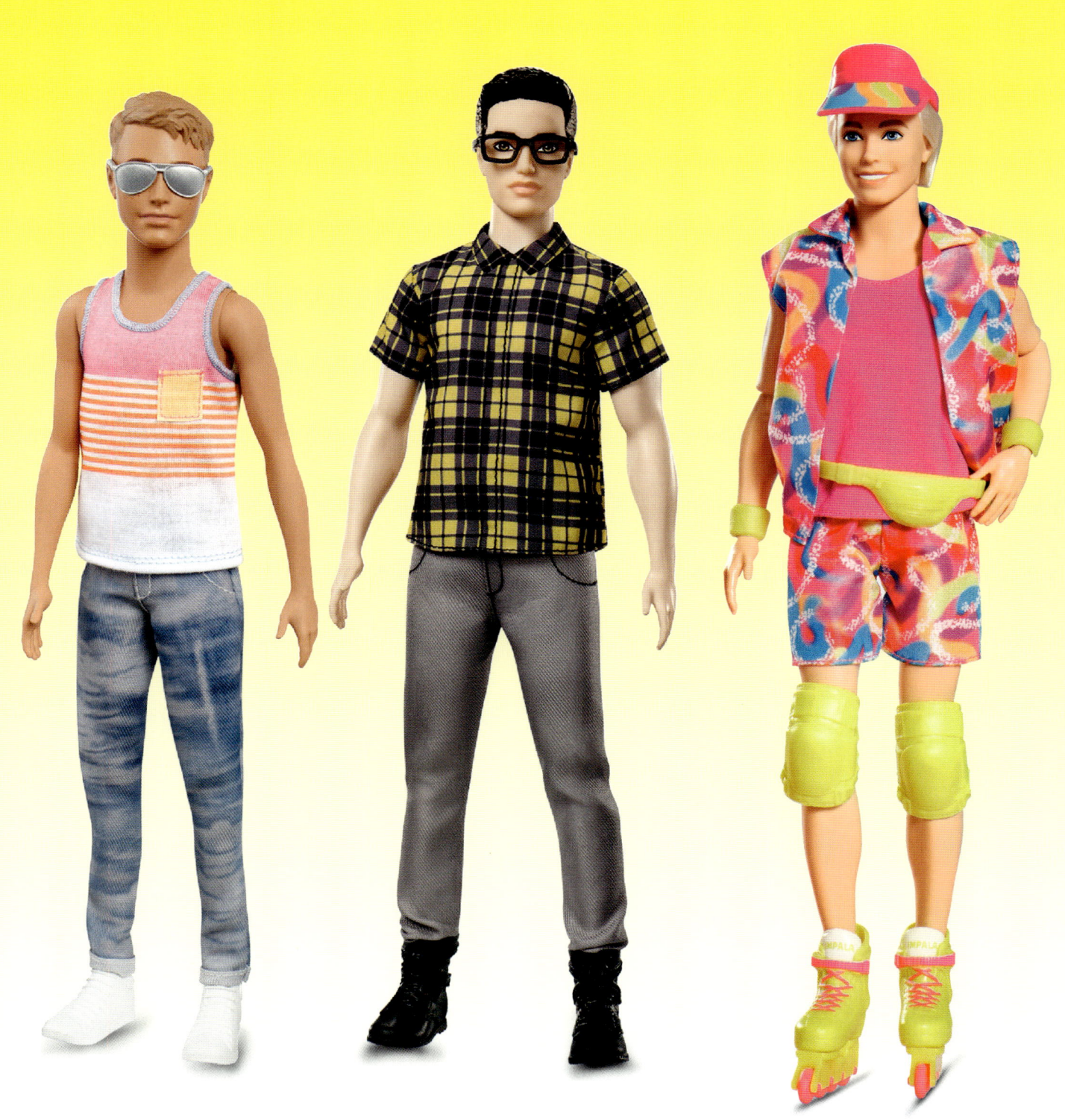

The Library of Congress Control Number has been requested from the Library of Congress.

ISBN: 978-1-4197-8459-0

Copyright © 2025 Mattel, Inc. All rights reserved.
Copyright © 2025 24 ORE Cultura S.r.l., Milano

Text by Massimiliano Capella
English translation by Antony Shugaar

Cover design © 2025 Abrams

Originally published in Italian in 2025 by 24 ORE Cultura Srl, Milano.

This edition published in 2025 by Cernunnos, an imprint of ABRAMS. All rights reserved. No portion of this book may be reproduced, stored in a retrieval system, or transmitted in any form or by any means, mechanical, electronic, photocopying, recording, or otherwise, without written permission from the publisher.

Printed and bound in China
10 9 8 7 6 5 4 3 2 1

Cernunnos books are available at special discounts when purchased in quantity for premiums and promotions as well as fundraising or educational use. Special editions can also be created to specification. For details, contact specialsales@abramsbooks.com or the address below.

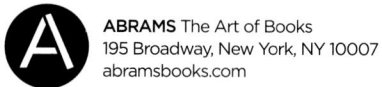

ABRAMS The Art of Books
195 Broadway, New York, NY 10007
abramsbooks.com

Barbie the Movie Ken, 2023.

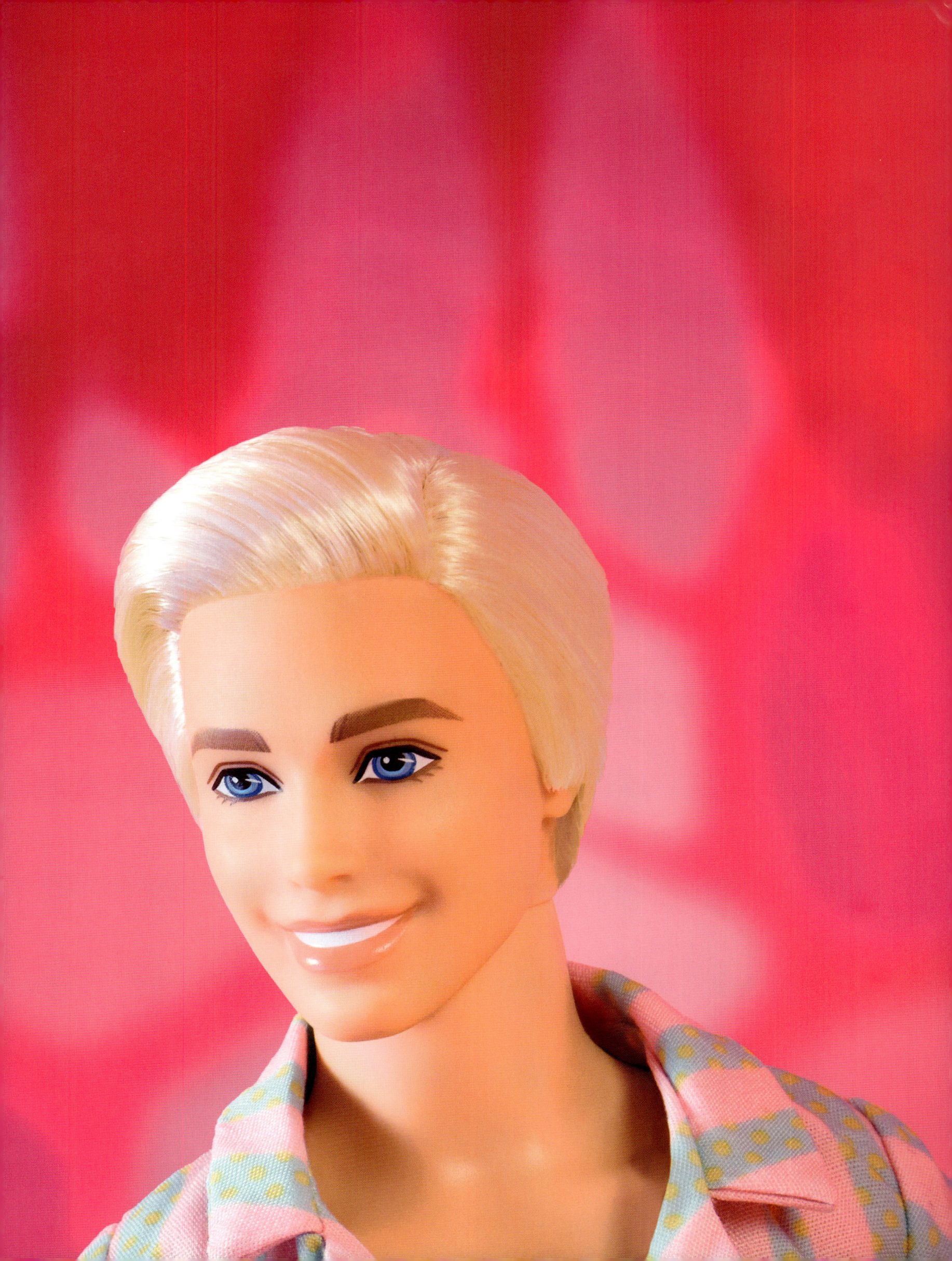

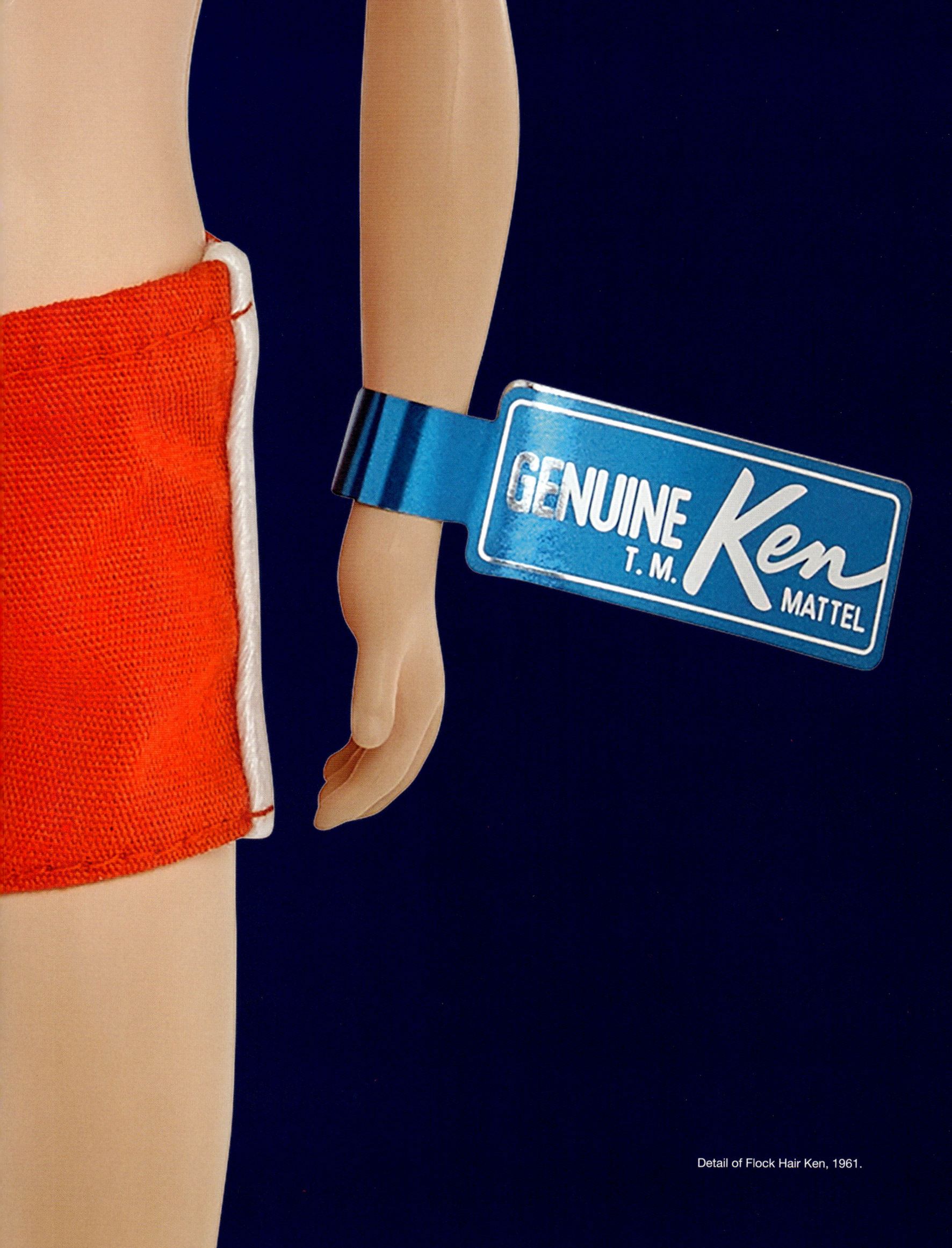

Detail of Flock Hair Ken, 1961.

CONTENTS

KEN 1961 — 11
THE ORIGINS OF THE MYTH

KEN'S EVOLUTION — 26

TIMELINE — 35
1961 – 2026

KEN—FUN FACTS — 110

KEN'S WARDROBE — 114
FROM BEACHWEAR TO TUXEDO

CAREERS AND SPORTS — 154

SOCIAL LIFE — 176

KEN + BARBIE — 180
IN SPORTS, FASHION, AND FILM

GLOBAL ICON — 190
EVERYONE NEEDS A KEN!

BIBLIOGRAPHY — 200

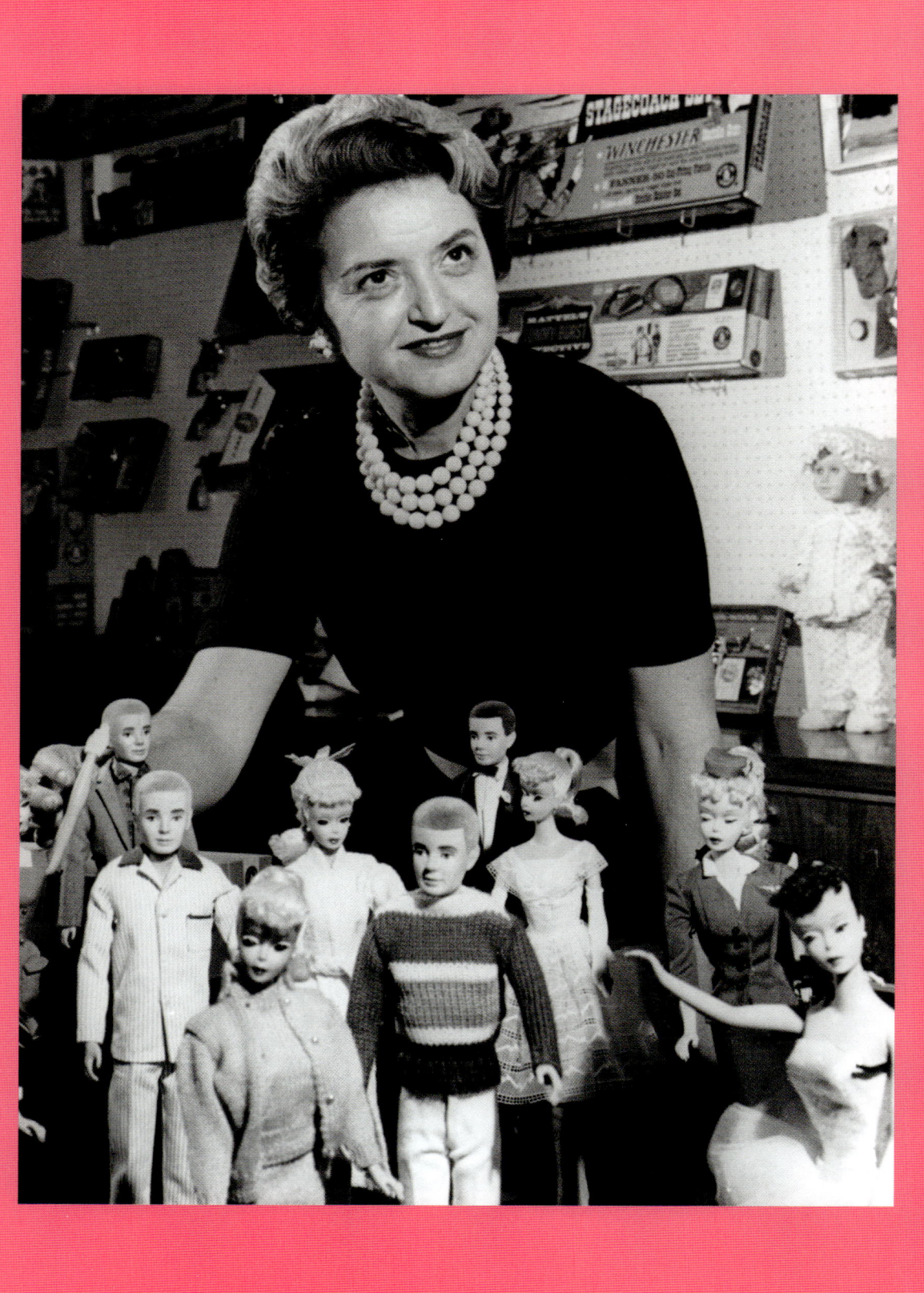

Ruth Handler in the early 1960s, surrounded by her creations: Barbie and Ken.

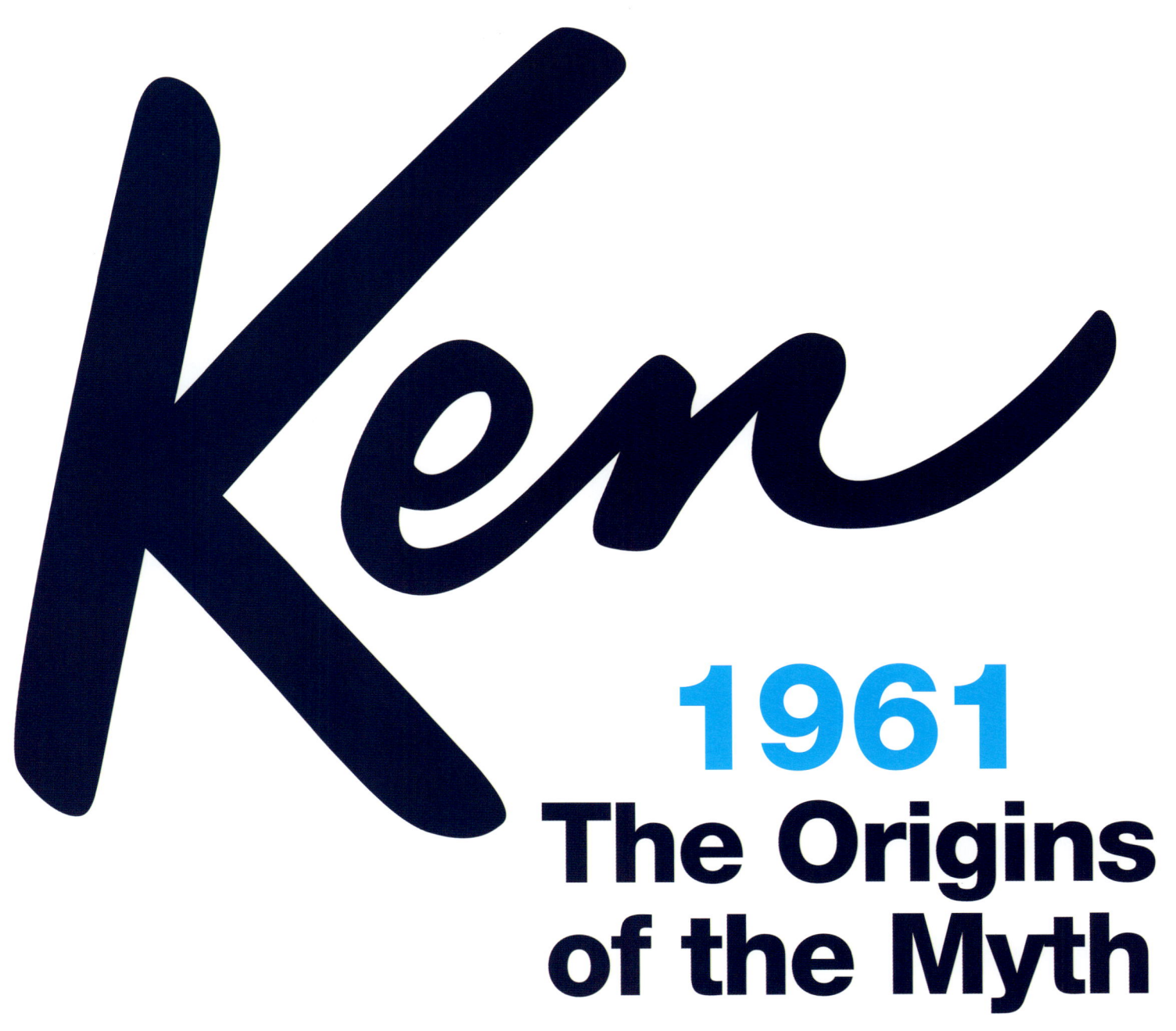

New York, March 11, 1961. Two years and two days after the launch of Barbie, Mattel launches Ken. Not long after the Barbie doll's debut as a "Teen Age Fashion Model," Ken is introduced at the New York Toy Fair with the unequivocal slogan: "He's a Doll! Barbie's Boyfriend." He has the look of the wholesome guy next door and comes with nine different outfits—many of which are sports-related, ideal for someone living a California lifestyle.

With Ken, Mattel thus began to expand the world of Barbie by creating a new character who, along with Barbie's sisters, breathed new life into an ever-expanding story.

Ken and Barbie's first meeting unfolds on the set of their debut television commercial, filmed in 1961 and set in the fictional town of Willows, Wisconsin, birthplace to both characters.

Ken wears a sleek tuxedo for the occasion, while Barbie, sporting her iconic ponytail, wears an evening gown and fur stole. The couple is ready to hit the dance floor and inaugurate one of the most iconic couples in the history of pop culture. Blending fiction and reality, Ken and Barbie are a glamorous duo with with a life full of possibilities.

Ken's formal evening outfit in that first televised appearance contrasts sharply with the casual beachwear he wore for his official introduction at the New York Toy Fair.

Just like Barbie, who made her debut on March 9, 1959, in a striped swimsuit, Ken first appeared in a basic bathing suit—red poplin shorts paired with cork sandals and a yellow towel.

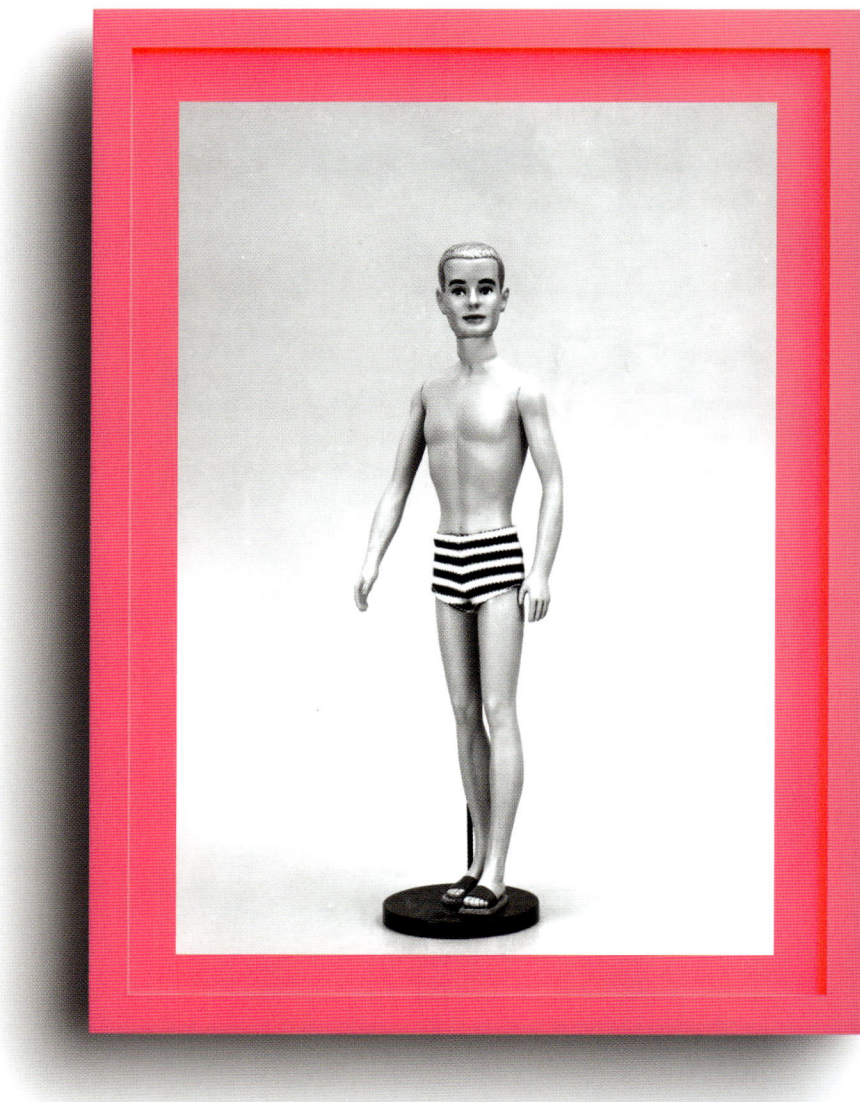

Above and opposite: Ken sporting the swimwear look created for his first promotional campaign, along with two outfits from his original 1961 wardrobe: Casual #782 and Dreamboat #785.

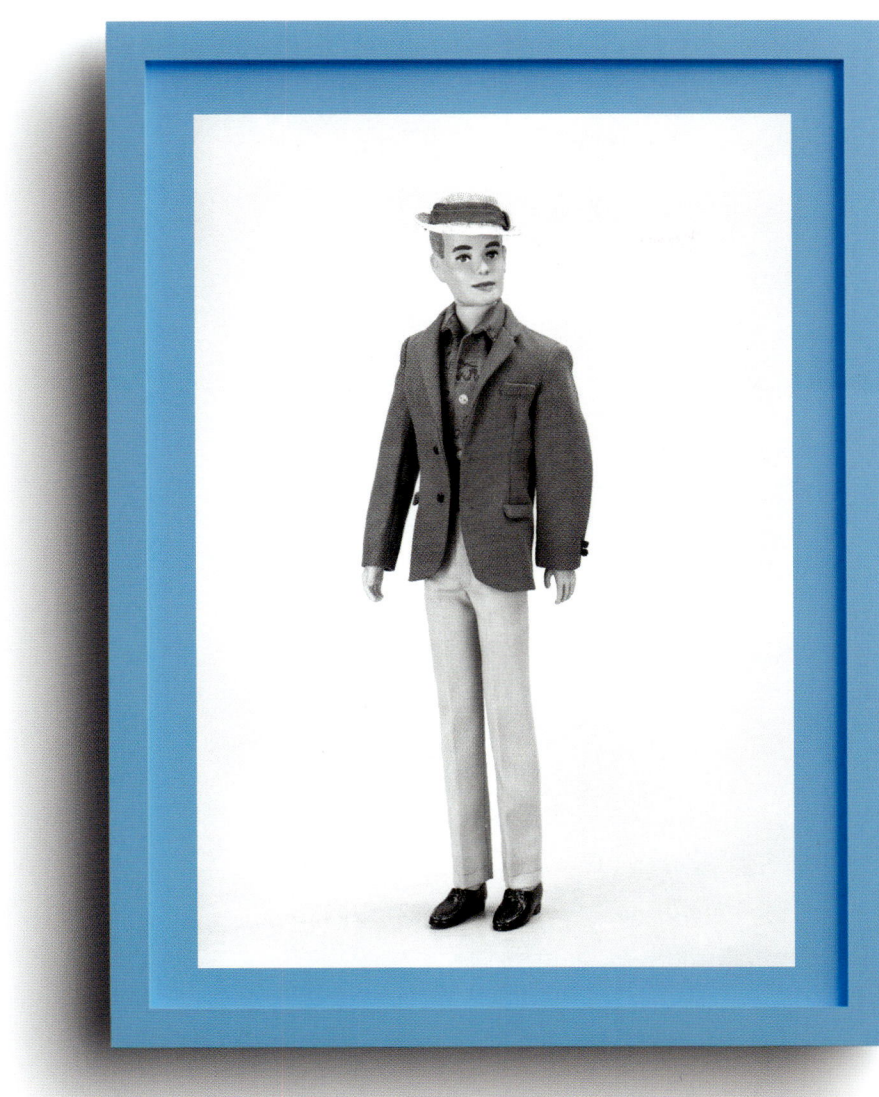
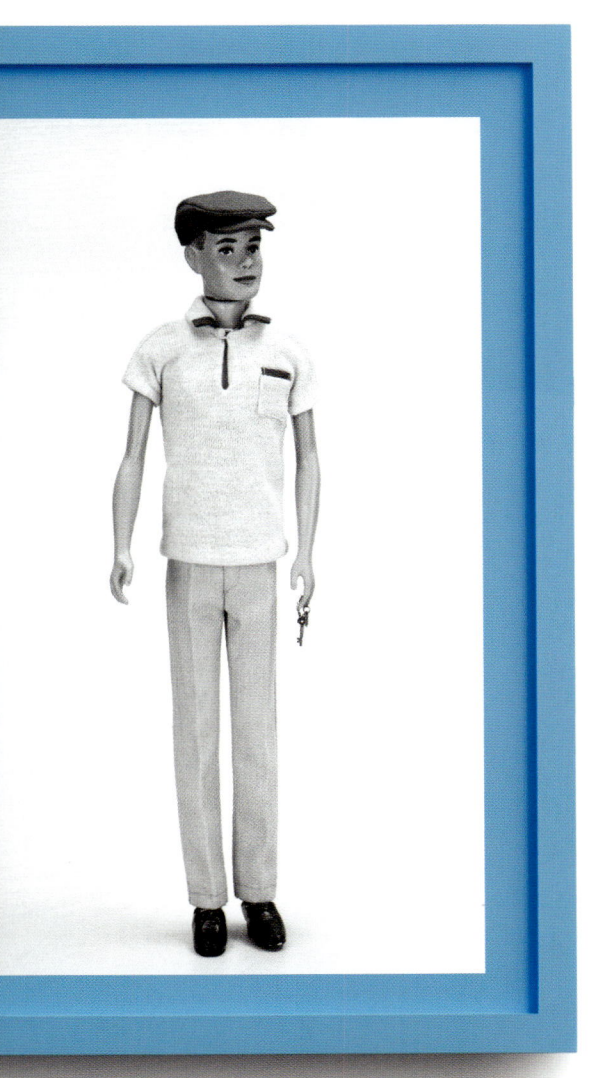
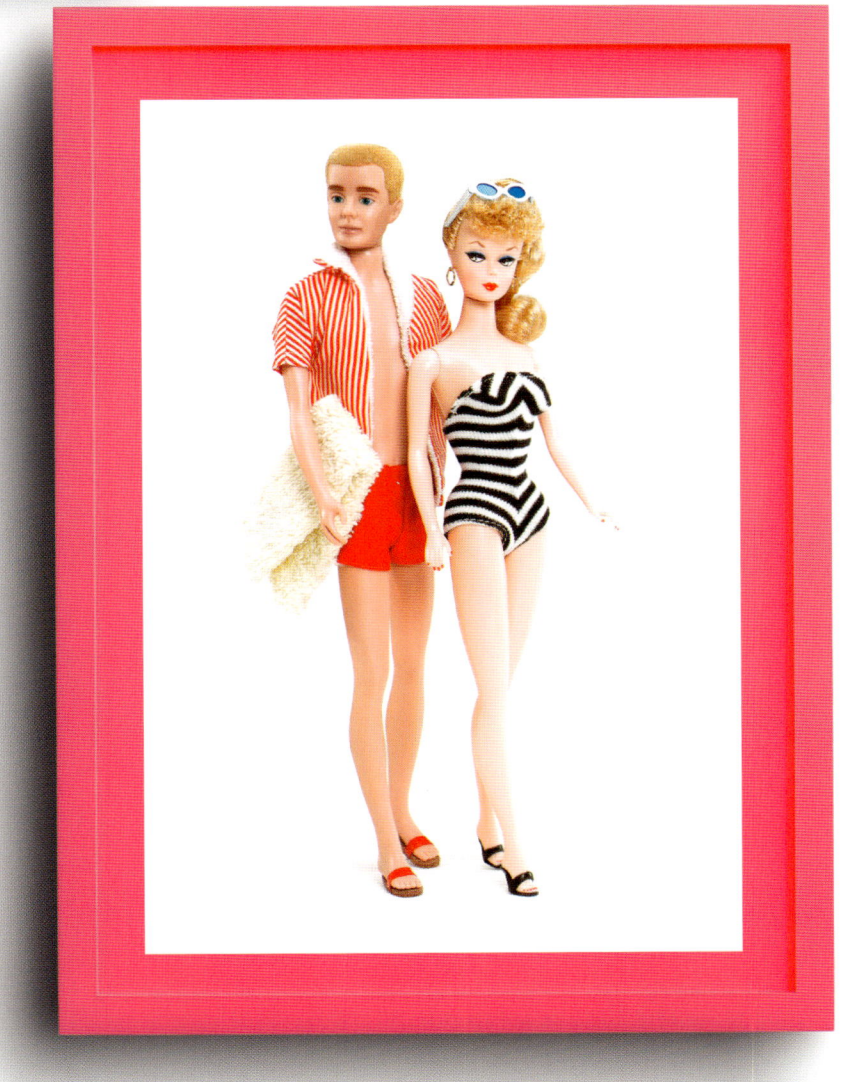

Ken and Barbie in one of their first appearances as a couple, 1961–1962.

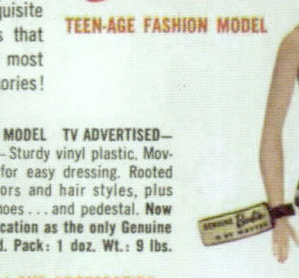
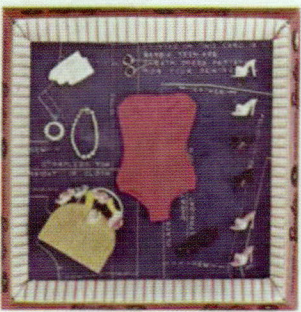
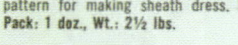
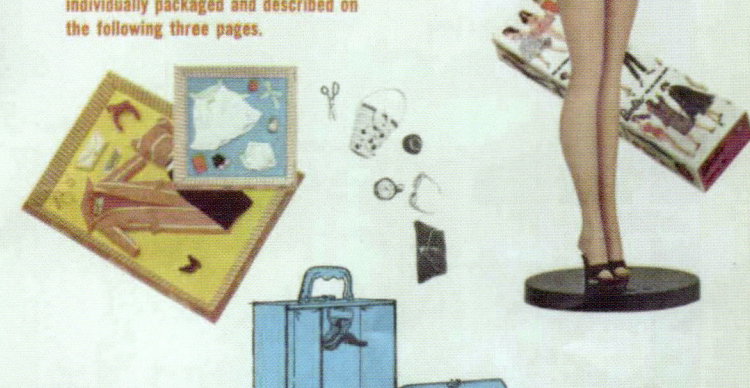
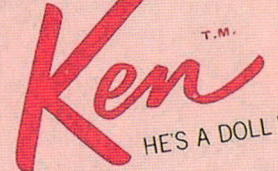
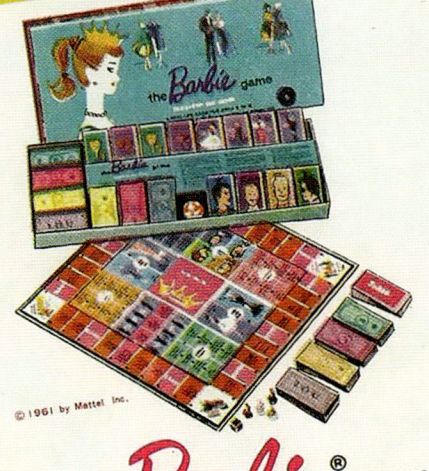

NEW FASHION APPEAL FOR GIRLS OF ALL AGES!

Here she is... Barbie... the most wanted doll of them all! The one-and-only Barbie is an exciting, uniquely appealing kind of doll, so curvy and lifelike, she almost breathes. Girls of all ages have become real Barbie fans, enchanted with her miniature wardrobe of fine-fabric fashions. They insist on the exquisite detailing found only in authentic Barbie costumes... the tiny zippers that really work... coats with luxurious, tailored linings... and always the most up-to-the-minute, most glamorous fashions and tiny coordinated accessories!

Barbie TEEN-AGE FASHION MODEL

BARBIE TEEN-AGE FASHION MODEL TV ADVERTISED— Stock #850 — Retail $3.00 — Sturdy vinyl plastic. Movable arms, legs, and head for easy dressing. Rooted Saran hair in assorted colors and hair styles, plus jersey swimsuit, earrings, shoes... and pedestal. Now with special arm tag identification as the only Genuine Barbie. Size: 11½" tall. Std. Pack: 1 doz. Wt.: 9 lbs.

COSTUMES (without dolls) AND ACCESSORIES — individually packaged and described on the following three pages.

BARBIE'S ACCESSORIES T.M.

Stock #923 — Retail Price $1.50 — All the little accessory extras that add to the fun of Barbie play. Delightful miniatures that look real. Coral bathing suit, white gloves, gold loop earrings, "pearl" necklace and matching earrings, straw purse, sunglasses, 3 pair shoes, printed pattern for making sheath dress. Std. Pack: 1 doz., Wt.: 2½ lbs.

NEW BARBIE® DOLL CASE

(licensed by Mattel, Inc.) Designed expressly for Barbie and her wardrobe! Colorful carrying case is just right for taking Barbie and her wardrobe travelling. Orders accepted by Standard Plastics, Inc., Plainfield, New Jersey.

the *Barbie*® game
QUEEN OF THE PROM
Be sure to play this exciting game of teen-age girl activities!
Available Now — $4.00

AND NOW...
PRESENTING
Ken T.M.
HE'S A DOLL!
BARBIE'S BOYFRIEND

Ken is the ideal boyfriend for Barbie, the Teen-Age Fashion Model. A complete wardrobe of exclusively-tailored men's clothes is available for Ken... plus the "right" accessories in the latest men's style... sports, business, semi-formal and formal wear.

Above and opposite:
On selected pages from Ken's original 1961 launch booklet introduced with the slogan "He's a Doll! Barbie's Boyfriend," Ken comes with a complete wardrobe featuring nine separate outfits.

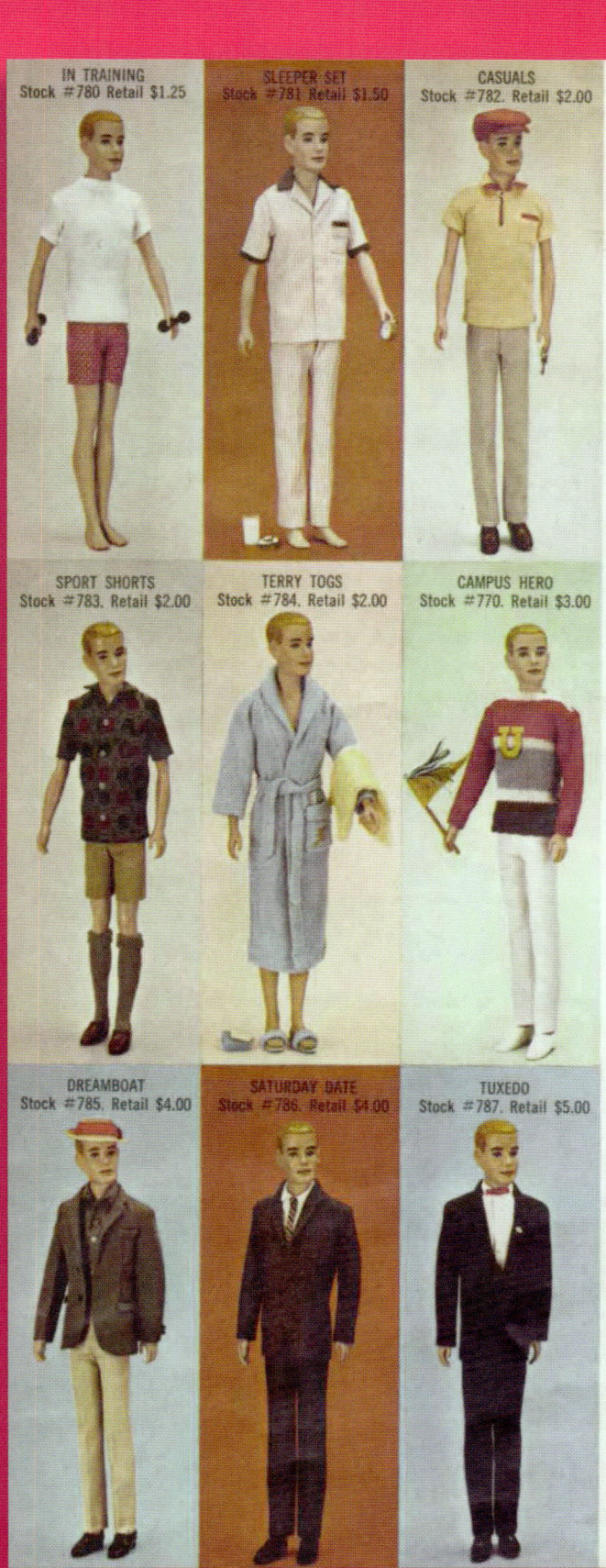
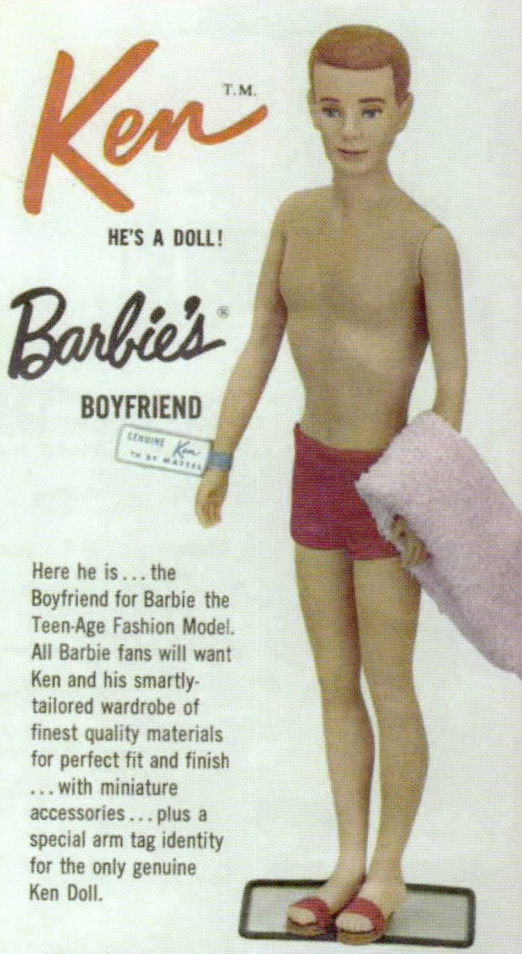

As you can see in the first promotional campaign in Mattel's 1961 catalog, Ken was originally supposed to wear a black-and-white striped swimsuit—a pattern matching Barbie's 1959 debut look as Teen Age Fashion Model Doll. That visual harmony of their launch outfits set the stage for their perfect harmony as a couple.

Ken's face mold presented a down-to-earth appearance with big eyes painted blue. His hairstyle—technically described as Flock Hair—was a velvety crew cut and offered in blond, black, or more rarely, brownette. The soft hair was replaced the following year because the flocked fabric fibers tended to detach if exposed to water. By 1962, Ken was produced with molded vinyl hair, subsequently painted.

His body stands 12 inches (30.5 cm) tall and comprises six separate parts: legs, arms, torso, and head. By 1963, a first restyling shortened Ken by half a centimeter (a fifth of an inch) and substituted a heavier vinyl version of his legs. Unchanged for many years, however, was Ken's defining boyish personality. What prompted the decision to create Ken, then? What determined his identity, so radically different from the popular American superheroes of the time? In 1960, just one year after the debut of the Barbie doll, it was the loyal buyers who demanded a companion for her. Mattel tasked Ruth Handler and Charlotte Johnson—respectively, the Barbie doll's creator and first fashion designer—with creating the first doll with male features. It was quite a challenge: nothing of

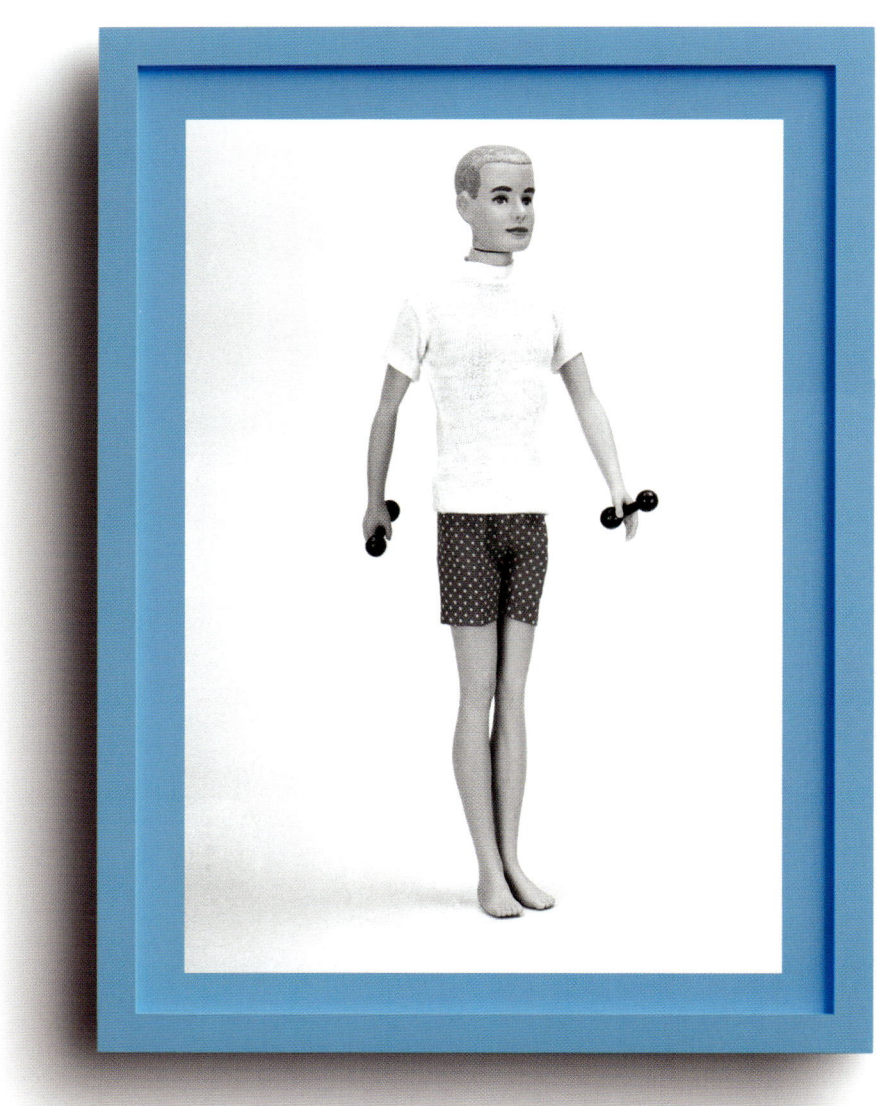

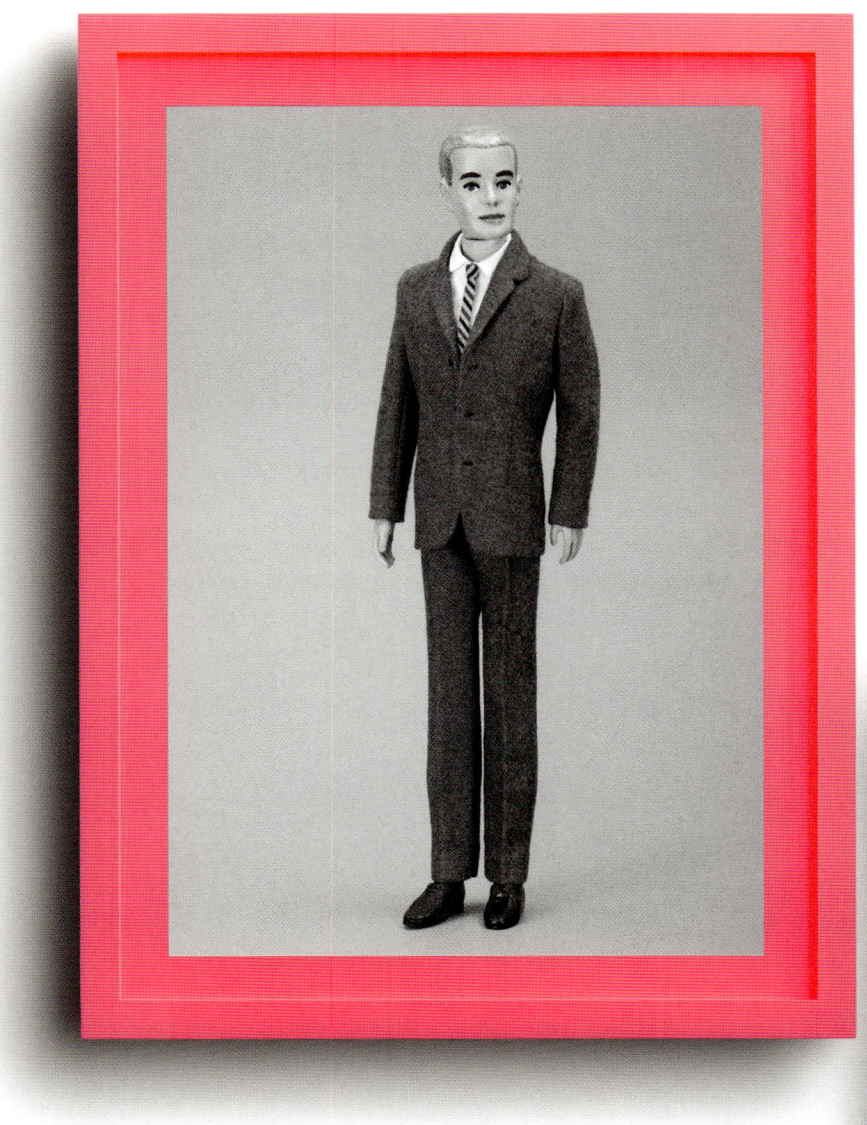
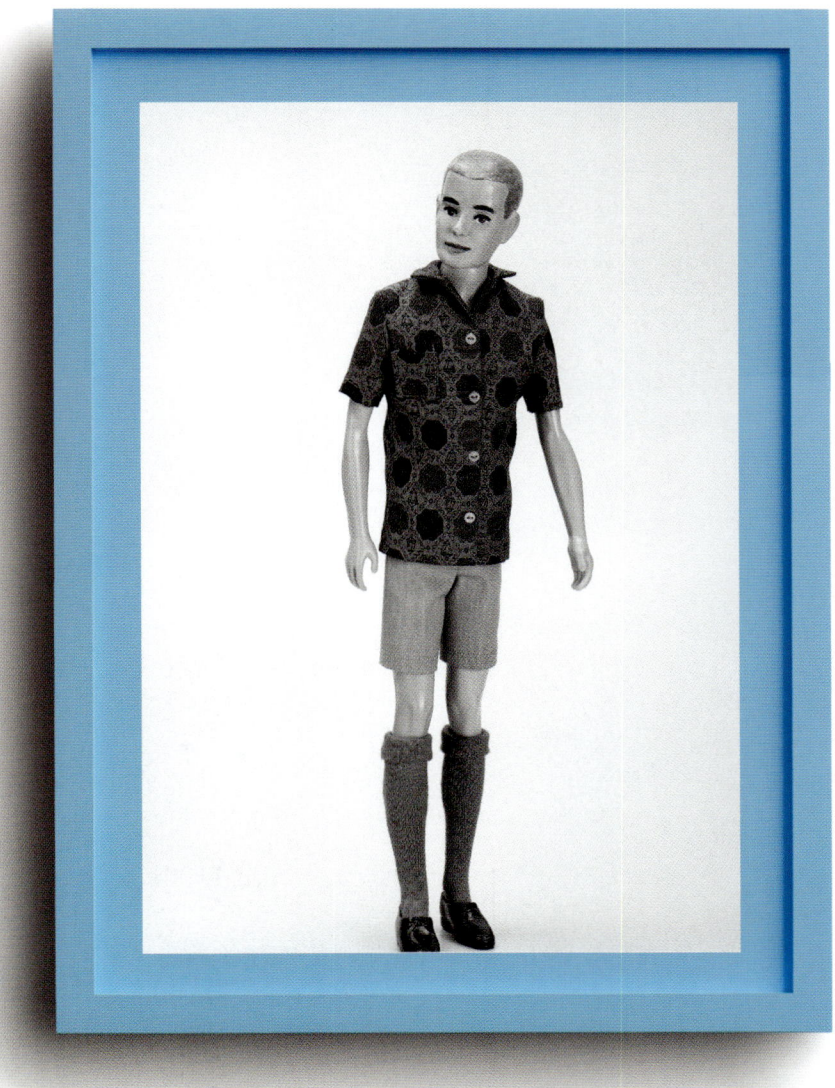

A selection of three outfits from Ken's iconic first wardrobe: In Training #780, Saturday Night Date #786, Sport Shorts #783.

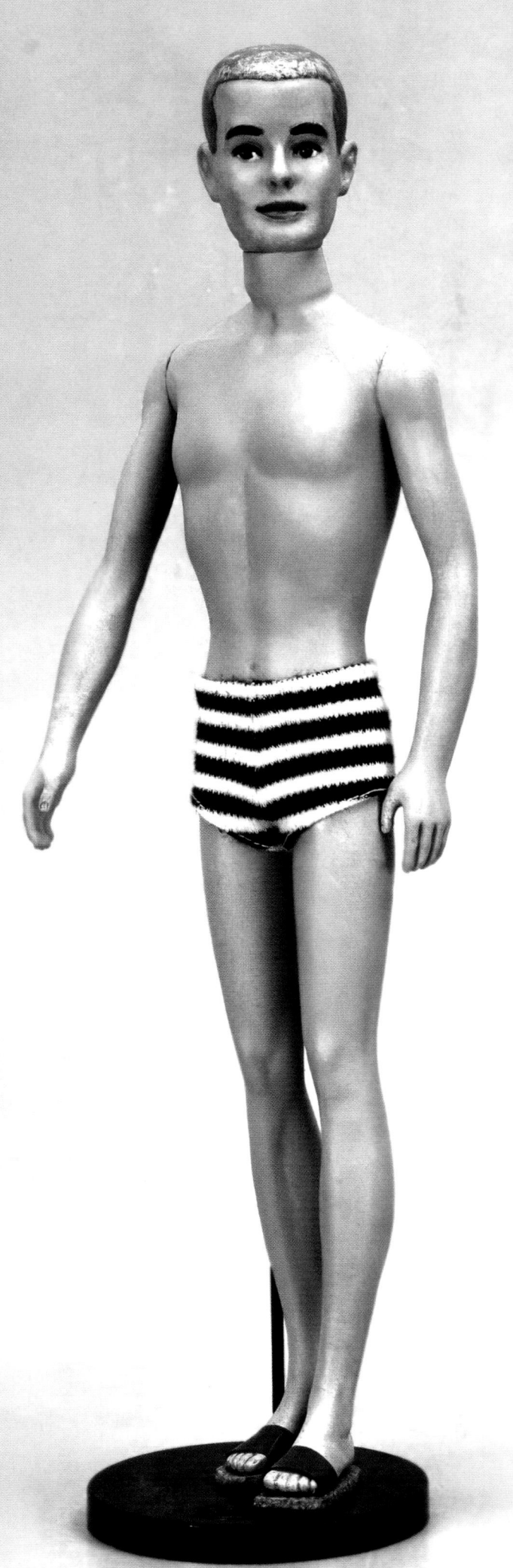

The first promotional shot of Ken in the 1961 Mattel catalog, wearing a swimsuit with black and white stripes—just like the one worn by Barbie as Teen Age Fashion Doll in 1959.

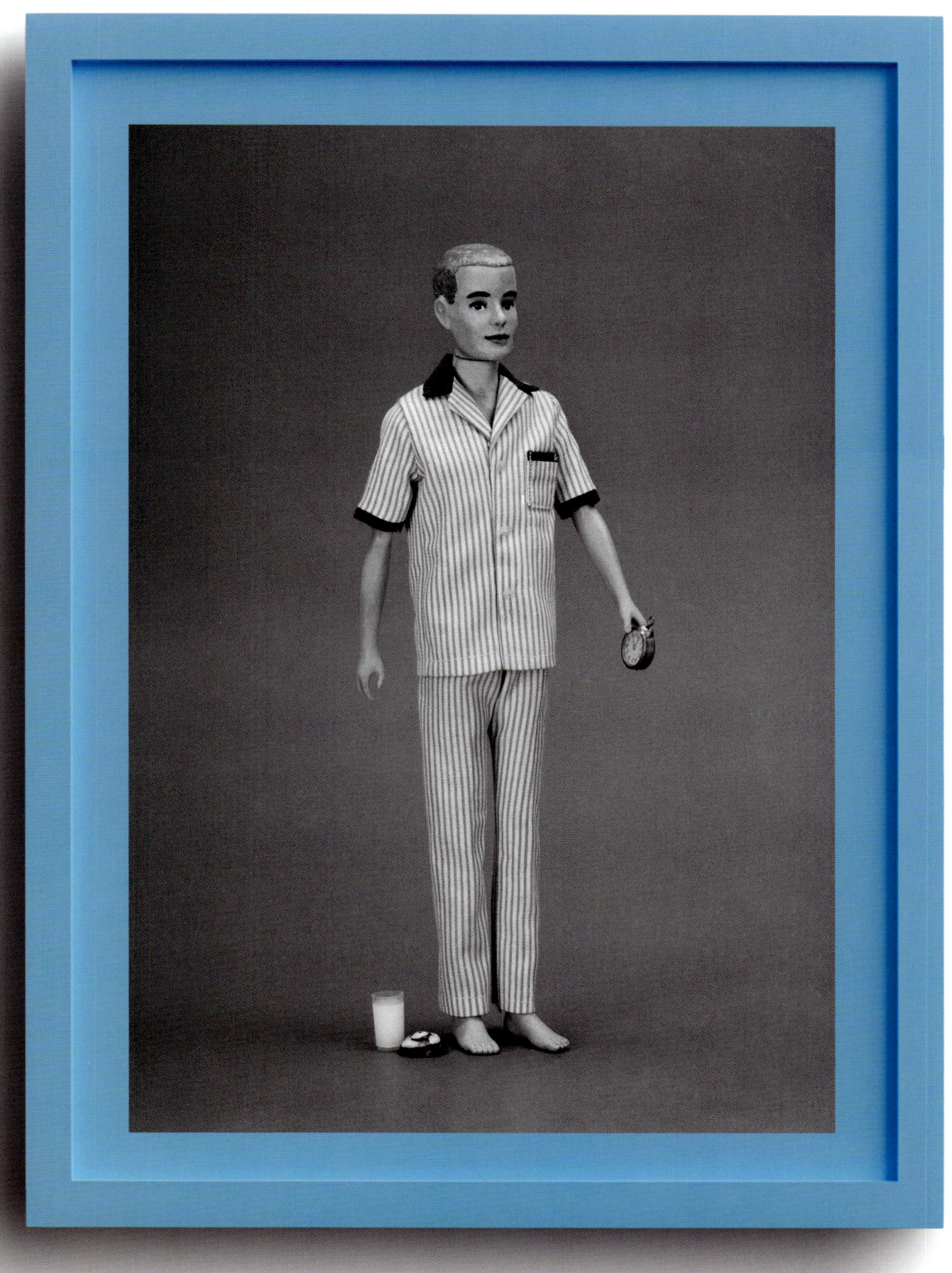

Ken in the Sleeper Set
#781 outfit, 1961.

the sort yet existed in the toy market. Every detail of the mold's prototype would have to be discussed in depth, to ensure it would satisfy market expectations and social values of the time. Among the potential role models offered by American film and television of the time was Dobie, lead character of the series *The Many Loves of Dobie Gillis*, played by Dwayne Hickman. The show ran on CBS from 1959 to 1963 and was a spin-off of the 1953 movie *The Affairs of Dobie Gillis*, starring Bobby Van and Debbie Reynolds. Dobie was the archetype of the easygoing middle-class American teenager of the era, and his escapades were chronicled through his high school and college years.

Despite drawing from many pop culture inspirations, the first Flock Hair #750 Ken was a man of his own, completely independent of any obvious reference to celebrity. In fact, the T-shirt and jeans look, popularized by the new generation of actors, didn't make it into Ken's original wardrobe, which leaned toward a mix of athletic casual wear and classic elegance, perfect for a lifestyle full of dates, dancing, and travel. At the core of Ken's original image is a sense of innocence and wholehearted devotion to Barbie.

Once the prototype mold and core personality traits were established, the next step would be choosing the doll's name. That came easily and naturally: he would be Ken. In the same way that Barbie was named after Ruth and Elliot Handler's daughter Barbara, Ken would be named after their son, Kenneth. His surname, Carson, was added later—introduced in Cynthia Lawrence's 1962 book *Here's Barbie: Stories About the Fabulous Barbie and Her Boyfriend Ken*, illustrated by Clyde Smith. That's where the first details of Ken's personality and family background were revealed. Ken was not only Barbie's devoted boyfriend and social companion—he was also the son of a lawyer, with a surname directly inspired by the Carson/Roberts advertising agency that served Mattel on the Barbie brand's earliest promotional campaigns. Barbie herself, of course, was given the surname Roberts (Barbara Millicent Roberts).

At that point, the work was complete. The legend of Ken could begin!

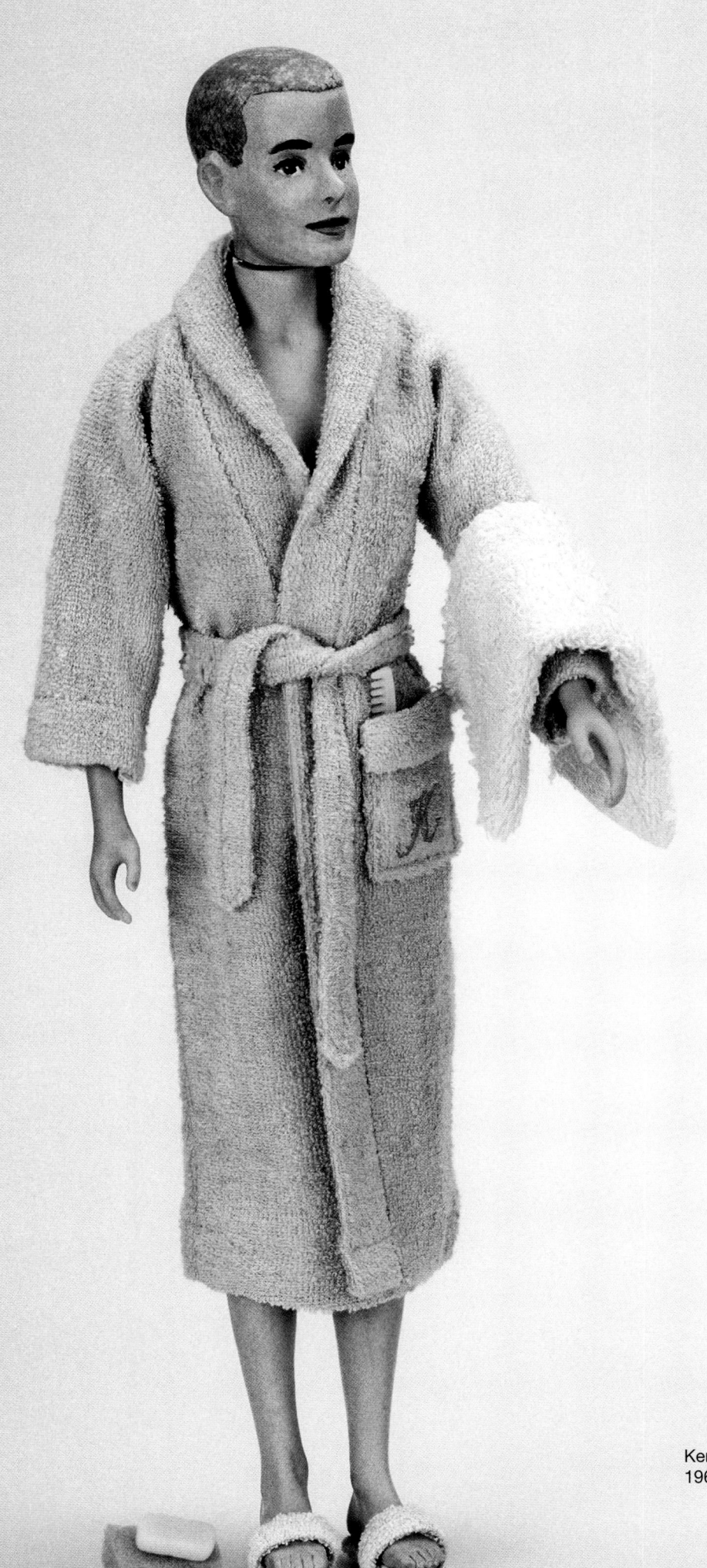

Ken in the Terry Togs #784 outfit, 1961.

"Ken Doll is Malibu—
he goes to the beach
and surfs.
When I was at Hamilton
High School in
Beverlywood,
I played the piano
and went to movies
with subtitles.
I was a real nerd."

—Kenneth Handler,
Los Angeles Times, 1989

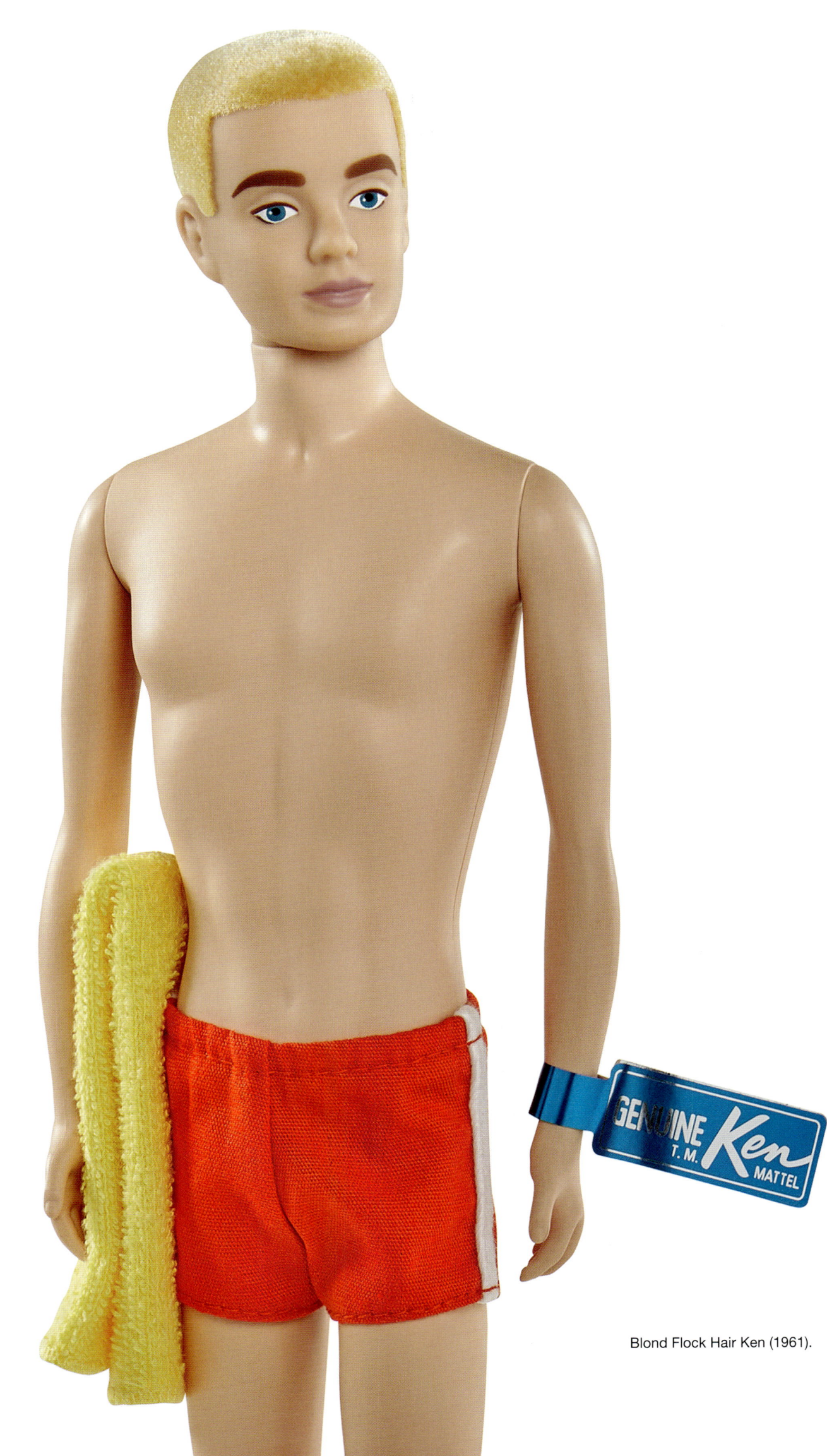

Blond Flock Hair Ken (1961).

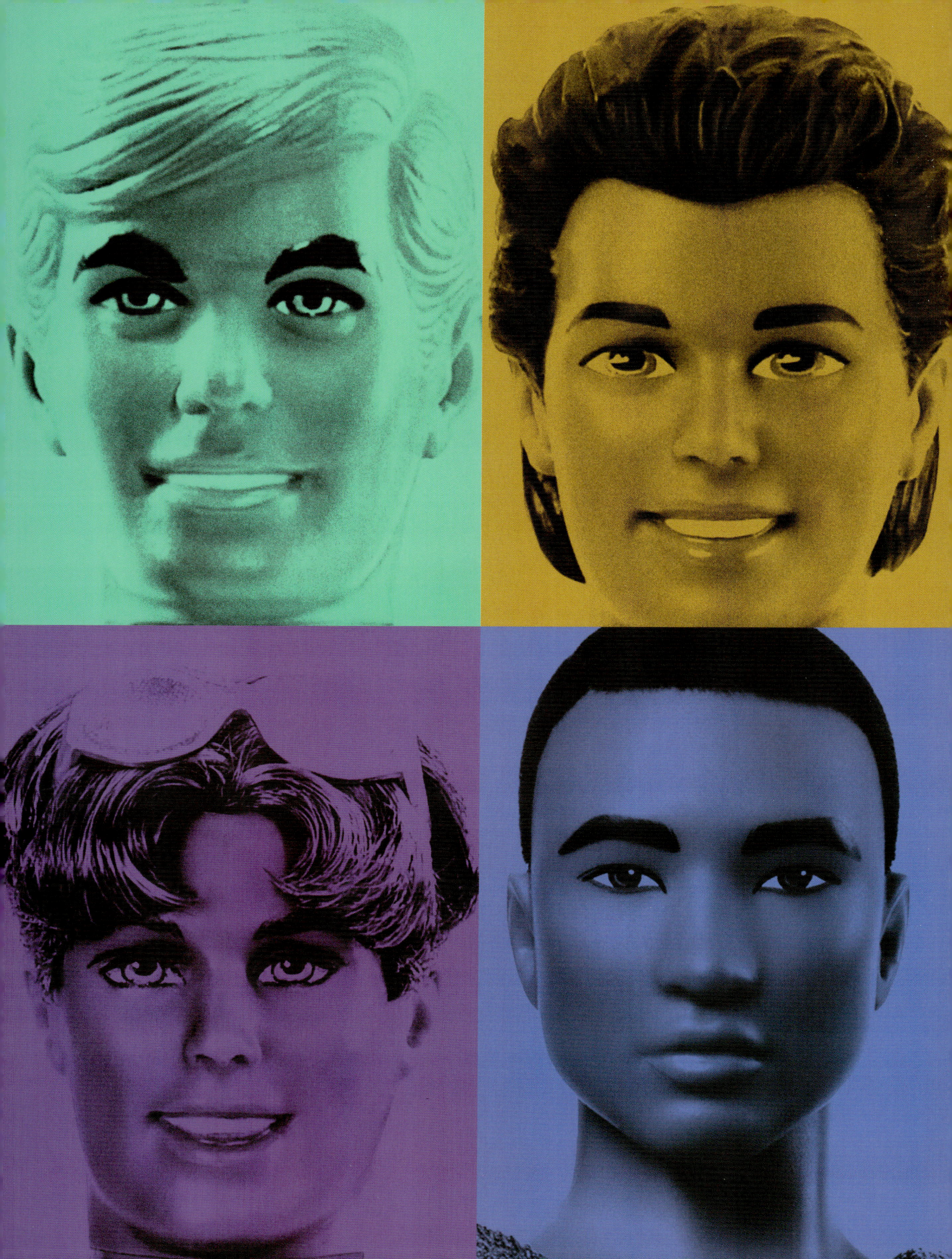

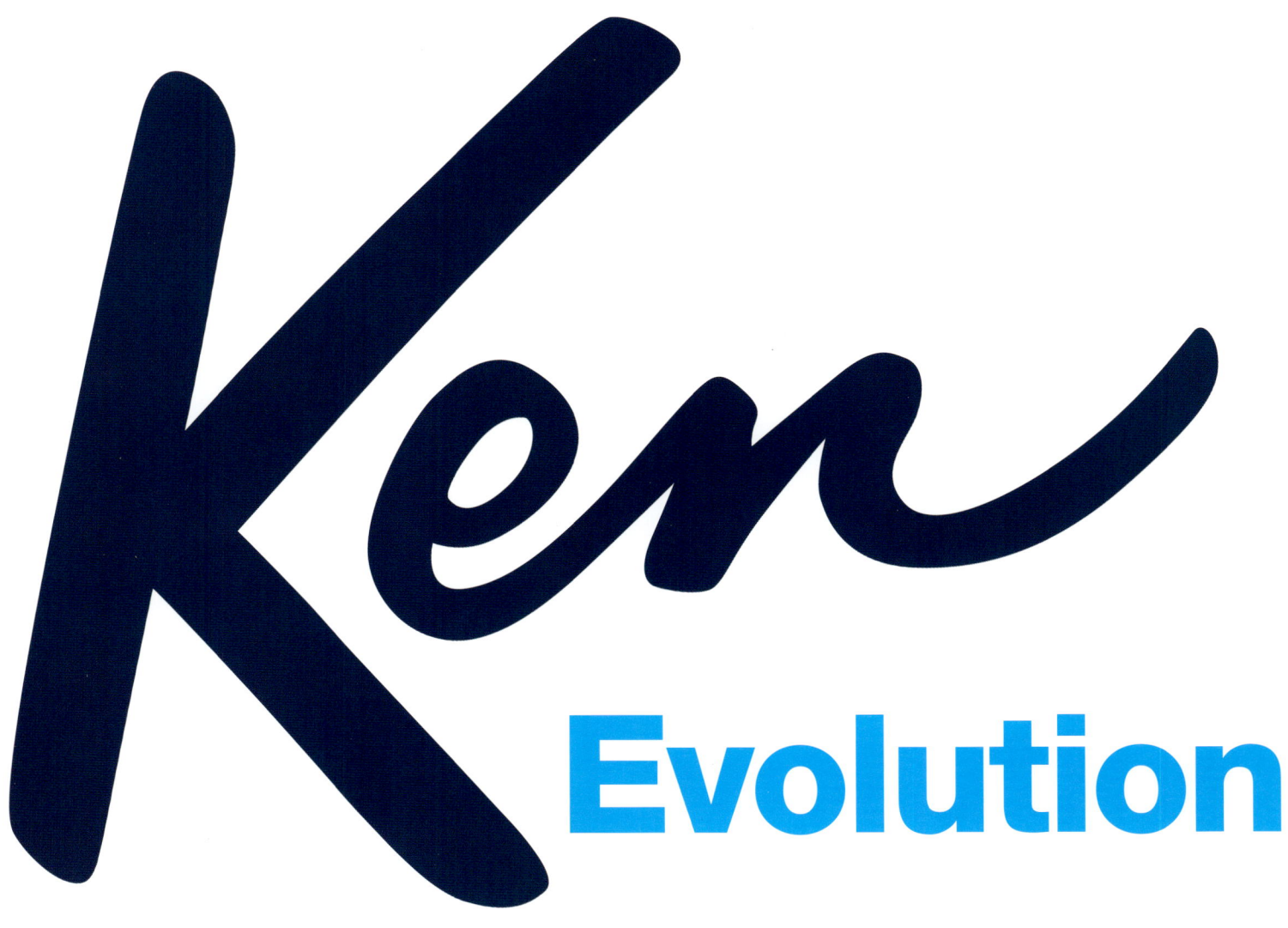

Ken Evolution

From his first appearance with the Flock Hair styling—in blond, black, or brownette—and a typical Californian style red swimsuit, Ken's image has transformed over the past six decades. He's spent every phase of his life evolving alongside fashion trends that have not only redefined his wardrobe but also, and more importantly, his hairstyle and facial features.

    And so we see Ken embodying the styles of each era: sporting thick beards and mustaches in the 1970s, a sideswept fringe haircut in the 1980s, sculpted gel hairstyles in the 1990s, quiff hairstyles with razor-cut sides in the 2000s, and finally, the longer, flowing hairstyles of today. Even more than his body, it's the sculpted vinyl head mold that defines Ken's personal identity and his identity through the decades. Most of those head molds have been production-stamped by Mattel with the year of creation (on the nape of the neck). The dates provided in this book refer to the year of production, not the date of market launch.

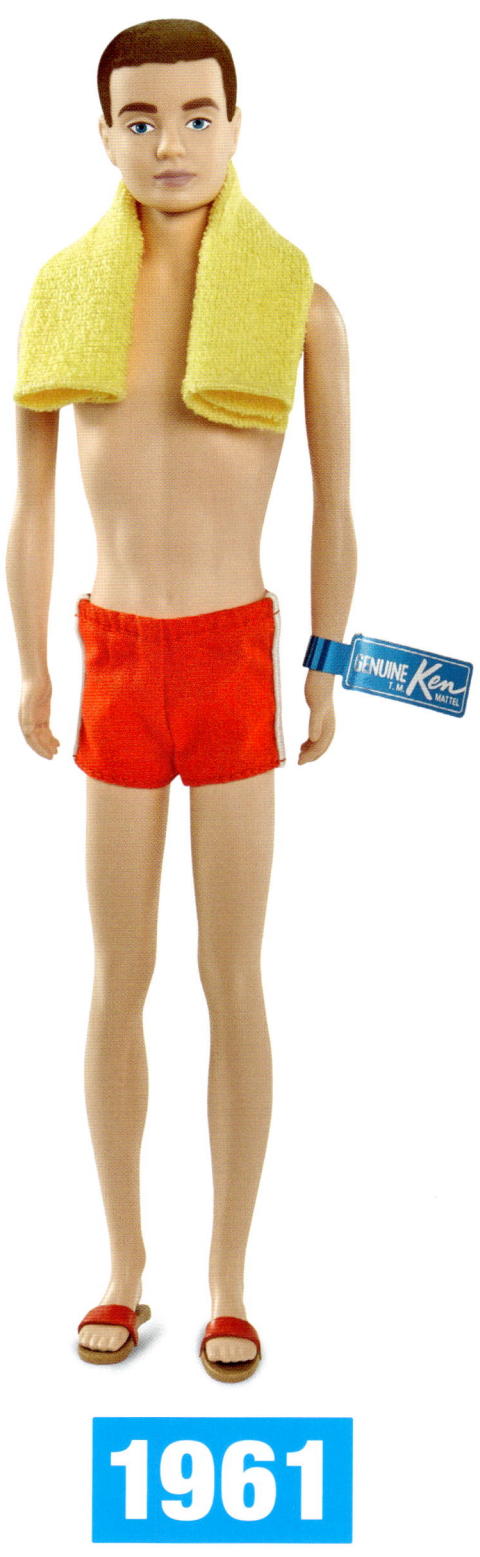

1961

Flock Hair Ken

Flock Hair Ken #750, the first model introduced by Mattel on March 11, 1961, is released in three versions—with blond, black, or brown flocked hair. His gaze is straight ahead, with painted blue eyes. The body mold is labeled "Tan Straight Leg" and stamped: Ken T.M./Pats. Pend/© MCMLX/by/Mattel/Inc. The face mold, used only for these early editions, is unmarked and is known as "FH Ken." The box bears the unequivocal slogan: "He's a Doll! Barbie's Boyfriend."

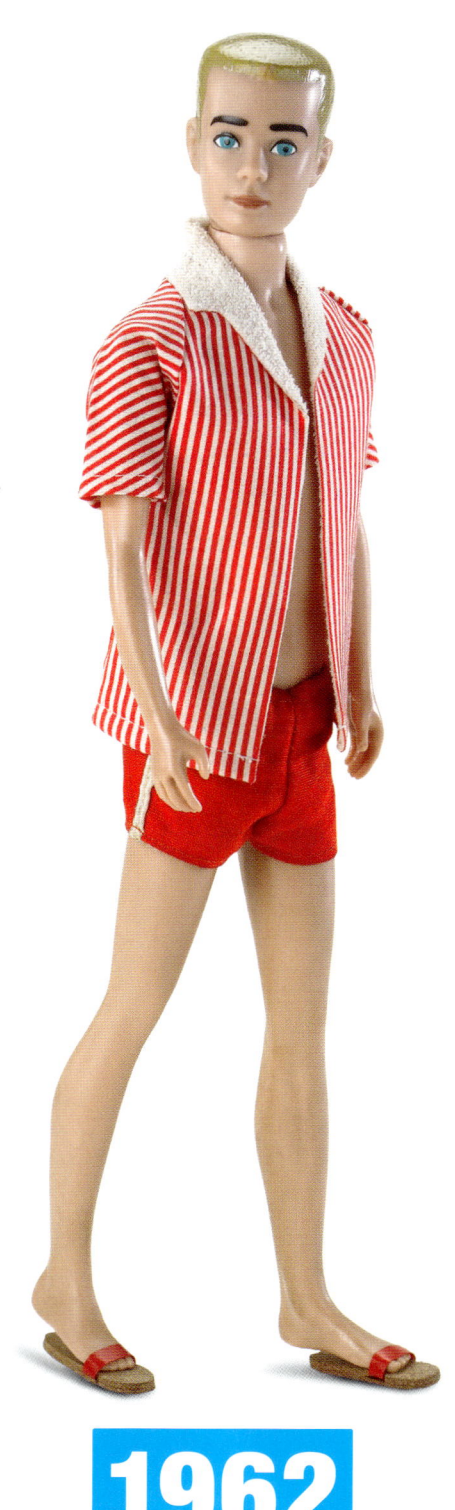

1962

Painted Hair Ken

Here Ken has painted, sculpted hair in molded plastic. The red shorts are paired with a red-and-white striped beach shirt, trimmed with a white terry collar. Some head molds are marked under the chin with a three-digit numerical code.

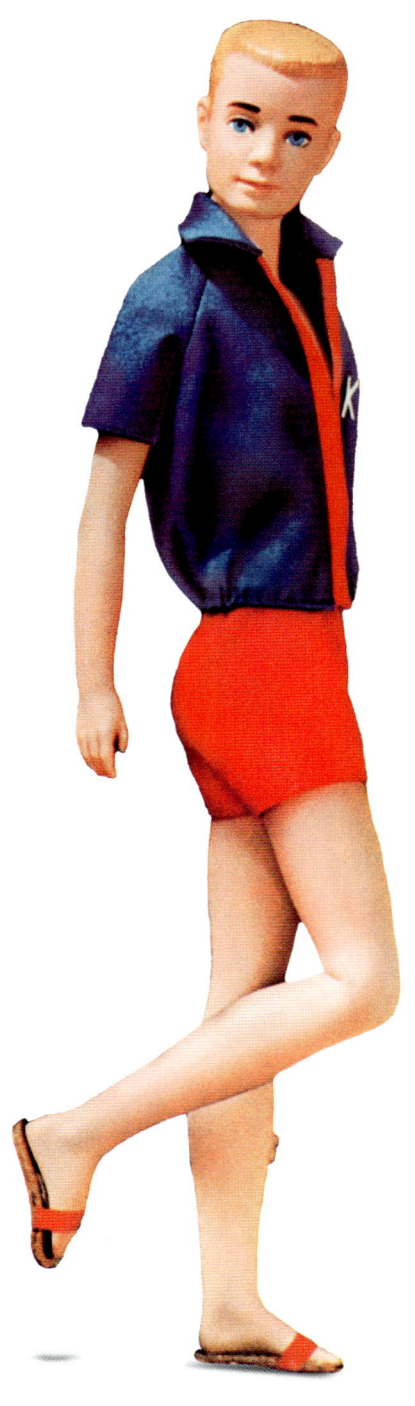

1964

Bendable Legs Ken

Now with bendable legs, Ken appears with blond or brown hair, wearing red swim trunks and a navy-blue jacket with red trim and a "K" monogram. On his feet: cork sandals.

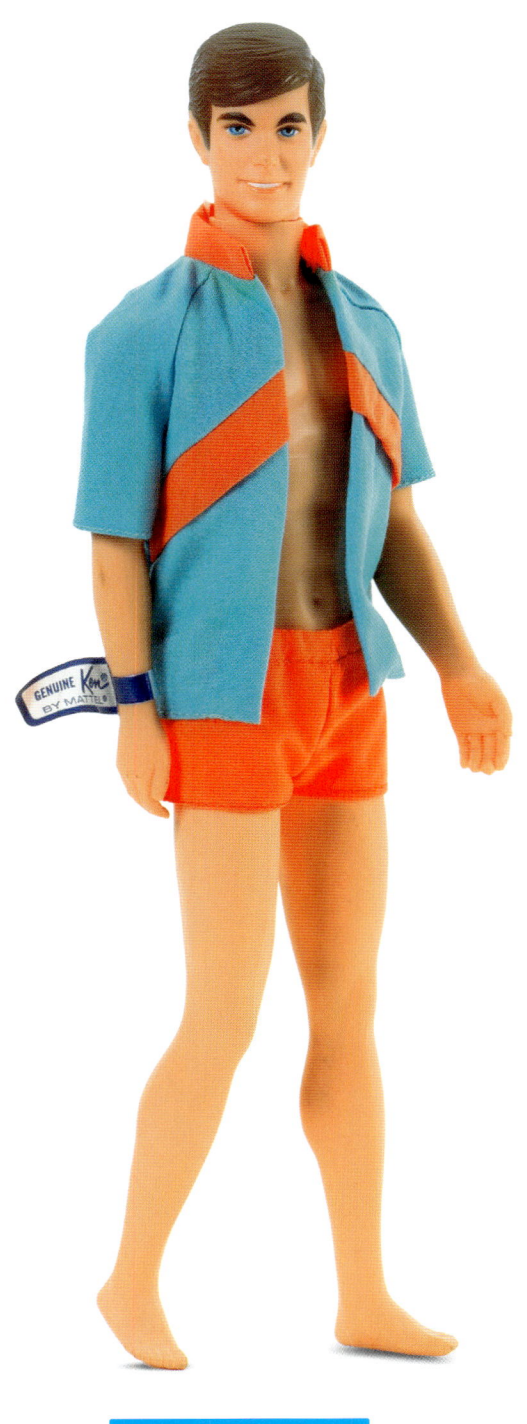

1969

New Good Lookin' Talking Ken

Blond or brown, Ken's hair is painted and molded in plastic with sideswept bangs, and Ken now smiles, showing a set of white teeth. He wears red shorts and a matching Nehru-style (so named for Jawaharlal Nehru, the former prime minister of India) summer shirt-jacket. This new face mold will be reused in many models in the 1970s including: Free Moving Ken (1975–1976), Malibu Ken (1971–1978), Olympic Skier Ken (1975–1976), and finally Hawaiian Ken (1978–1979).

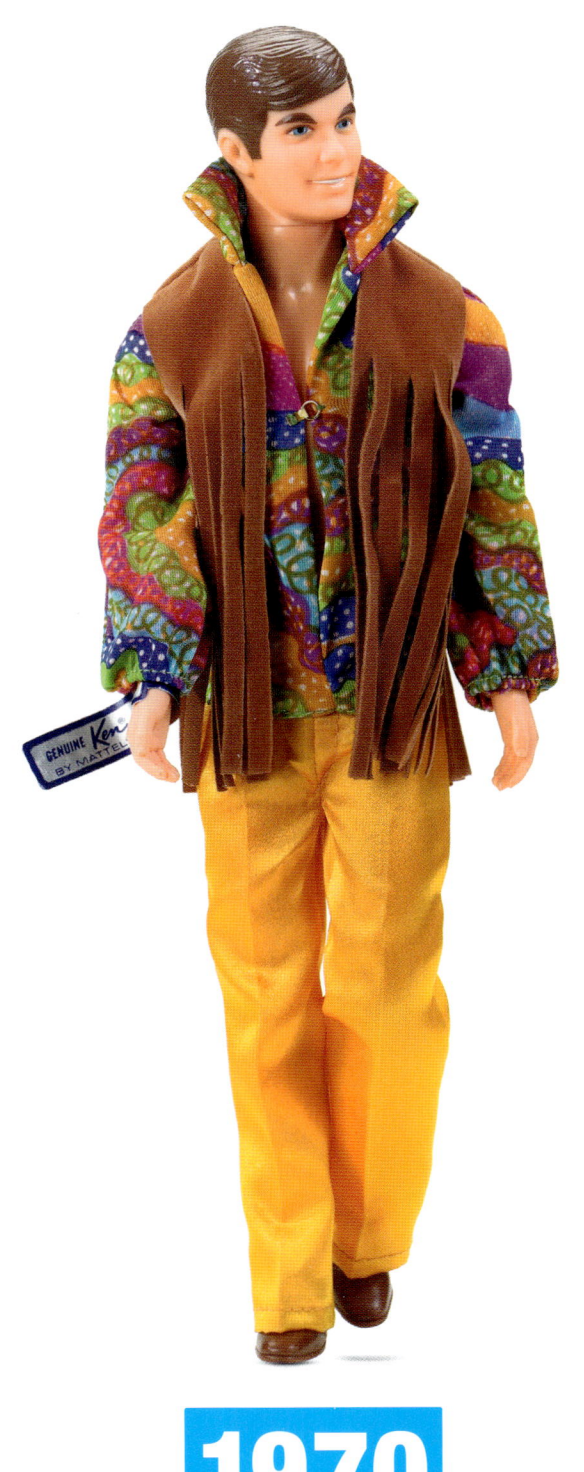

1970

Live Action on Stage Ken

Wearing gold satin pants, a brown Western-style vest with fringe, a multicolor shirt, and brown loafers, Live Action On Stage Ken (#1172) moves with a motorized base and comes with a disk that plays two hits: "A Little Bit of That Sky" and an instrumental track. The nape of the neck reads either "Hong Kong" or "Taiwan."

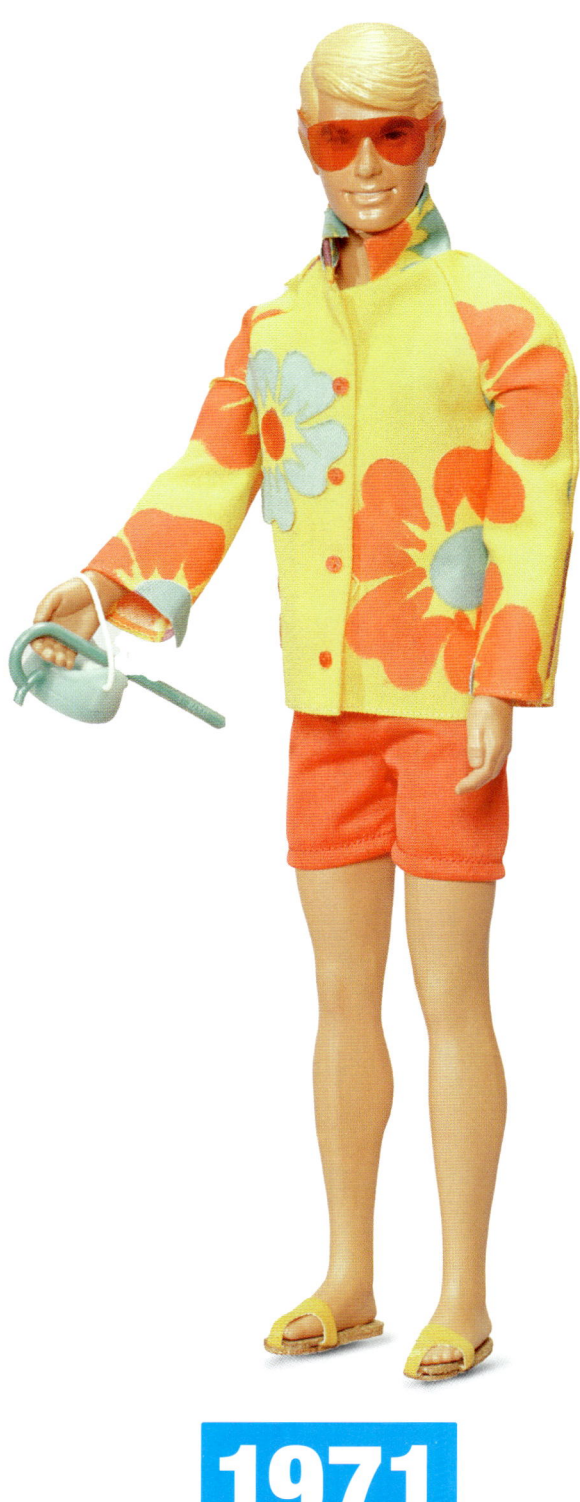

1971

Malibu Ken Surf's Up

Now Ken has become a true California Guy—blond and ready to hit the beach, with a golden tan that pops against his orange swim trunks. He sports a yellow floral Nehru-collared shirt and is equipped with a blue towel, diving mask, snorkel, flippers, sunglasses, and signature cork sandals.

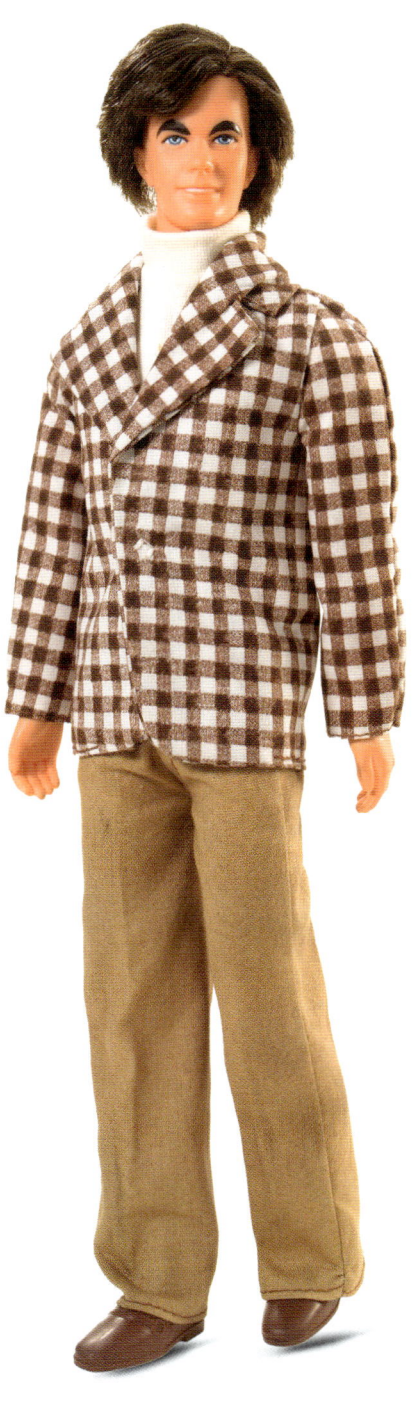

1972

Mod Hair Ken

Ken returns with rooted fiber hair—straight or curly—offering a more natural look than the sculpted plastic hair of earlier versions, alternately with beard, mustache, goatee, and sideburns. In perfect seventies style, he sports beige trousers paired with brown loafers, a white turtleneck, and a brown-and-white checkered blazer.

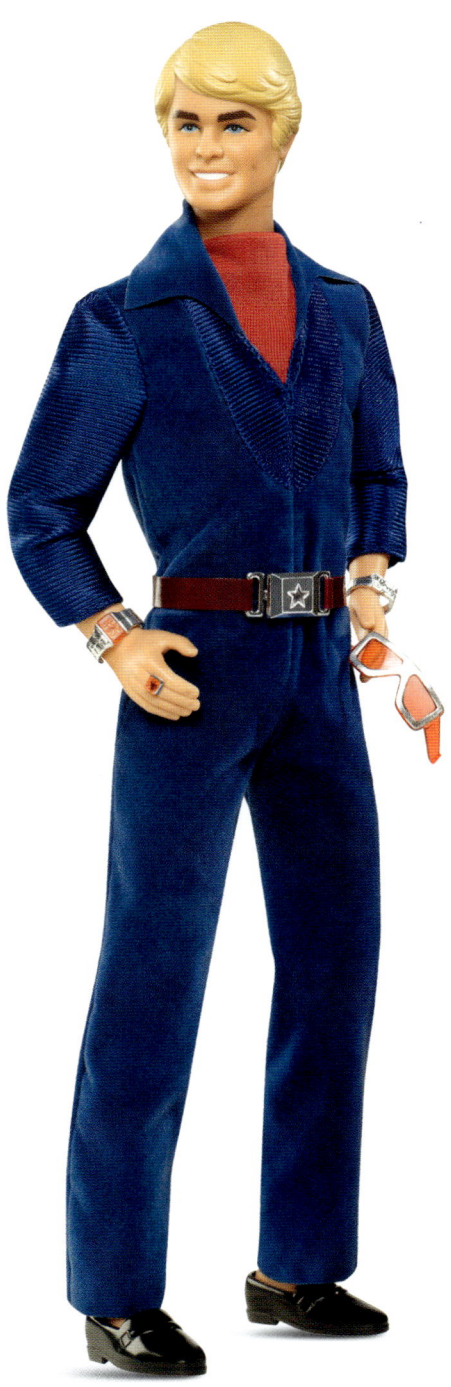

1978

SuperStar Ken

Ken is transformed into an icon of disco culture and fashion. Blond like Robert Redford, he's ready to hit the dance floor in a super cobalt-blue jumpsuit cinched at the waist with a belt, and wearing a red scarf around his neck. His accessories include a silver watch that matches the frame of his sunglasses, as well as a bracelet and a ruby ring.

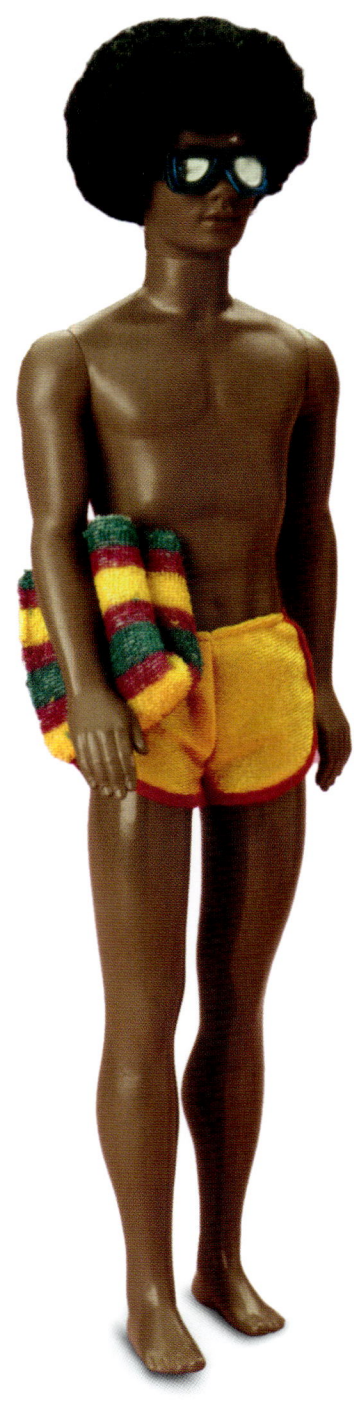

1981

Sunsational Malibu Ken

The first Black Ken features a unique face mold and a fashionable Afro hairstyle. Sunsational Malibu Ken wears a yellow swimsuit with orange trim, mirrored sunglasses, and a striped towel in purple, green, and yellow. A new version of this model appears as early as 1983, with a redefined face featuring molded and painted plastic hair—released at the same time as a brand-new Hispanic Ken.

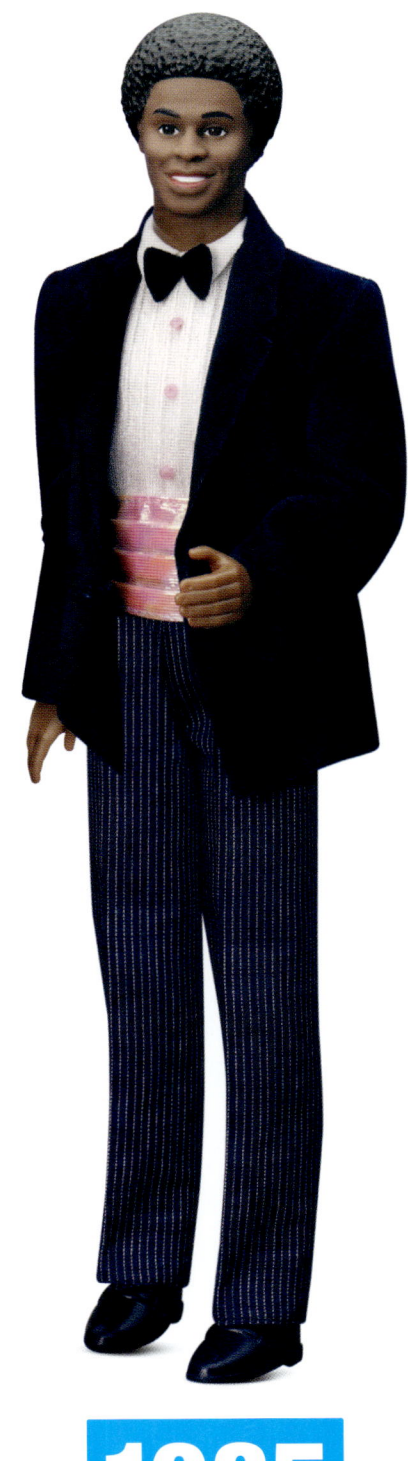

1985

Day-to-Night Ken

Ken dresses fancier than ever for his date with Barbie. For the occasion, he wears a black tuxedo jacket paired with a matching bow tie, loafers, and overcoat, with silver contrasting trousers. A bright pink cummerbund and a matching boutonniere on the lapel complete his look.

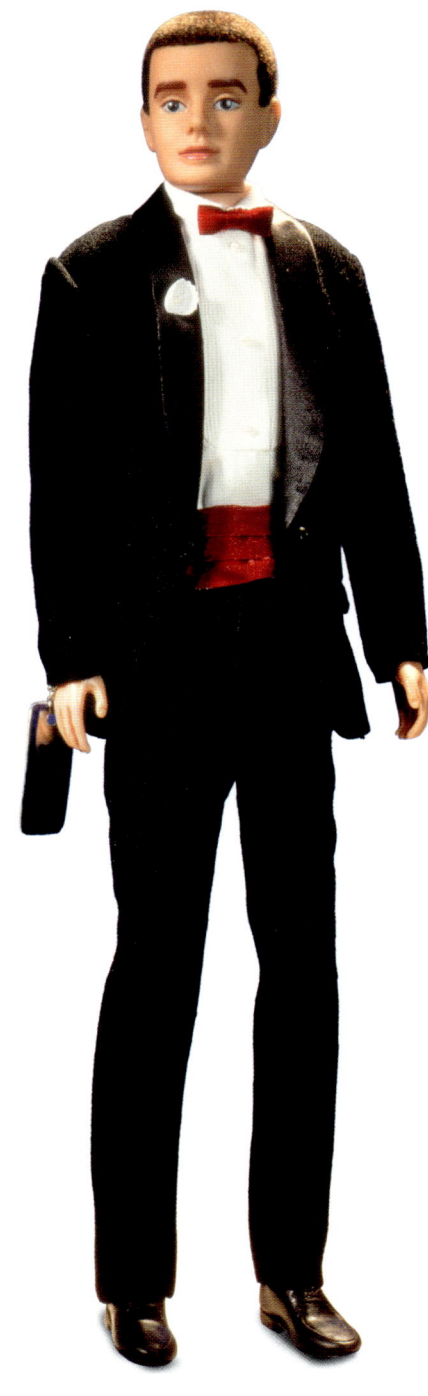

1991

30th Anniversary
Porcelain Ken

Sculptor John Gardner reimagines the original 1961 Flock Hair Ken #750, creating a special limited edition in matte bisque porcelain with a hand-painted face to celebrate Ken's thirtieth anniversary. His blue eyes are framed by dark brows and brown hair. The refined tuxedo—an homage to the original 1961 model #787—is paired with a white shirt, burgundy bow tie and cummerbund, and meticulously detailed accessories: a tank top, white boxers, black socks, black garters, and classic Oxford shoes for the dance floor.

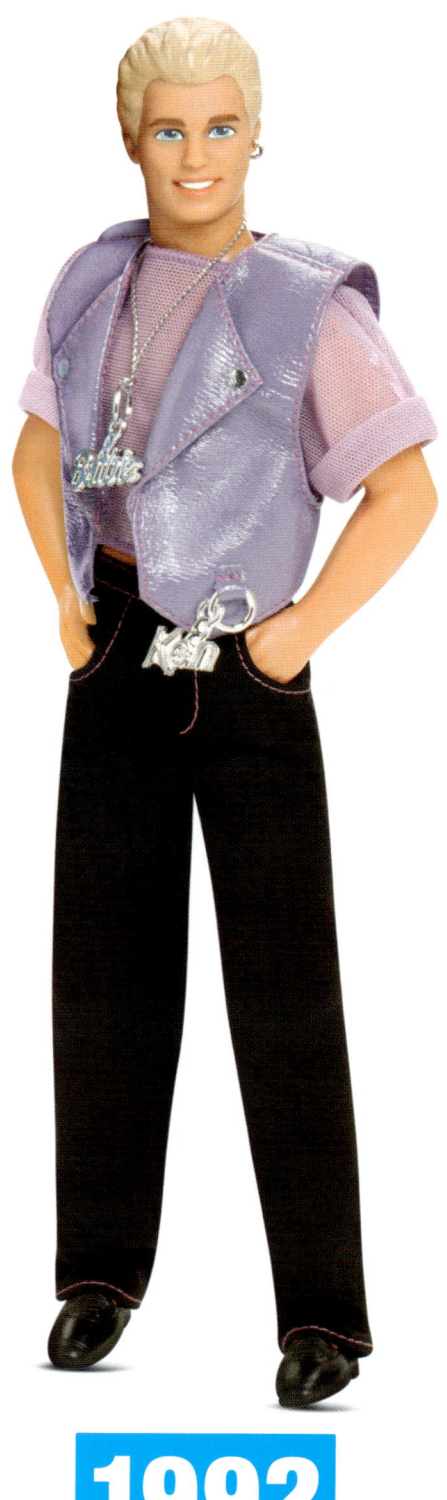

1992

Earring Magic Ken.

Earring Magic Ken—released to accompany Barbie Earring Magic—sparks unprecedented media buzz, even landing on the first page of the *New York Times* Arts & Leisure section. A radically reimagined Ken with a look that prompts much discussion, he sports platinum-blond highlights, with a faux leather lilac vest (reminiscent of the Jean Paul Gaultier look), mesh T-shirt, black jeans, a chain, and a silver hoop earring in his left ear—transforming the boy next door. This doll becomes the best-selling Ken in history.

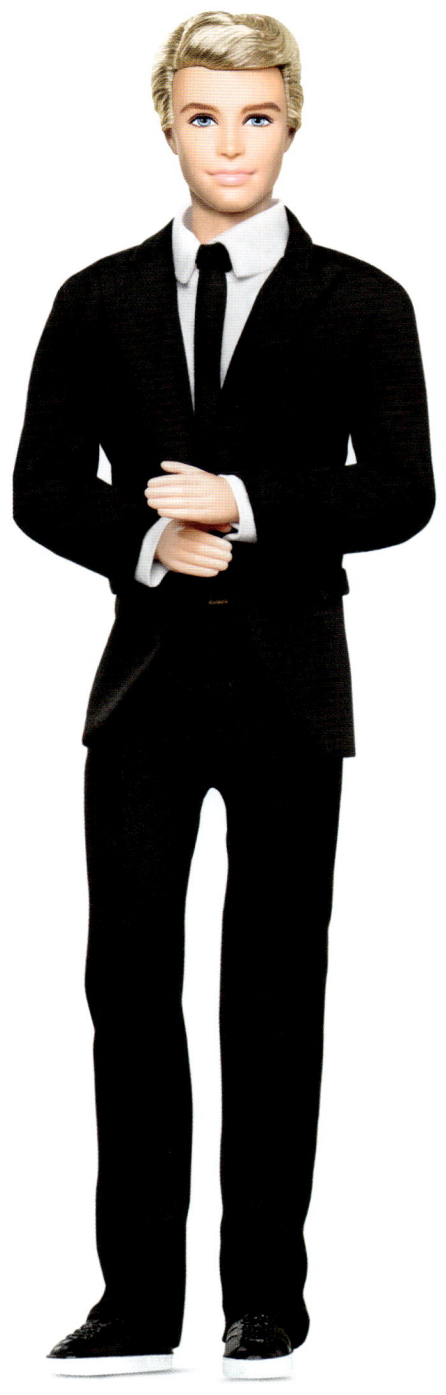

2011

BRB Ken
Breakup / get-back-together campaign: 50th anniversary

The Ken of reconciliation! Blond and dashing in a black tuxedo, Ken—having appeared with Barbie in *Toy Story 3*—takes the spotlight in a Times Square ad campaign to win back Barbie, his longtime girlfriend. On Valentine's Day, February 14, 2011, Barbie and Ken officially became a couple again.

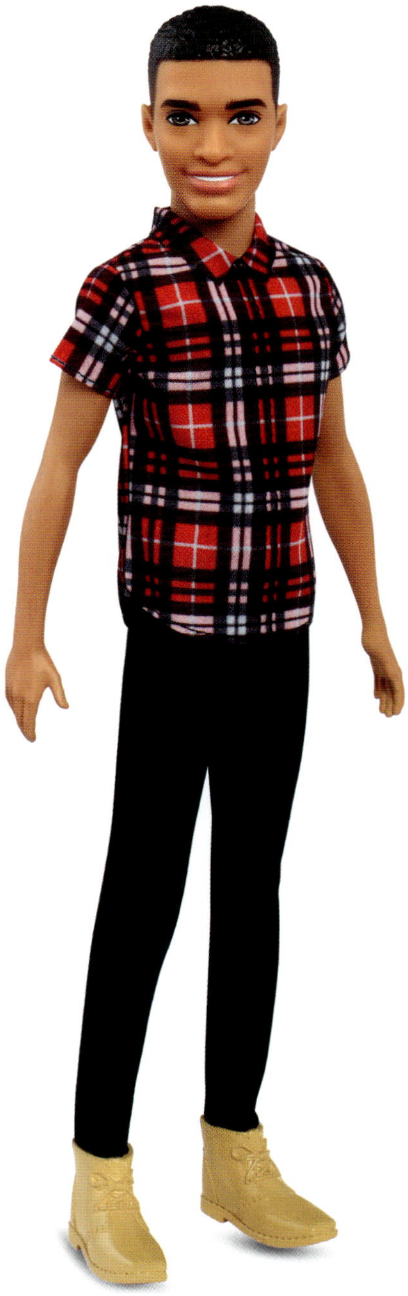

2017

Fashionistas Ken

A total reinvention, from head to toe, in the Fashionistas line, embodying every possible expression of modern masculinity. Fifteen new Ken dolls with three body types (original, slim, and stocky), seven skin tones, nine face shapes, eight hair colors, and nine hairstyles.

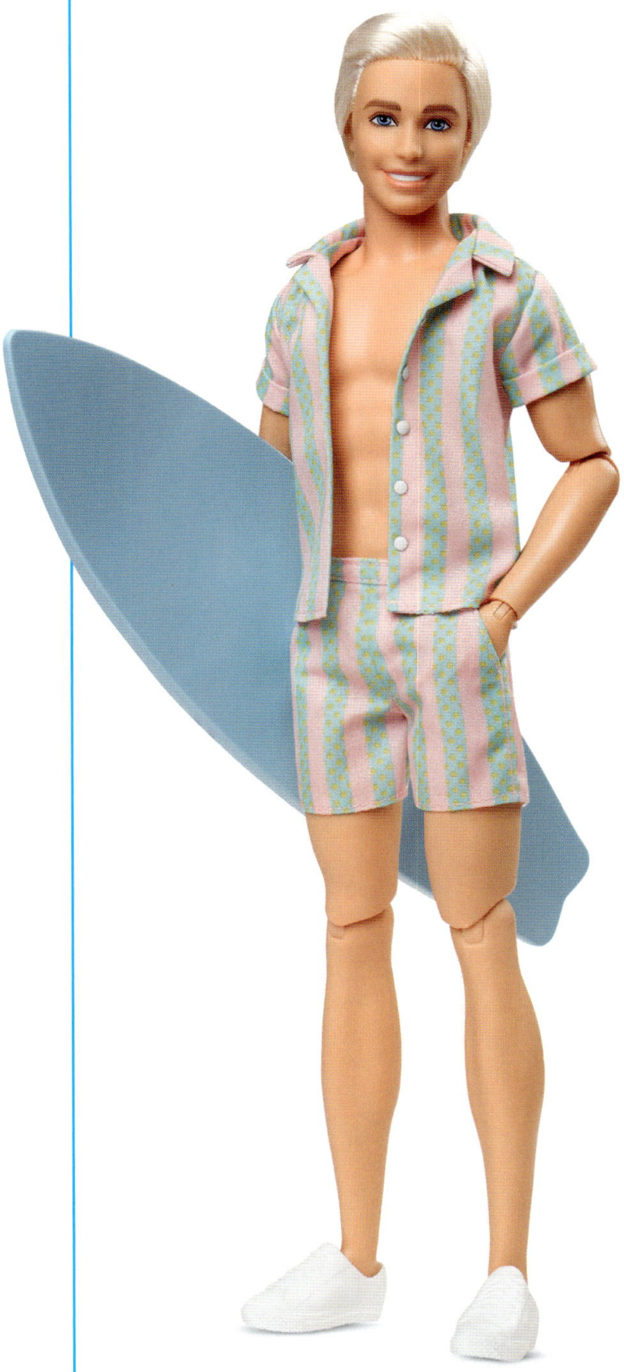

2023

The Movie Ken

Ryan Gosling earns an Oscar nomination for his portrayal of Ken in *Barbie*, directed by Greta Gerwig. As portrayed by Ryan Gosling, Ken launches a genuine "Kenaissance"—catapulting the character back into the zeitgeist. To mark the occasion, Mattel releases several platinum-blond versions, including one in full denim and another with a surfboard and beach outfit.

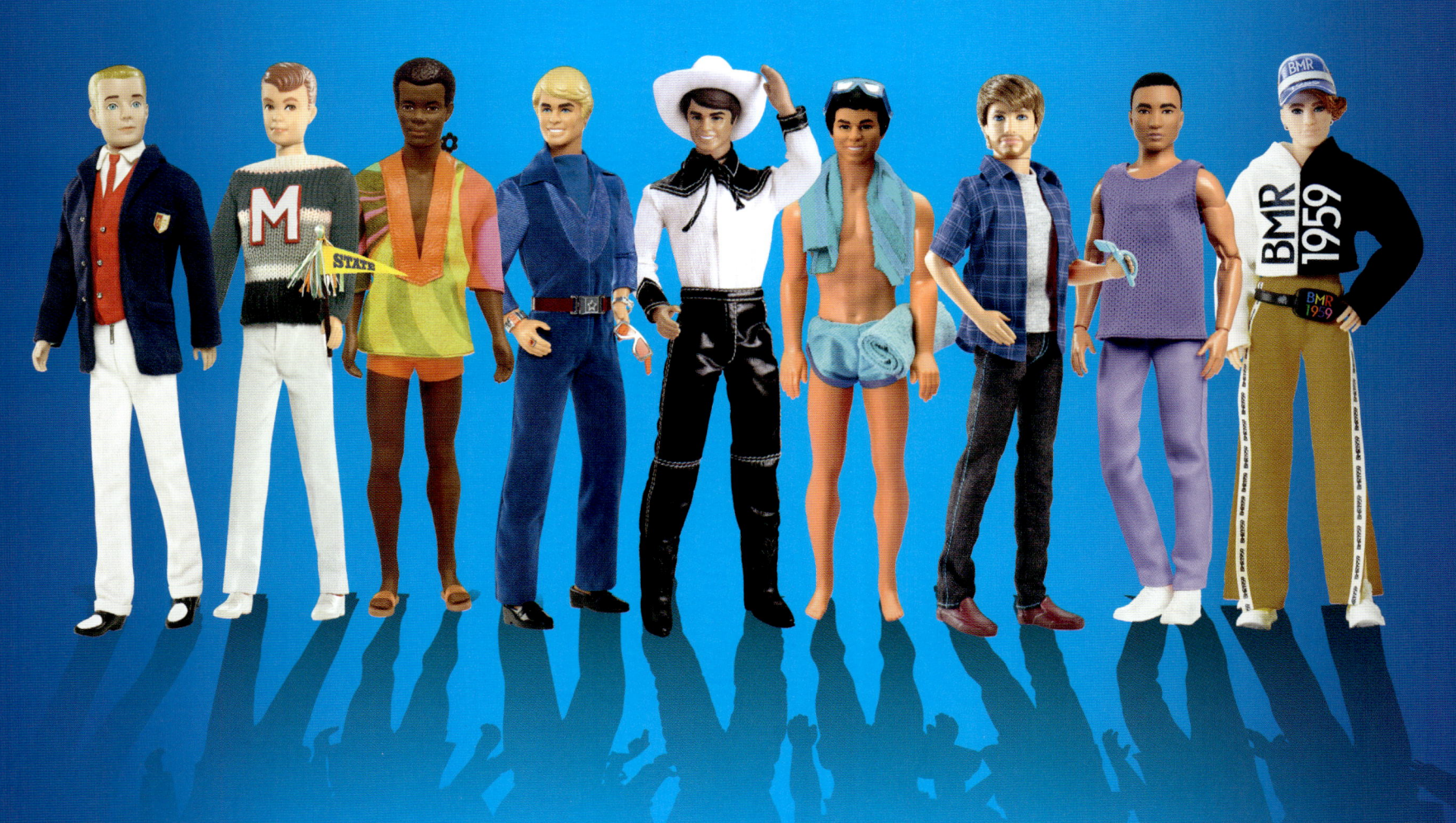

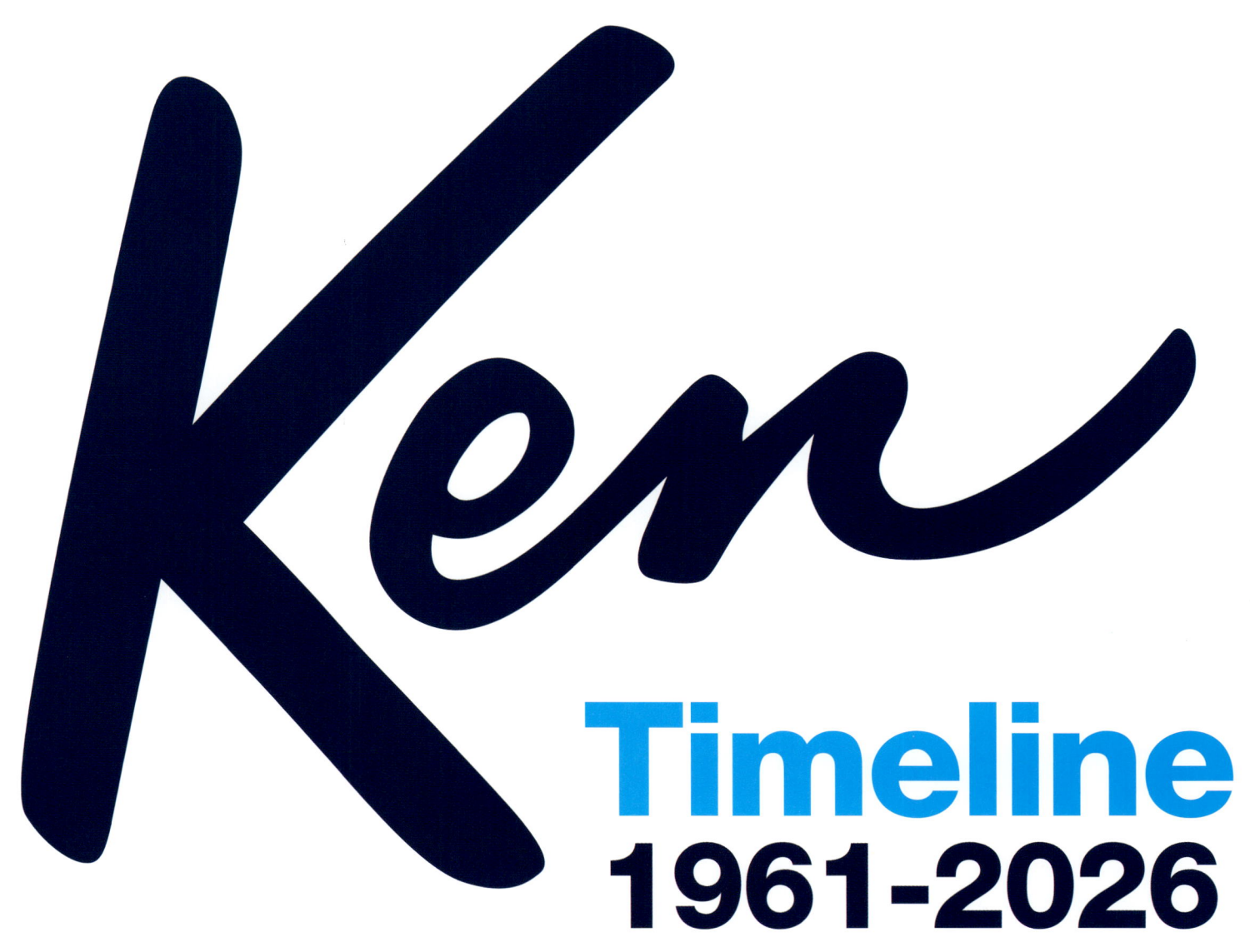

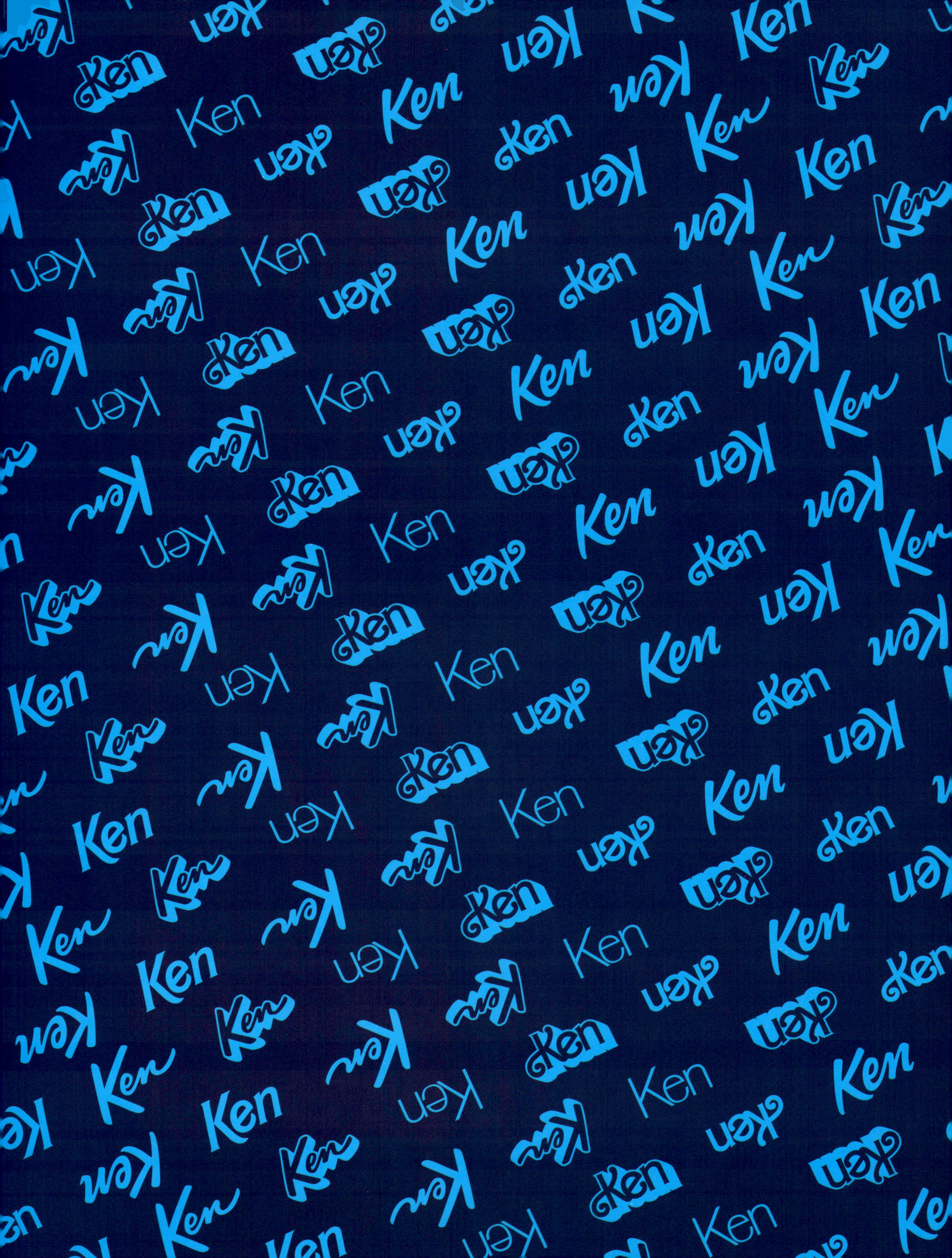

The 60s

1960-1969

1961

Flock Hair Ken

On March 11, 1961, Mattel launches the first official Ken model: Flock Hair Ken, released in three different versions—with blond, black, or brownette flocked hair. The box features an unequivocal slogan: "He's a Doll! Barbie's Boyfriend." His full name is Kenneth Sean Carson Jr., and his gaze is straightforward, with painted blue eyes.

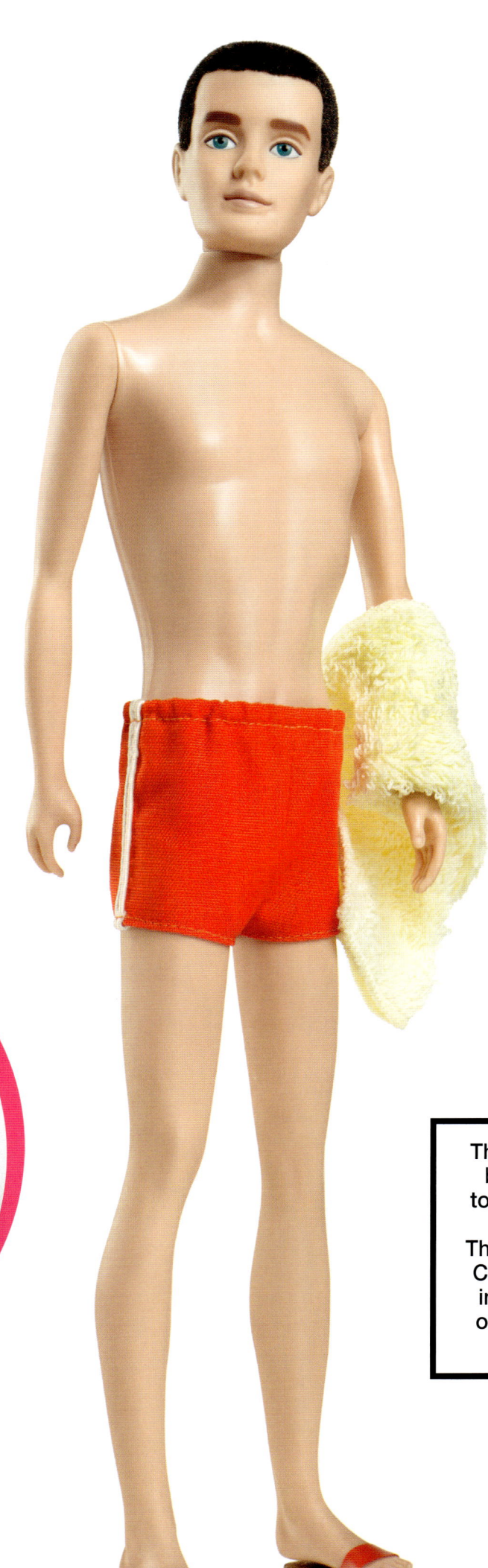

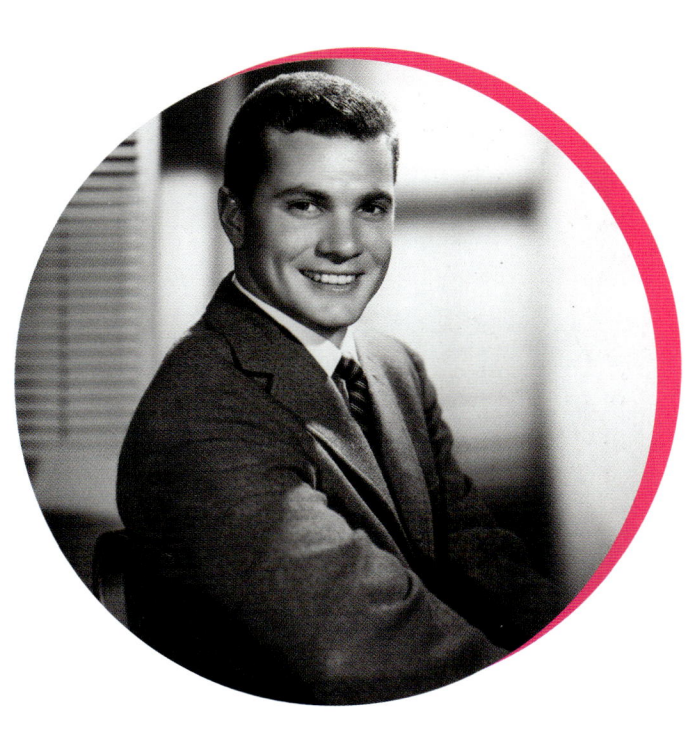

Dwayne Hickman stars as Dobie—the all-American boy next door—in the series *The Many Loves of Dobie Gillis*, which airs on American television from 1959 to 1963. The series is considered a spin-off of the 1953 film *The Affairs of Dobie Gillis*, starring Bobby Van and Debbie Reynolds.

The iconic Beach Boys begin making music together in Hawthorne, near Los Angeles. Their songs immortalize California in the public imagination as a land of sunshine, beaches, and surf culture.

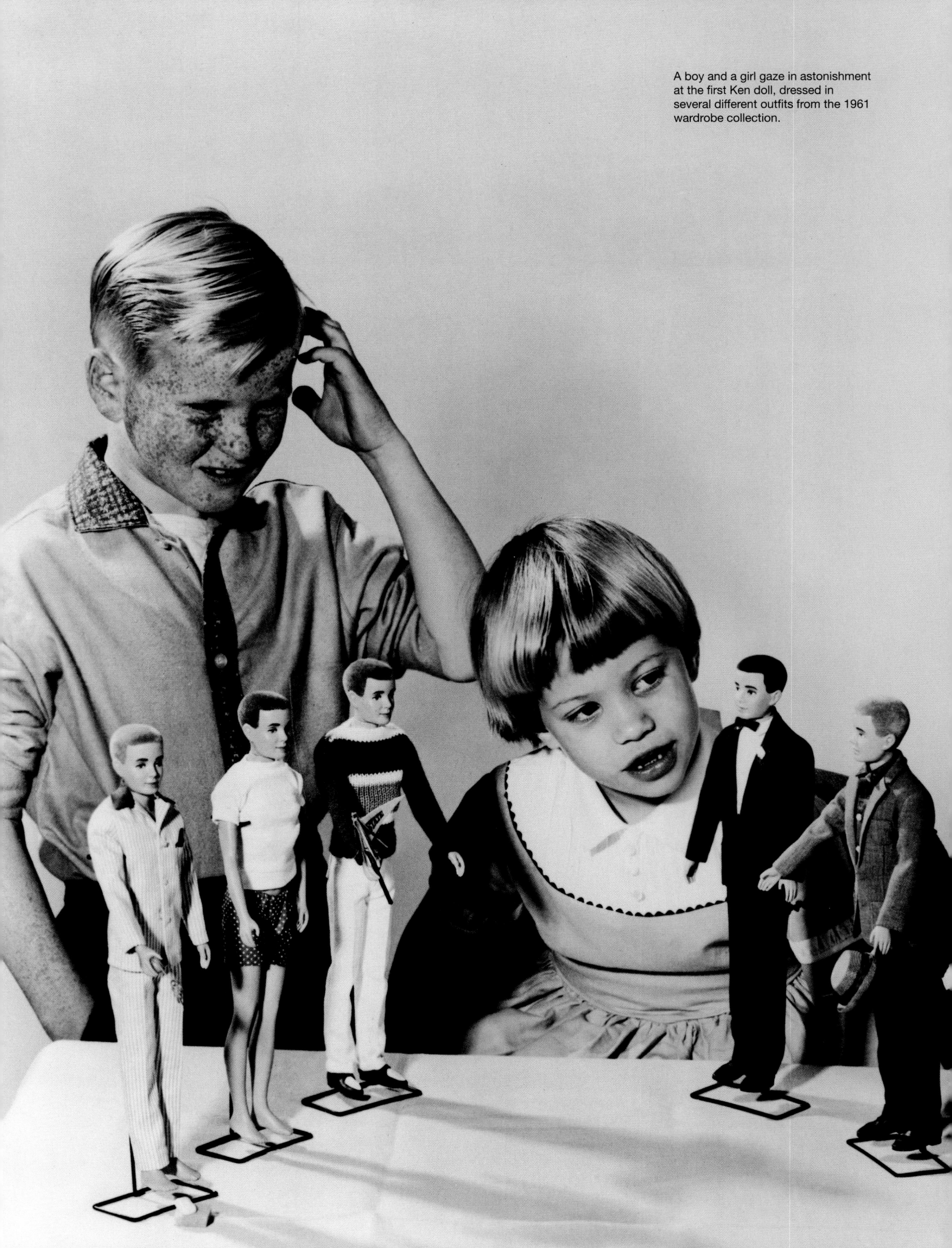

A boy and a girl gaze in astonishment at the first Ken doll, dressed in several different outfits from the 1961 wardrobe collection.

1962

Painted Hair Ken

Ken's hair is now plastic-molded and painted. The red shorts are now paired with a red-and-white striped beach shirt trimmed with white terry cloth.

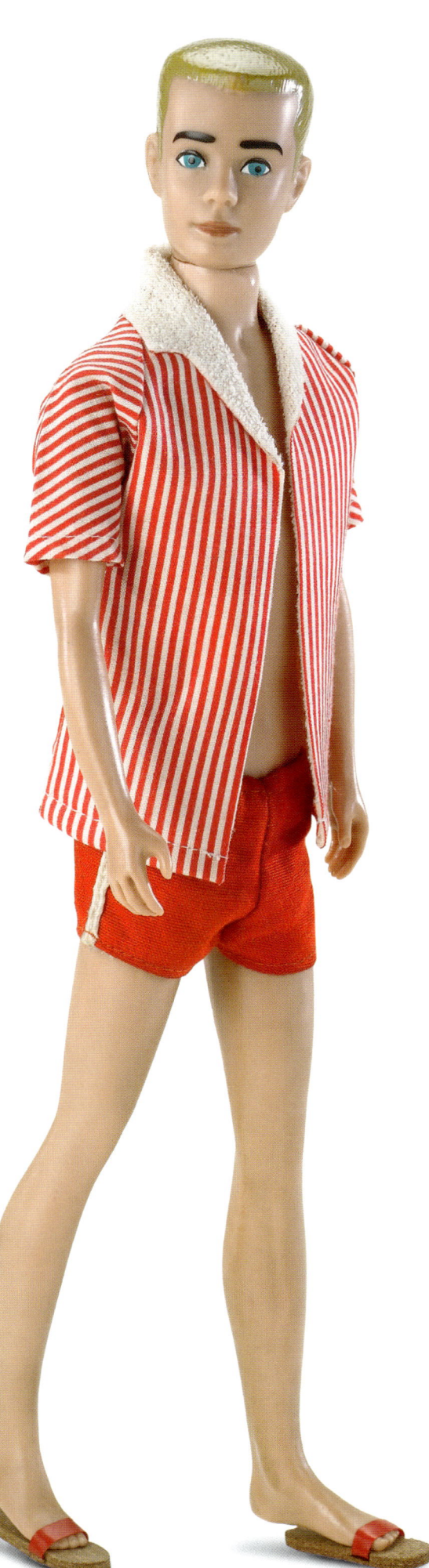

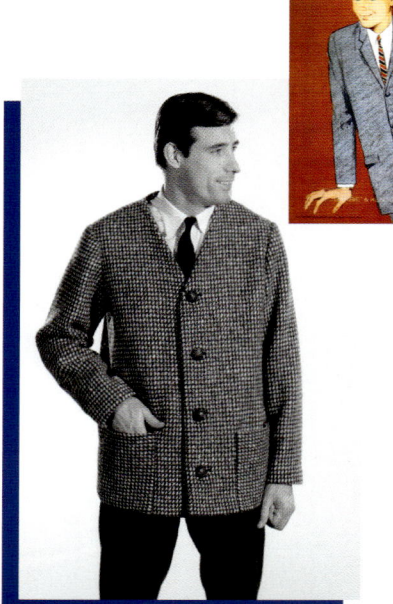

Model Peter Antony wears a tweed jacket suit.

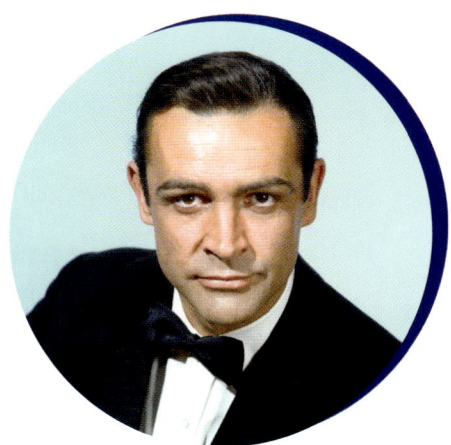

A new icon of masculine style is born—British secret agent James Bond! He is portrayed by Sean Connery, who stars in the first film in the series: *Dr. No*.

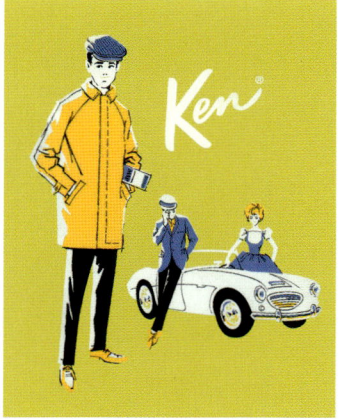

Ken's wardrobe continues to expand with new styles and accessories inspired by European sartorial elegance and American casual style, available in ensemble packs. On this occasion, Ken also becomes a race car driver, wearing the Ken Rally Day Fashion outfit.

On July 19, Valentino Garavani debuts on the catwalks of Palazzo Pitti. As the youngest designer on the schedule, he is given the final time slot on the last day—in spite of that, one hour before the show ends, his collection has already sold out.

Federico Fellini's *La Dolce Vita* wins the Oscar for costume design by Pietro Gherardi. Italian style—embodied by Marcello Mastroianni—conquers the world.

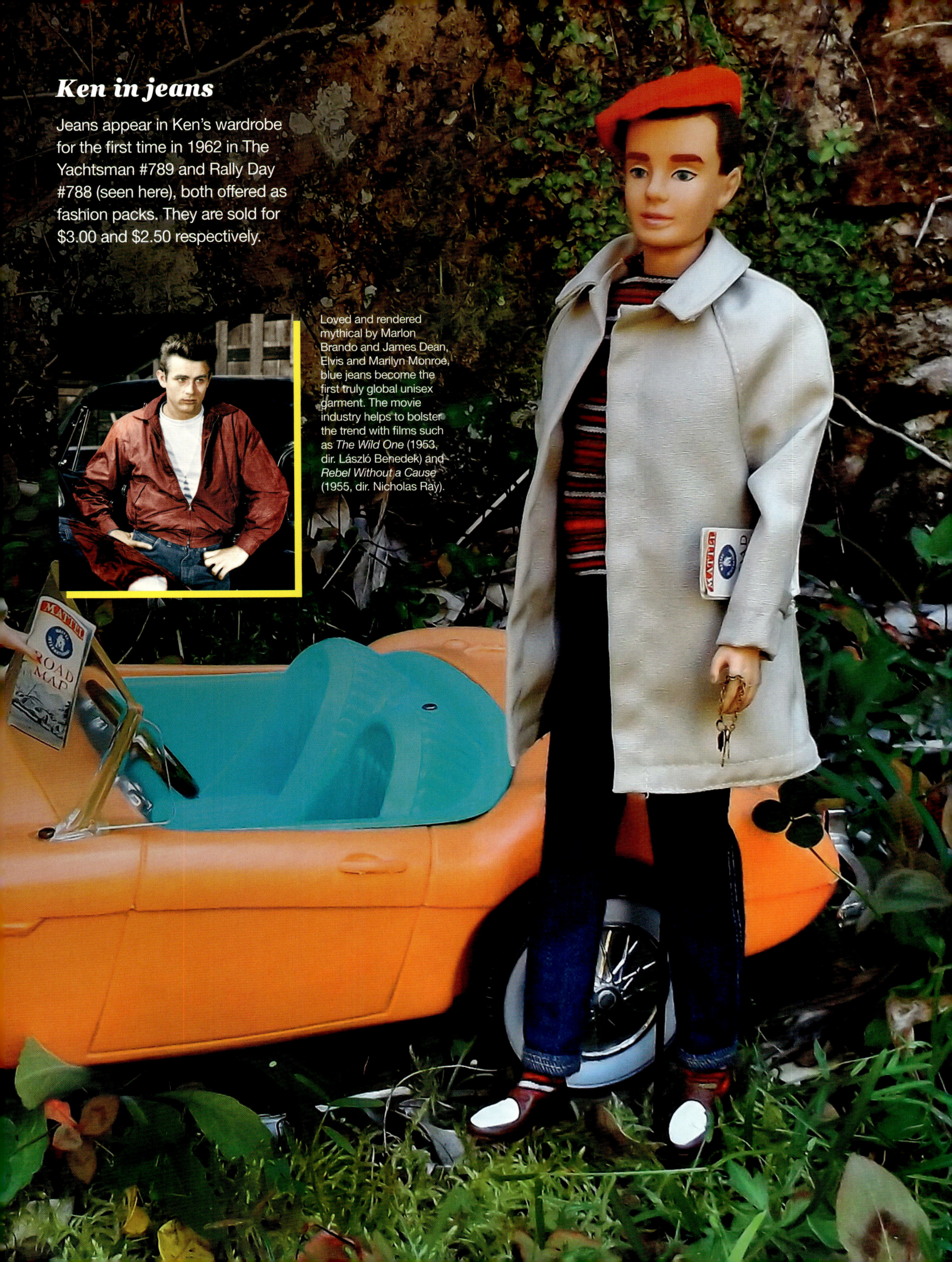

Ken in jeans

Jeans appear in Ken's wardrobe for the first time in 1962 in The Yachtsman #789 and Rally Day #788 (seen here), both offered as fashion packs. They are sold for $3.00 and $2.50 respectively.

Loved and rendered mythical by Marlon Brando and James Dean, Elvis and Marilyn Monroe, blue jeans become the first truly global unisex garment. The movie industry helps to bolster the trend with films such as *The Wild One* (1953, dir. László Benedek) and *Rebel Without a Cause* (1955, dir. Nicholas Ray).

1964

Victory Dance Ken

Alongside his traditional outfits and the elegant fashion of Victory Dance Ken, Ken's wardrobe grows to include three theatrical costumes and four outfits inspired by the traditional attire of Mexico, Hawaii, the Netherlands, and Switzerland.

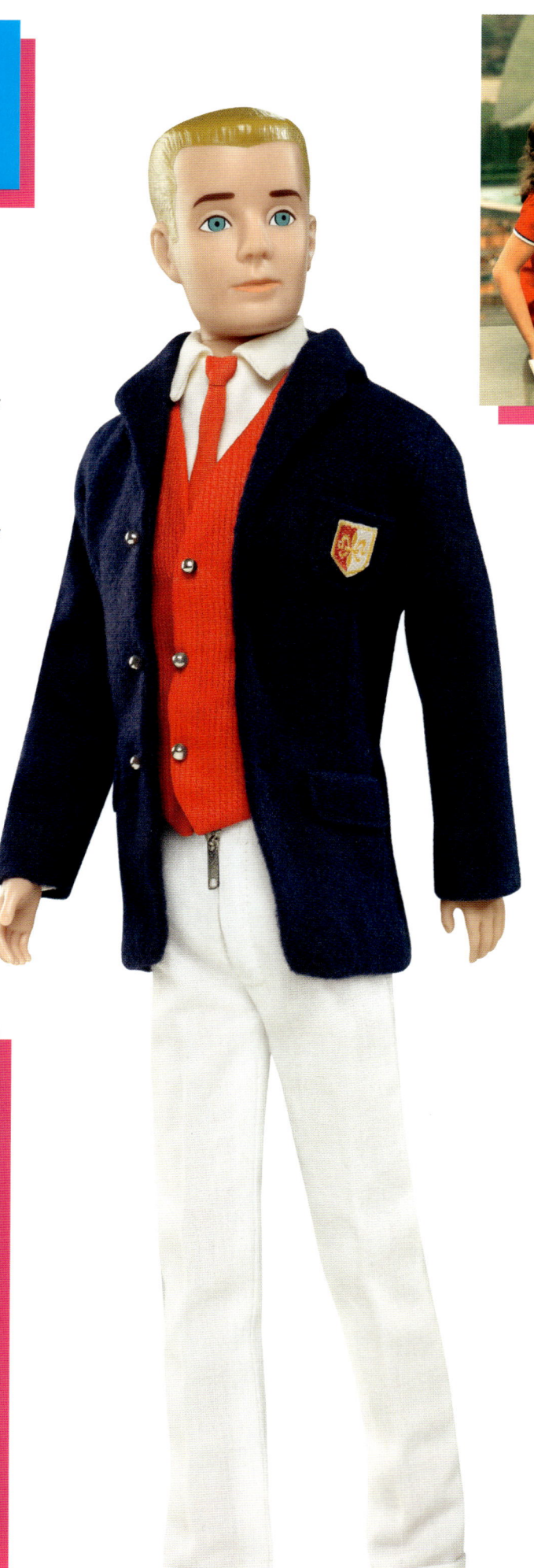

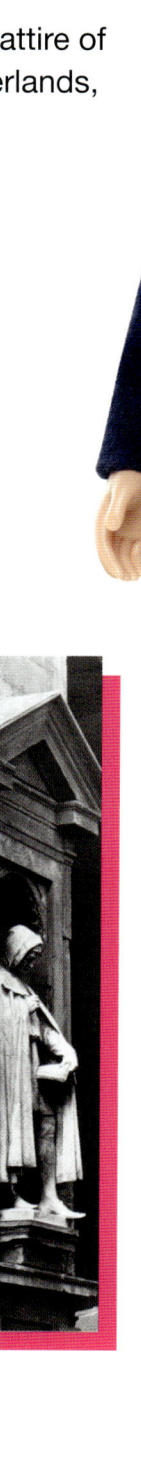

A model poses in an alcove of the loggia in Florence's Piazza del Mercato Nuovo, wearing a double-breasted blazer. Brioni transforms men's elegance into an art form!

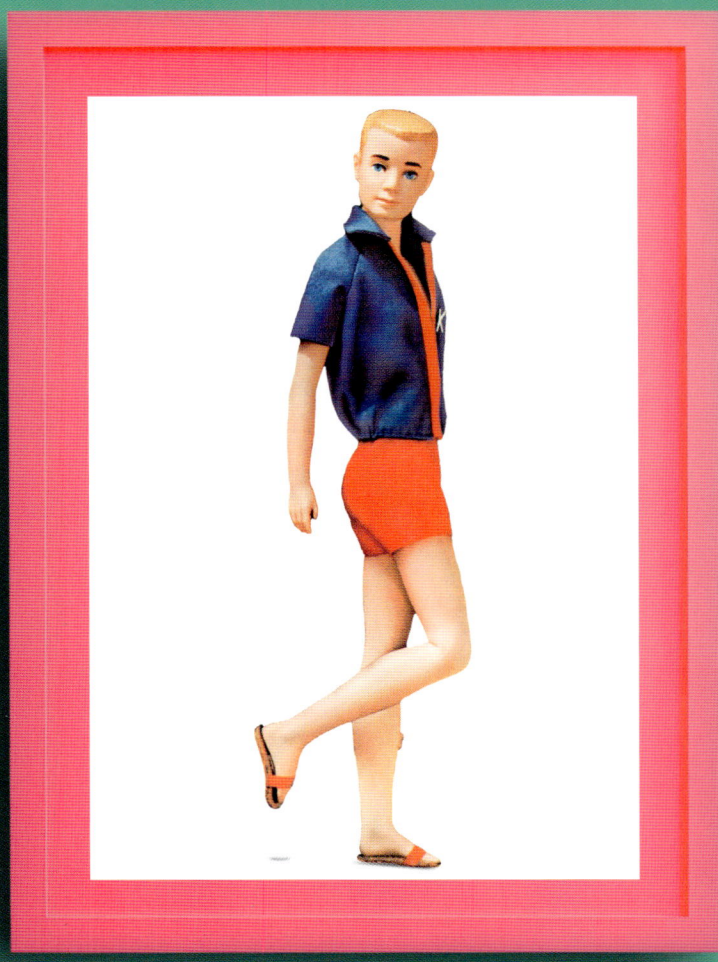

Allan

A new friend enters Ken's world: Allan Sherwood, who shares many items from Ken's wardrobe.

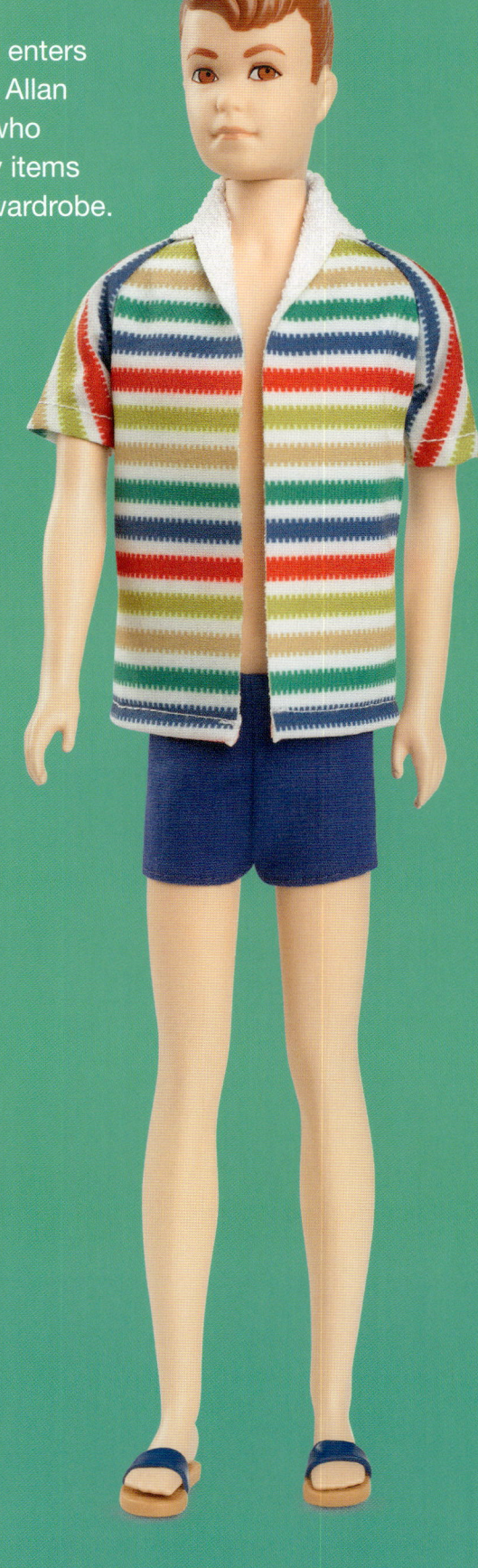

Bendable Leg Ken

Ken becomes increasingly fashionable and flexible—literally, in perfect time with a culture increasingly enchanted with free-wheeling dance moves. Now, both Ken and Allan appear in bendable-leg versions. Ken, in blond or brunette versions, wears red swim trunks and a navy jacket with red trim and a "K" monogram and cork sandals. Allan sports the same look, but with reversed colors and an "A" on his jacket.

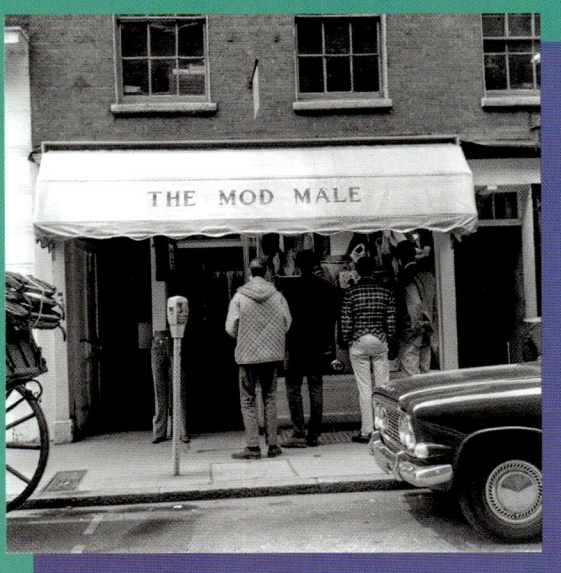

In London, Mary Quant launches the miniskirt. The Swinging London era begins, centered on Carnaby Street as the global hub of youth fashion. The Mod Male becomes one of the most popular clothing shops, with young Londoners following "Mod" culture.

The body is in constant and increasing motion—especially on the dance floor. The craze for the Twist takes the world by storm.

1966

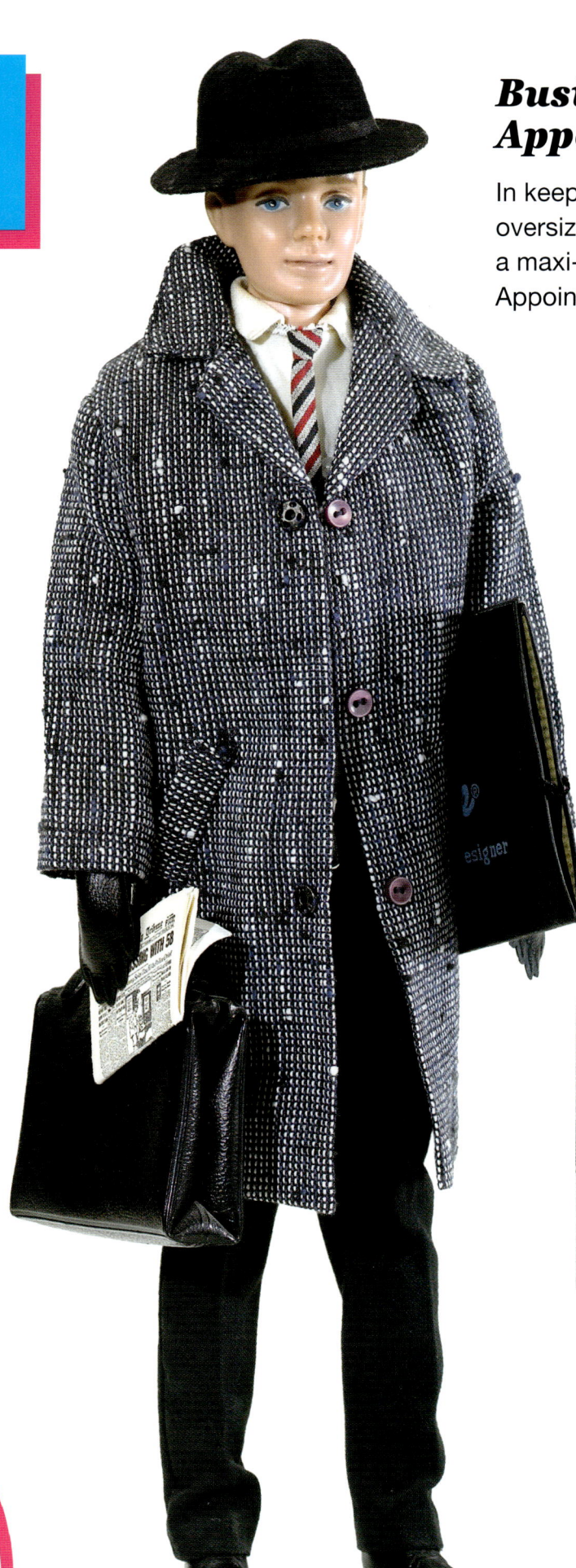

Business Appointment Ken

In keeping with the trend toward oversized silhouettes, Ken sports a maxi-coat for his Business Appointment look.

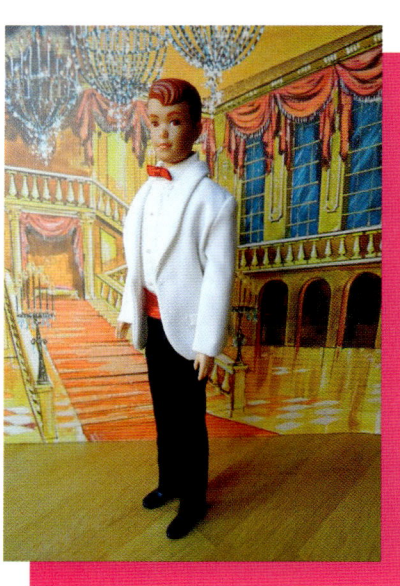

Best Man

All tuxed up: Ken, along with Allan, becomes a best man and wears a white tuxedo jacket with shawl collar, black cotton twill trousers with a side stripe, a white ruffled shirt with pearl buttons, and a red satin bow tie and cummerbund.

Riding the popularity of the film *Doctor Zhivago* (1965), the fashion market embraces the maxi-coat, dutifully paired with a warm fur hat. Mini and maxi styles coexist for a few years, before settling into the midi length that closes out the 1960s.

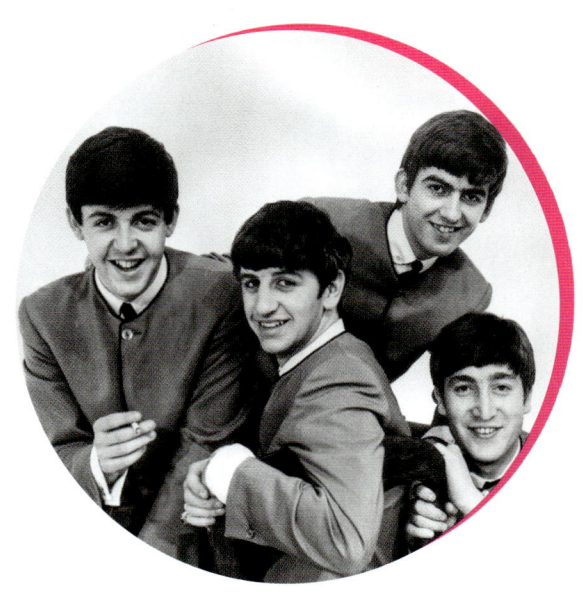

Pierre Cardin introduces cigarette trousers and collarless suit jackets in men's fashion. The collarless "Cylinder Look" jacket shapes the Beatles early look. The worldwide Beatles phenomenon, sparked by their appearance on *The Ed Sullivan Show*, launches a true British invasion.

From a masculine wardrobe item, by virtue of the genius of Yves Saint Laurent, the tux becomes a unisex piece of apparel.

1967

Pilot Ken by Pucci

The Montgomery Ward Christmas catalog presents an exciting novelty: Ken in a Braniff International Airways pilot uniform created by Italian fashion designer Emilio Pucci.

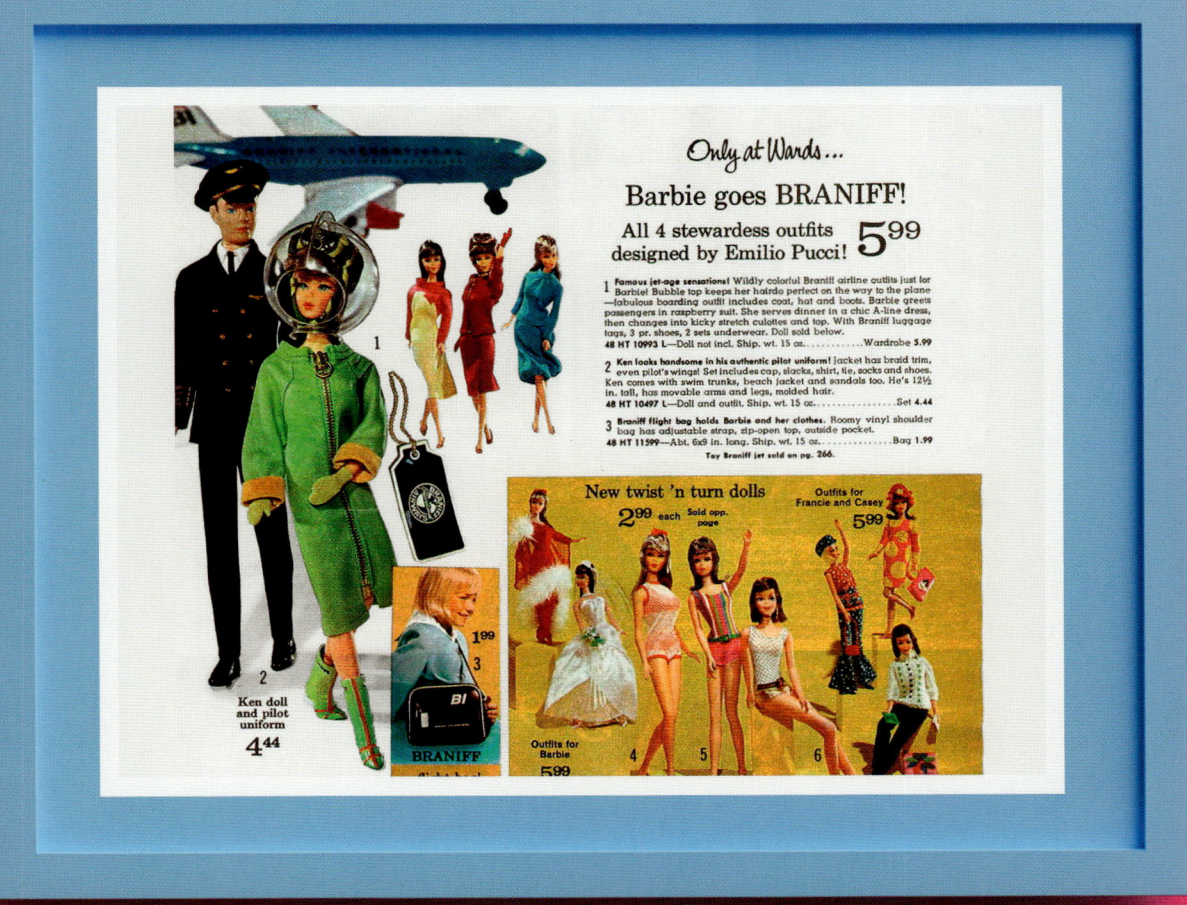

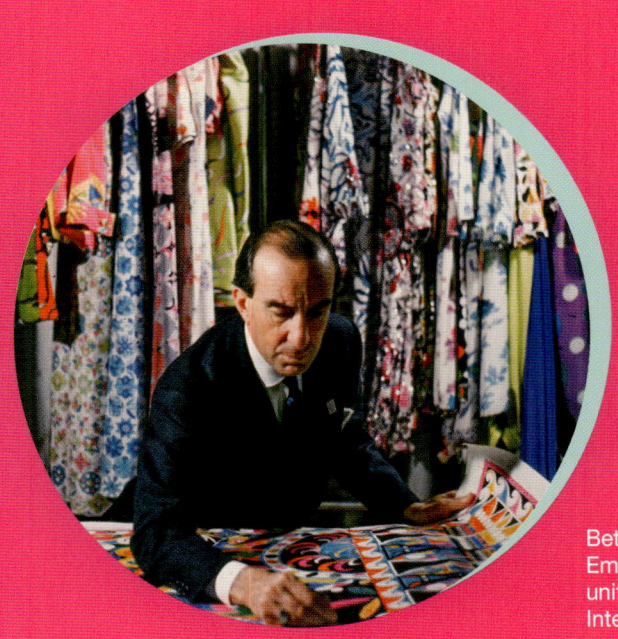

Between 1965 and 1973, Emilio Pucci designs uniforms for Braniff International Airways.

Men's Vogue: The fashion magazine *L'Uomo Vogue* is founded by Flavio Lucchini as a supplement to *Vogue Italia*. It is the first fashion magazine dedicated to men published by Condé Nast, and will remain the only one until *Men's Vogue* launches in the United States in 2005.

1969

New Good-Lookin' Talking Ken

A real game changer: Ken now has molded, painted plastic hair with sideswept bangs. Now he smiles, revealing his white teeth. Ken wears red shorts and a matching Nehru-style summer shirt-jacket. His body is more muscular and defined, and he presents a new face mold—one of the most iconic of the following decade—used for Free Moving Ken (1975–1976), Malibu Ken (1971–1978), Olympic Skier Ken (1975–1976), and last of all, Hawaiian Ken (1978–1979).

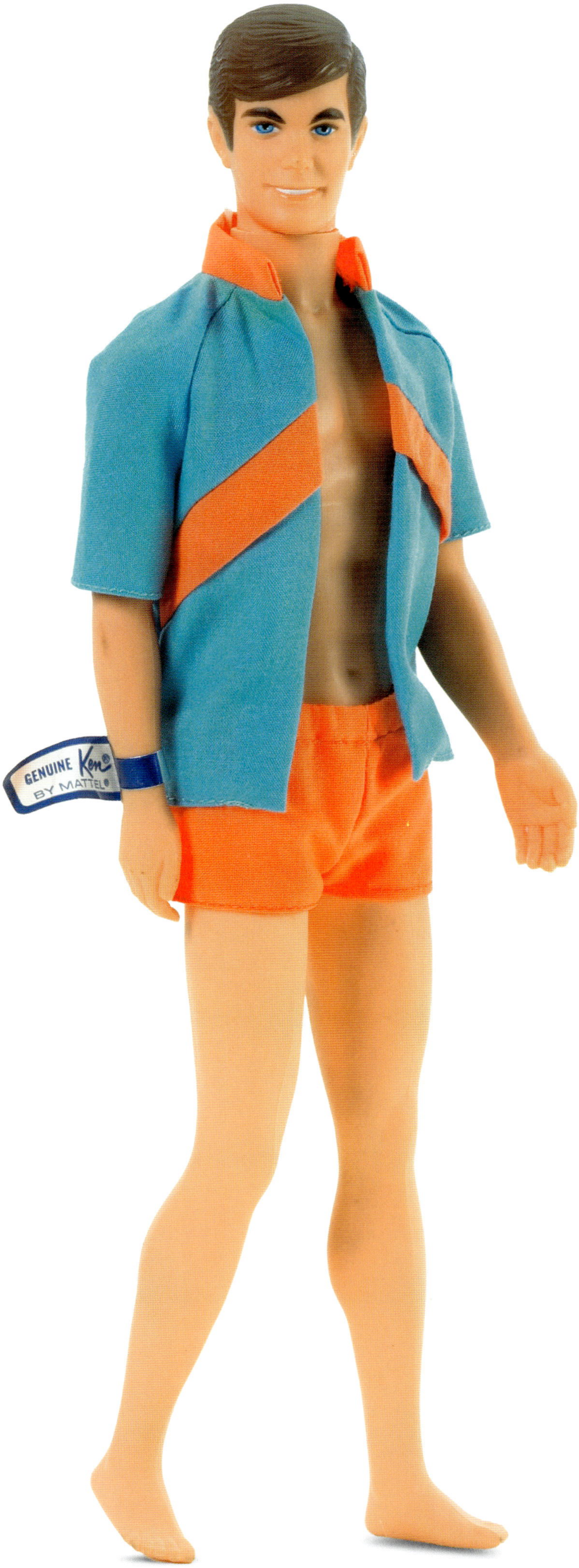

Danilo Donati wins the Oscar for Best Costume Design for Franco Zeffirelli's *Romeo and Juliet*.

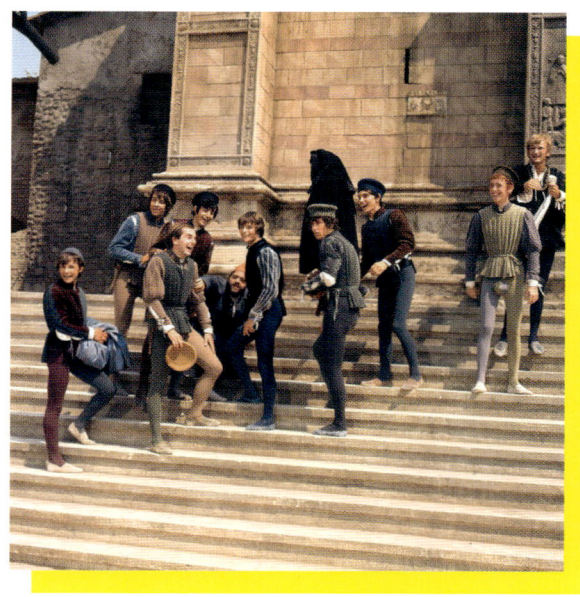

Brad

Brad is introduced as the first Black male character. New Talking Brad features a unique face mold and utters several phrases, including:
"My name is Brad."
"Christie is the best."
"Baseball is my favorite sport."
"Let's go to the movies."
"I like the Mod look."
"Hey, let's all go for a ride."
He is produced until 1972.

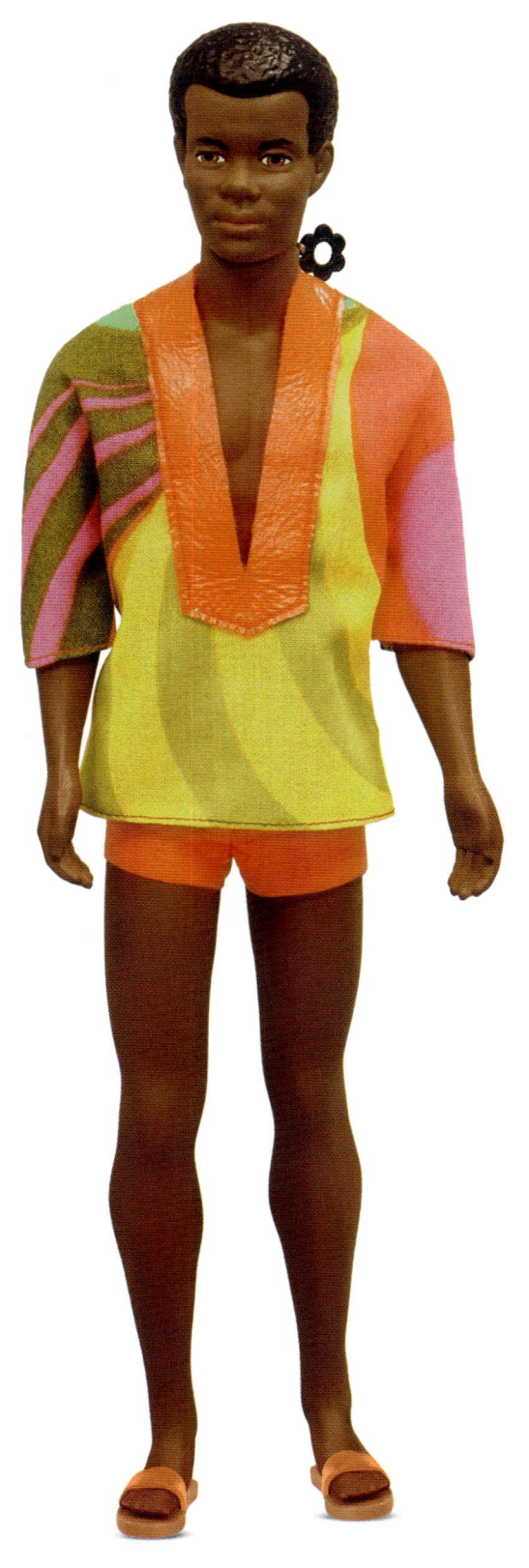

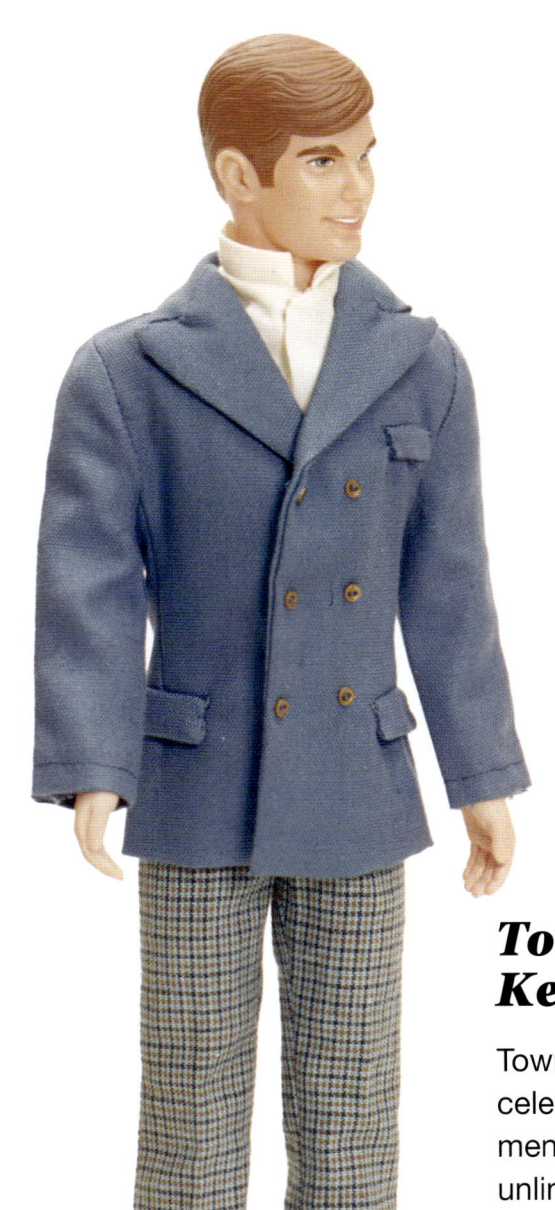

Town Turtle Ken

Town Turtle Ken offers a celebration of Edwardian menswear style with an unlined double-breasted navy jacket, a white Nehru shirt, slim-fit blue-and-white checkered trousers, knitted blue socks, and black loafers.

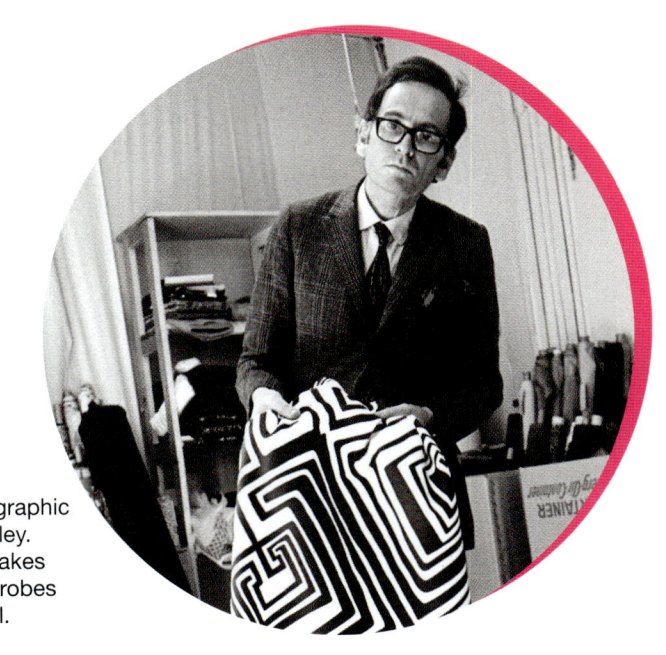

Pierre Cardin designs outfits inspired by the graphic art of Bridget Riley. Op Art fashion takes menswear wardrobes by storm as well.

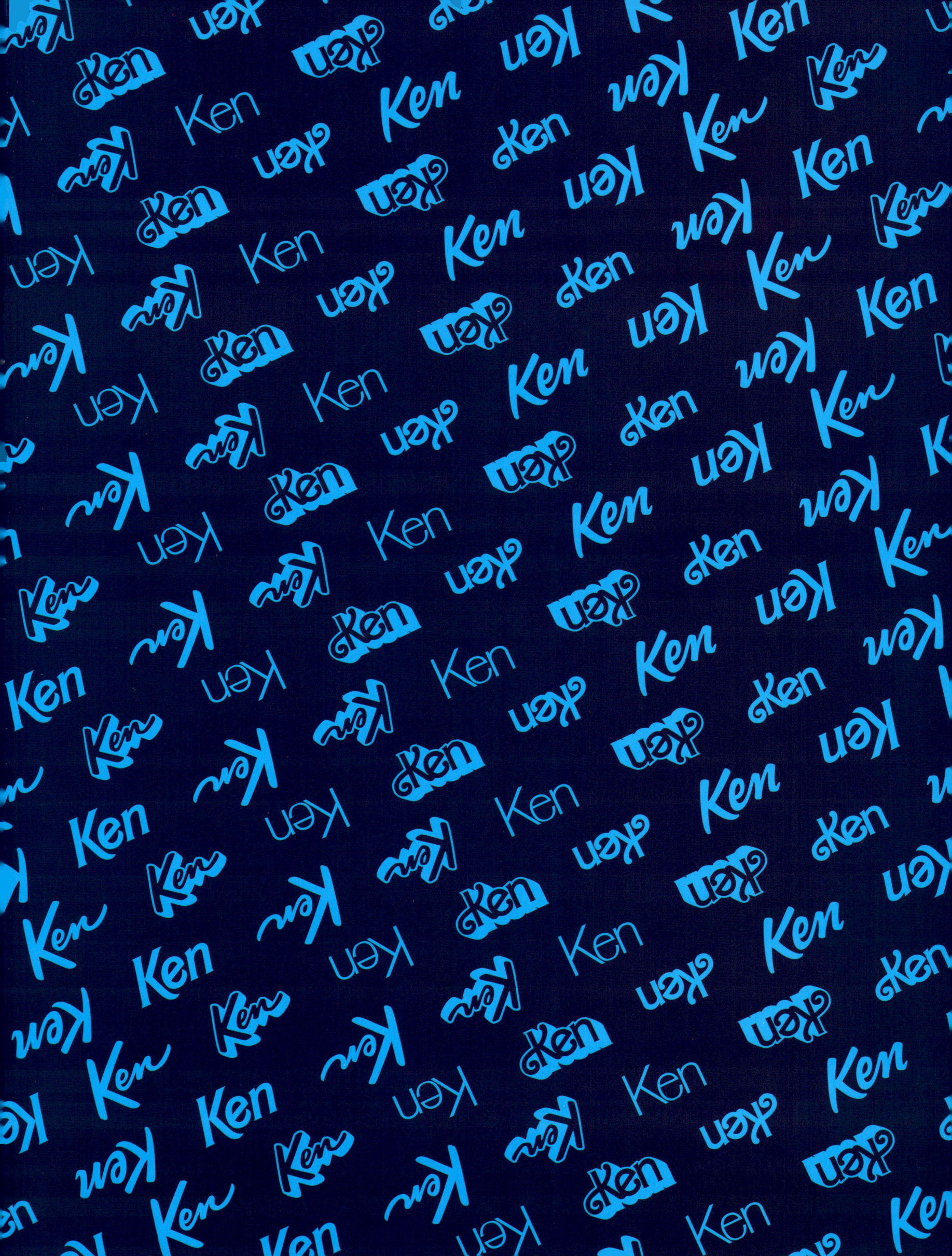

The 70s

1970-1979

1970

Live Action On Stage Ken

Live Action On Stage Ken once again shakes up his wardrobe with gold satin pants, a fringed brown Western-style vest, a multicolor shirt, and brown loafers. The On Stage model is more dynamic, featuring a motorized base and a disk that plays two hit songs: "A Little Bit of That Sky" and an instrumental track.

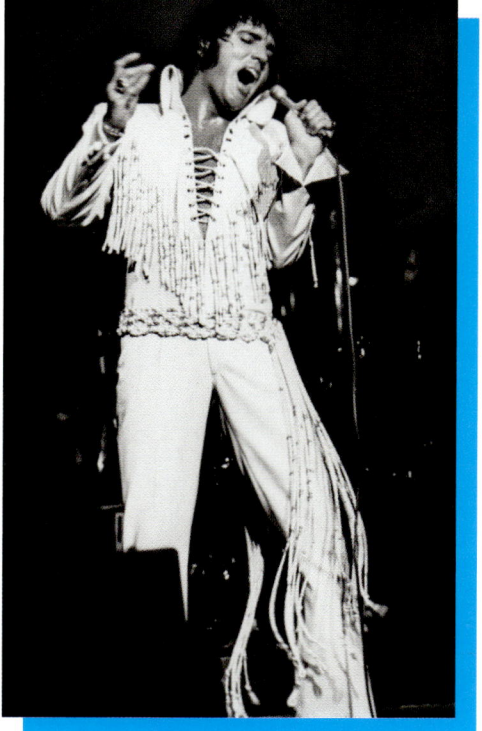

Elvis Presley performs in Las Vegas in one of his legendary outfits—a mix of leather, fringe, and studs!

> Japanese fashion design arrives in France with KENZO, while in America, Issey Miyake launches his Tattoo Collection.

> On April 22, the first worldwide event for environmental protection is held: Earth Day. Fashion inevitably responds to this newfound spirit of environmentalism and multiculturalism.

48

Riding the wave of the layered hippie look (Peruvian ponchos, capes, and raw wool sweaters), numerous fashion lines inspired by global style hit the scene. Ken and Barbie will also be influenced by these innovative trends.

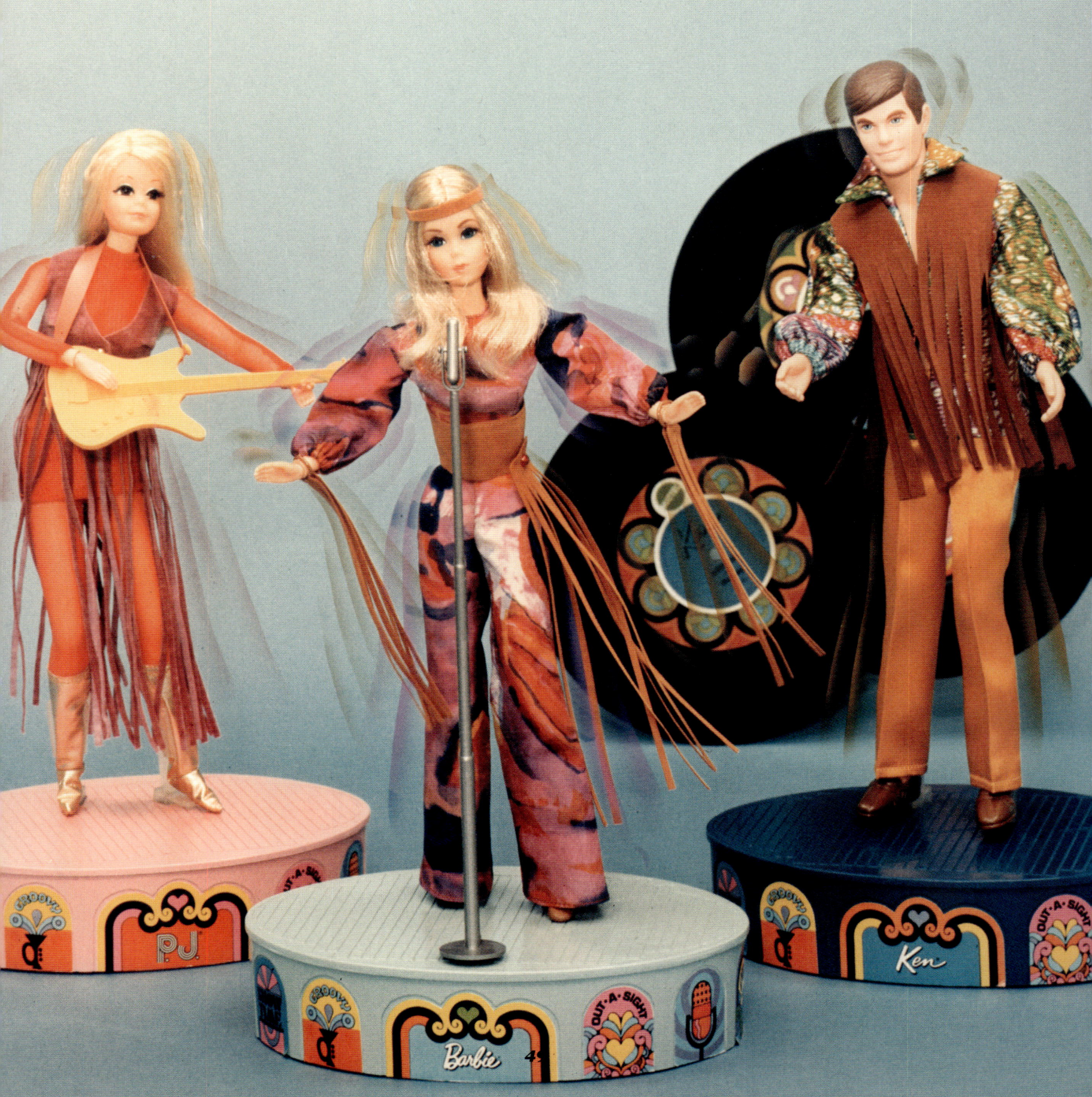

1971

Busy Ken

Busy Ken premieres as a more mobile version, with the unmistakable slogan on the box: "My hands open, close, hold things too!" He comes with accessories like a TV, valise, telephone, record player, and a tray with two glasses. Busy Ken is the first Ken model launched for the European market. For the occasion, he wears jeans and a textured orange tank top (red in the US version).

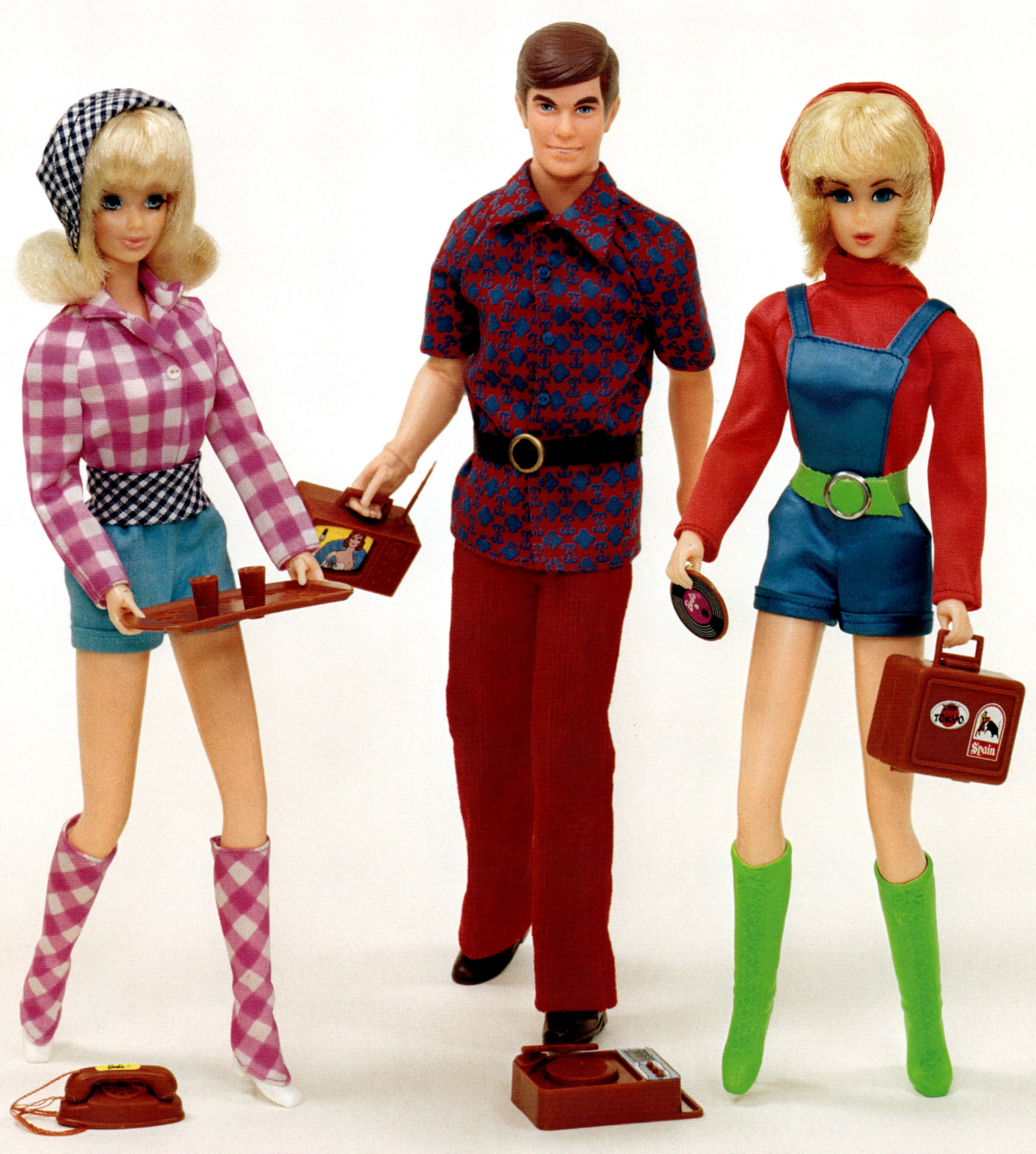

Malibu Ken Surf's Up

The ultimate California boy. Malibu Ken is unmistakably blond, ready to hit the beach and ride his surfboard. His golden tan is accentuated by his outfit: orange swim trunks and a yellow floral shirt with a Nehru collar. He's equipped with a blue towel, dive mask, snorkel, flippers, sunglasses, and the classic cork sandals.

> **Lloyd Johnson** launches the Sea Cruise Jacket, with neo-deco graphics by Sue Saunders.

> **Andy Warhol** designs one of the most controversial album covers in history for *Sticky Fingers* by the Rolling Stones: a pair of jeans with a real zipper, worn by Joe Dallesandro.

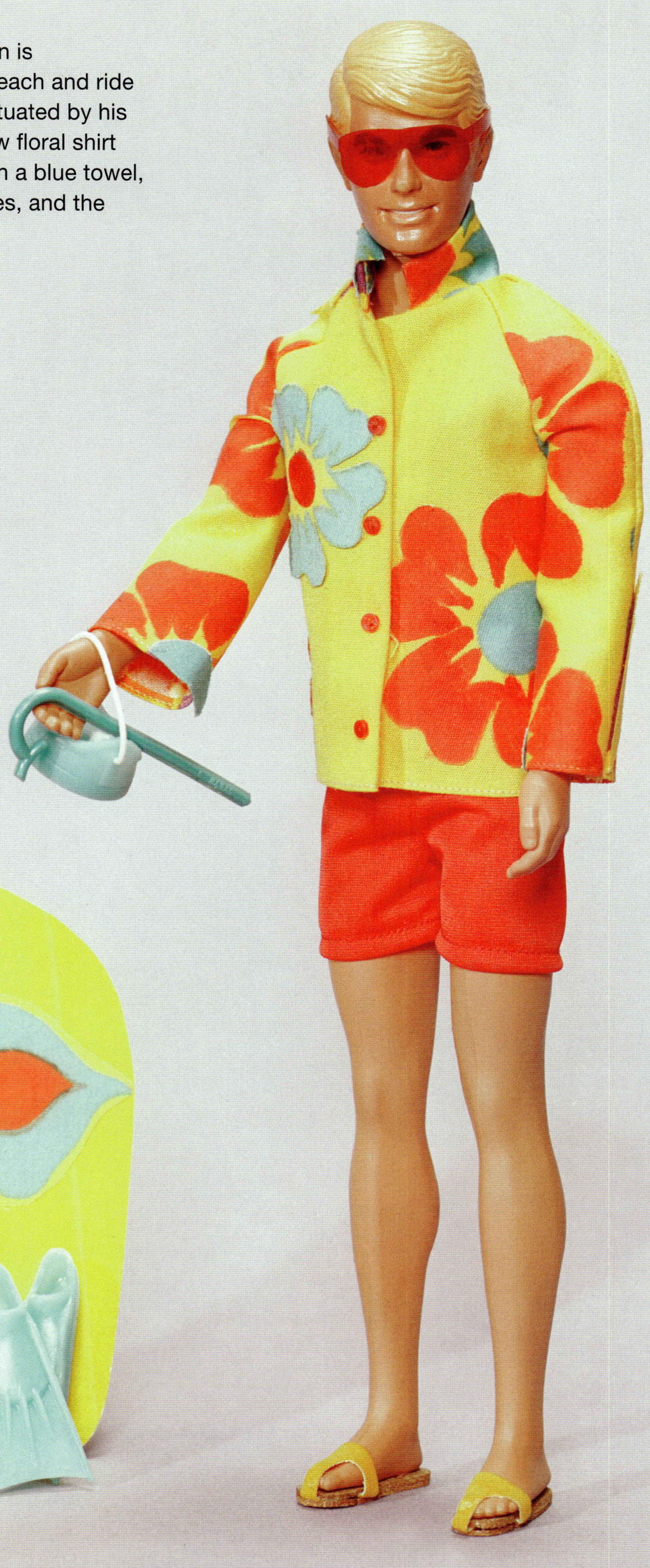

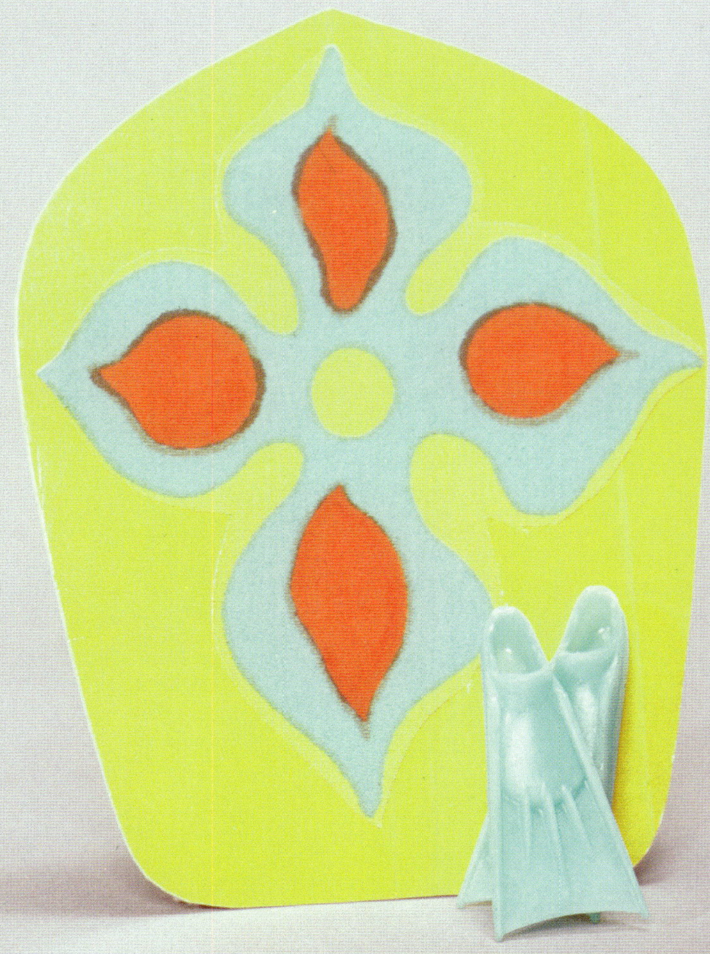

1972

Mod Hair Ken

Mod Hair Ken returns with more natural hair, replacing the molded plastic look. This new model alternates styles with beard, mustache, goatee, sideburns, and long, straight or curly hair. He wears beige slacks with brown loafers, a white turtleneck, and a brown-and-white plaid blazer.

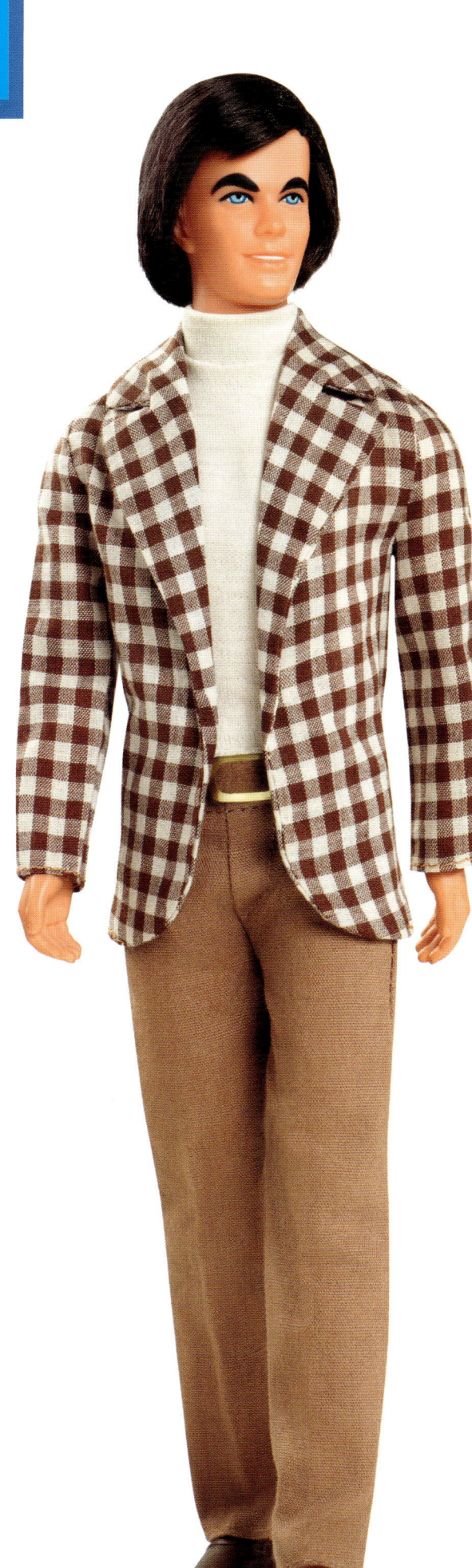

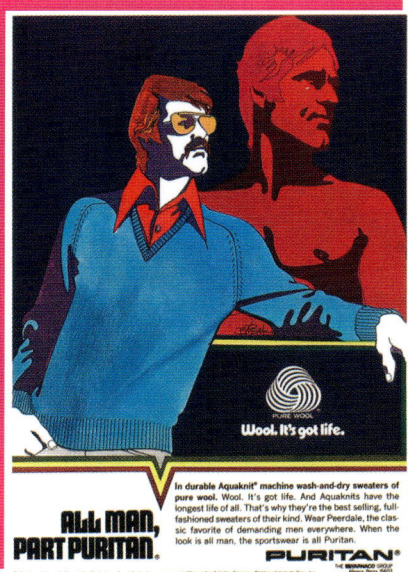

The seventies look brings us a colorful man with flowing hair, a beard, and a mustache.

After Brioni's first menswear show at Florence's Palazzo Pitti, in the Sala Bianca, in 1952, Pitti Uomo is officially founded in Florence—becoming the most important international event for men's fashion.

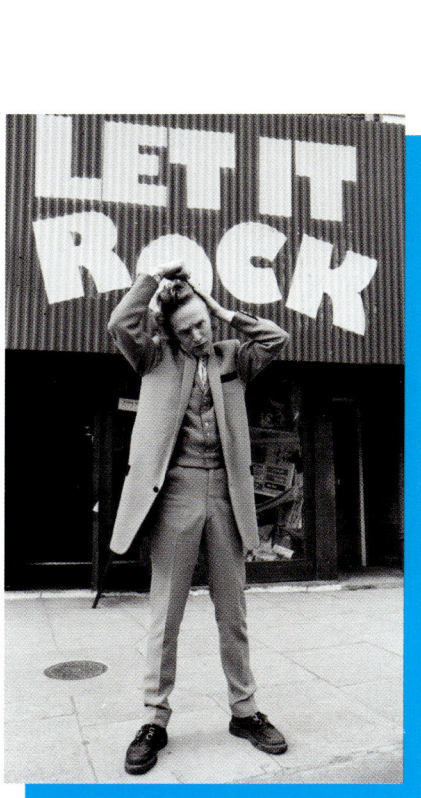

While American hippie fashion still reigns, new punk and rock trends begin to take hold among young people. Vivienne Westwood opens her first London boutique, Let It Rock, at 430 King's Road.

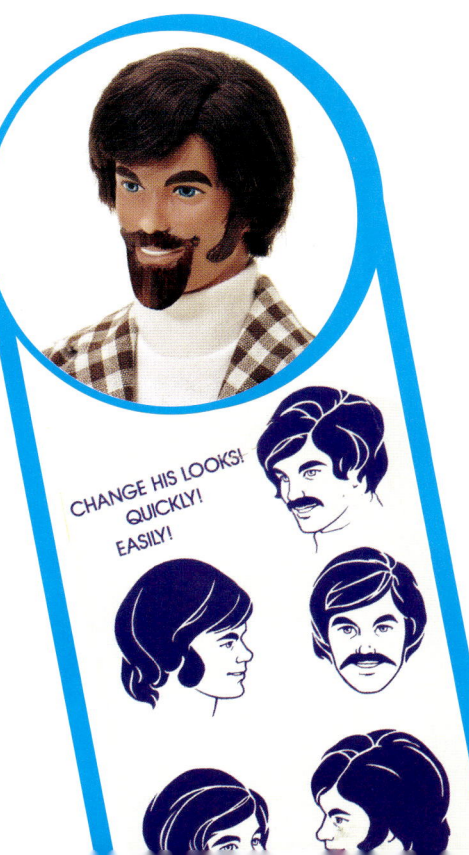

1974

Mod Hair Ken (Montgomery Ward)

Ken wears Bridegroom #7836 Get-Ups 'N Go Fashions line. That same year, Mod Hair Ken is released in an exclusive edition in which he wears an ultra-elegant look: a brocade tuxedo with black lapels, black trousers, a ruffled light blue shirt with black bow tie, mesh socks, and black loafers. This exclusive set is created for the Montgomery Ward mail-order catalog, following the model previously tested by Sears between 1969 and 1972 with the Red White 'N Wild Gift Set and Malibu Ken Surf's Up Gift Set, and later with Flight Time Ken (1989).

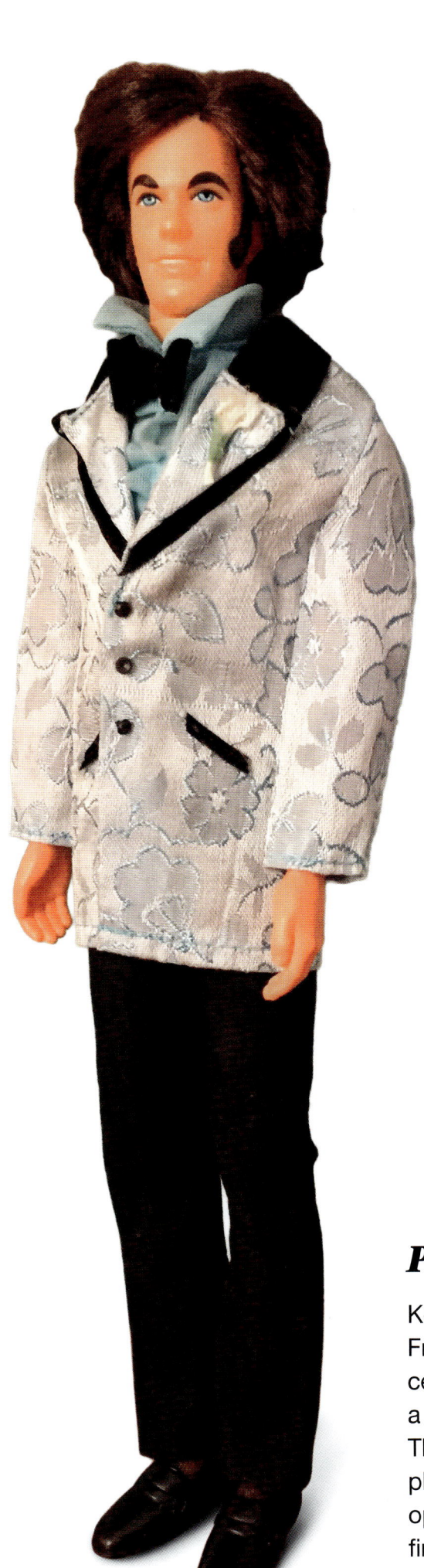

Pepsi Ken

Ken, along with Barbie, Francie, and Skipper, celebrates Pepsi Cola with a specially dedicated outfit. That same year, a Soviet bottling plant for the American beverage opens in Novorossiysk—the first Western product sold and produced in the Soviet market.

1974

Free Moving Ken and Curtis

Curtis is Ken's new friend.
The new Free Moving models, which include Barbie and Cara, pursue their passion for sports, from tennis to golf.

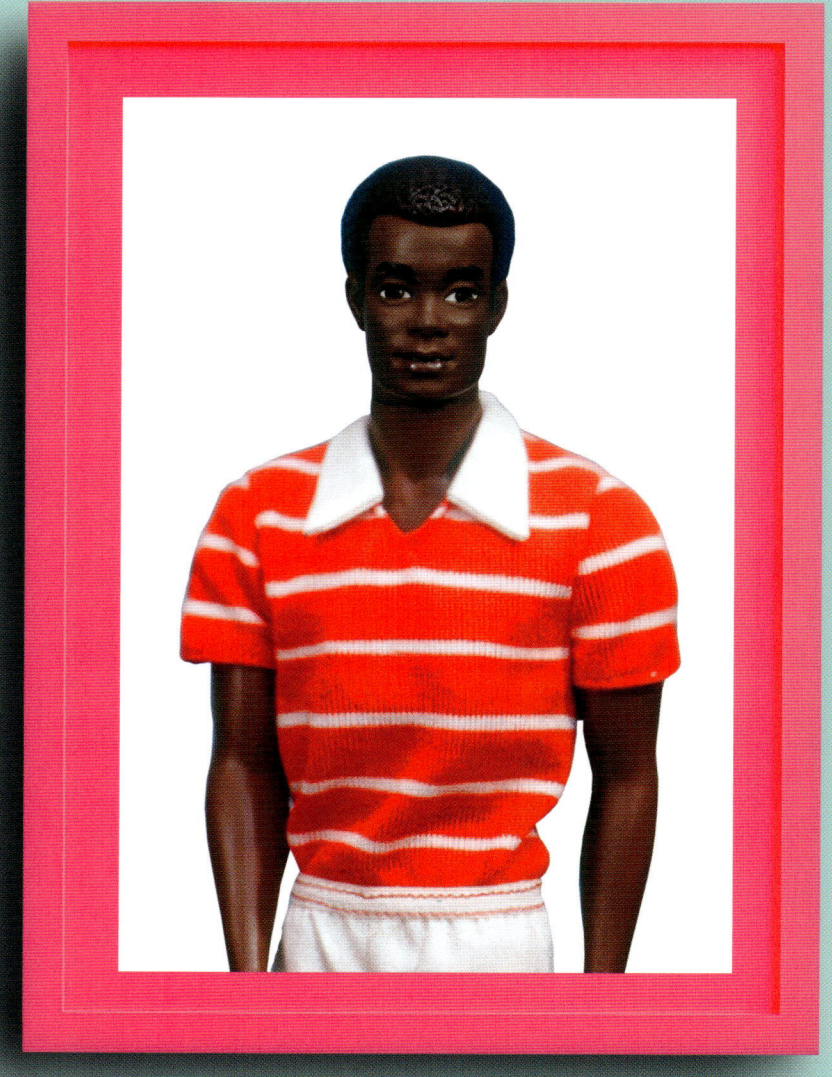

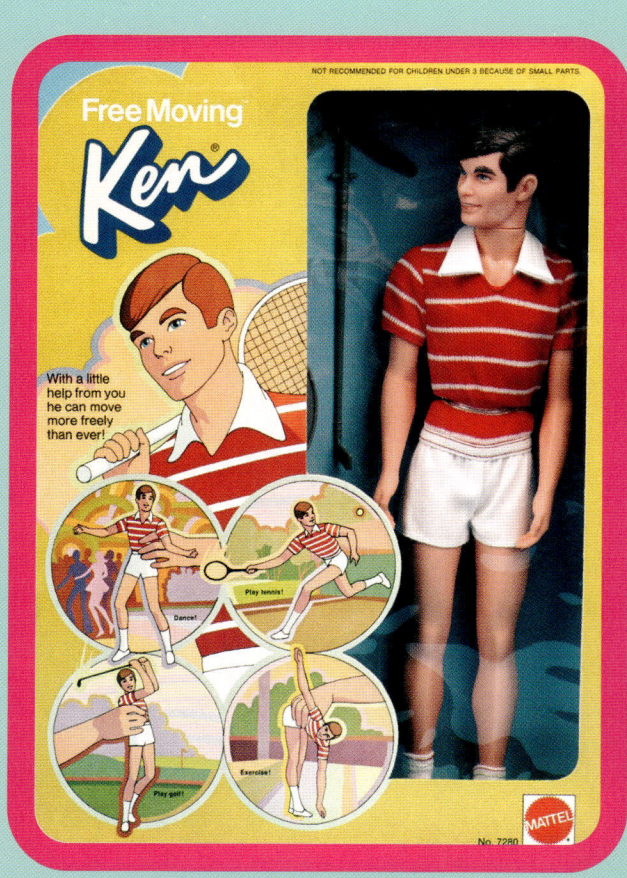

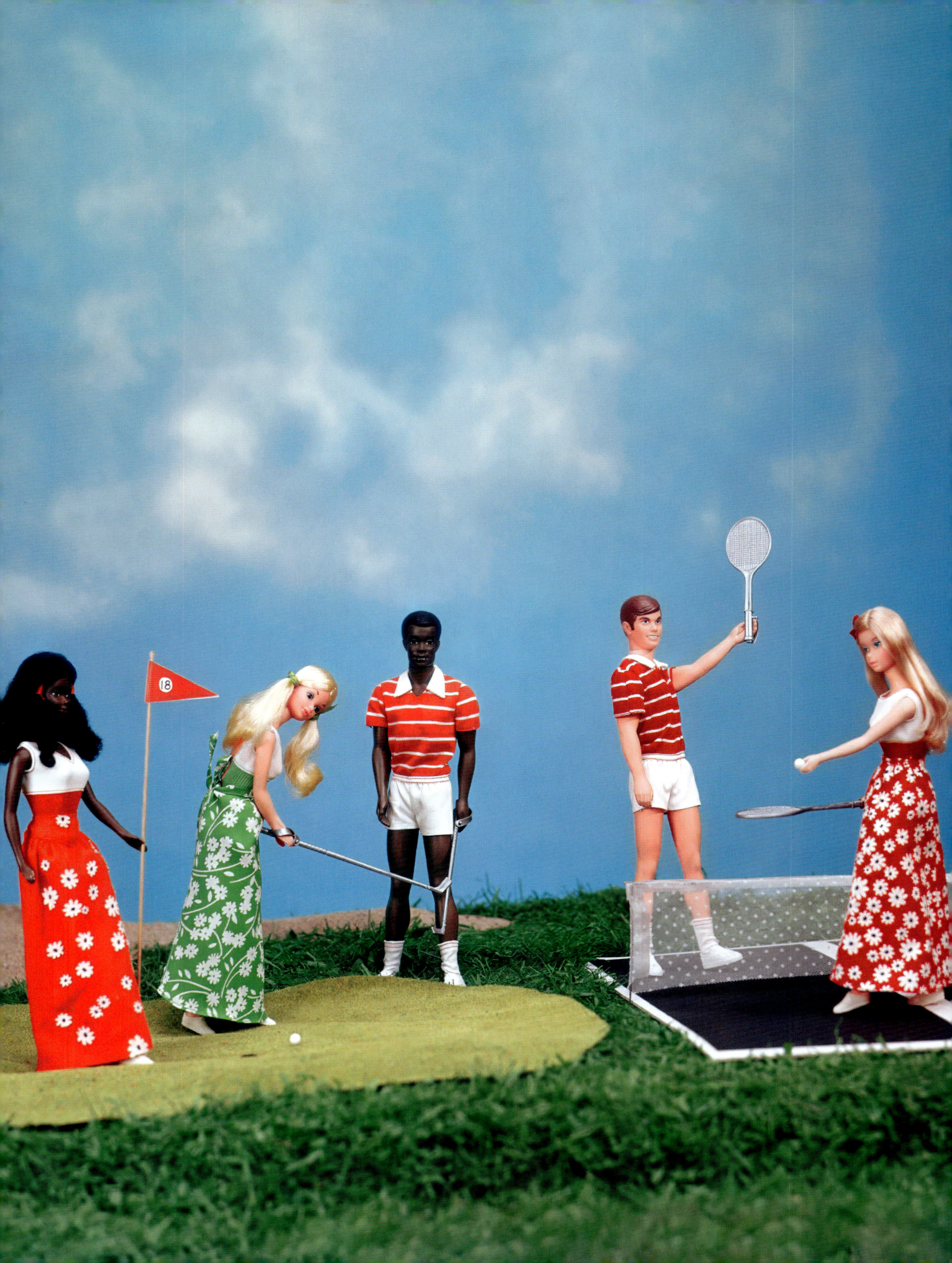

1975

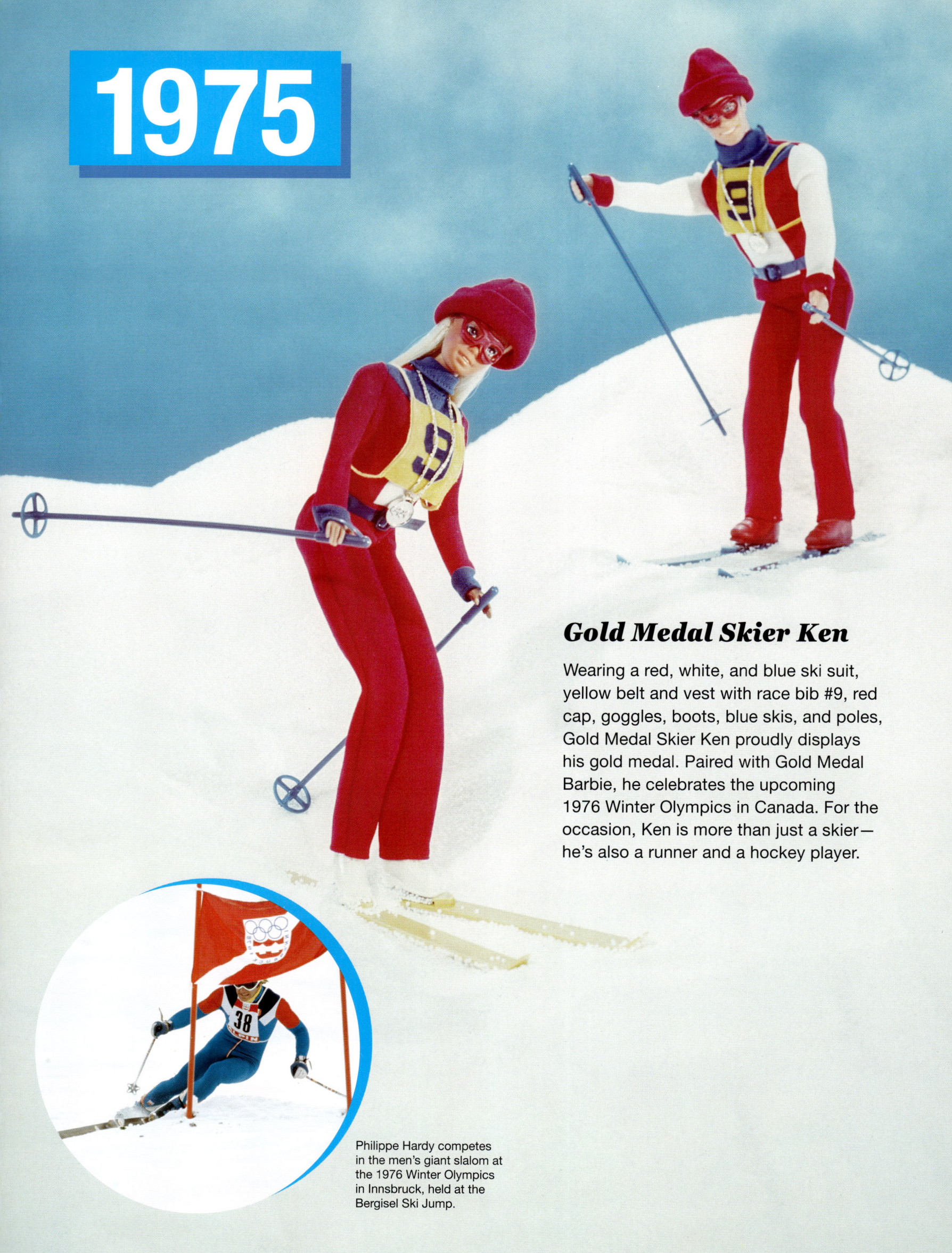

Gold Medal Skier Ken

Wearing a red, white, and blue ski suit, yellow belt and vest with race bib #9, red cap, goggles, boots, blue skis, and poles, Gold Medal Skier Ken proudly displays his gold medal. Paired with Gold Medal Barbie, he celebrates the upcoming 1976 Winter Olympics in Canada. For the occasion, Ken is more than just a skier—he's also a runner and a hockey player.

Philippe Hardy competes in the men's giant slalom at the 1976 Winter Olympics in Innsbruck, held at the Bergisel Ski Jump.

1976

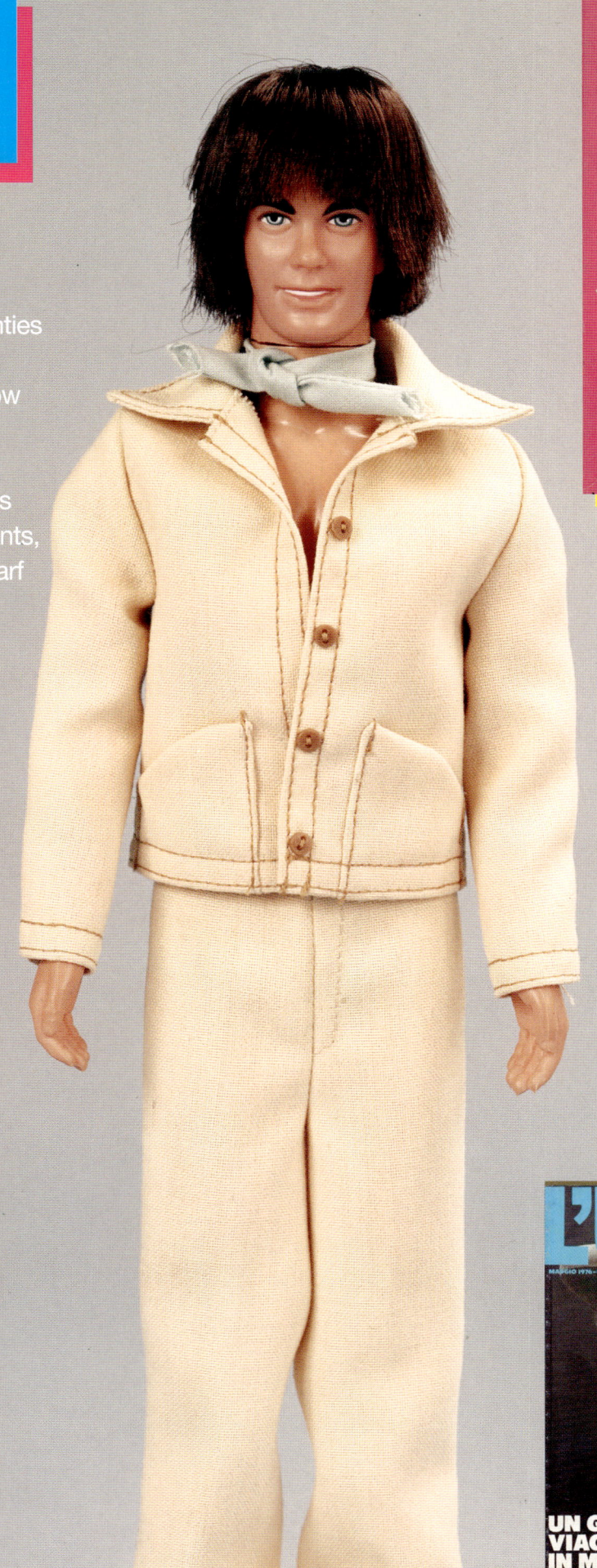

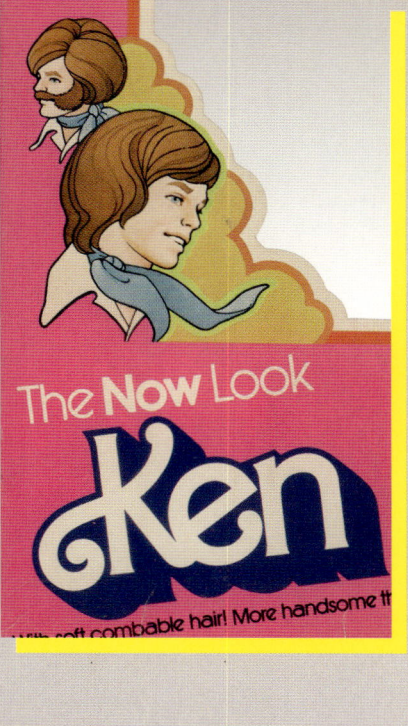

Now Look Ken

A refreshed look with a full-on seventies face mold: long hair, pronounced jawline, and a new feathered eyebrow design—no longer the perfect half-moon shape. Ken now sports a beard, mustache, and sideburns. His outfit features a beige jacket and pants, brightened by a stylish turquoise scarf knotted at the neck.

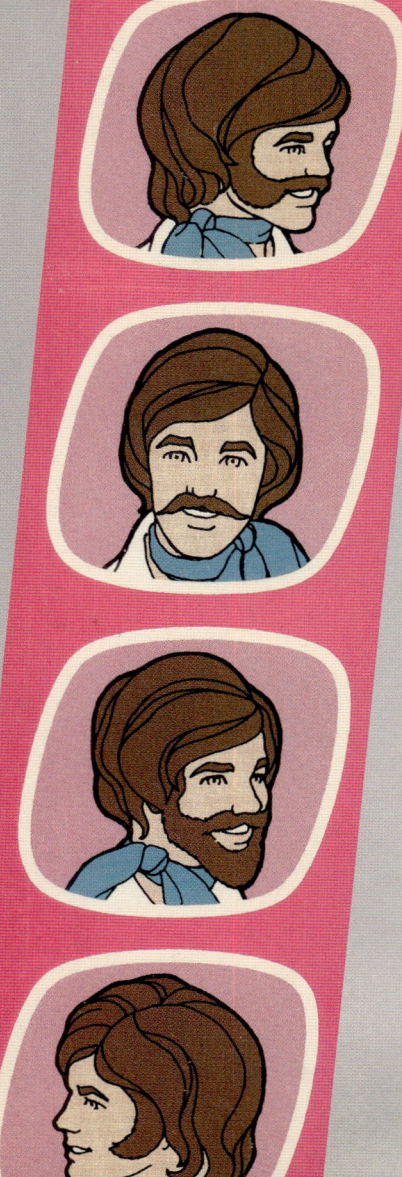

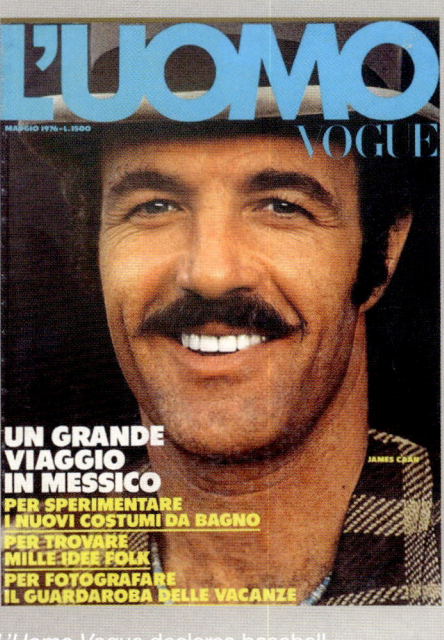

L'Uomo Vogue declares baseball shirts and mustaches to be the year's breakout fashion trends.

1978

SuperStar Ken

The disco jumpsuit era officially begins for men: a second skin in Lycra or lamé in pop colors. SuperStar Ken hits the dance floor and becomes "Barbie Doll's boyfriend with the movie star look!" Blond in Robert Redford style, he dons a cobalt blue jumpsuit, cinched at the waist with a star-buckled belt. The accessories: a red cravat, silver watch, KEN bracelet, and ruby ring. He also sports silver-framed sunglasses with red lenses. This Ken is the ultimate expression of disco culture and fashion, then dominating the United States and spreading worldwide.

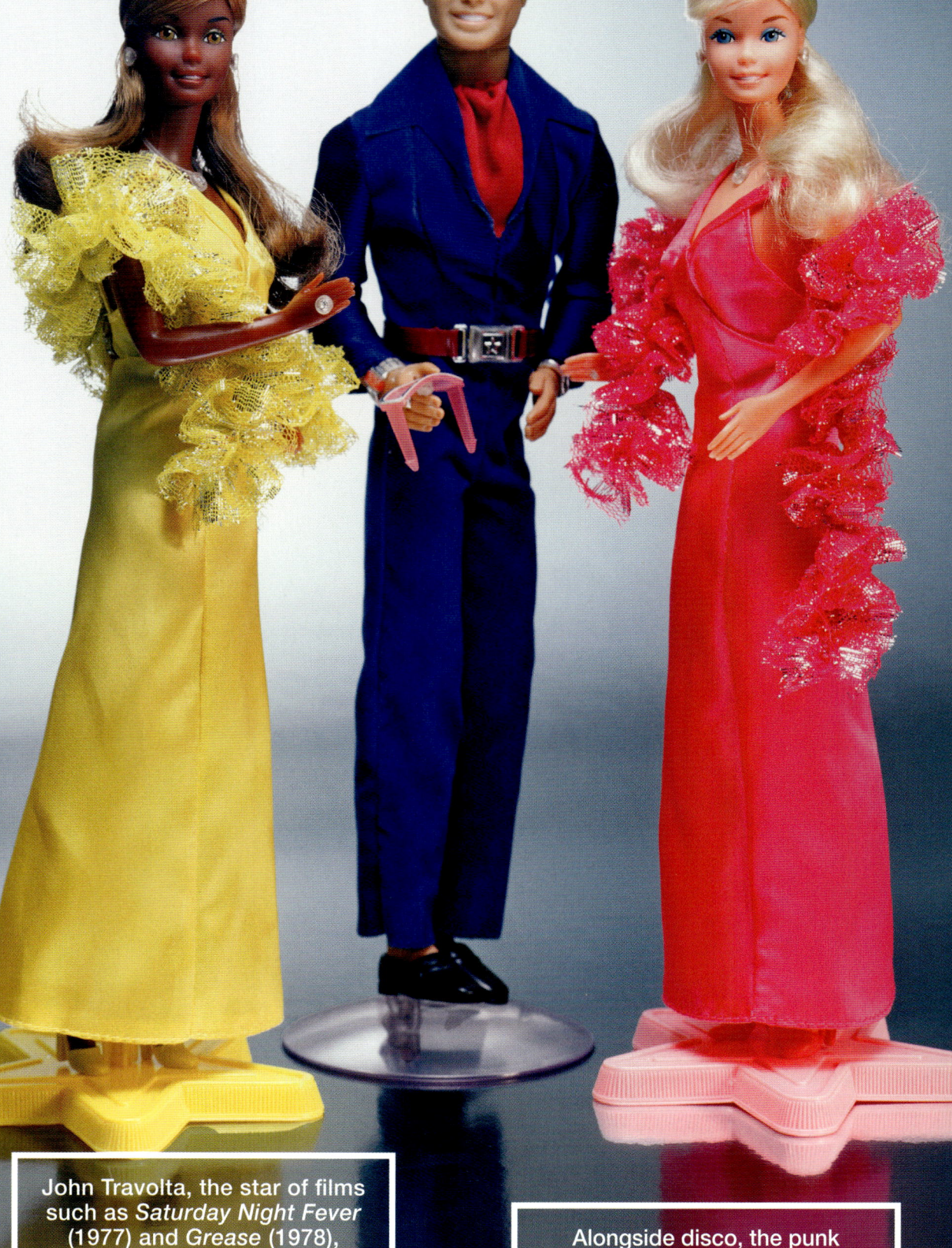

Robert Redford stars in the ensemble film *A Bridge Too Far*, directed by Richard Attenborough and nominated for eight BAFTA awards.

John Travolta, the star of films such as *Saturday Night Fever* (1977) and *Grease* (1978), becomes a full-fledged youth idol. His style takes an entire generation by storm, leading to a fever for disco music and dance.

Alongside disco, the punk movement gains traction. Vivienne Westwood unveils her punk collection in London, becoming the pioneer of a new lifestyle.

Hawaiian Ken

With a deeper tan than usual, Ken becomes the perfect Hawaiian man—wearing a colorful floral swimsuit, a lei, and carrying a pink surfboard decorated with floral appliqués under his arm. Just like Hawaiian Barbie in 1975, it's time for Ken to devote himself to sun, surf, and sand.

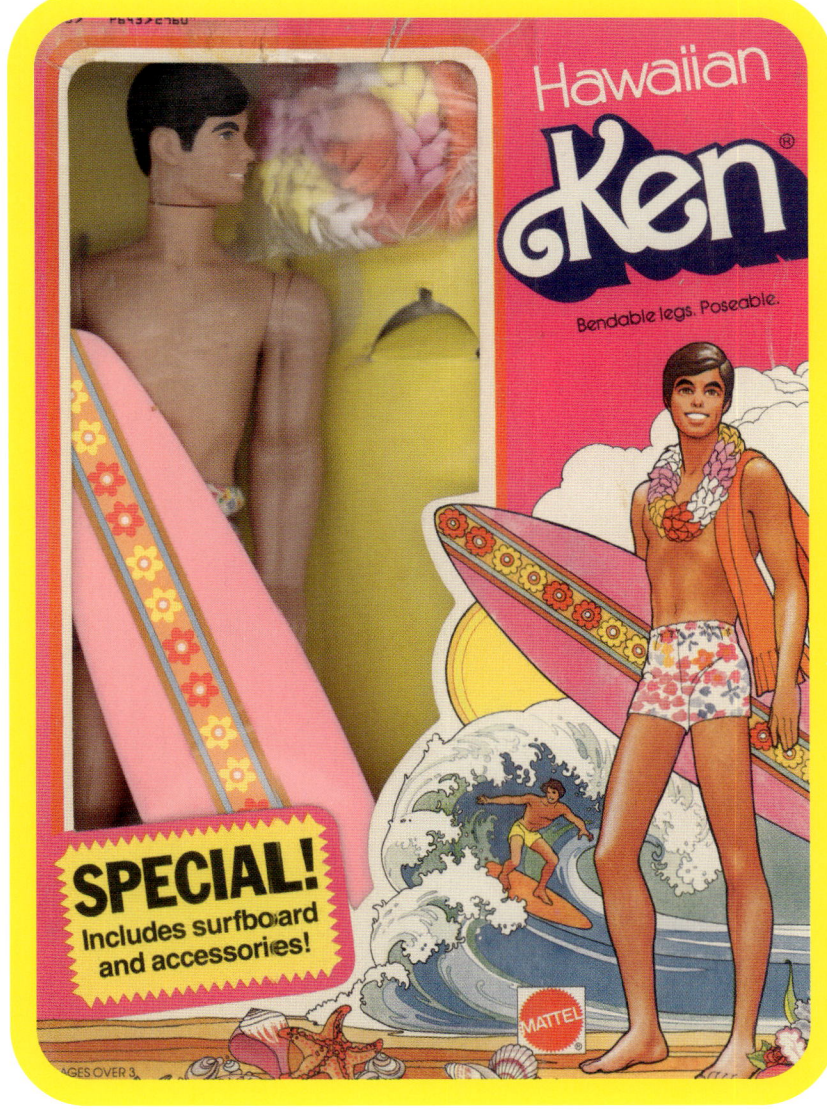

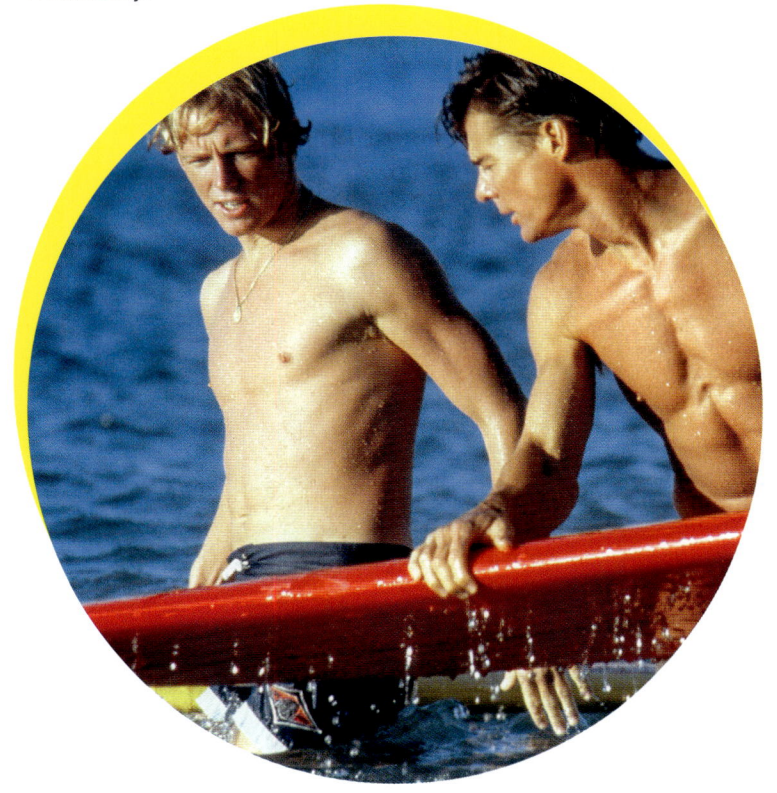

The Malibu surfer community of the 1960s and 1970s reaches peak global fame—later celebrated in John Milius's 1978 film *Big Wednesday*.

> On April 26, New York's Studio 54 opens—soon to become the cathedral of disco music and fashion. A cultural phenomenon like no other.

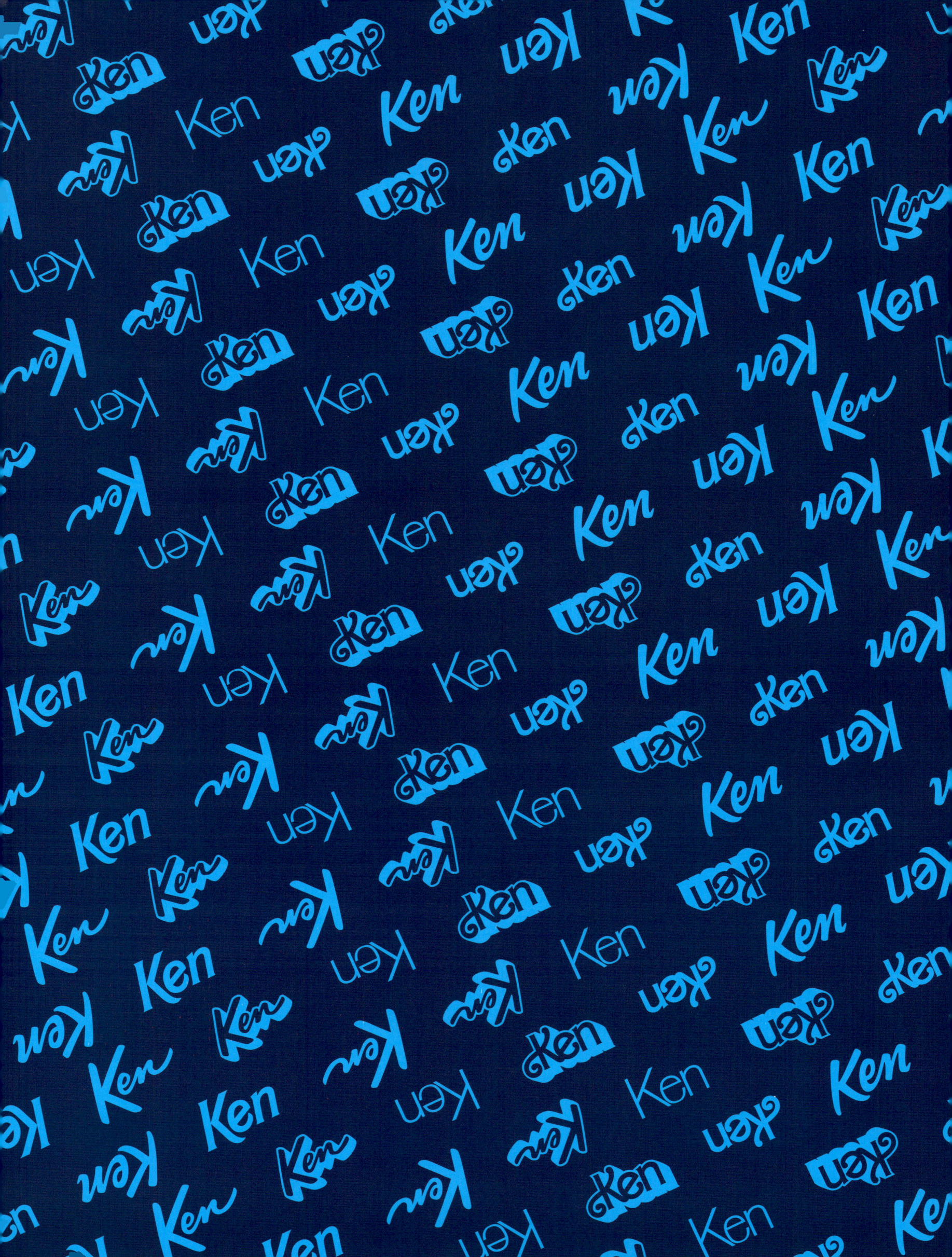

The 80s

1980-1989

1980

Western Ken

Western Ken celebrates cowboy culture. He wears black vinyl pants with white topstitching, a white shirt with black vinyl accents, a KEN-buckled belt, black boots, and a white cowboy hat.

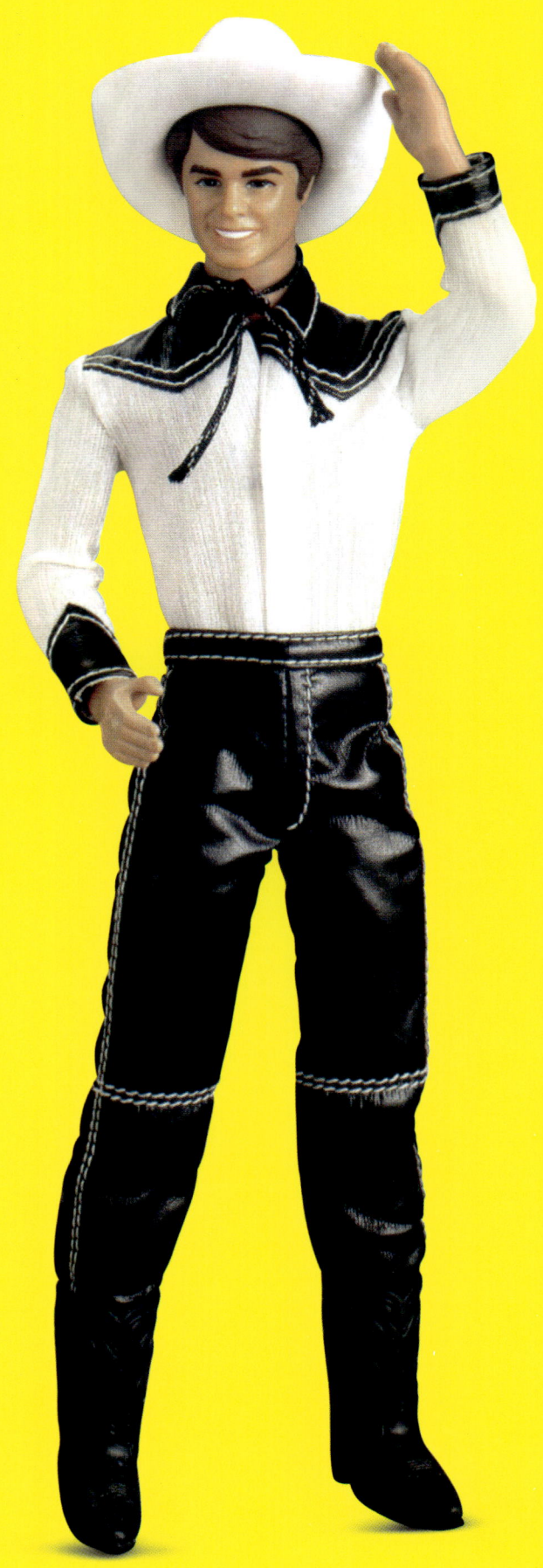

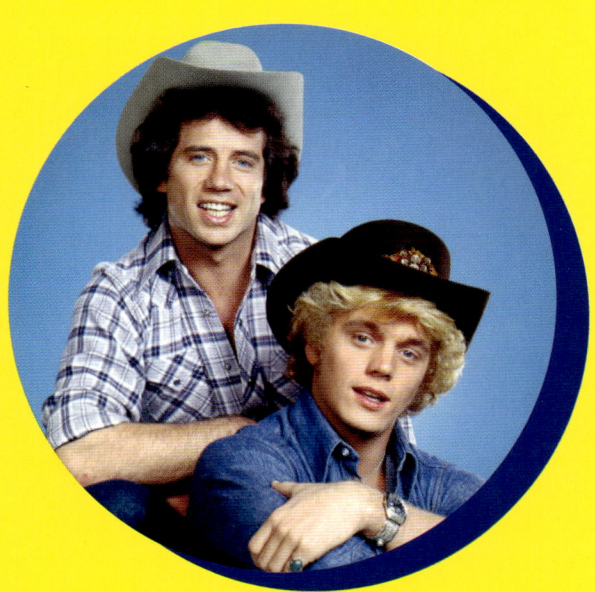

Country style fuels the cowboy craze with *The Dukes of Hazzard*, starring Tom Wopat and John Schneider as Luke and Bo Duke.

The hugely popular show *Dallas*, on air since 1978, becomes the first soap opera broadcasted globally, sharing the charm of country living and Texas style with the world.

Giorgio Armani defines the sleek look of *American Gigolo*, starring Richard Gere and directed by Paul Schrader. A new ideal of male sartorial elegance is born.

1981

Sunsational Malibu Ken

Ken appears for the first time as a Black doll, one year after the premiere of Black Barbie. He features a unique face mold and Afro hairstyle and wears a yellow swimsuit with orange trim and mirrored sunglasses. The look is finished with a striped towel in purple, green, and yellow.

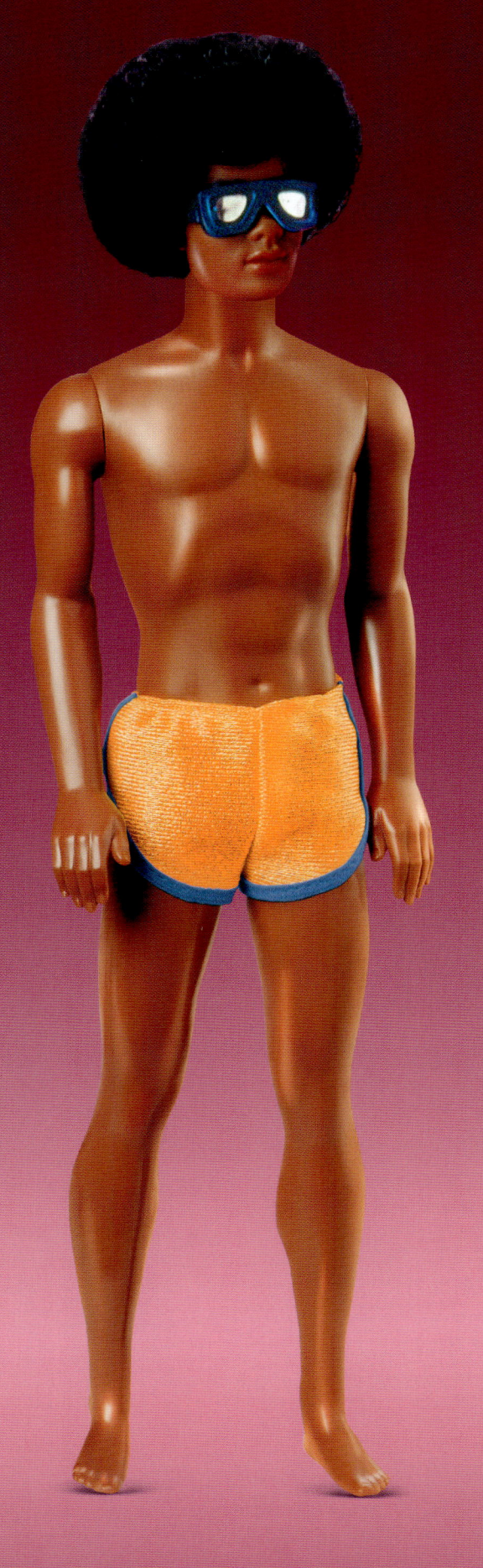

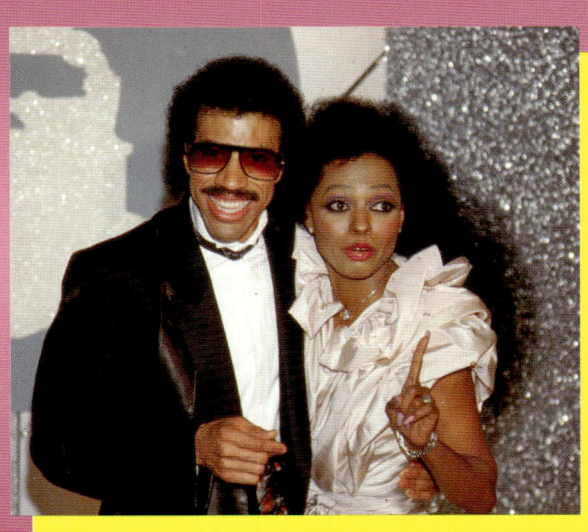

"Endless Love," sung by Lionel Richie and Diana Ross, tops the *Billboard* Hot 100 for nine straight weeks and twenty-six weeks total—an RIAA-certified record. It goes platinum with more than two million US sales and earns Oscar and Golden Globe nominations.

On May 11, reggae legend Bob Marley dies in Miami.

Vivienne Westwood launches her Pirate Collection for Fall/Winter 1981–1982, beginning her personal historic costume revival.

1982

Dream Date Ken

With the slogan "He's everybody's dream date!" Dream Date Ken looks snazzier than ever next to Dream Date Barbie. He wears a black jacket, a hot pink cummerbund and boutonniere, a white muslin shirt with plastic collar, black bow tie, black loafers, and a matching overcoat.

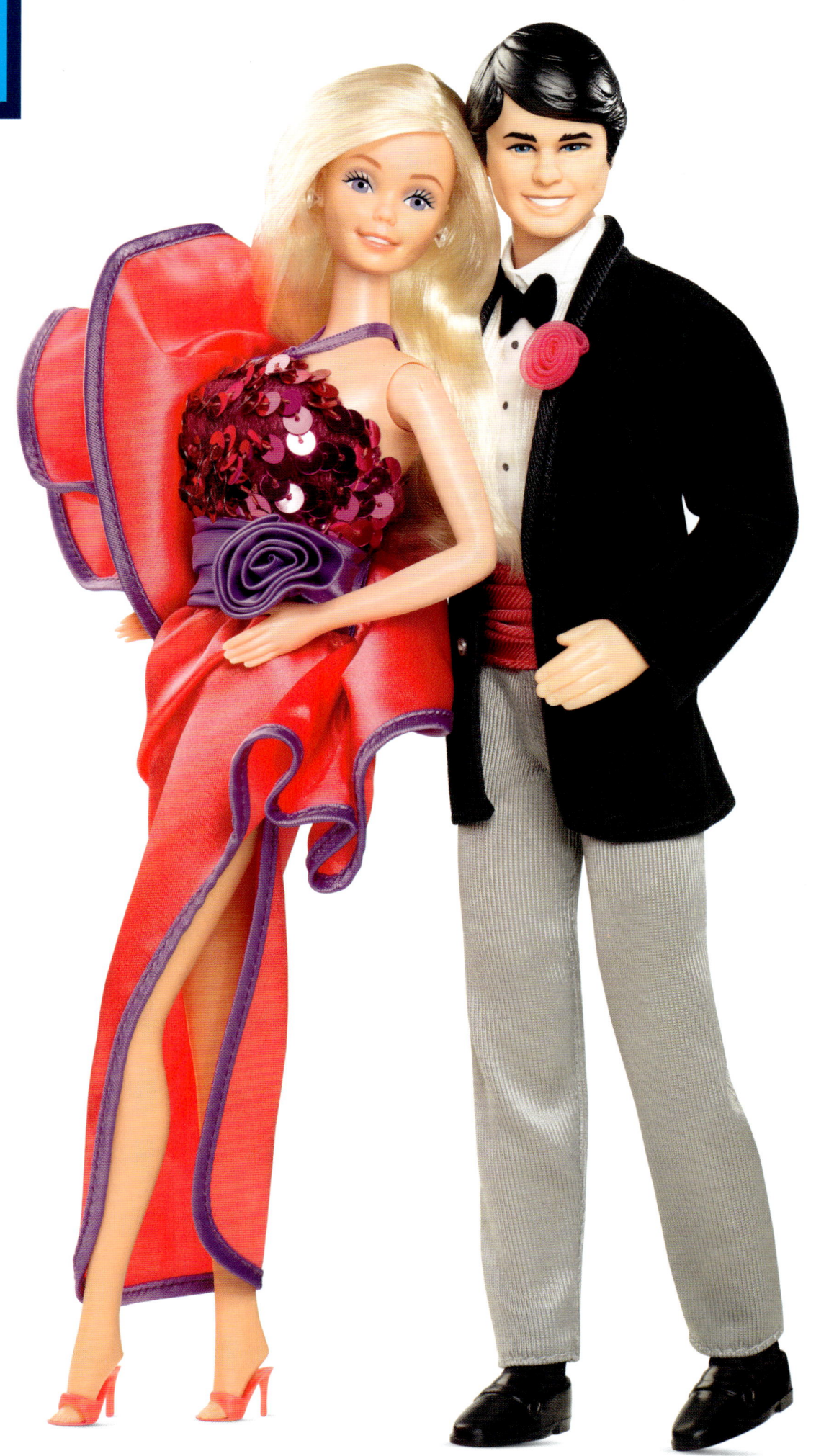

Andy Warhol designs an ad campaign for a menswear collection by Halston, the new king of New York fashion.

TIME magazine features Giorgio Armani on a cover, while Artforum celebrates Issey Miyake—editorial prestige for fashion's new faces.

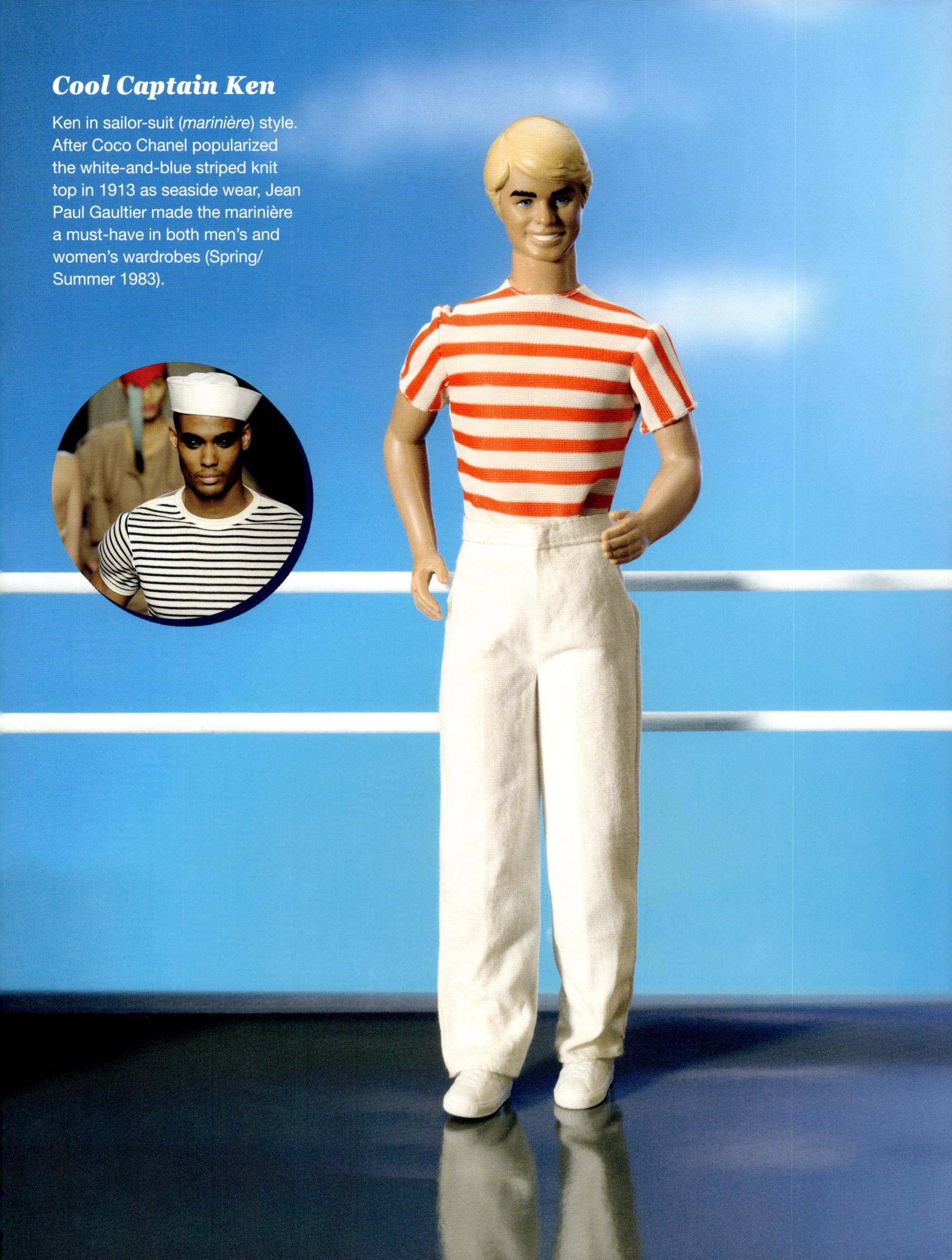

Cool Captain Ken

Ken in sailor-suit (*marinière*) style. After Coco Chanel popularized the white-and-blue striped knit top in 1913 as seaside wear, Jean Paul Gaultier made the marinière a must-have in both men's and women's wardrobes (Spring/Summer 1983).

1985

Day-to-Night Ken

Day-to-Night Ken perfectly embodies the fast-paced lifestyle of New York yuppies, with two looks: one for day, one for night. By day, he's a business executive in an elegant pinstripe suit with matching vest, white shirt with pink buttons, and a striped pink-and-white tie. For evening wear, he adds a pink cummerbund and black bow tie to transform his look.

The fashion designer BillyBoy* creates a series of sketches and prototypes for Mattel, in which Barbie and Ken show off haute couture creations—including these fashions designed by Jean Paul Gaultier. BillyBoys*'s creations are presented in Paris at an exhibition celebrating the Barbie brand's twenty-sixth anniversary.

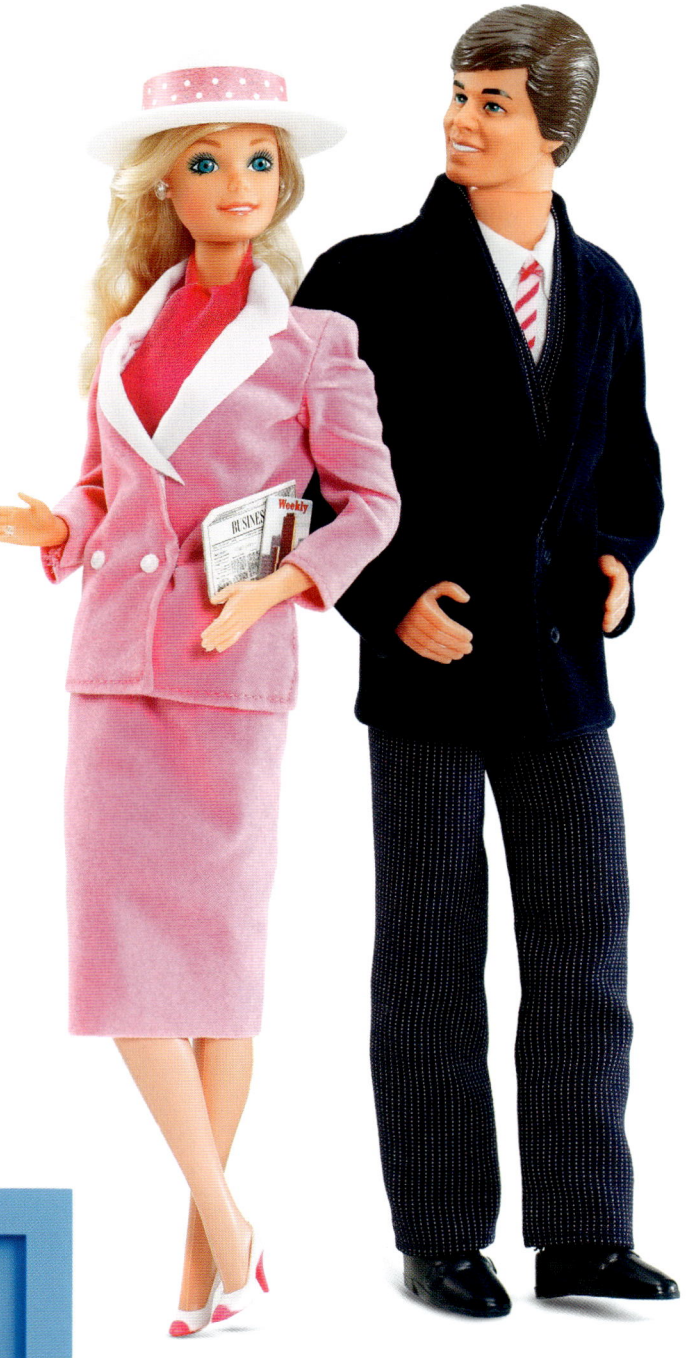

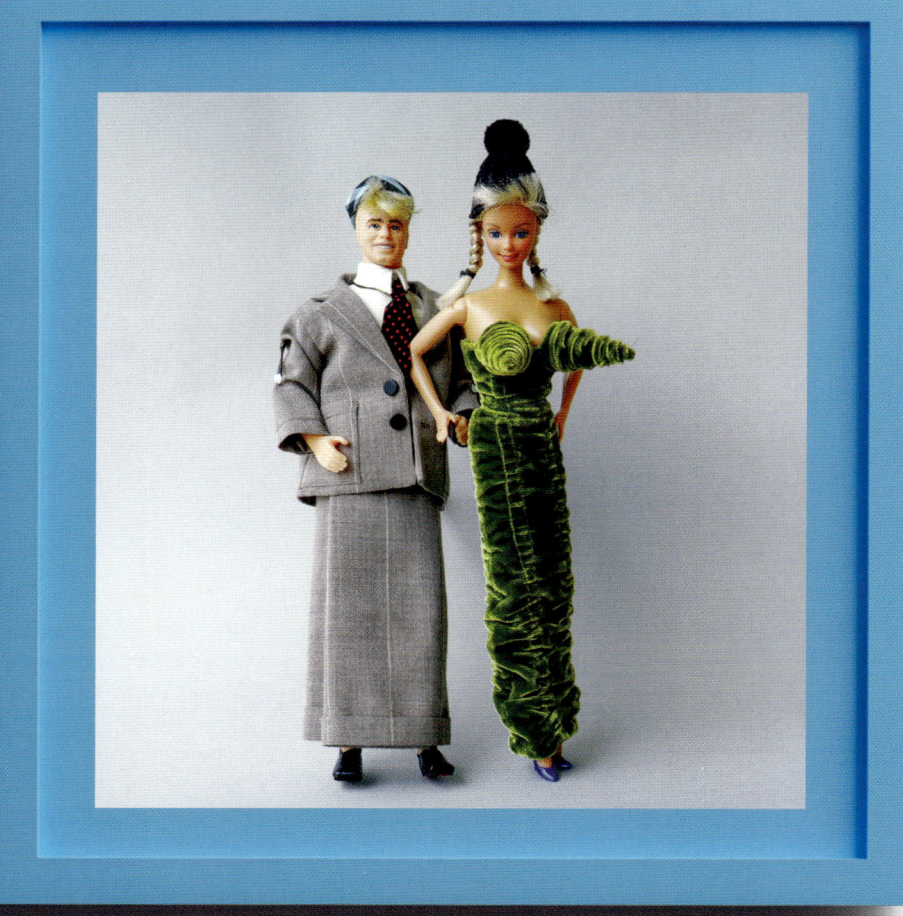

Oscar de la Renta becomes the first designer to create a haute couture collection for Barbie.

These are the years of brash, fast-moving yuppies—ambitious, young American college graduates hungry for wealth and success. They work in Manhattan skyscrapers, dress in Armani or Versace, collect works by Jean-Michel Basquiat, and spend their nights at restaurants and clubs like Studio 54.
Dorian Walker's 1984 film *Making the Grade* spreads the culture of this new generation worldwide.

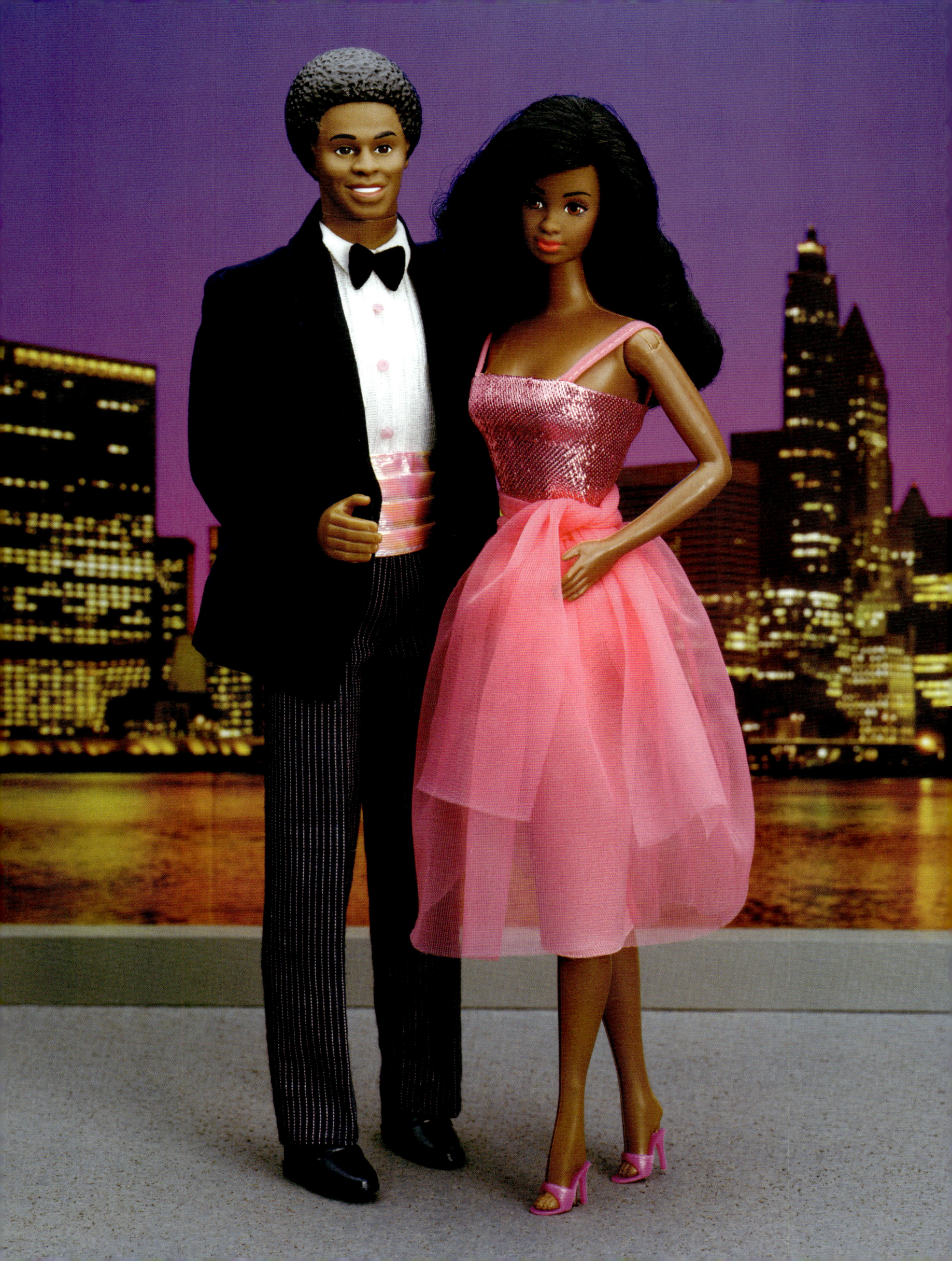

1985

Music Lovin' Ken

Ken dresses in a sporty outfit with a white jacket cinched at the waist (with his name embroidered on the chest), a Nehru collar, yellow three-quarter sleeves, white sneakers, and—essential for the eighties—headphones and a Walkman for music during workouts!

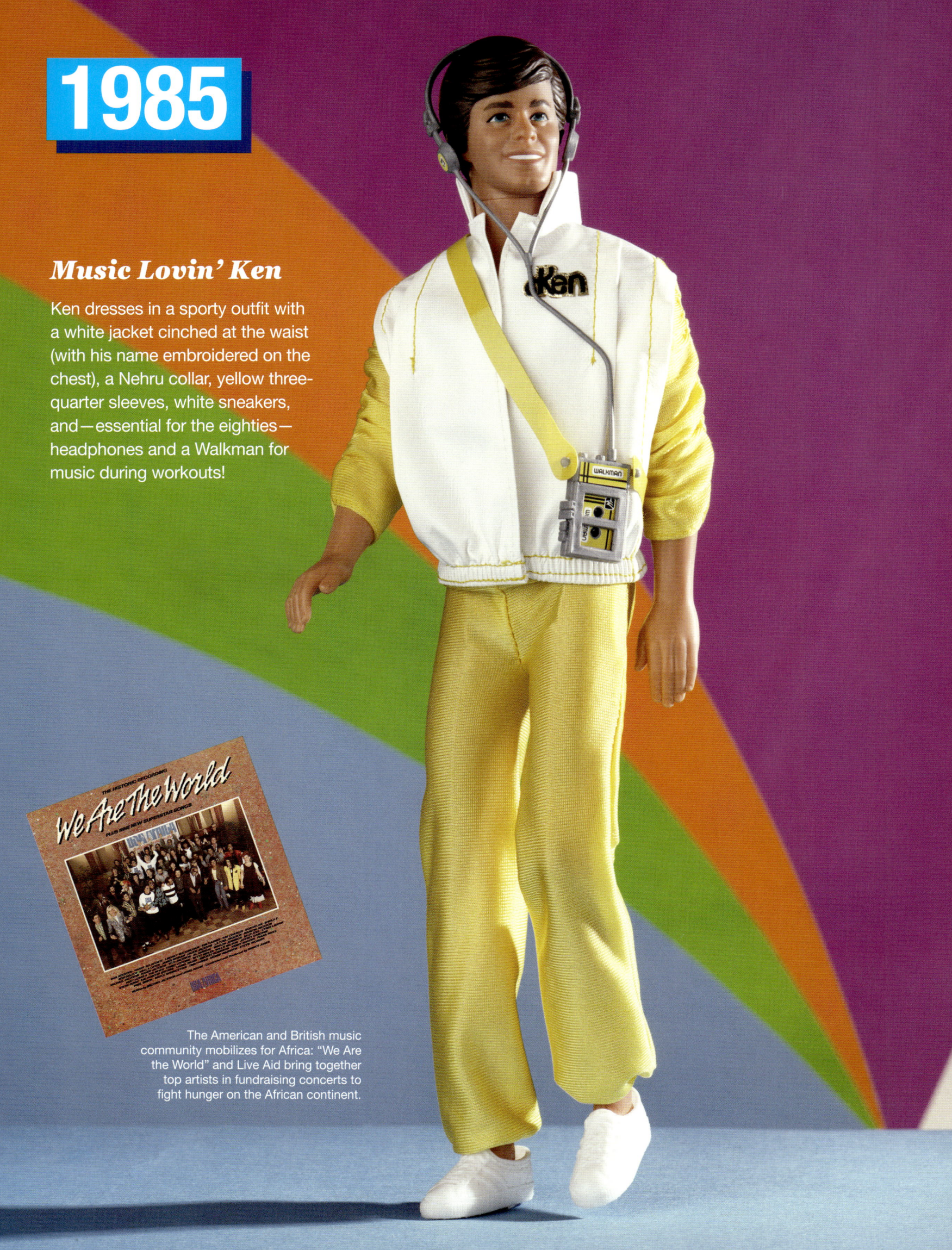

The American and British music community mobilizes for Africa: "We Are the World" and Live Aid bring together top artists in fundraising concerts to fight hunger on the African continent.

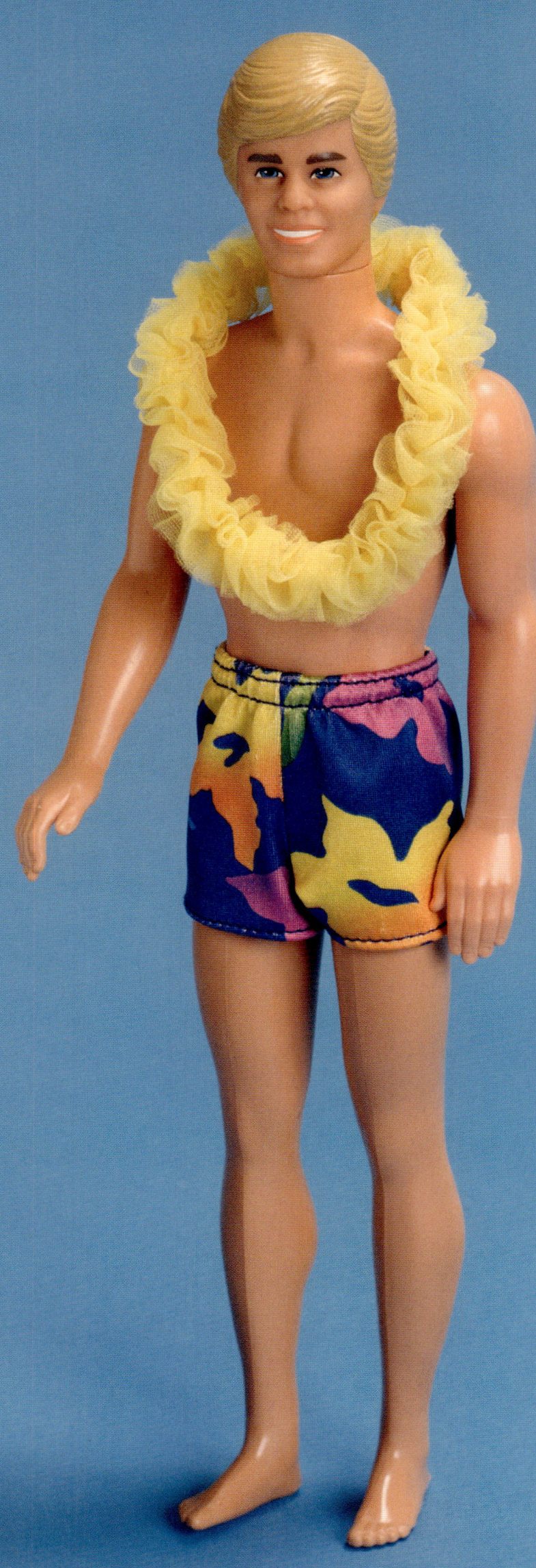

Tropical Ken

In a world that's becoming ever more pop and colorful, Ken goes tropical too!

> Andy Warhol pays tribute to his friend BillyBoy* with a portrait of Barbie, inspired by BillyBoy*'s comment: "If you want to do my portrait, do Barbie, because Barbie *c'est moi*." Barbie has officially become an artwork.

> Keith Haring paints singer and model Grace Jones, who is then photographed by Robert Mapplethorpe.

1986

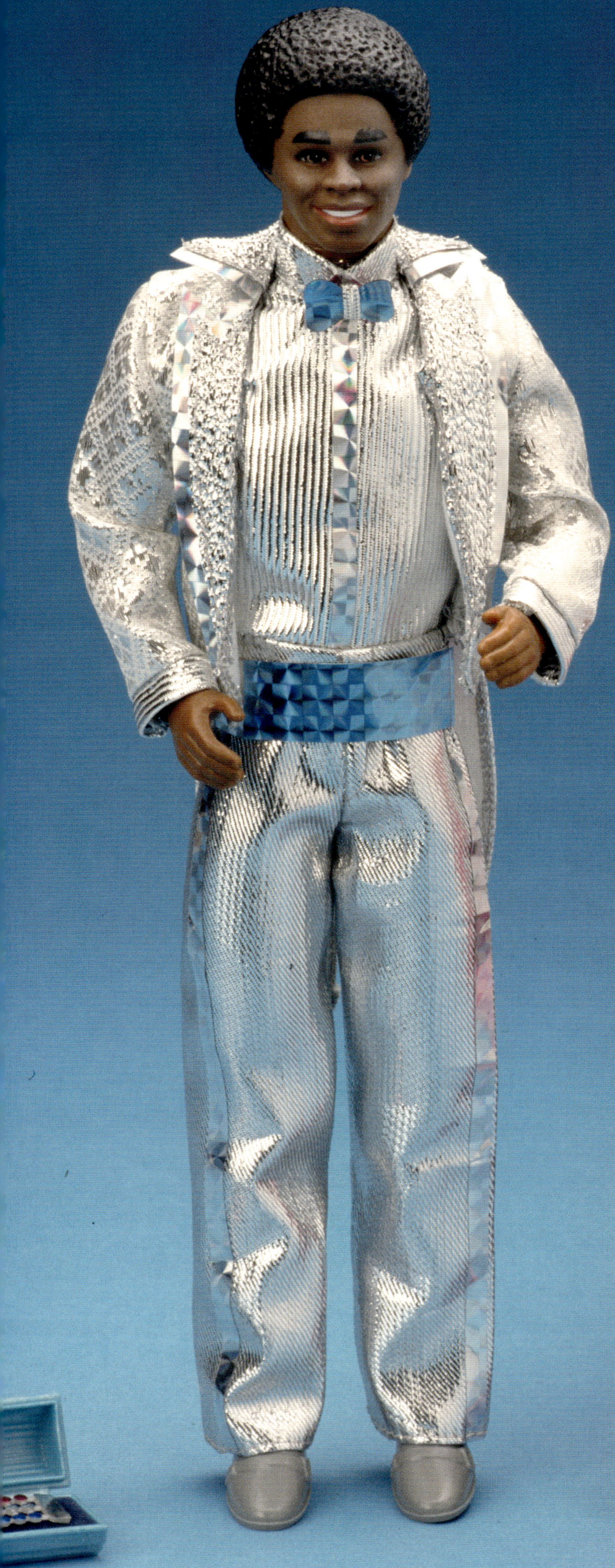

Jewel Secrets Ken

For the twenty-fifth anniversary of Ken, the Jewel Secrets version of the doll appears with a redesigned face mold. Jewel Secrets Ken comes with a mini-booklet titled "Mystery at Sea," which tells the tale of Ken's birthday party as organized by Barbie aboard the Glamour II. For the occasion, Ken wears a completely silver tuxedo with bow tie and a reversible cummerbund in aqua and fuchsia. The white and Hispanic versions come with rooted hair and a hairbrush.

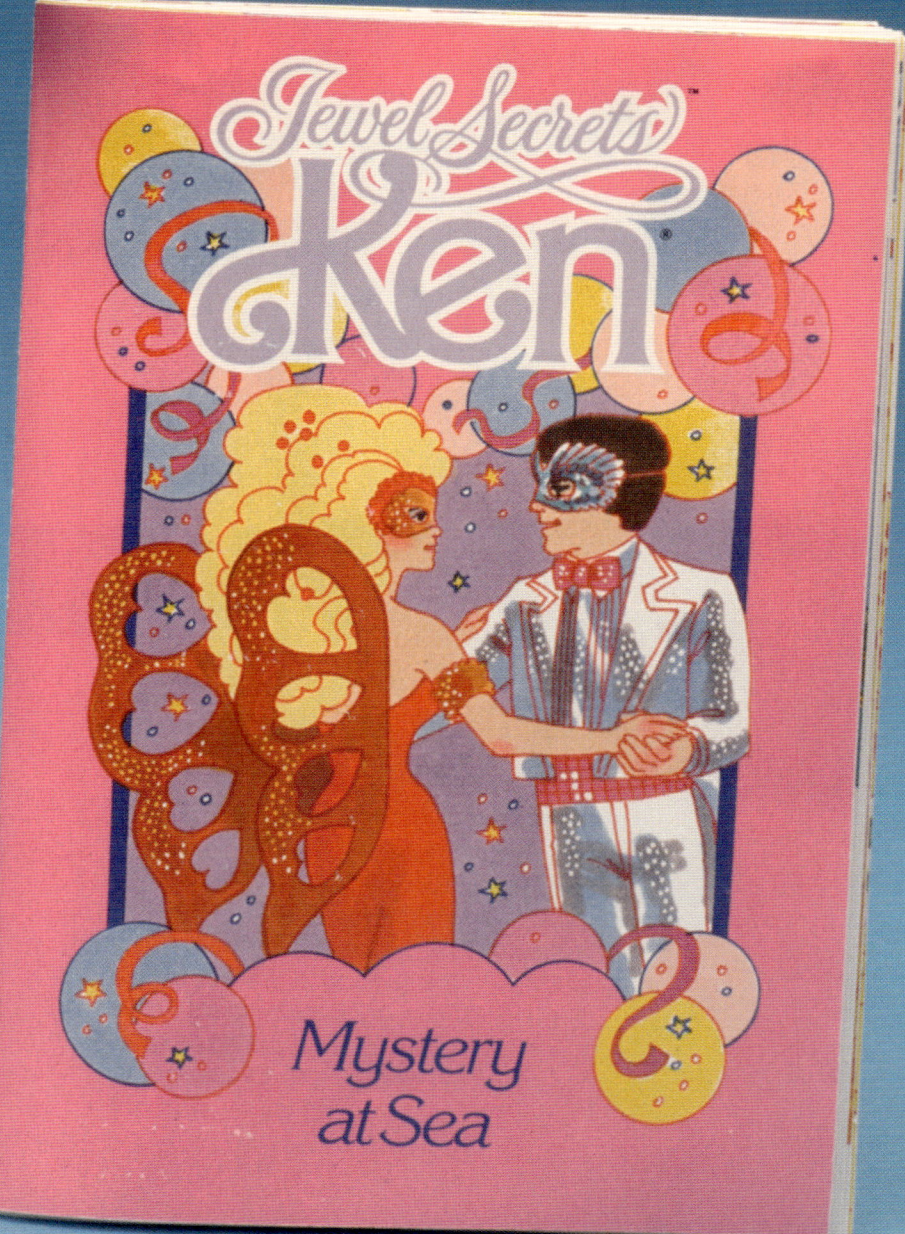

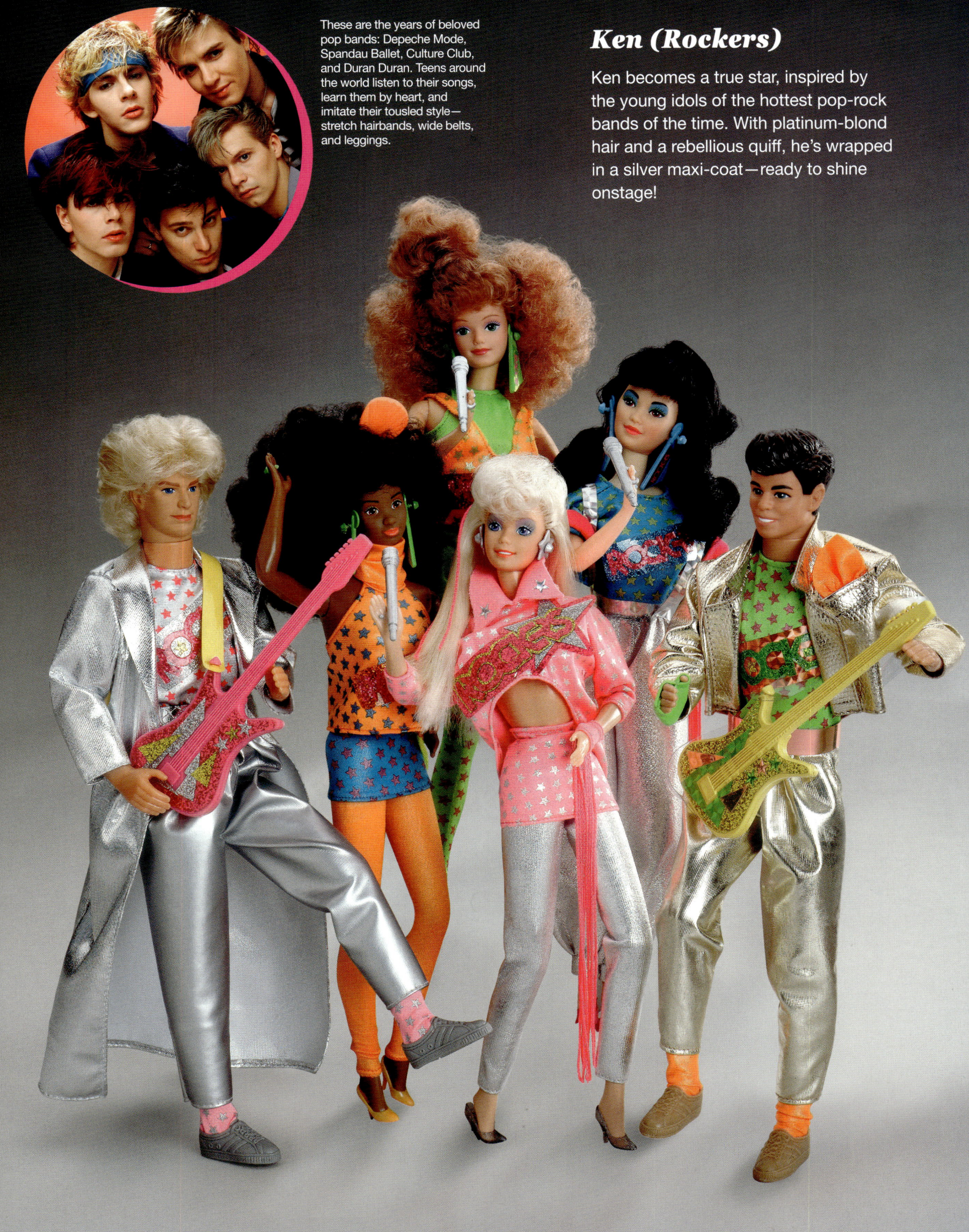

1988

Island Fun Steven

Steven becomes Ken's new friend.

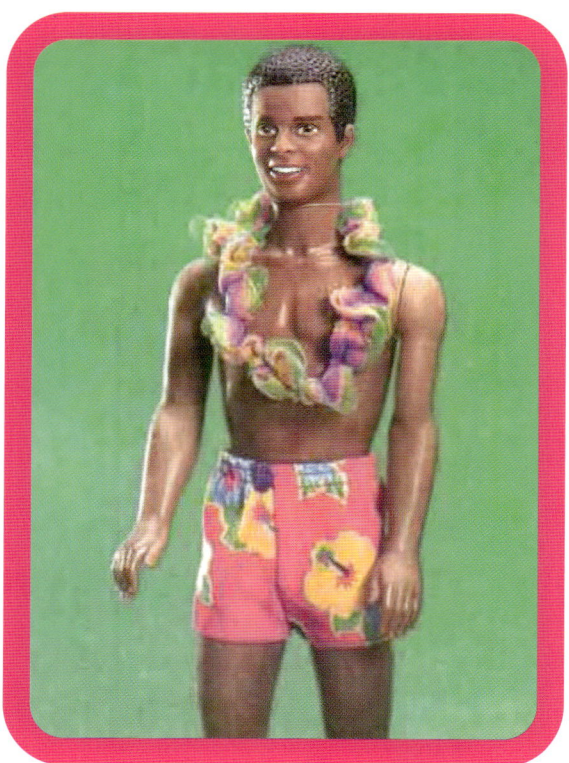

1989

All Stars Ken

Ken and the All Stars (All Stars Ken) sports a champion's outfit: light blue shorts, a white tank top with metallic lilac stars, calf-high white socks, a gym bag that transforms into pants, and white sneakers. To the left: the 1982 version of All Star Ken.

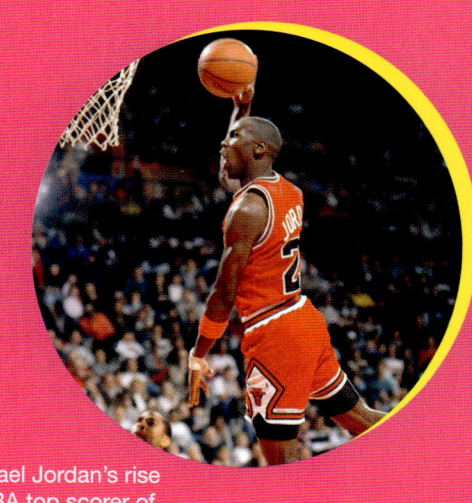

Michael Jordan's rise to NBA top scorer of the year helps turn basketball into a global phenomenon.

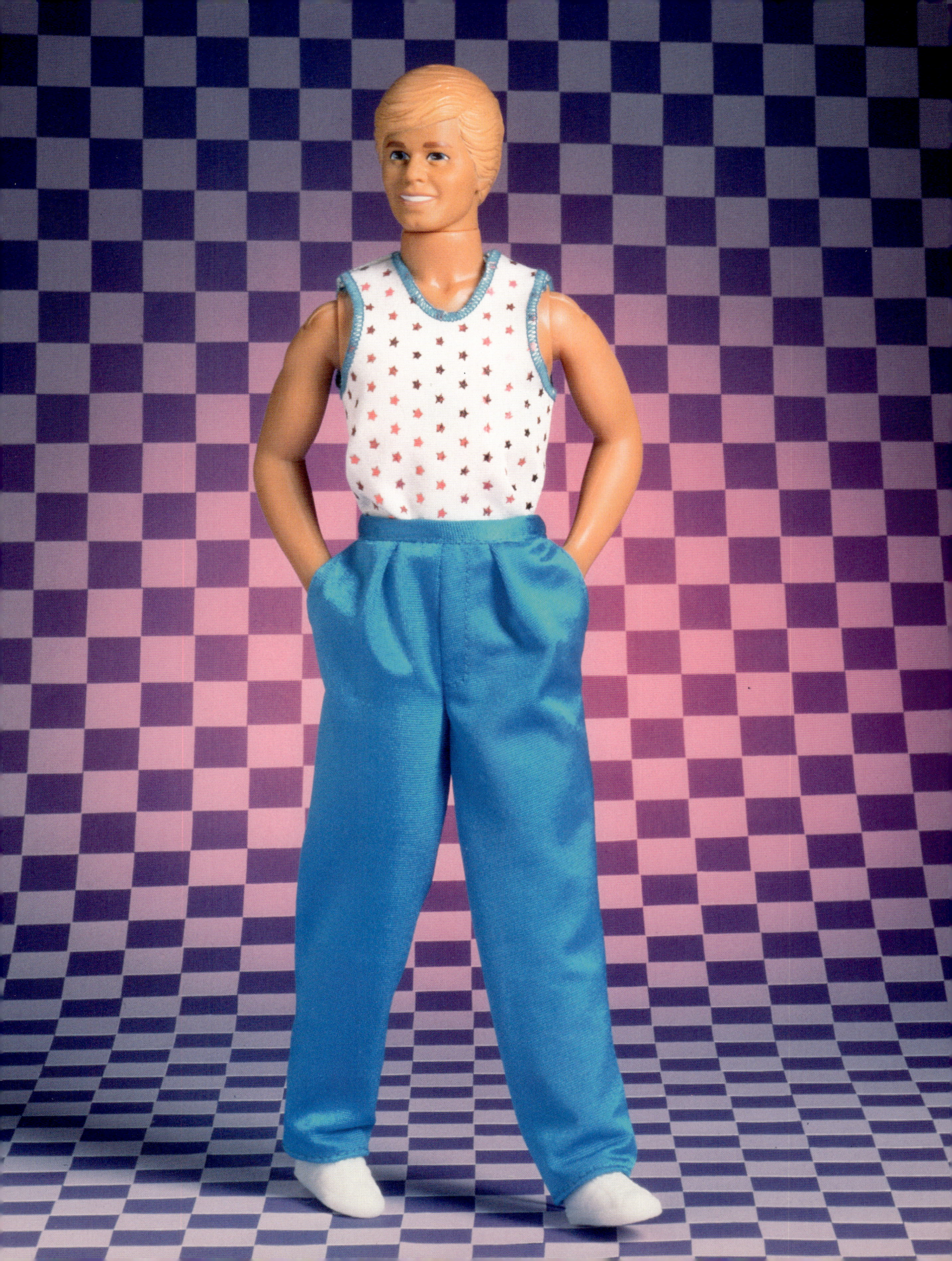

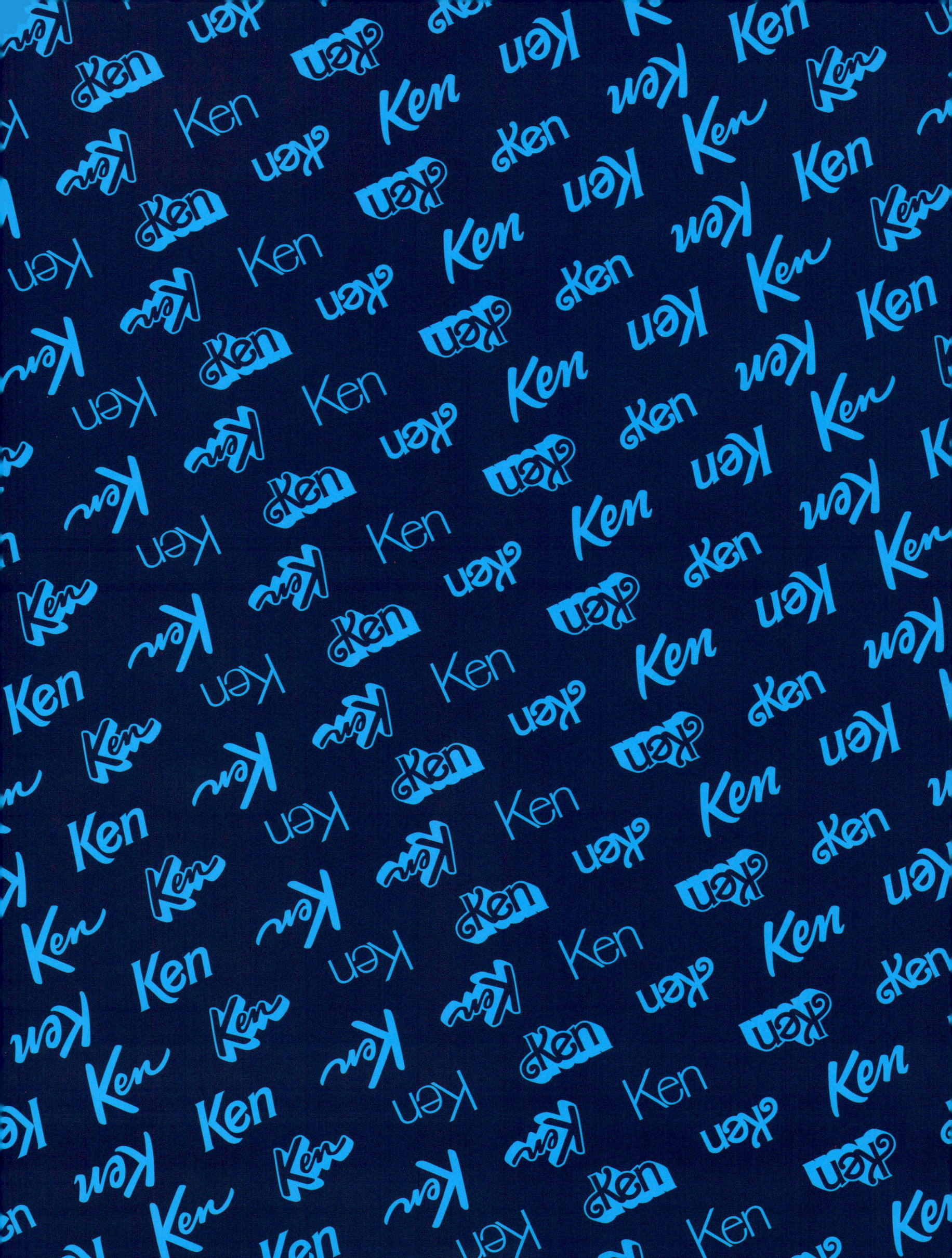

The 90s

1990-1999

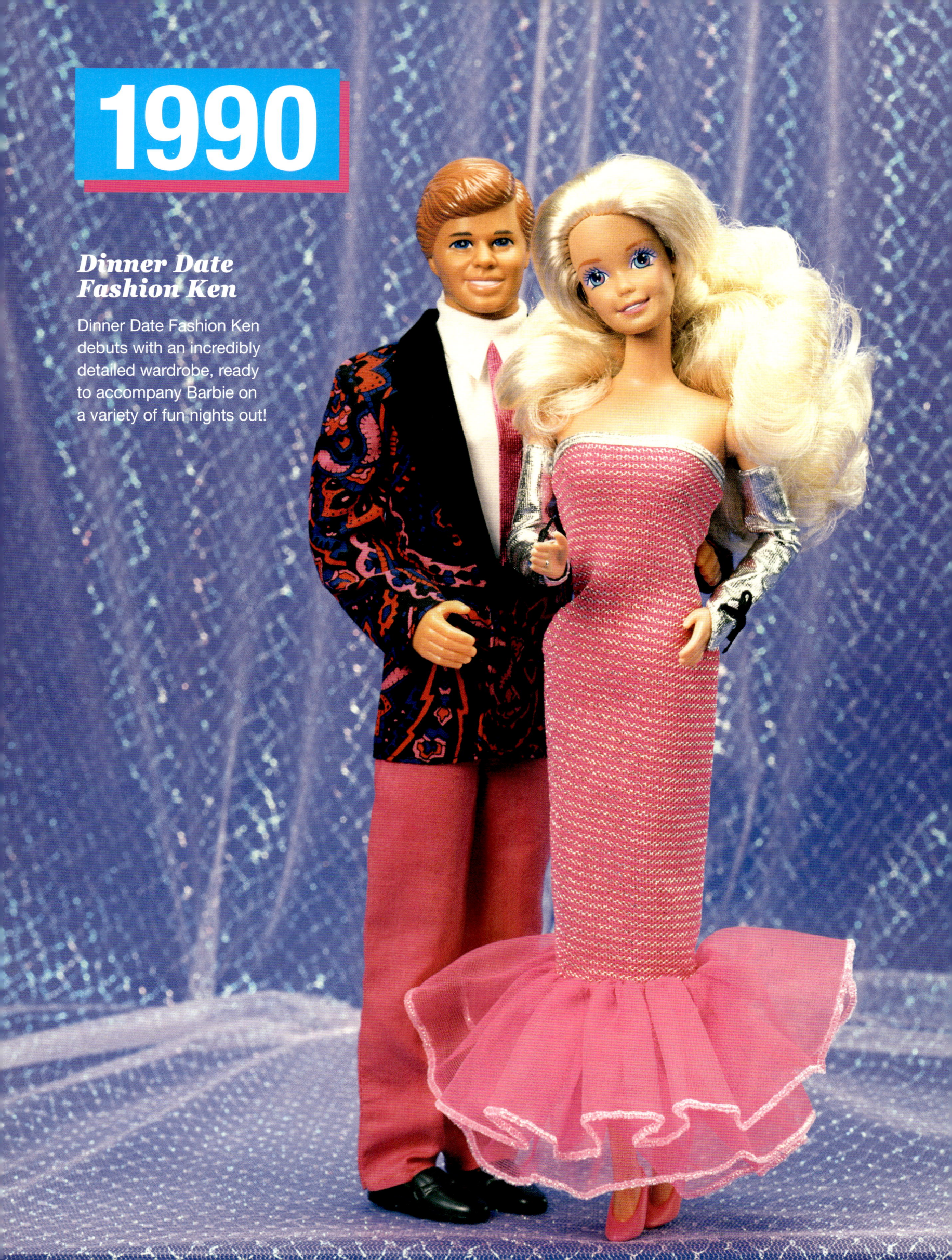

1990

Dinner Date Fashion Ken

Dinner Date Fashion Ken debuts with an incredibly detailed wardrobe, ready to accompany Barbie on a variety of fun nights out!

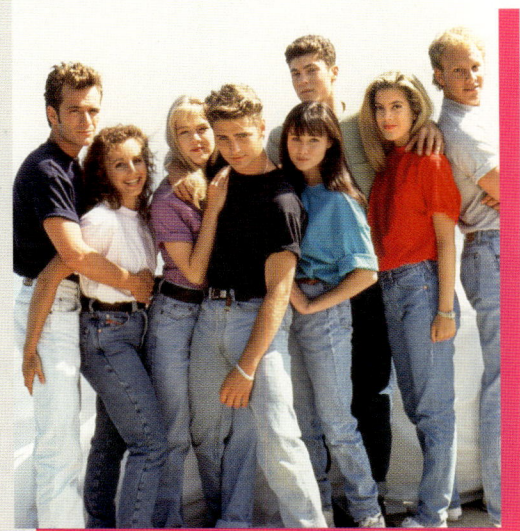

The global phenomenon of *Beverly Hills 90210* launches two new teen idols: Brandon (Jason Priestley) and Dylan (Luke Perry), celebrated by Mattel in a 1991 doll collection.

Benetton Ken

After wearing a Braniff International Airline uniform designed by Emilio Pucci, Ken dons a new Italian wardrobe brand: United Colors of Benetton creates two vibrant, pop-inspired outfits just for him!

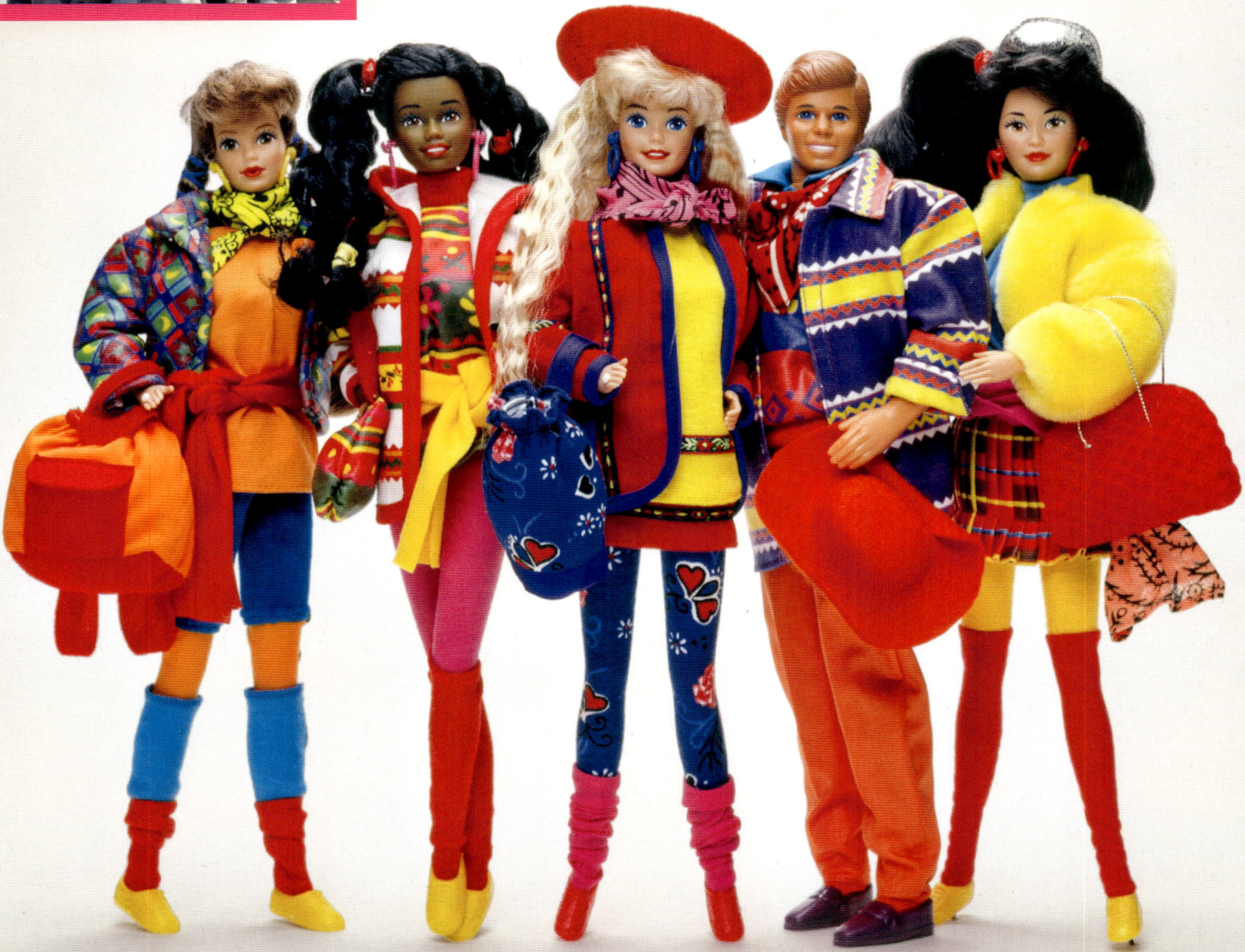

In both men's and women's runway collections, pop culture triumphs: from Versace's dress inspired by Warhol's work, to Christian Lacroix and Moschino's Cheap and Chic collection.

The relationship between fashion and photography also becomes a form of social commentary through Oliviero Toscani's advertising campaigns for United Colors of Benetton—a collaboration that began in 1982.

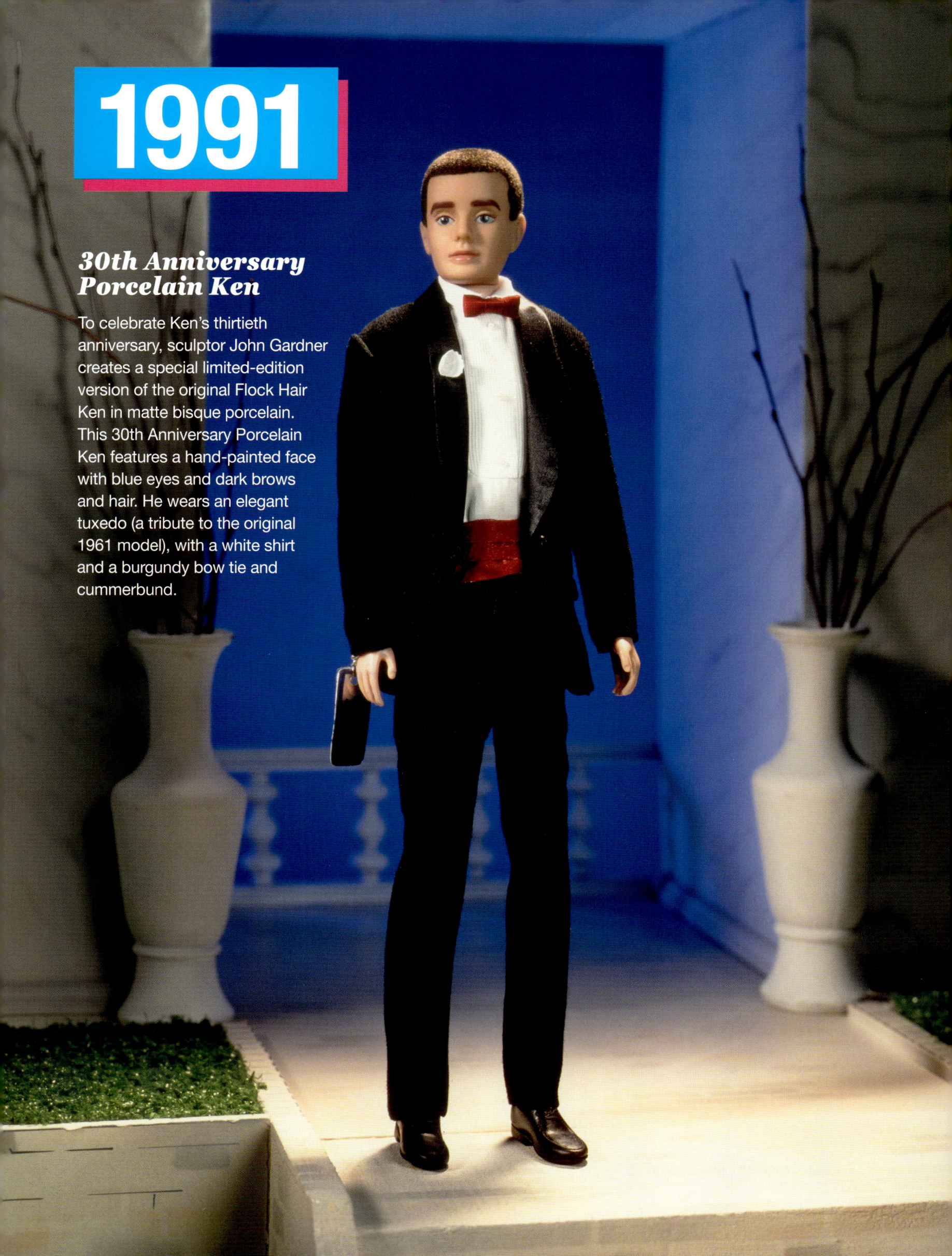

1991

30th Anniversary Porcelain Ken

To celebrate Ken's thirtieth anniversary, sculptor John Gardner creates a special limited-edition version of the original Flock Hair Ken in matte bisque porcelain. This 30th Anniversary Porcelain Ken features a hand-painted face with blue eyes and dark brows and hair. He wears an elegant tuxedo (a tribute to the original 1961 model), with a white shirt and a burgundy bow tie and cummerbund.

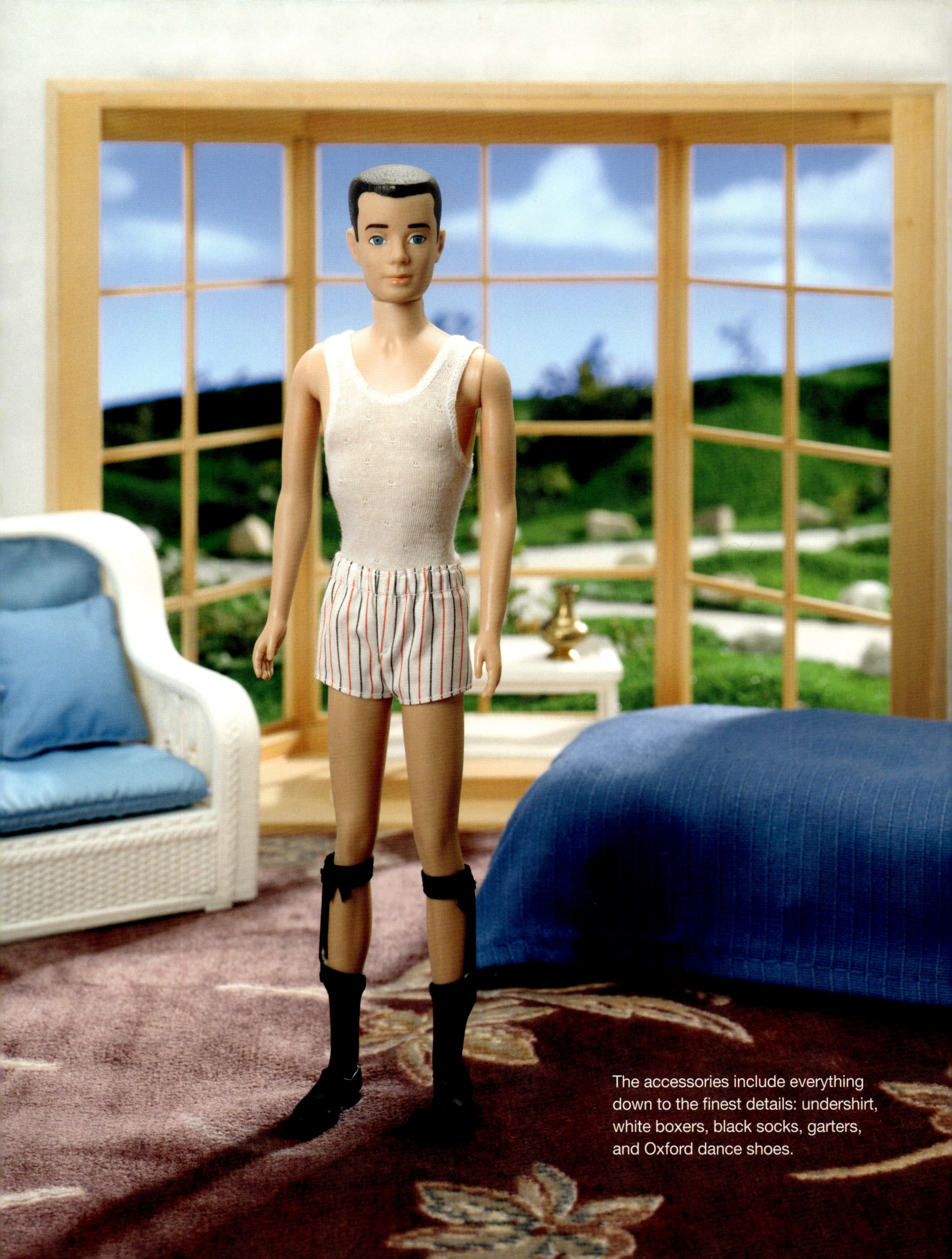

The accessories include everything down to the finest details: undershirt, white boxers, black socks, garters, and Oxford dance shoes.

1992

Totally Hair Ken

A defining model of early '90s pop culture, Totally Hair Ken debuts alongside the best-selling Totally Hair Barbie (who holds the all-time Barbie sales record to this day). His look bursts with color, and his innovative face mold remains unique, topped by a thick, tousled mane. For the occasion, he wears branded puffed purple pants and a multicolor graphic shirt reminiscent of Pucci and Versace creations.

Accessories include white loafers, a lilac comb to restyle his hair, a tube of Dep gel (first sold in 1954), and a booklet of on-trend nineties hairstyles.

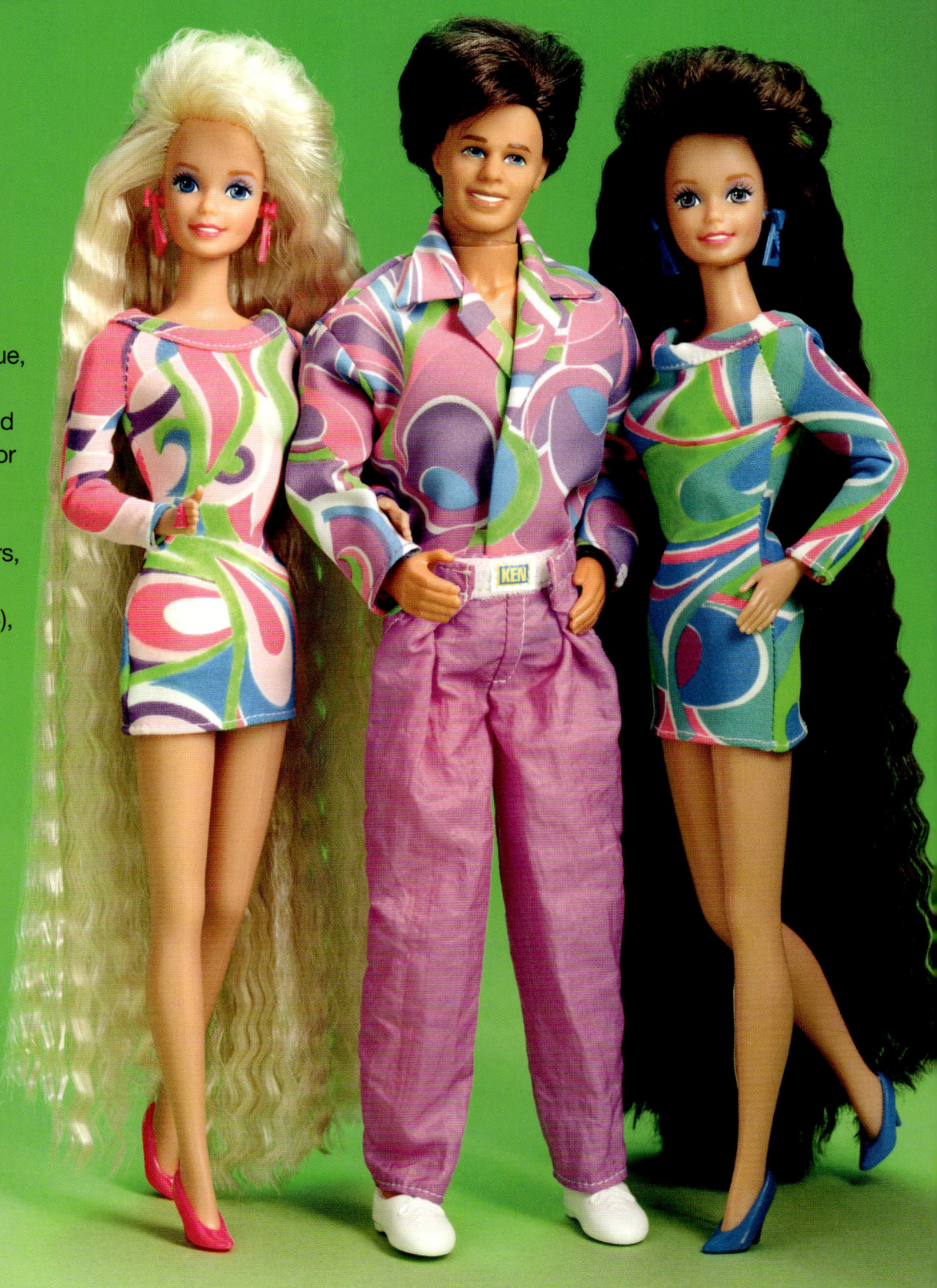

Earring Magic Ken

The most widely collected, most controversial, and best-selling Ken in history, Earring Magic Ken is created alongside Earring Magic Barbie. His accessory-heavy look sparks fierce debate in the mass media, landing him on the first page of the *New York Times* Arts & Leisure section. The new model features platinum-blond highlights and wears a lilac faux-leather vest reminiscent of Jean Paul Gaultier's designs, a mesh T-shirt, black jeans, a necklace with a pendant, and a silver hoop earring in his left ear—a decidedly bold look.

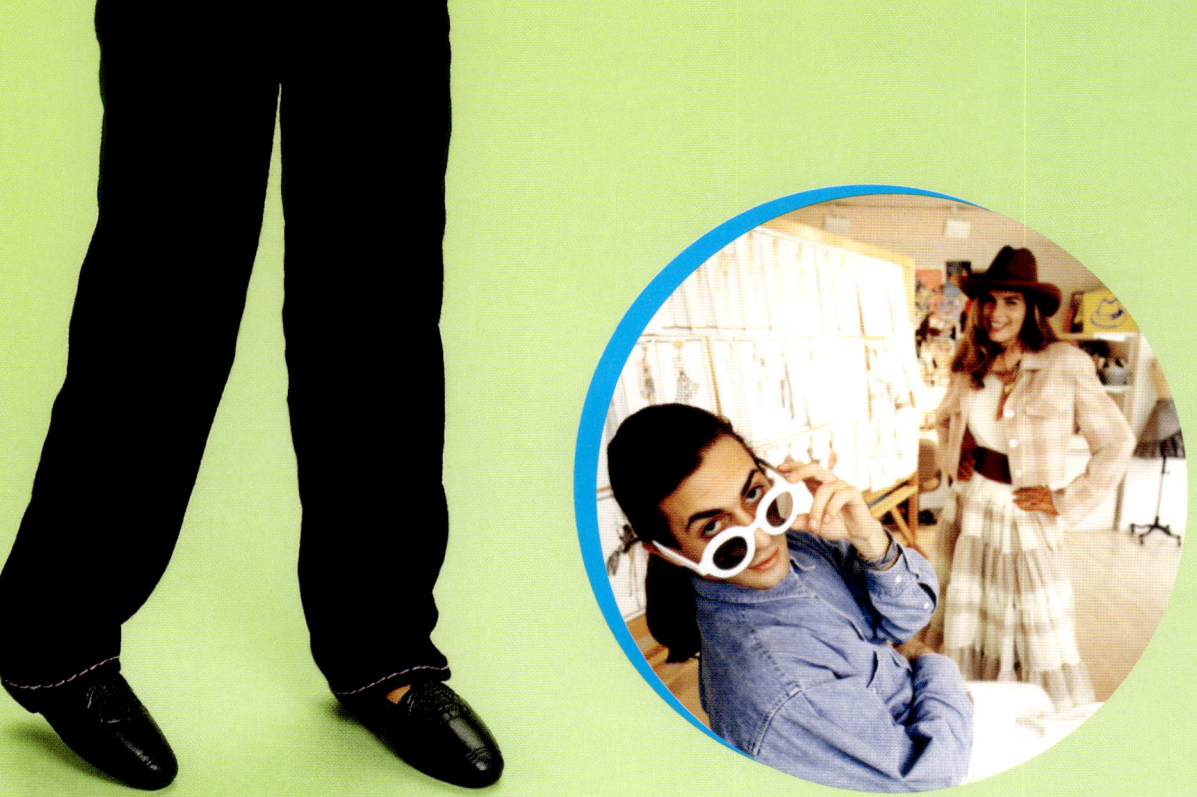

Marc Jacobs debuts his Grunge Collection for Perry Ellis (S/S 1992). Jacobs becomes one of the most acclaimed designers of his generation.

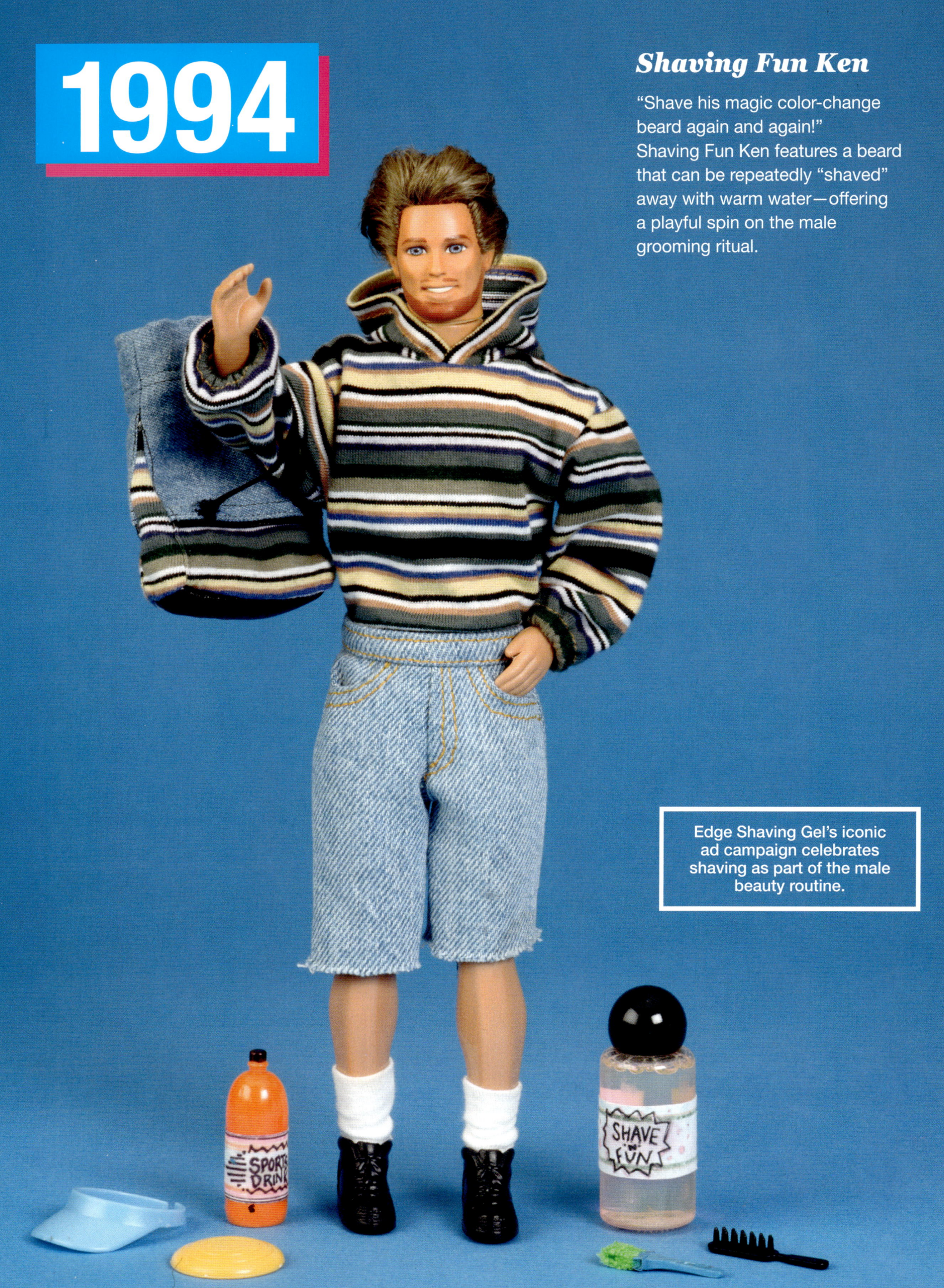

1994

Shaving Fun Ken

"Shave his magic color-change beard again and again!" Shaving Fun Ken features a beard that can be repeatedly "shaved" away with warm water—offering a playful spin on the male grooming ritual.

Edge Shaving Gel's iconic ad campaign celebrates shaving as part of the male beauty routine.

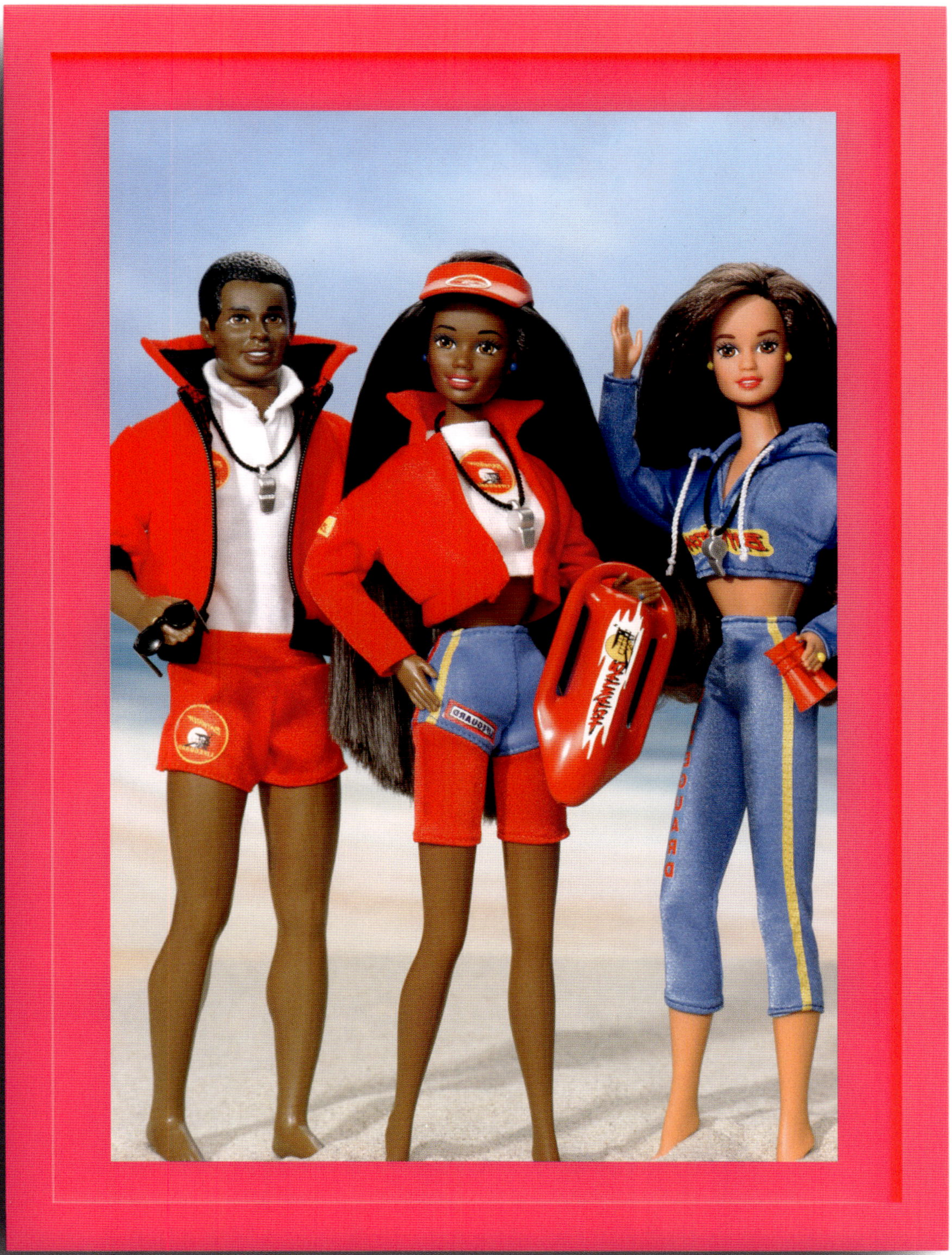

Baywatch Ken

Ken becomes *Baywatch* lifeguard. He wears red swim trunks with a *Baywatch* Lifeguard patch, a white T-shirt, red nylon windbreaker, white tennis shoes, and all the beach rescue gear he'll need.

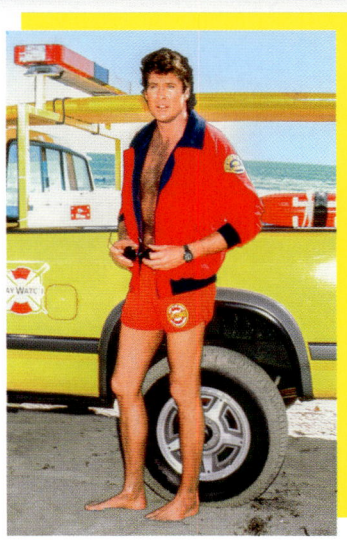

Everyone in red swim trunks! The iconic lifeguards of Malibu Beach, Los Angeles, were celebrated in the 1989 TV series *Baywatch*, starring David Hasselhoff as Mitch Buchannon.

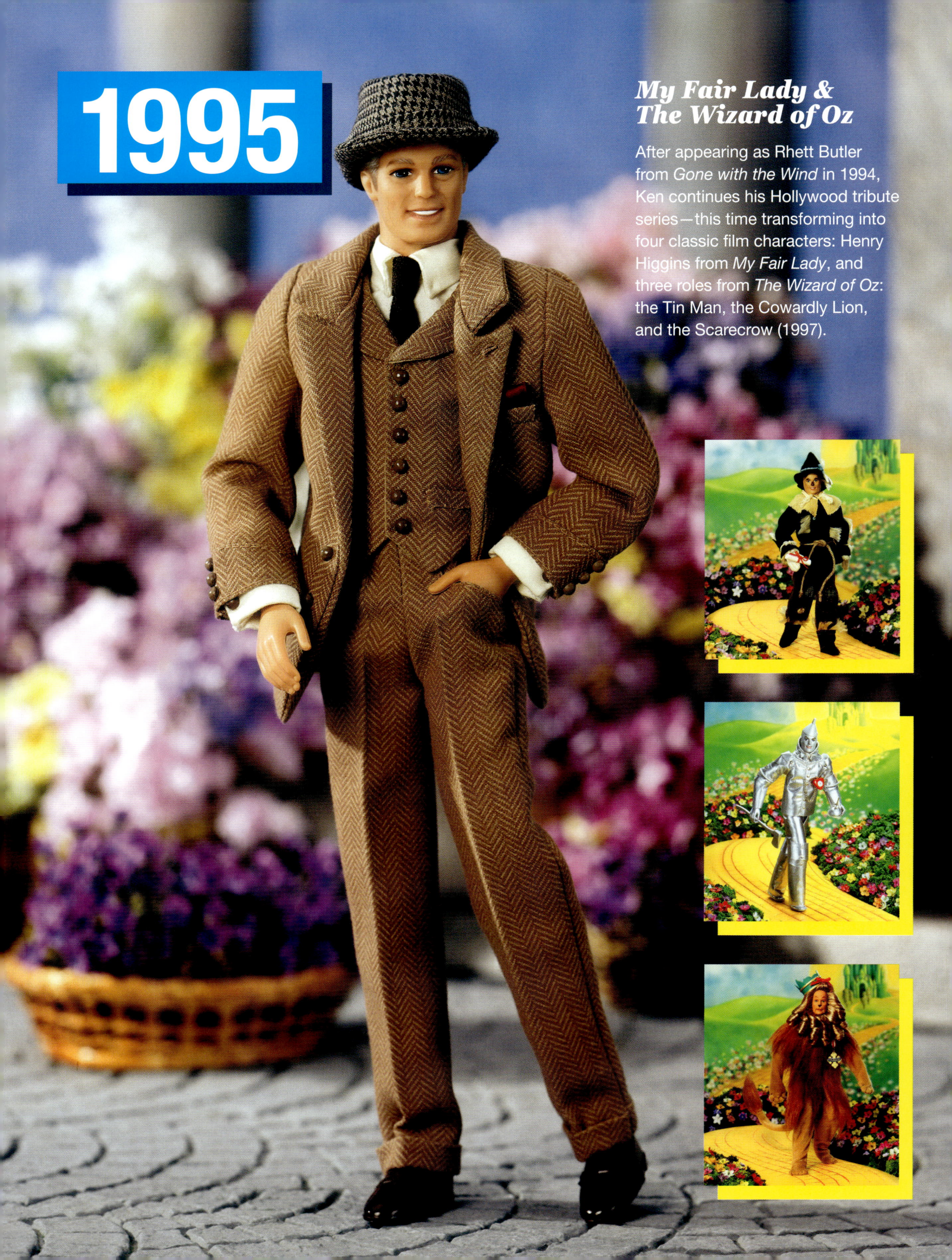

1995

My Fair Lady & The Wizard of Oz

After appearing as Rhett Butler from *Gone with the Wind* in 1994, Ken continues his Hollywood tribute series—this time transforming into four classic film characters: Henry Higgins from *My Fair Lady*, and three roles from *The Wizard of Oz*: the Tin Man, the Cowardly Lion, and the Scarecrow (1997).

1997

Ken and Little Tommy

Ken gets a little brother: Tommy, the first relative to be introduced as a doll. Tommy is three years old and comes with Ken, who carries him in a backpack-style baby carrier.

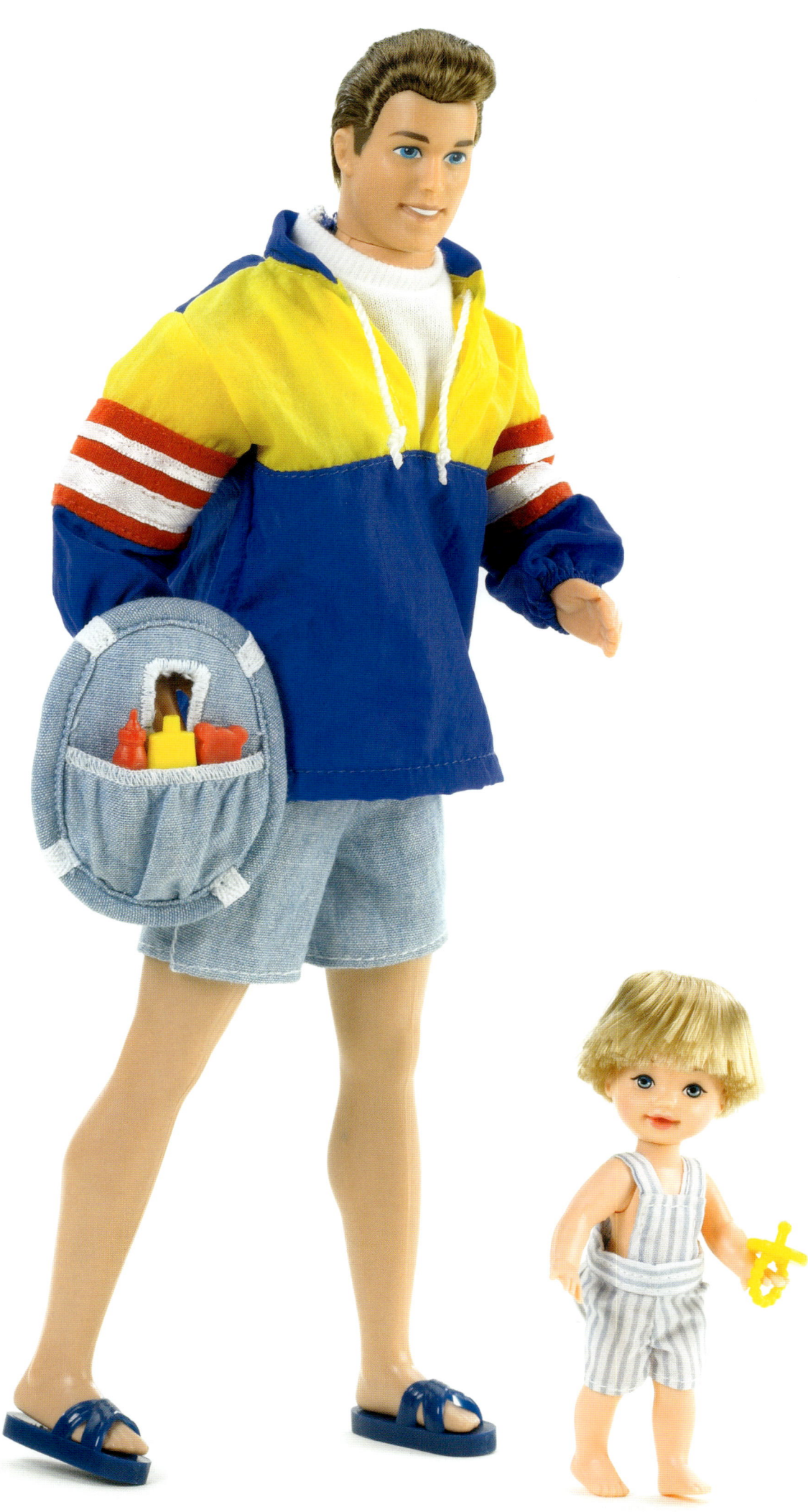

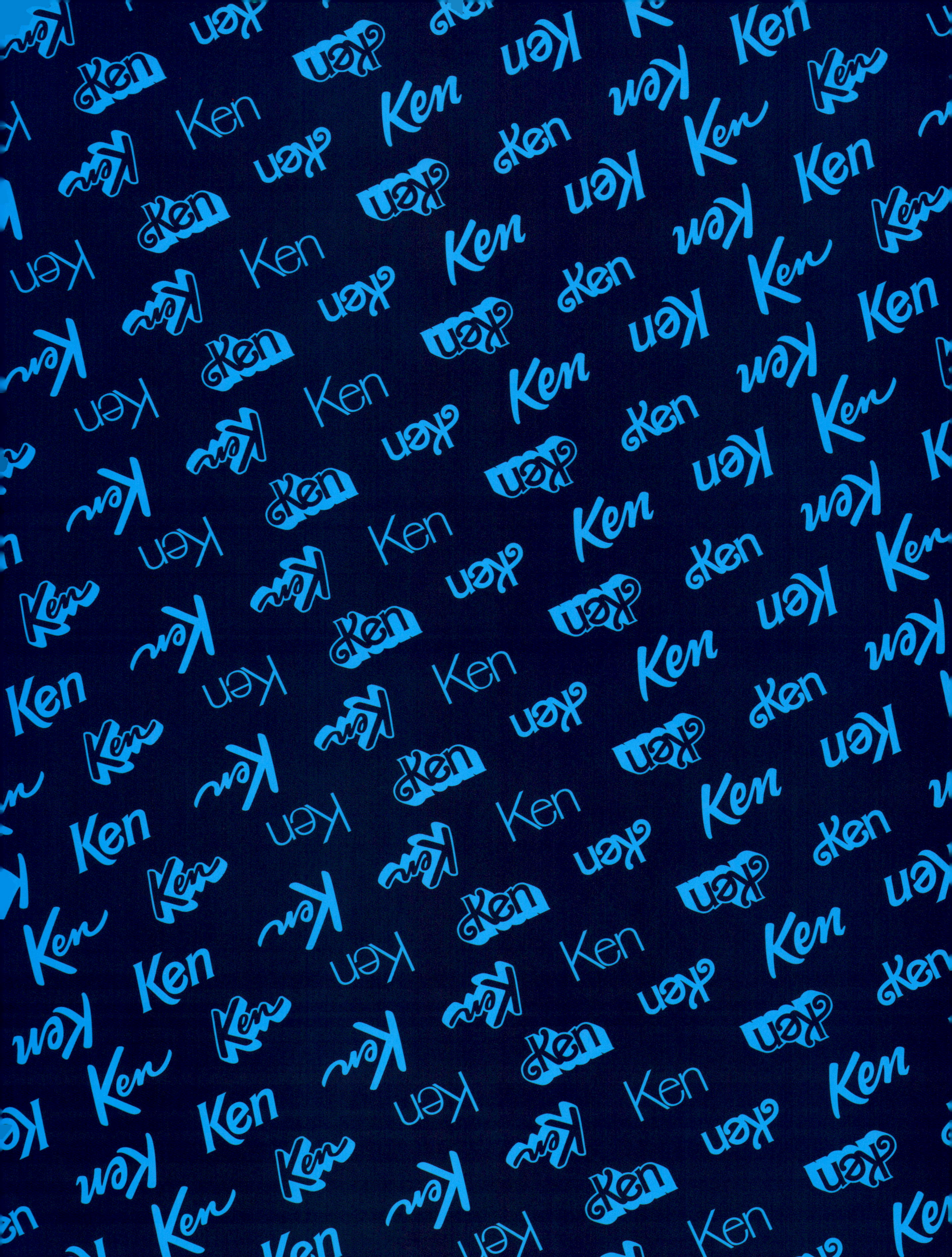

The 2000s

2000-2025

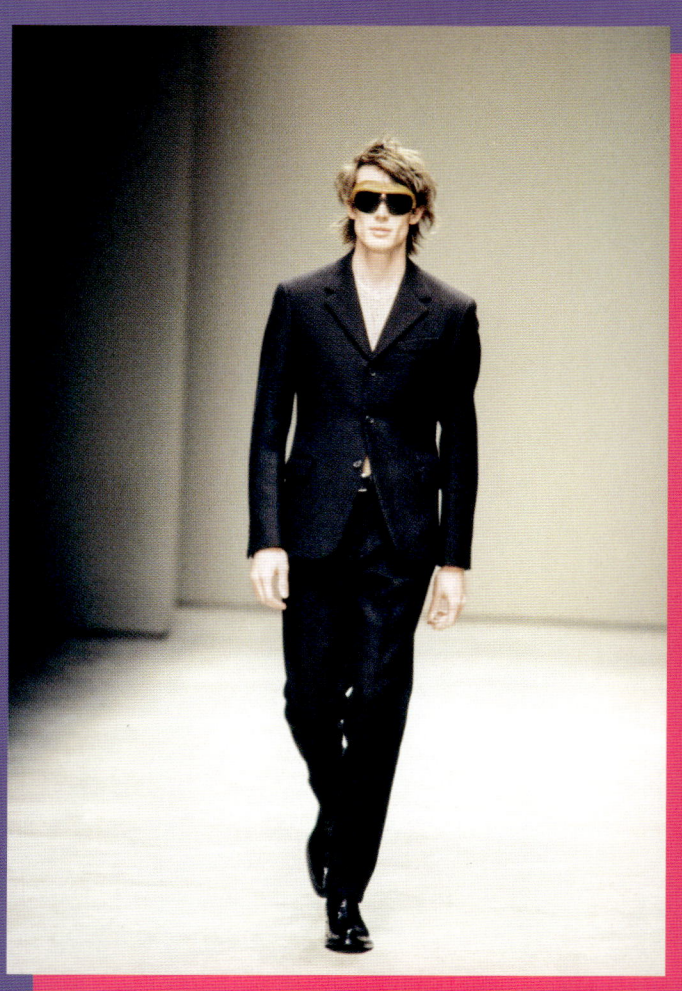

Prada's minimalist fashion triumphs on the runway, with menswear dominated by black fabric and clean, classic lines (menswear Fall/Winter 2001).

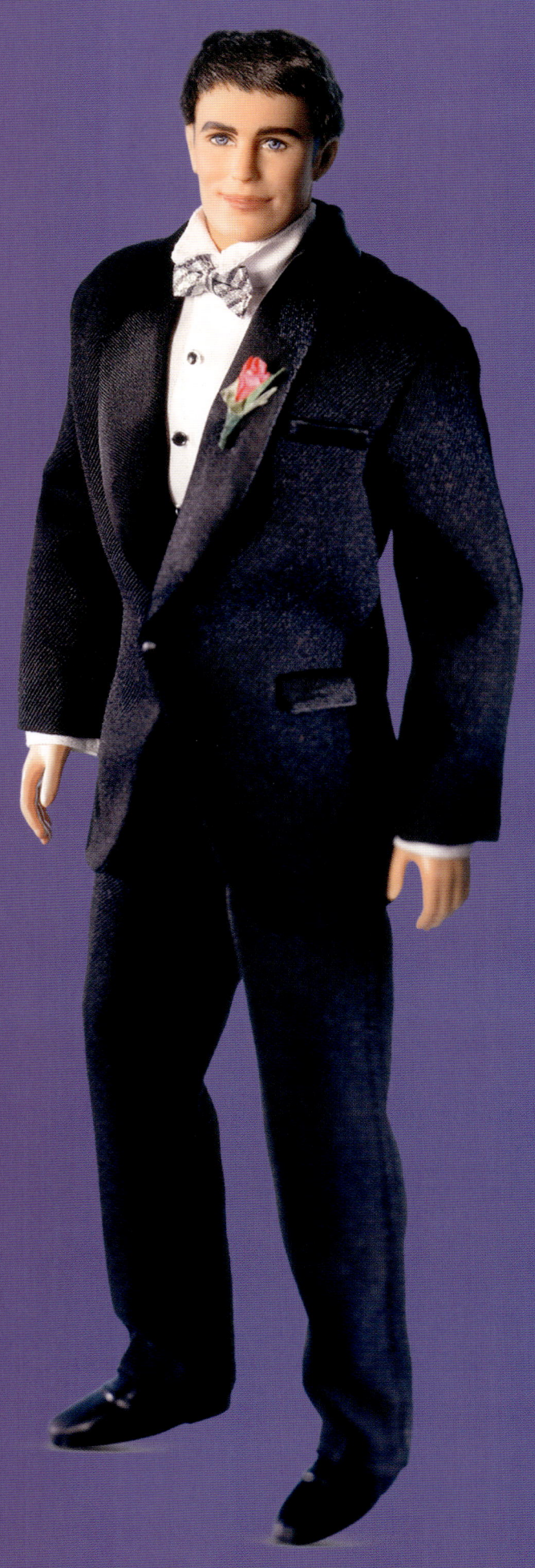

2001

40th Anniversary Ken

With dark hair and striking blue eyes, Ken marks his fortieth anniversary with a classic look that resists the minimalist trends of contemporary fashion. He wears an elegant black tuxedo with a satin shawl collar, a white shirt, silver cummerbund and bow tie, and a pink boutonniere on his lapel. For the occasion, Mattel also returns to his origins with a replica of the 1961 Flock Hair Ken.

2003

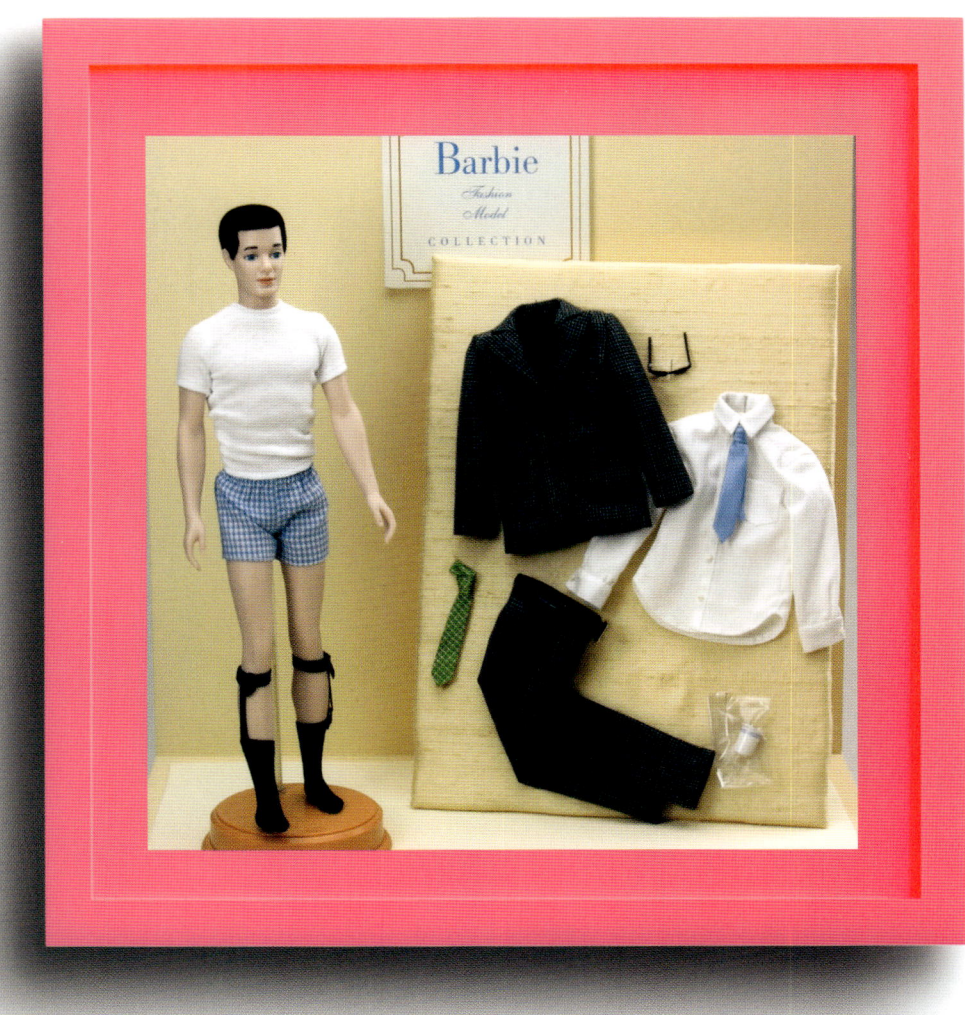

To mark their forty-fifth anniversary, Barbie and Ken appear together in a special Silkstone edition.

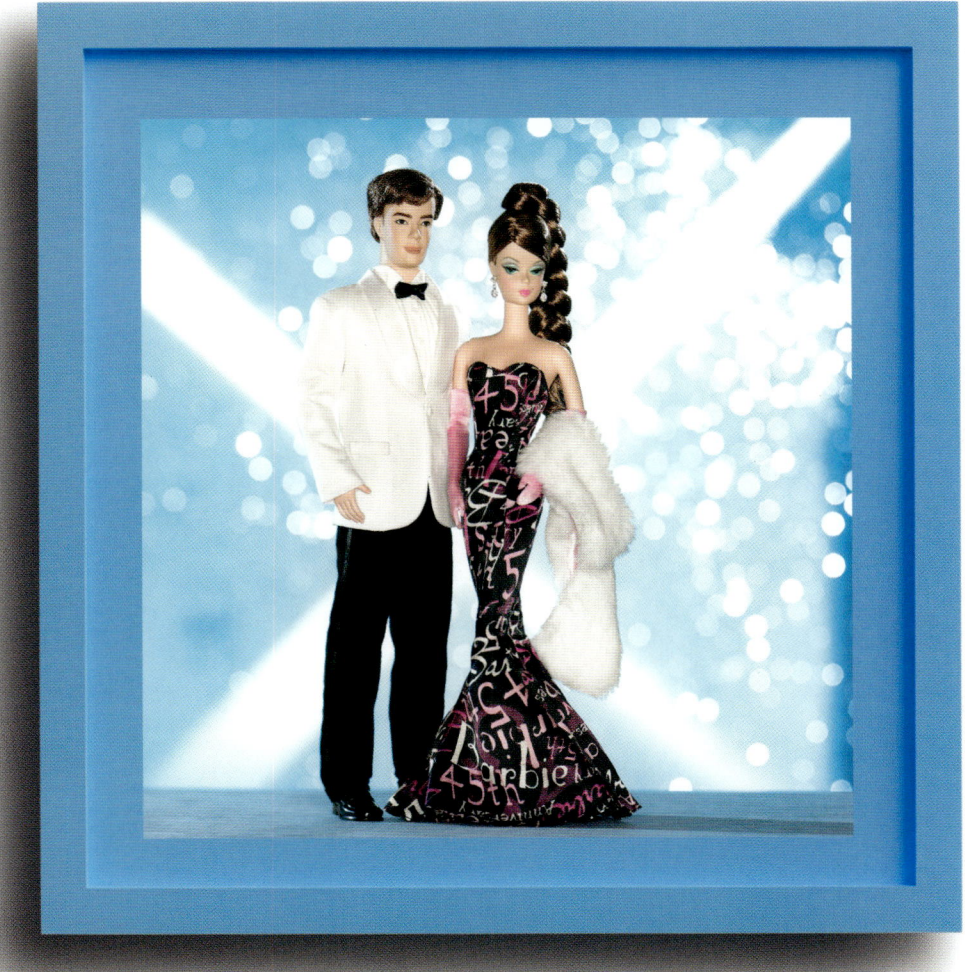

Fashion Insider Ken Doll Gift Set

In 2000, Mattel launched the Silkstone Barbie Dolls line, designed by Robert Best. These dolls, styled with vintage elegance, are made from "silkstone," a soft plastic that mimics porcelain. In this special edition, the Fashion Insider Ken Doll Gift Set debuts with a refined black-and-white ensemble packed with accessories: blue-and-white checkered boxers, white T-shirt, black socks with garters, white jacquard shirt, and a blue satin tie. The details are meticulous, from the black belt to silver-framed blue-lens glasses and newly-designed black loafers.

2004

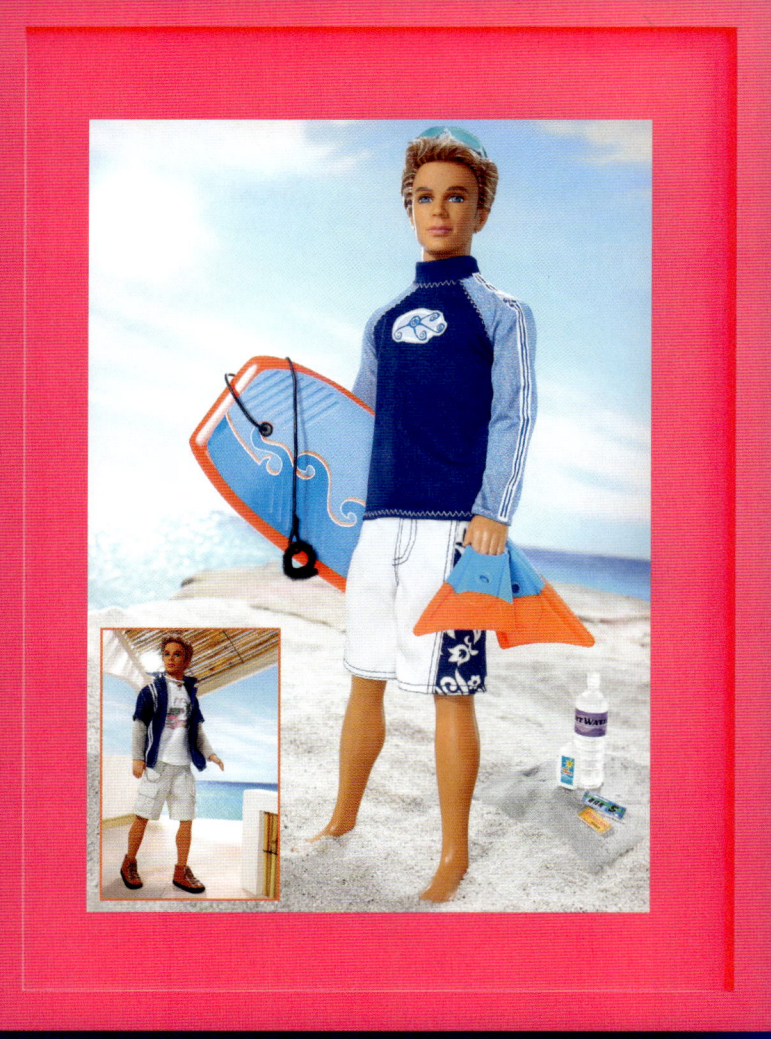

After forty-three years together, Barbie and Ken break up!

Barbie meets Blaine, an Australian surfer doll inspired by boy band heartthrobs like the Backstreet Boys (and reintroduced this year after previously debuting with the Generation Girl line in 1999).

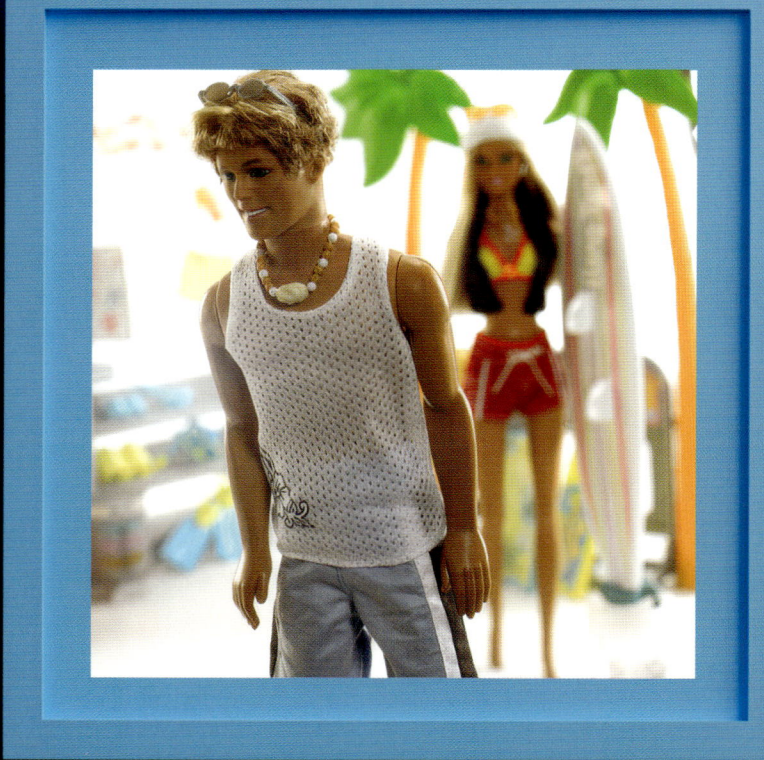

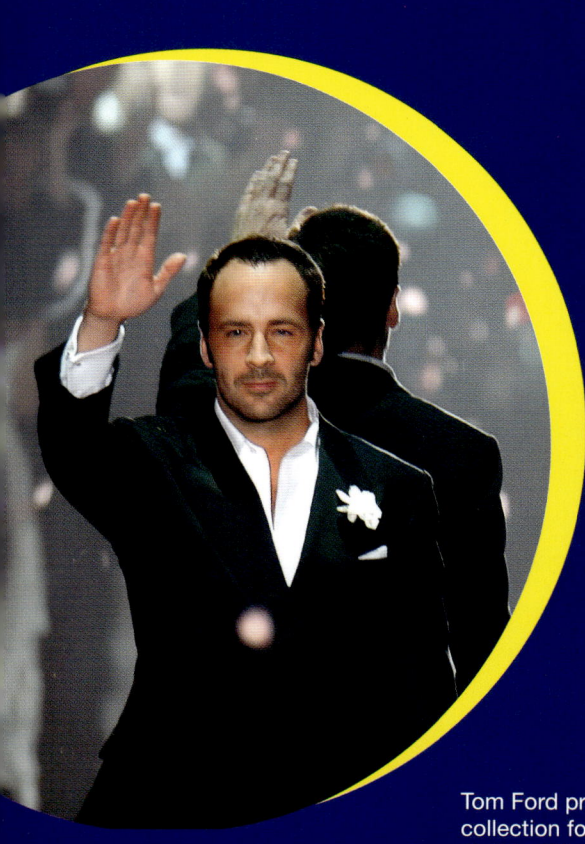

Tom Ford presents his final collection for Gucci at Milan Fashion Week on February 25, 2004 (F/W 2004/2005).

Facebook is founded. Communication becomes truly global.

2005

The New Look Ken

Ken is back! With a redesigned face mold featuring a sharper jawline and softer eyes, this Ken shows off an updated look styled by renowned fashion designer Phillip Bloch. Available in blond and brunette versions, he sports a streetwear-influenced wardrobe: cargo pants, leather jacket, bold chain necklaces—alternating with sportier outfits like jeans and a T-shirt printed with "I'M BACK!"—plus his signature beachwear, of course.

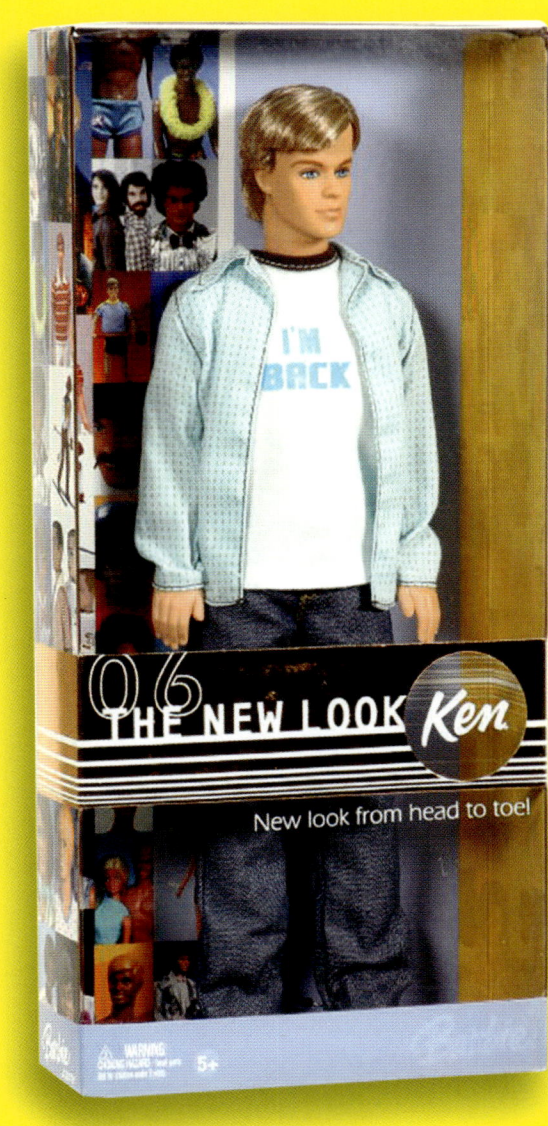

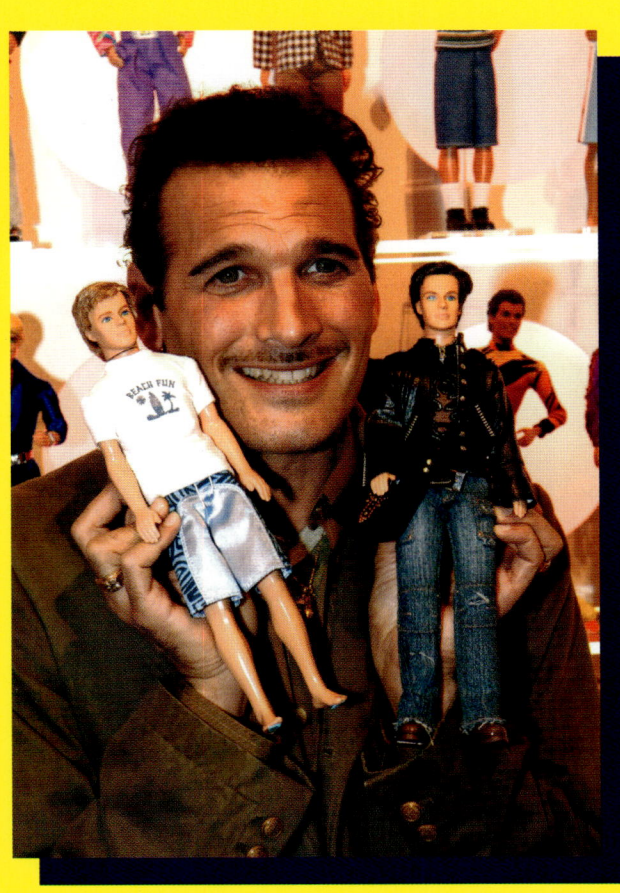

Philip Bloch brings Ken's style into the modern era.

2009

Elvis Presley Jailhouse Rock Doll and Star Trek

Ken becomes Elvis, and at the same time appears as Mr. Spock and Captain Kirk, from the beloved sci-fi series known as *Star Trek*.

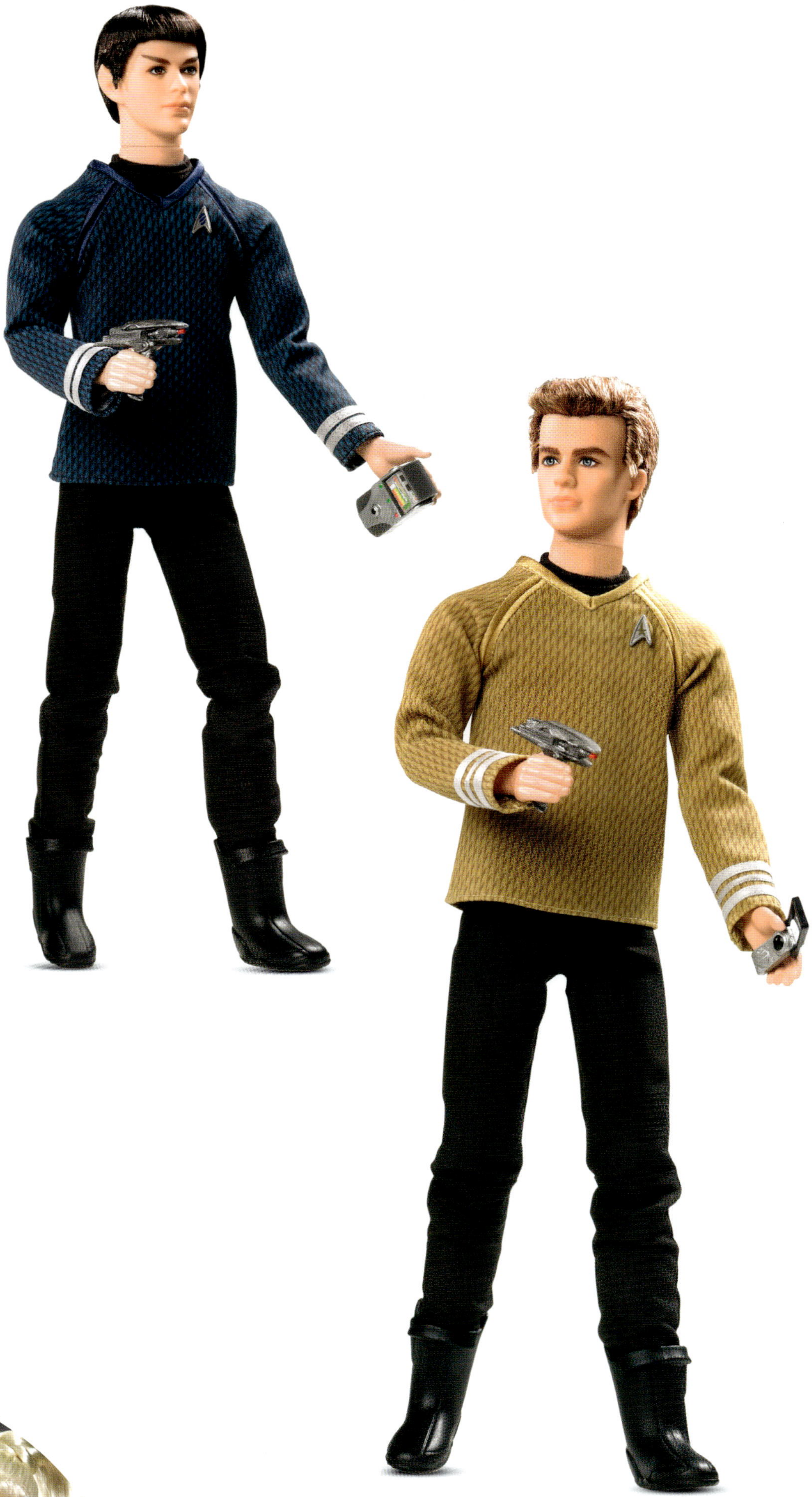

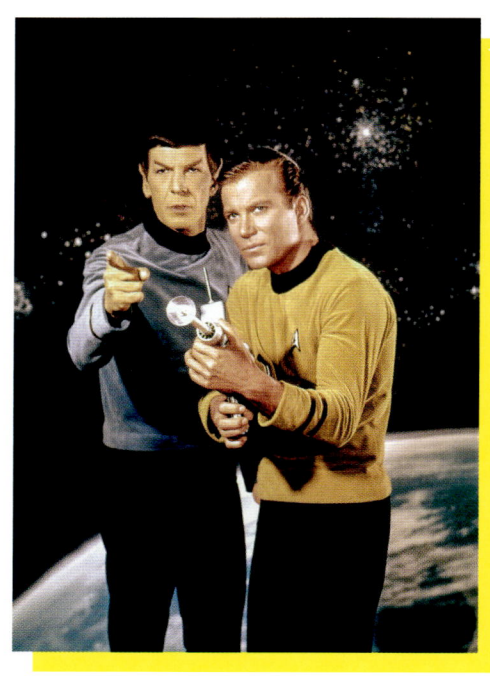

Mr. Spock and Captain Kirk in *Star Trek: The Motion Picture* (1979).

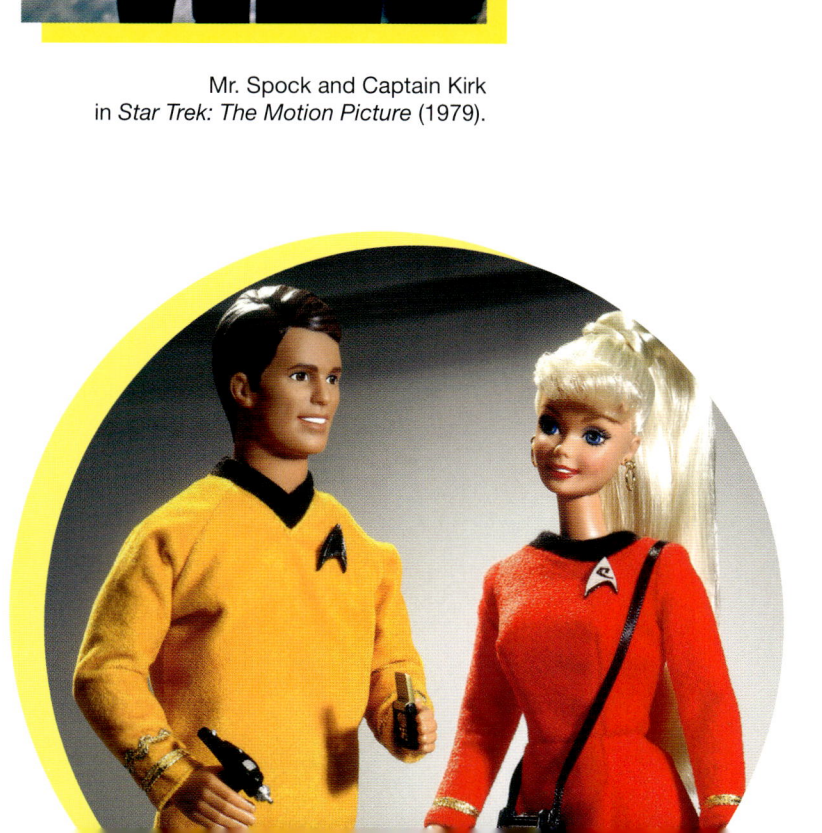

The eleventh *Star Trek* film is released, starring Chris Pine (as Captain Kirk) and Zachary Quinto (as Spock).

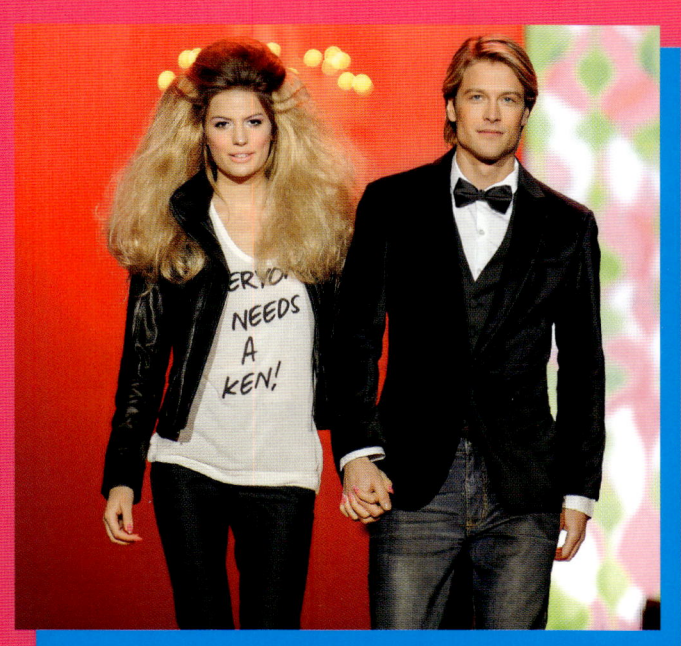

"Everyone needs a Ken!": this is the slogan Barbie sports on the runway at New York Fashion Week, with Ken at her side. At the Barbie Runway Show (Bryant Park, New York, February 14, 2009), the creations of fifty fashion designers, including Kenneth Cole, celebrate the fiftieth birthday of the world's most famous fashion doll!

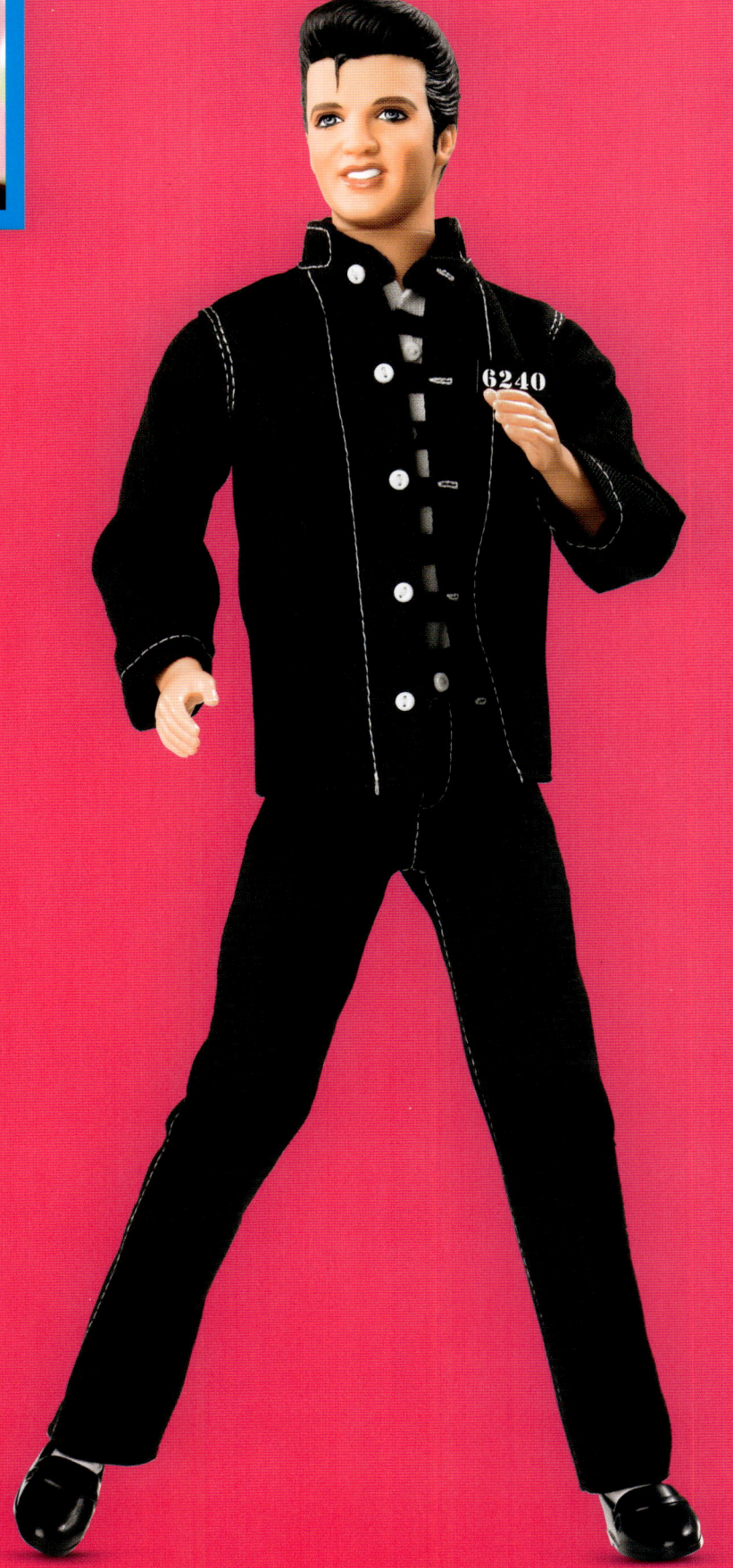

2009

Gareth Pugh Ken

In Paris, chez Colette, London designer Gareth Pugh pays tribute to Ken with fifty handmade dolls featuring a complete punk makeover. Inspired by Pugh's F/W 2009/2010 menswear debut, the look emphasizes glossy/matte contrasts in patent black leather—a decidedly dark aesthetic.

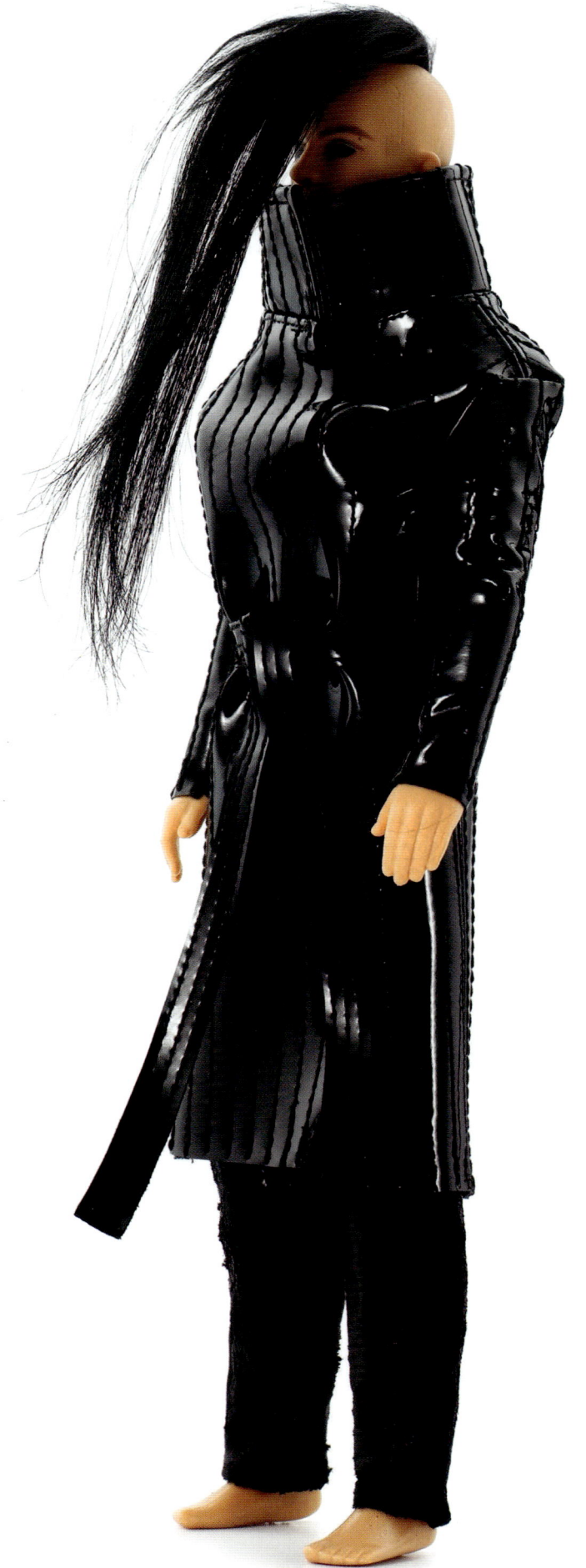

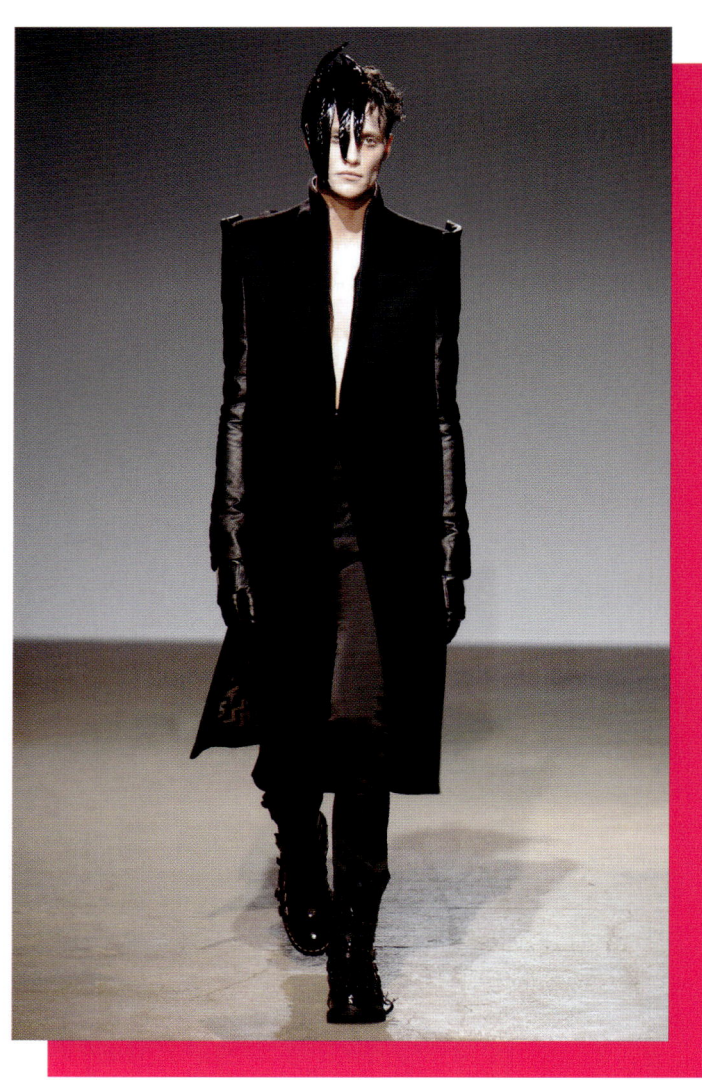

Gareth Pugh, Paris Fashion Week Menswear F/W 2009/2010.

"Ken came backstage at my Fall/Winter 2009/10 show and selected his favorite outfit for me to recreate exclusively for him."

—Gareth Pugh, 2009

2010

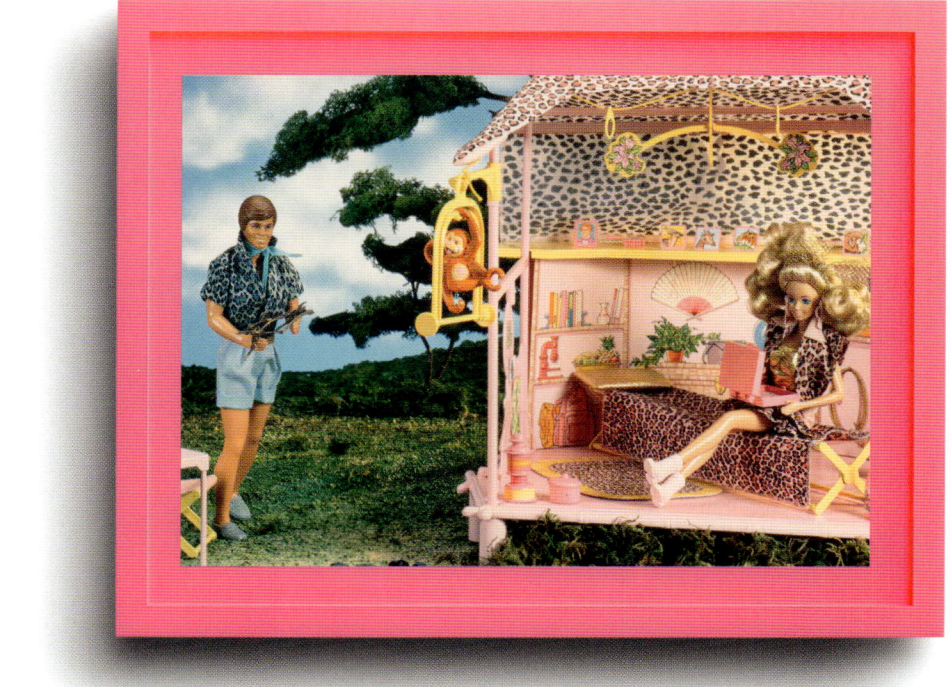

Toy Story 3 Ken

In 1988, Ken and Barbie camped out in the savannah, dressed in elegant animal-printed outfits. In the blockbusting *Toy Story 3*, Ken reprises his look—blue shorts and a leopard-print shirt, inspired by Animal Lovin' Ken.

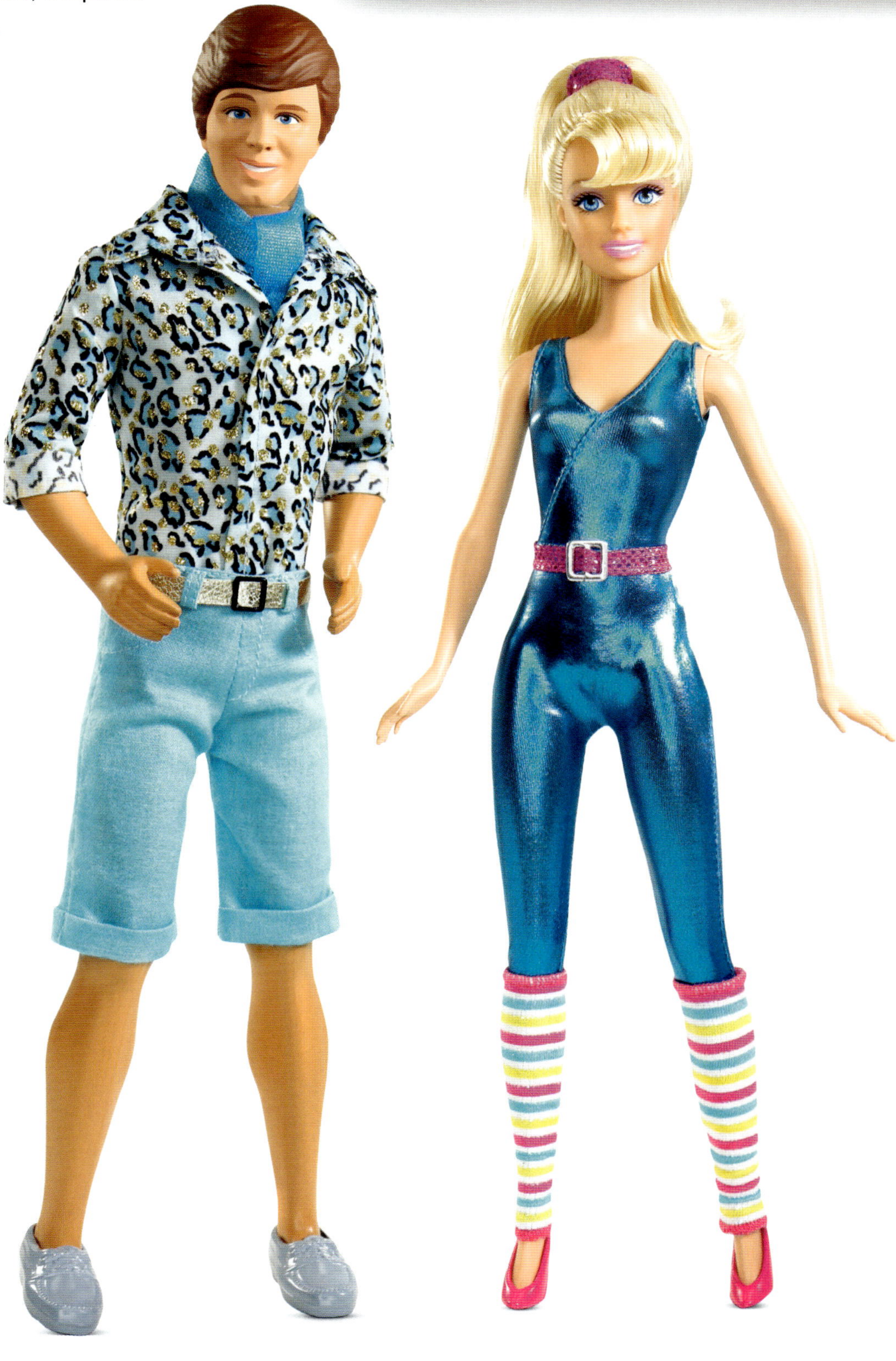

2011

Ken Basics 2.0

Ken's many faces are celebrated in the Ken Basics 2.0 line: jeans and a black top in the spirit of Calvin Klein minimalism.

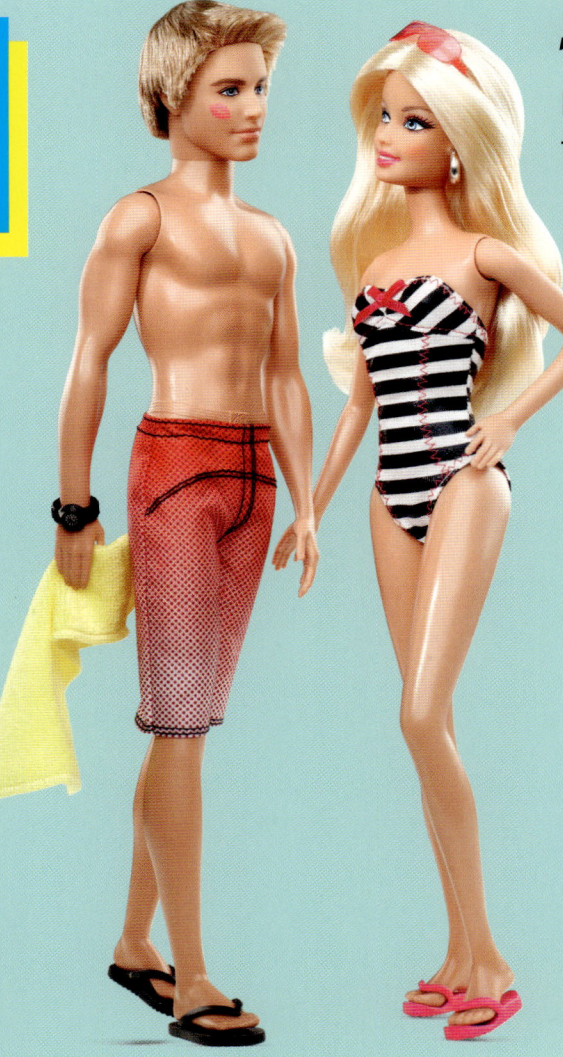

She said yes!

Blond and dashing in a black tuxedo, Ken reappears for his fiftieth anniversary after co-starring with Barbie in *Toy Story 3*. He also stars in a Times Square ad campaign to win back his longtime love. On Valentine's Day, February 14, 2011, Barbie and Ken reunite.

2013

Tailored Tuxedo Ken

A sophisticated, classic tuxedo with single-breasted jacket and black trousers, white shirt, vest, and bow tie. Tailored Tuxedo Ken is a Silkstone doll designed by Robert Best.

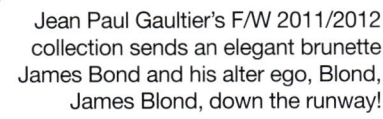

Jean Paul Gaultier's F/W 2011/2012 collection sends an elegant brunette James Bond and his alter ego, Blond, James Blond, down the runway!

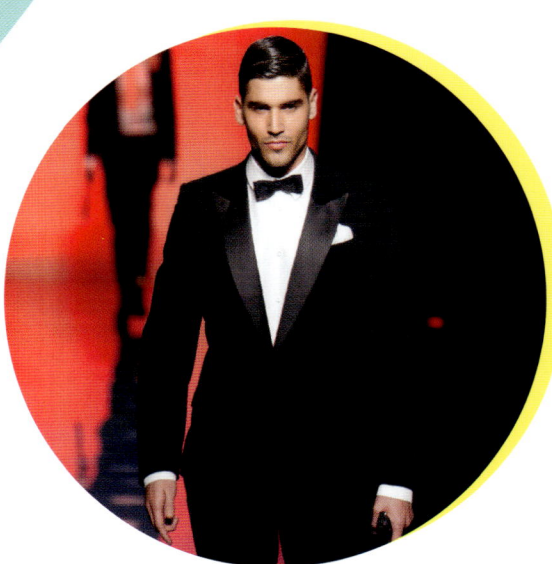

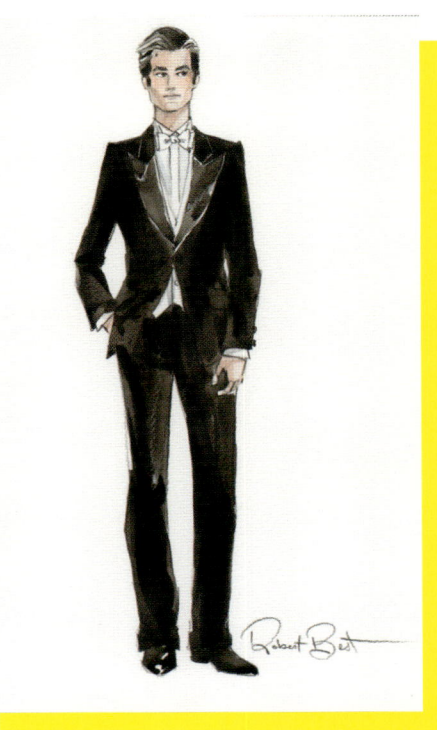

2016

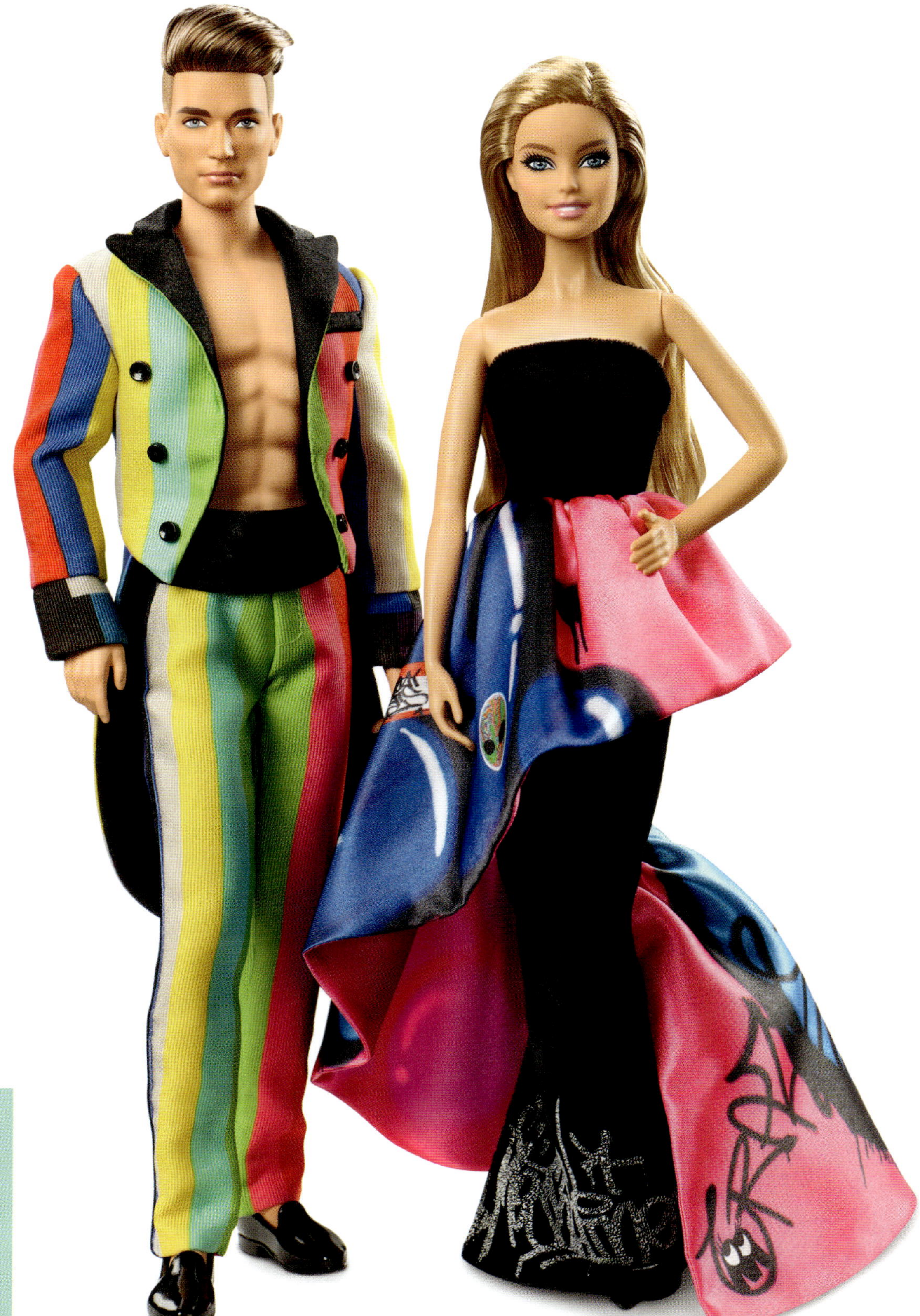

Moschino Ken

Barbie and Ken wear custom Moschino by Jeremy Scott—replicating Scott and Maxwell's red carpet look from the 2015 MTV VMAs.

At the 2015 MTV VMAs, Jeremy Scott and supermodel Stella Maxwell hit the red carpet in coordinated outfits.

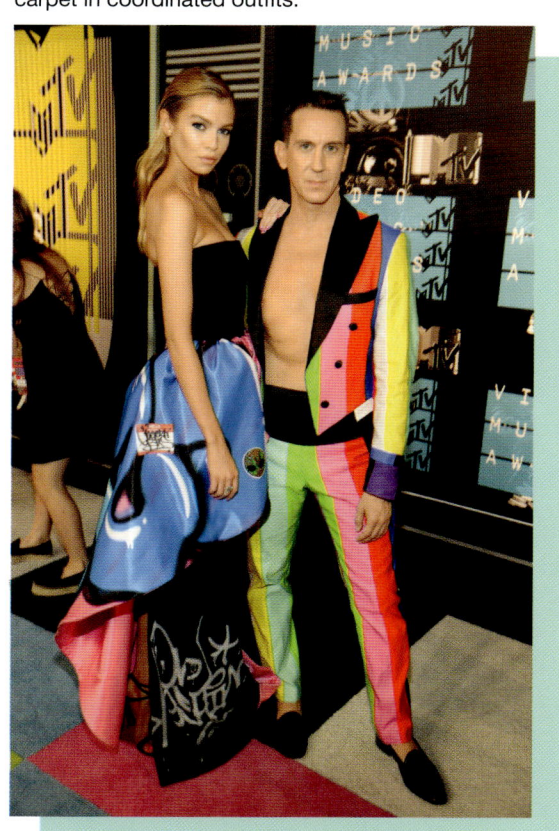

Philipp Plein brings a bold glam-rock edge to menswear (F/W 2016/2017).

2017

Ken Fashionistas

Ken gets a total refresh in the Fashionistas line, with fifteen new versions featuring three body types (original, slim, broad), seven skin tones, nine face shapes, eight hair colors, and nine hairstyles.

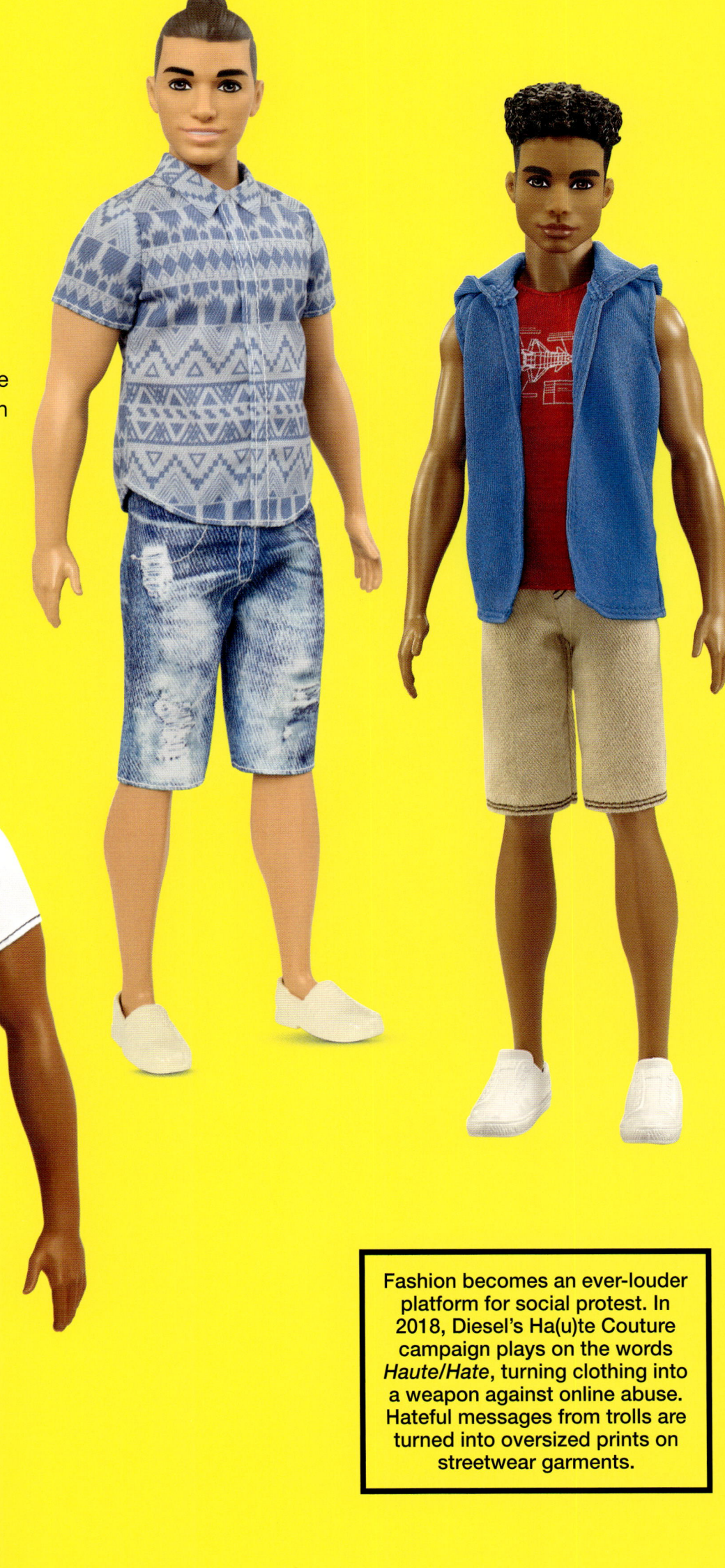

Fashion becomes an ever-louder platform for social protest. In 2018, Diesel's Ha(u)te Couture campaign plays on the words *Haute/Hate*, turning clothing into a weapon against online abuse. Hateful messages from trolls are turned into oversized prints on streetwear garments.

2019

The Ken line becomes more diverse and representative of the world around us.

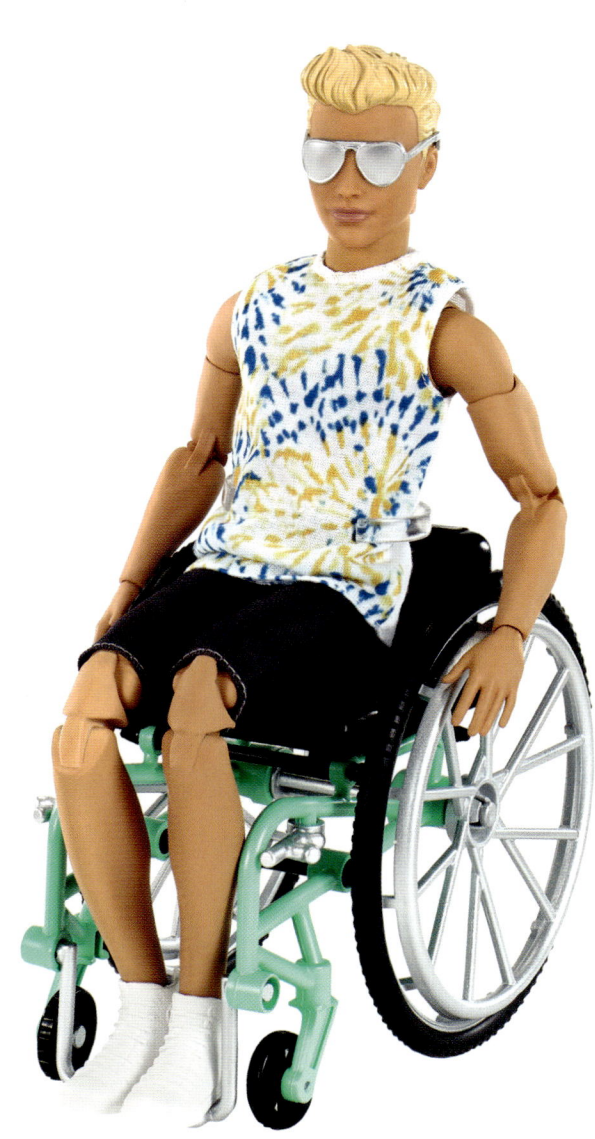

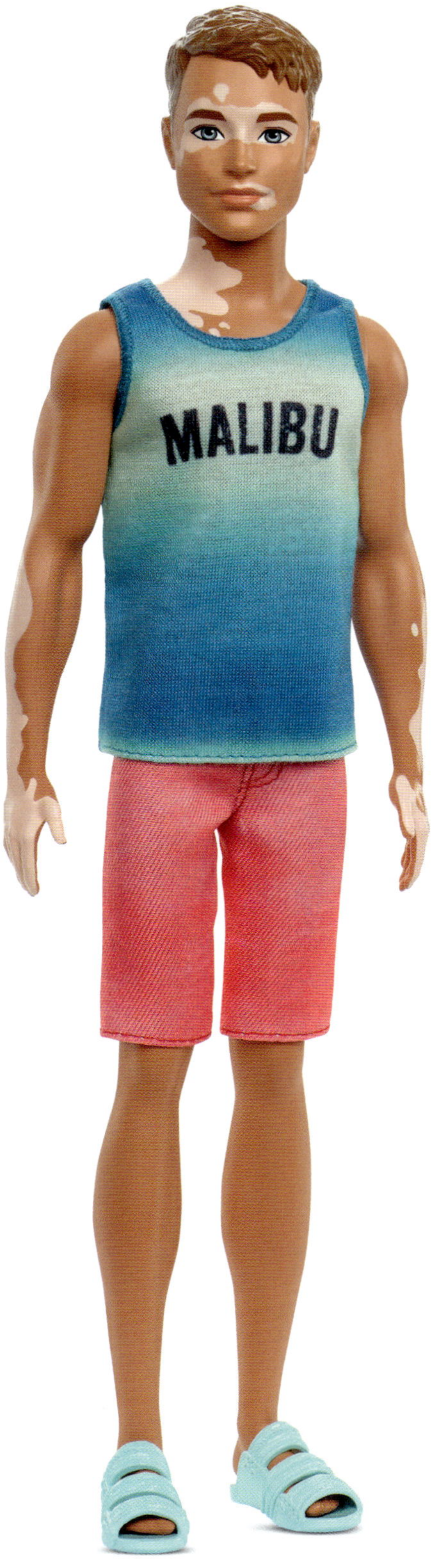

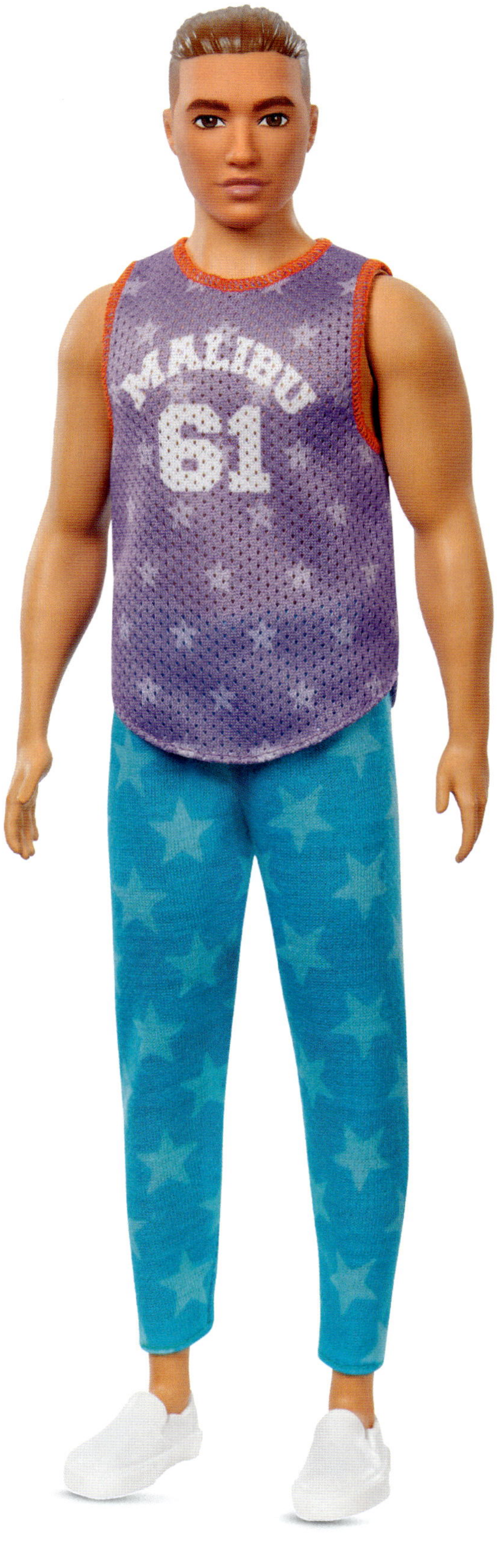

In September 2020, TikTok launches the viral #MachoPink challenge, inspired by a user celebrating pink style. The hashtag racks up 130 million views—with sixty-six percent of followers identifying as male.

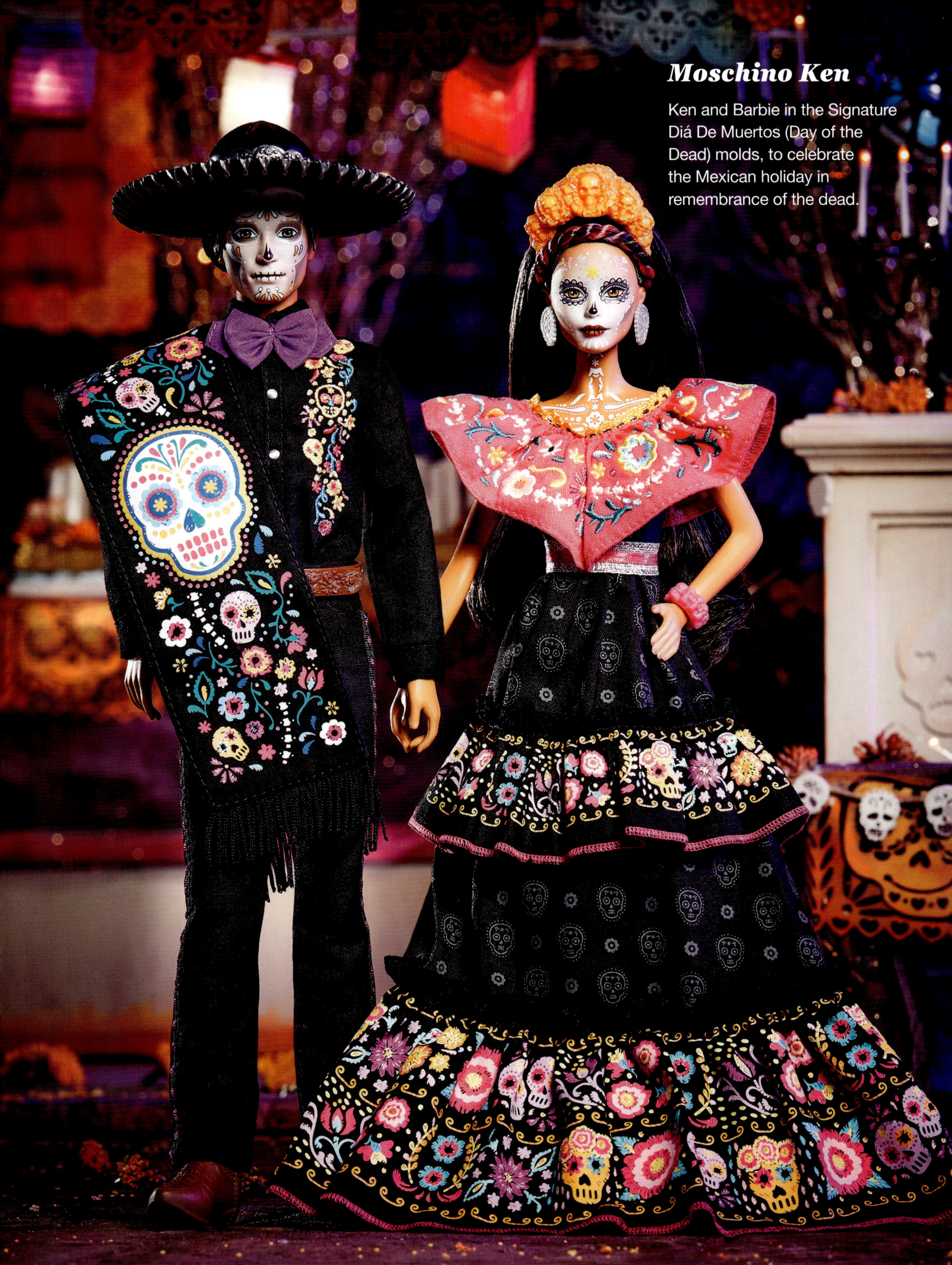

Moschino Ken

Ken and Barbie in the Signature Diá De Muertos (Day of the Dead) molds, to celebrate the Mexican holiday in remembrance of the dead.

2019

BMR1959

BMR1959 celebrates Barbie's sixtieth anniversary with a fresh, new aesthetic—the mood is contemporary, urban, and on-trend.

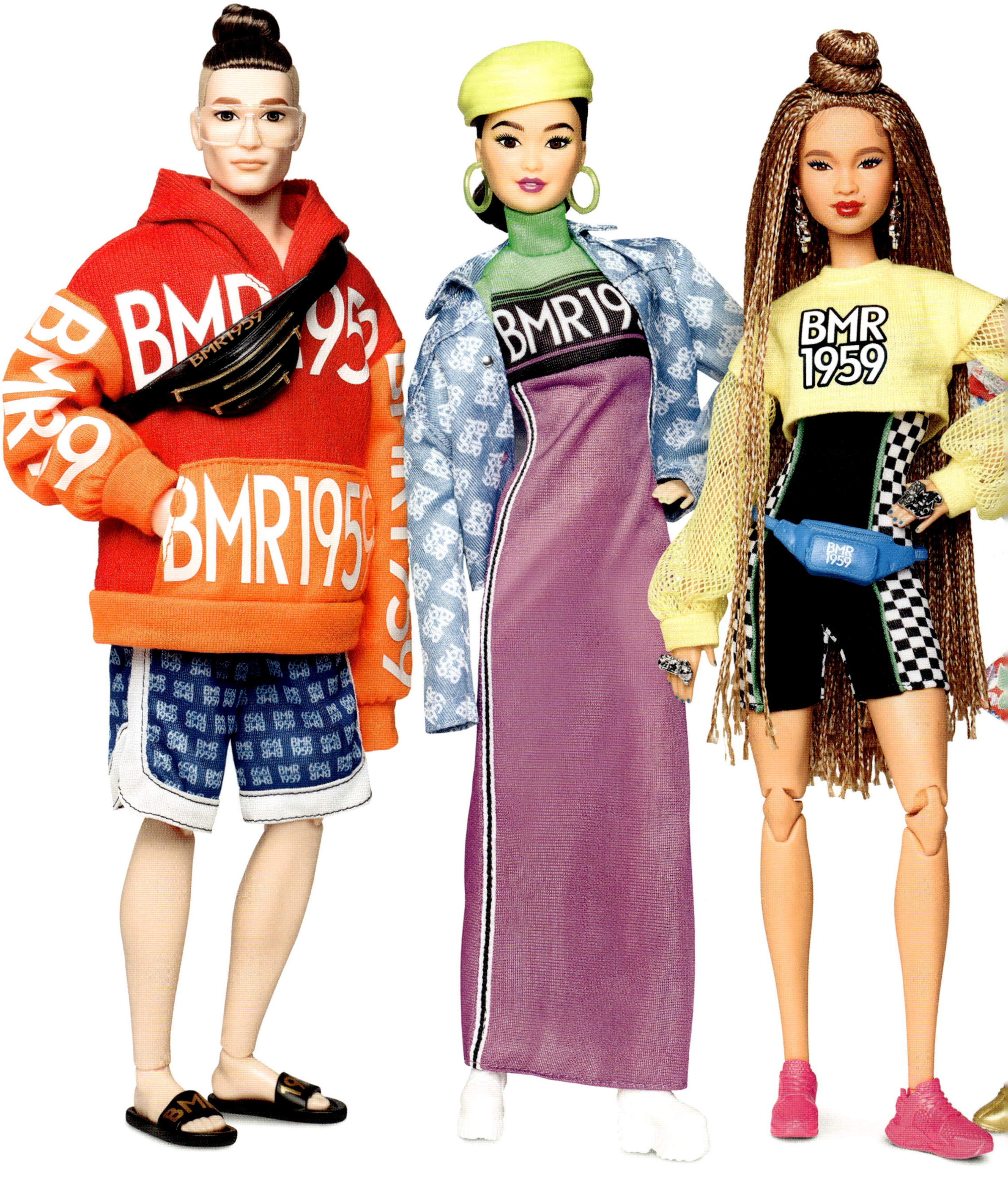

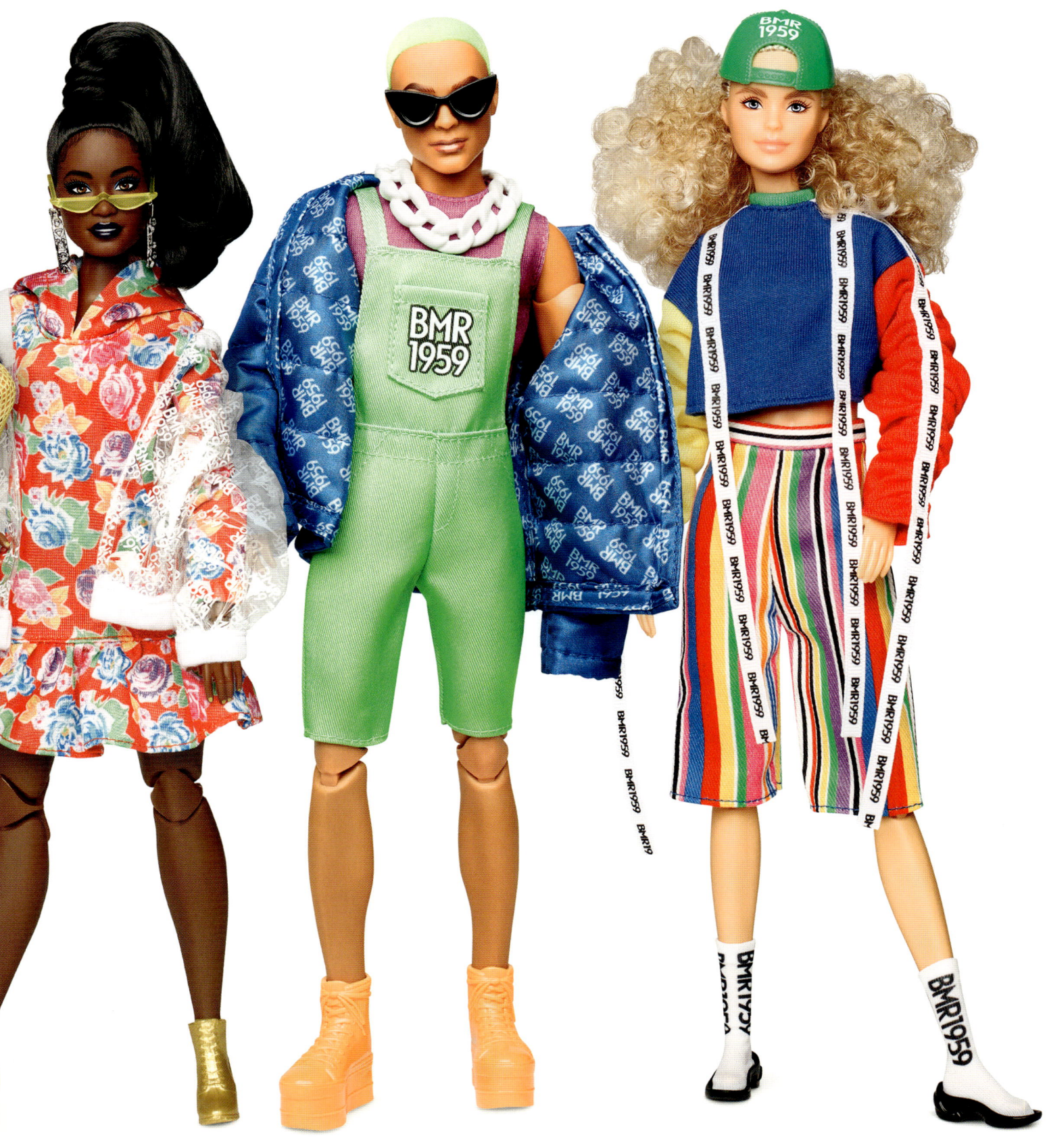

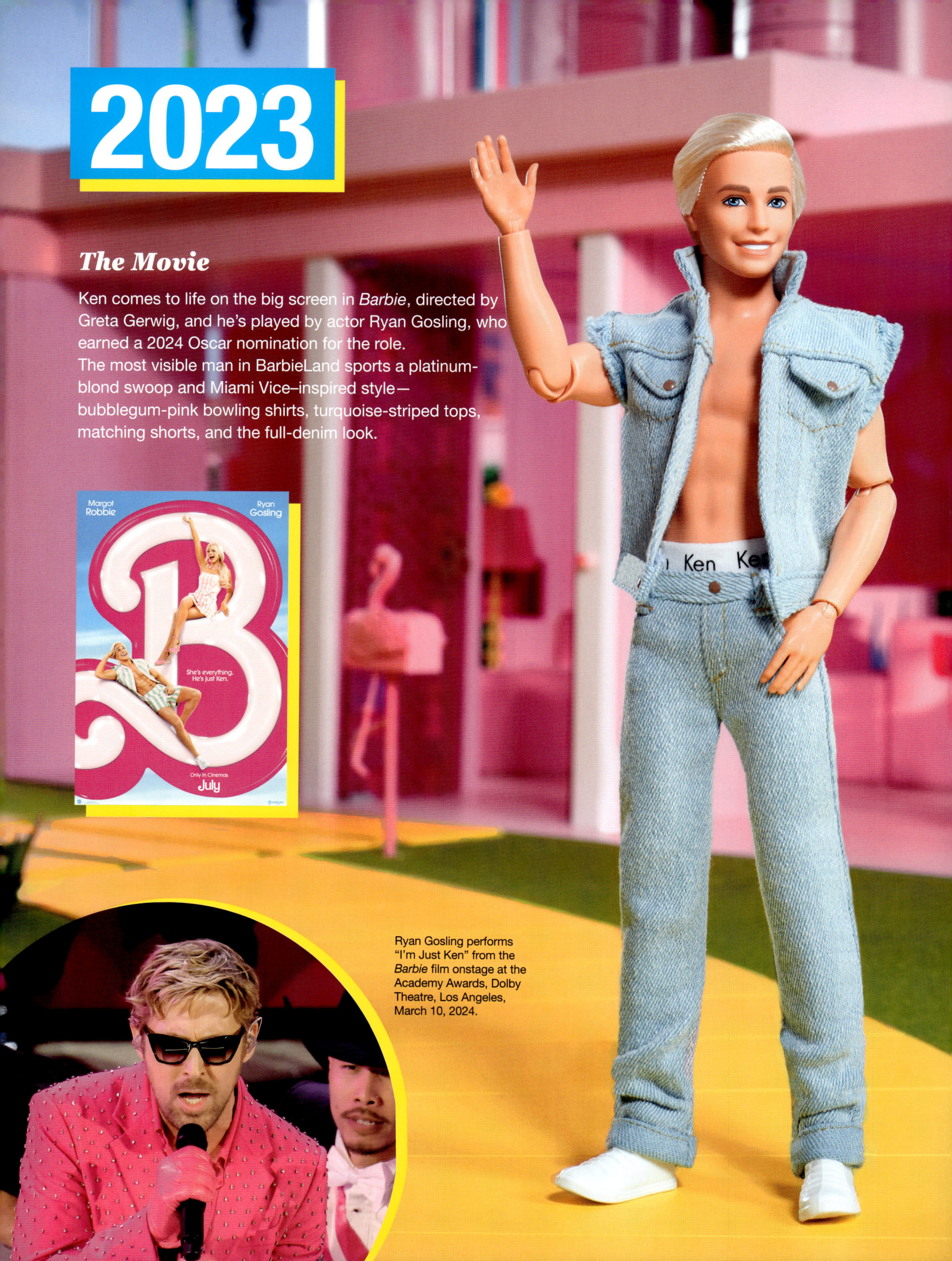

2023

The Movie

Ken comes to life on the big screen in *Barbie*, directed by Greta Gerwig, and he's played by actor Ryan Gosling, who earned a 2024 Oscar nomination for the role.
The most visible man in BarbieLand sports a platinum-blond swoop and Miami Vice–inspired style—bubblegum-pink bowling shirts, turquoise-striped tops, matching shorts, and the full-denim look.

Ryan Gosling performs "I'm Just Ken" from the *Barbie* film onstage at the Academy Awards, Dolby Theatre, Los Angeles, March 10, 2024.

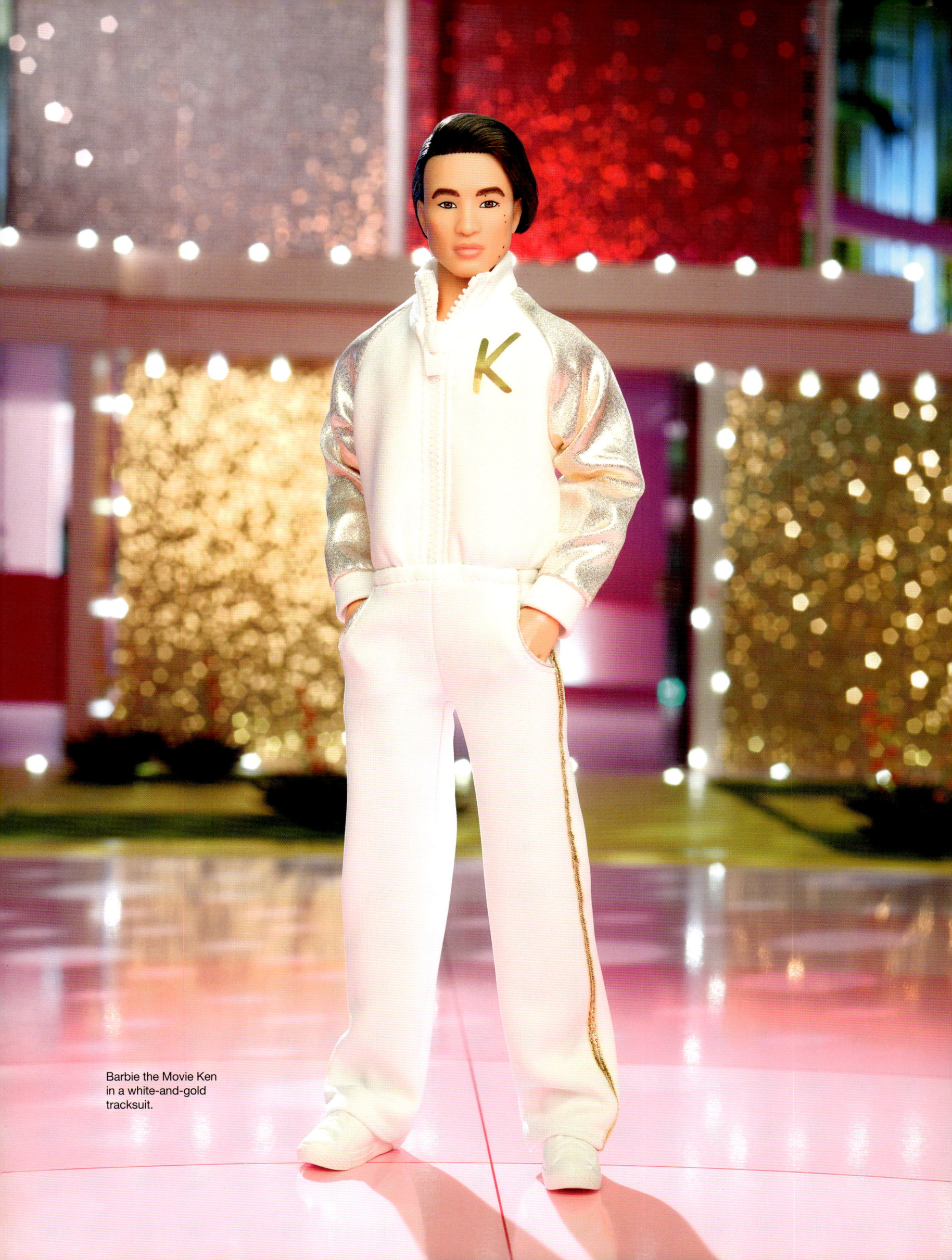

Barbie the Movie Ken in a white-and-gold tracksuit.

2023

Sugar Daddy Ken

With a more mature look—gray hair, lime-green jacquard blazer, pink polo, pleated white pants—and accompanied by a West Highland terrier named Sugar, this Ken appears in the Barbie Collector line. He's inspired by modern fashion trends and Slim Aarons's Palm Beach party photography.

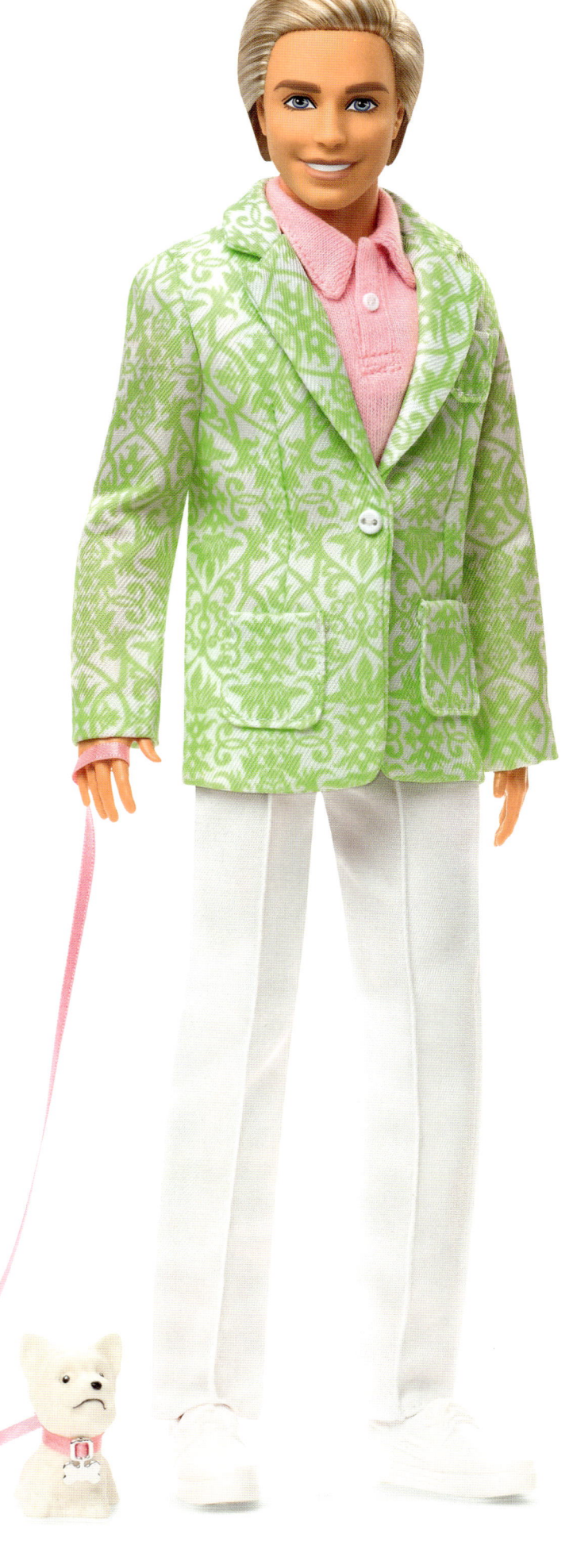

Slim Aarons, *Poolside*, 2007.

2026

The Ken brand's 65th anniversary

Ken celebrates his sixty-fifth anniversary with a perfect beach style, inspired by two models from the 1970s and 1980s: California Dream (1987) and Beach Fun (1993).

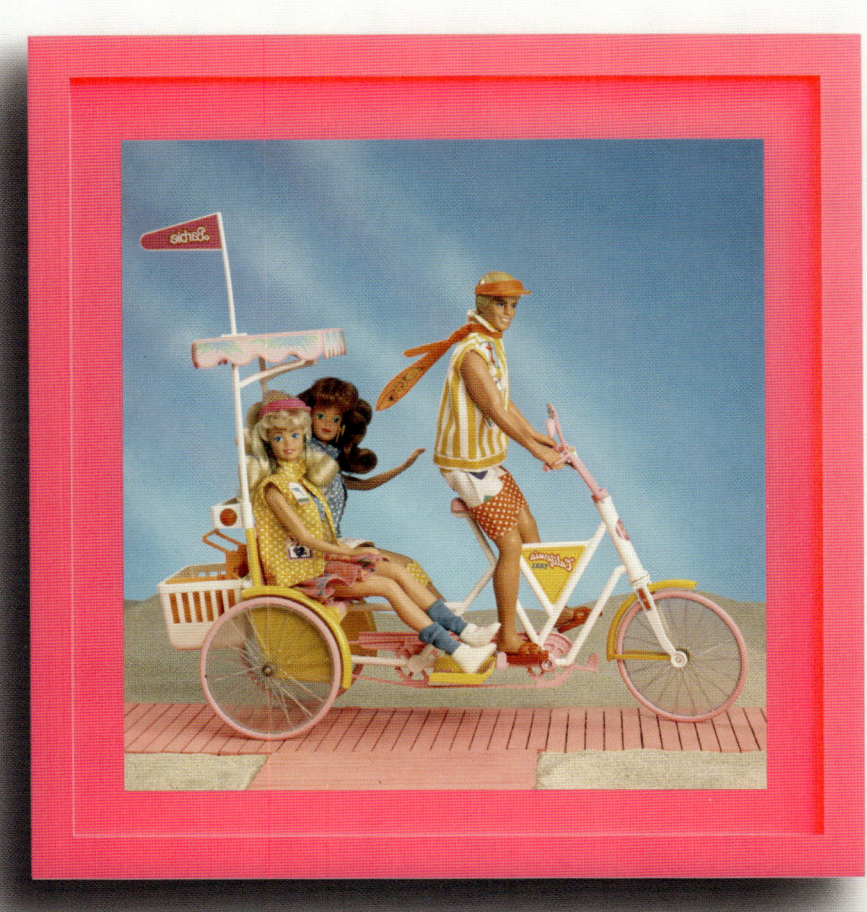

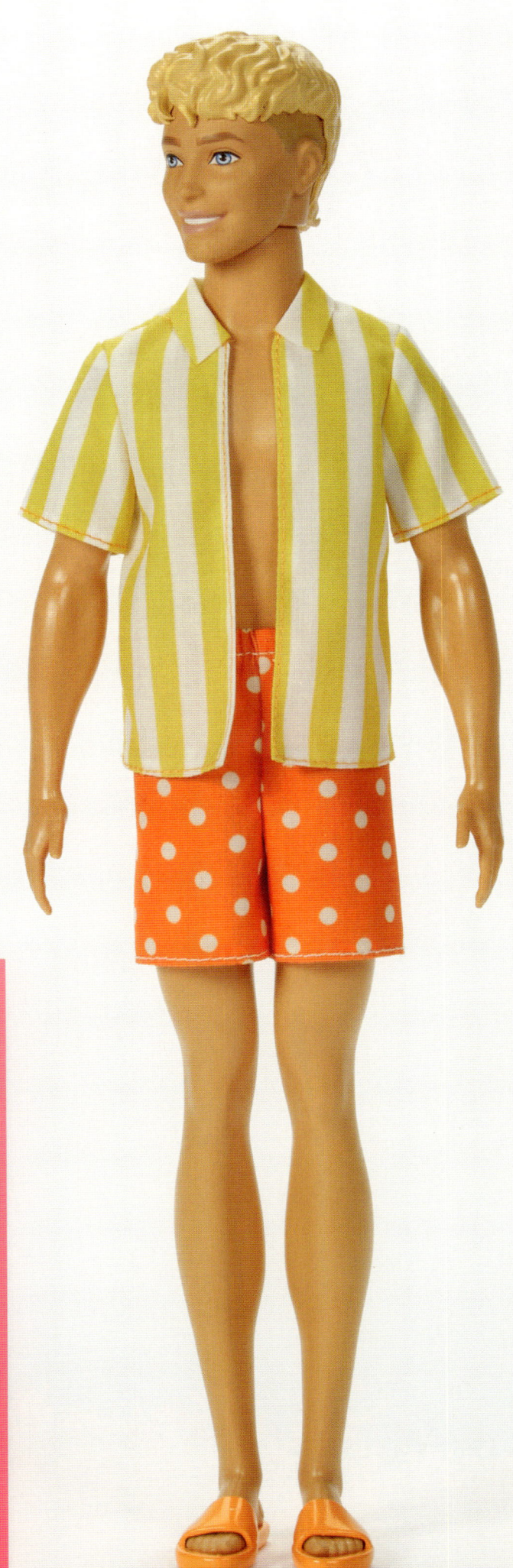

"I care about this dude now. I'm like his representative."

—Ryan Gosling, 2023

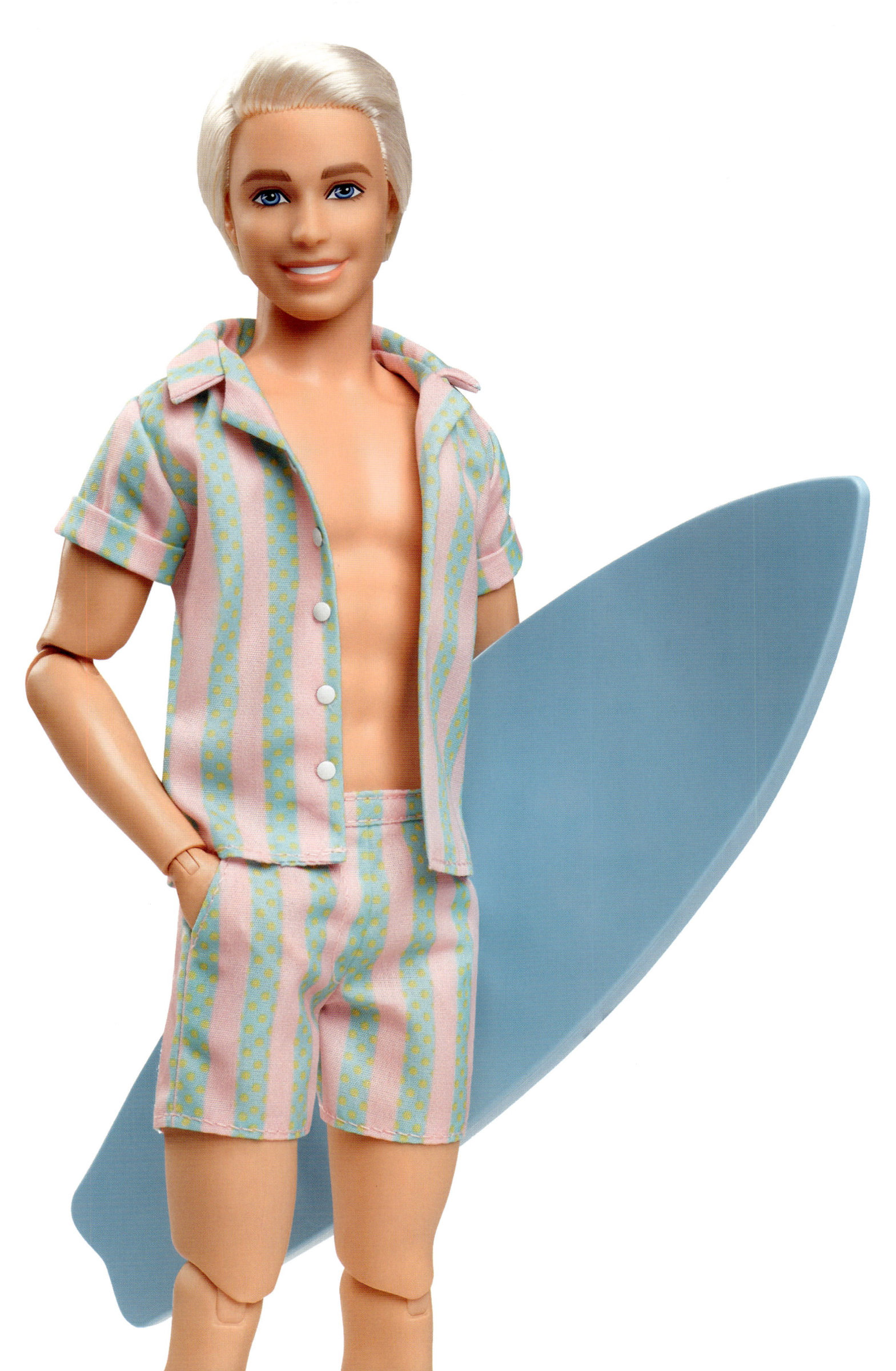

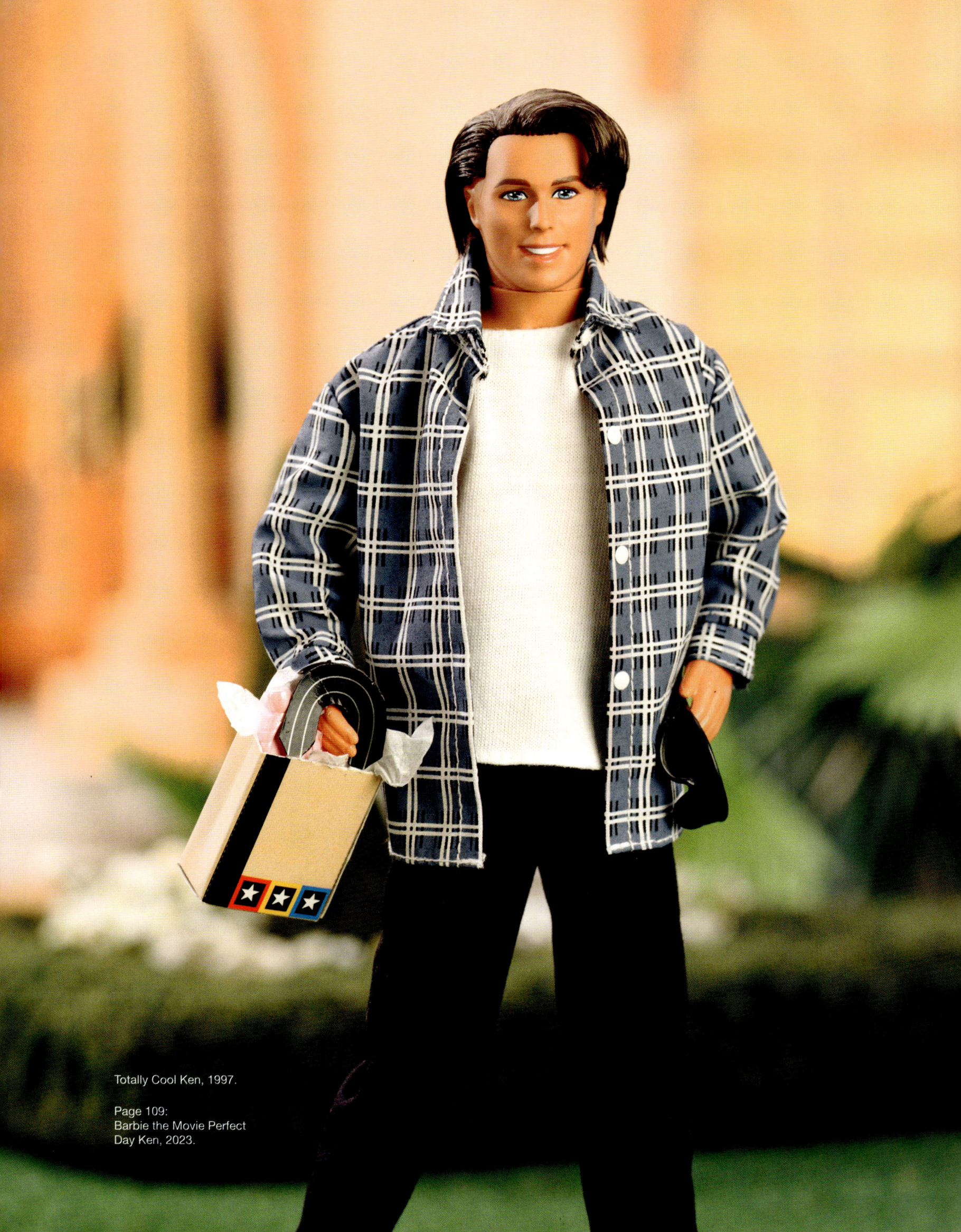

Totally Cool Ken, 1997.

Page 109:
Barbie the Movie Perfect Day Ken, 2023.

Ken

Fun Facts

Ken is a man full of quirks and idiosyncrasies—many of which he's revealed himself in interviews authorized by Mattel.

Ken was born on March 11, 1961, under the sign of Pisces. He describes himself as steadfast, loyal, compassionate, and a DREAMER!

KEN'S FULL NAME IS Ken Sean Carson Jr.

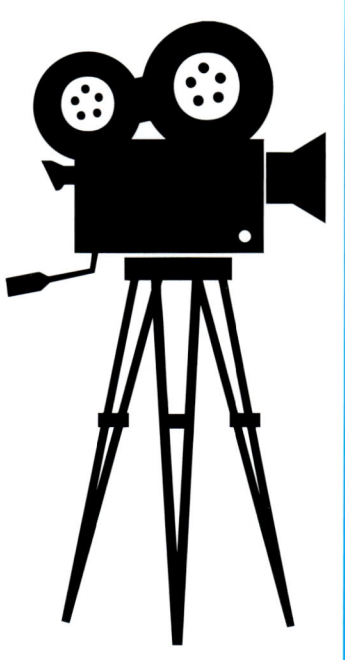

HE was named after **KENNETH**, the son of Barbie creators Ruth and Elliot Handler.

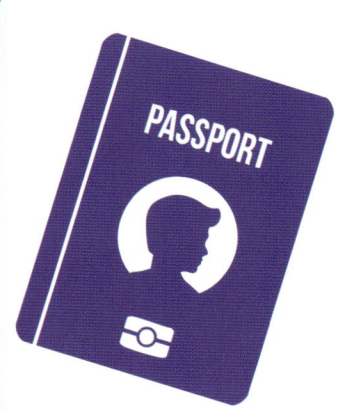

KEN'S FIRST JOB was as a **LIFEGUARD**. He would go on to have dozens more professions.

KEN IS ALSO A MOVIE STAR. On various occasions, he has portrayed iconic film and TV characters including **James Bond 007** (*Die Another Day*), Mulder from *The X-Files,* Gomez from *The Addams Family,* the **Tin Man** from *The Wizard of Oz,* Captain Kirk and **Spock** from *Star Trek,* and Edward from the *Twilight* saga.

Like Barbie, **KEN'S** hometown is **WILLOWS,** a make-believe town in Wisconsin inspired by the real village of Willow (population under 500) in Richland County.

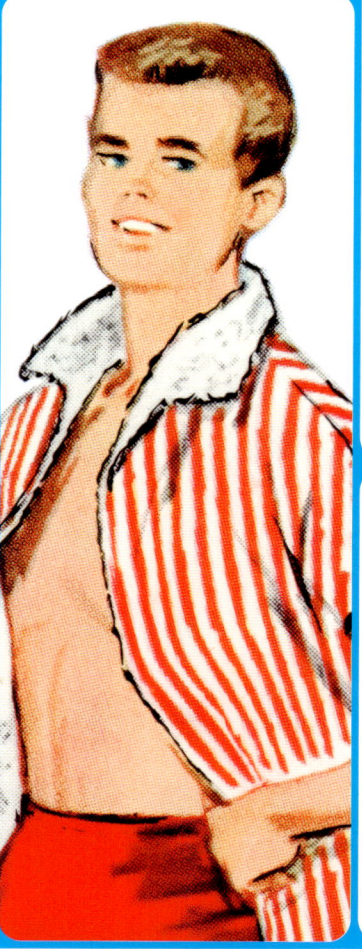

THE FIRST MODEL of Ken sold in 1961 for **$3.50** while **his outfits were sold separately** for prices ranging **from $1.50 to $5.00.**

KEN'S BUDDIES are Brad, Curtis, Steven, Todd, Derek, Darren, Ryan, and, of course, his best friend Allan.

When Mattel released The Barbie Game–Queen of the Prom in 1961, **KEN WAS JUST ONE OF BARBIE'S POTENTIAL BOYFRIENDS,** alongside Bob, Tom, and Poindexter. But Ken—the perfect gentleman—won out.

Ken is **TWO YEARS AND TWO DAYS** younger than Barbie.

The original 1961 **Ken came in three versions:** blond, brownette, and black hair.

KEN ARRIVED ON THE EUROPEAN MARKET in 1964, first in Sweden and then in France, where he was initially described as **BARBIE'S BROTHER!**

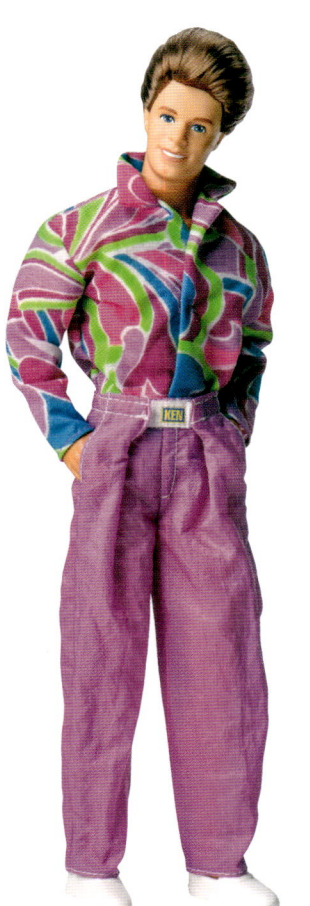

IN 1978, Ken was produced in the *SUPERSTAR* mold—pure triumph of disco style!

IN 1982, *Sunsational Malibu Ken* **DEBUTED AS THE FIRST BLACK VERSION OF KEN, FEATURING HAIR STYLED IN AN AFRO.**

THE ORIGINAL VOICE of Ken in television commercials was that of **BILL CUNNINGHAM** (1927-2023).

KEN STANDS AT 12 INCHES, just half an inch taller than Barbie.

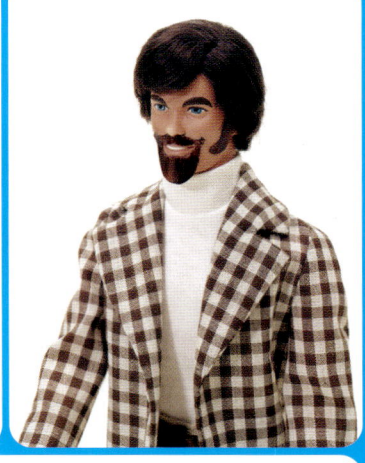

IN 1992, two different versions of *Totally Hair Ken* were created, both using a unique 1991 face mold. The first version had a higher hairline, glossier face finish, and included a promotional coupon. The second version had a lower hairline, more oval eyes, and a matte finish—and did not include the coupon.

After the breakup with Barbie in 2004, Ken made headlines again in 2011 with a sensational marketing campaign in New York's Times Square and in Los Angeles to win her back. New York lit up with slogans from Ken like **"BARBIE, YOU'RE THE ONLY DOLL FOR ME!"** For the occasion, Ken even commissioned custom cupcakes from Magnolia Bakery.

In 1986, Ken got his **FIRST CAR:** a Dream'Vette. In 2012 he picked out a red Mini Cooper with a custom **"KEN"** license plate.

IN 1972, Ken appeared with a more natural hairstyle—straight or curly—and sported **A MUSTACHE, BEARD, AND SIDEBURNS.**

IN THE SUMMER OF 2010, Ken made his big screen debut **IN *TOY STORY 3.*** For the shoot, Ken wore more than fifty different outfits!

KEN HAS A YOUNGER BROTHER, TOMMY (1997).

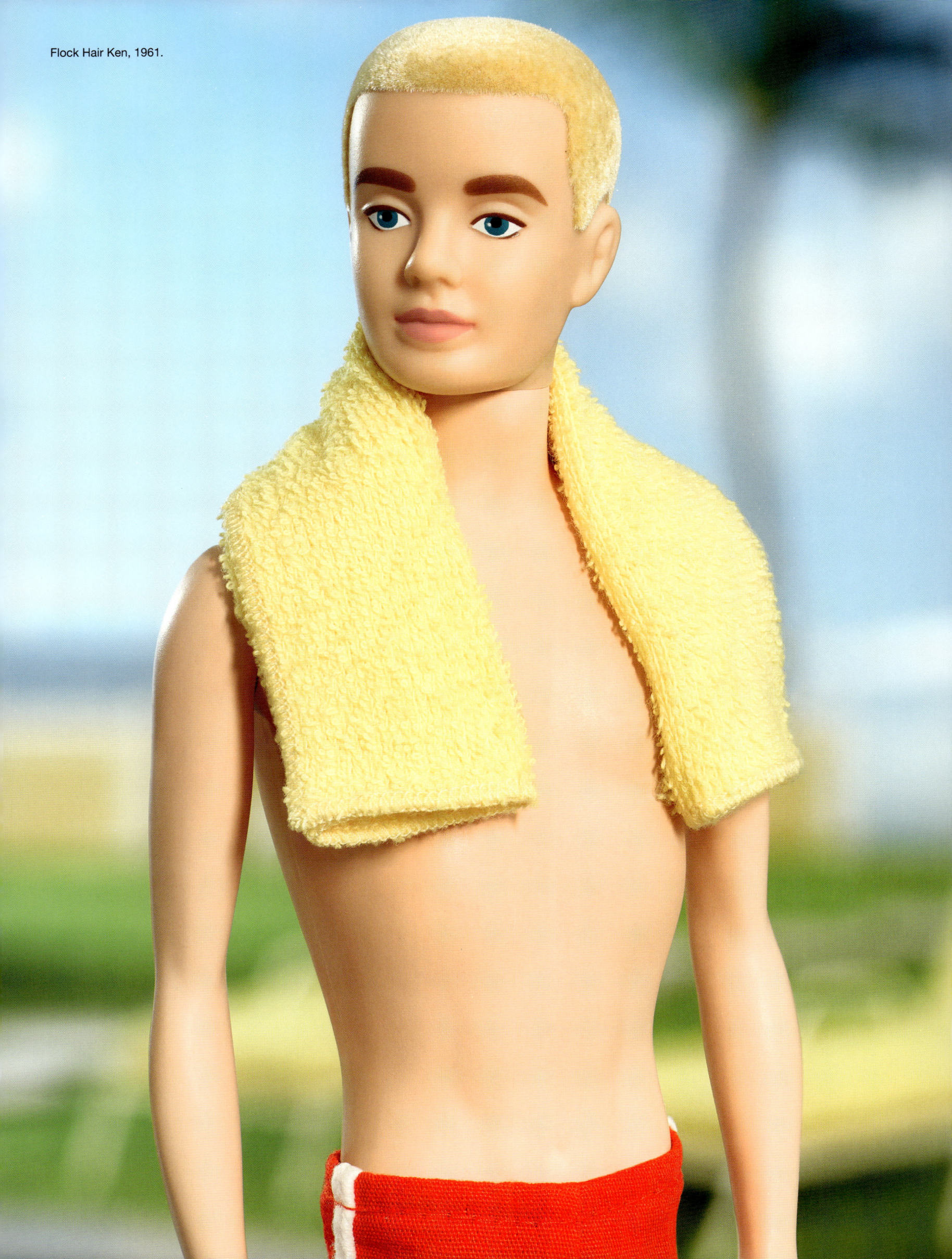
Flock Hair Ken, 1961.

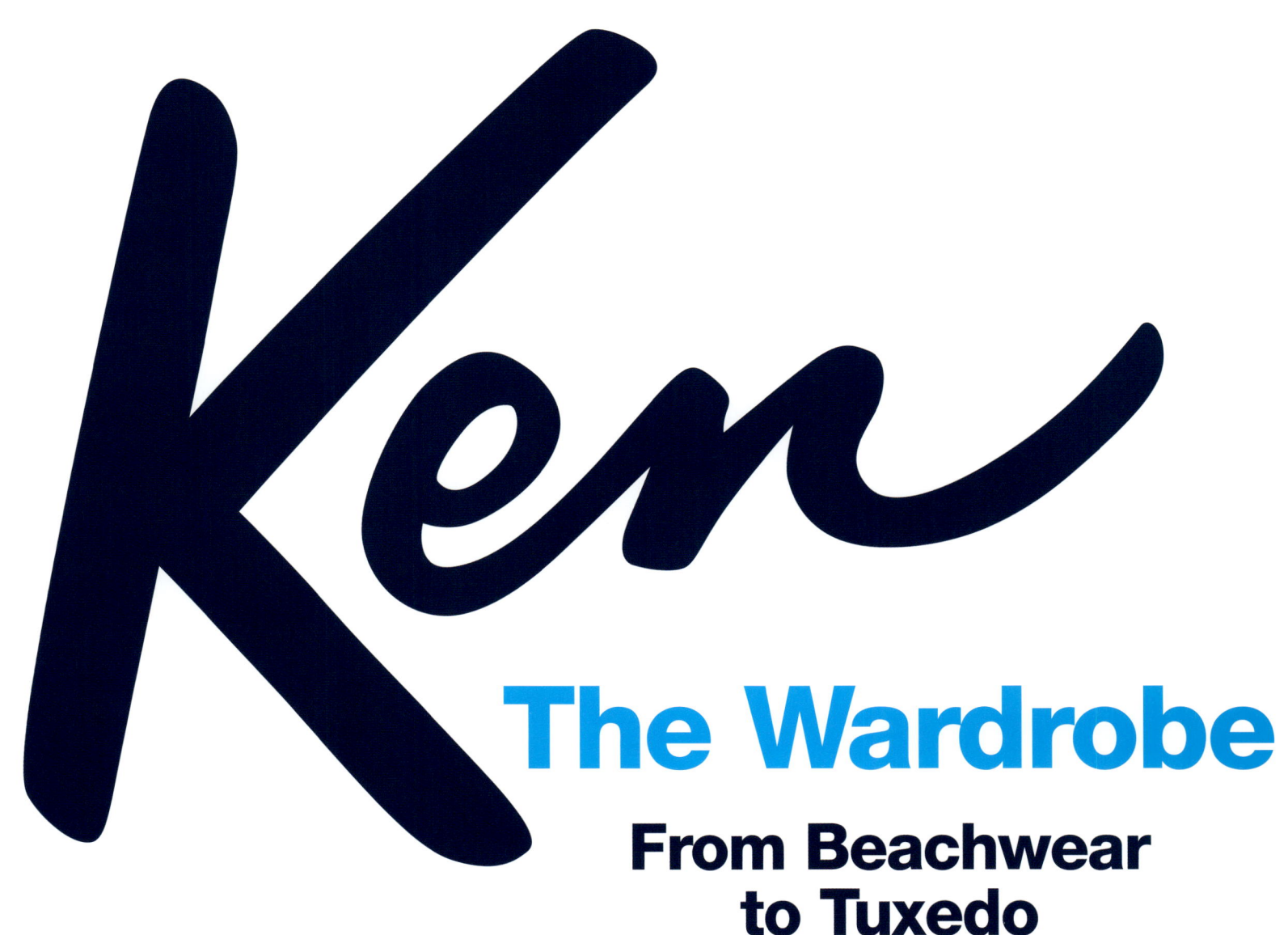

KEN: THE FIRST ICONIC COLLECTION

1961

The very first image of Ken evokes a distinctly summery vibe of a young athlete in a red swimsuit, complete with a beach towel and cork sandals. His subsequent wardrobe offered later that year is surprisingly complete. It includes nine different outfits, each one perfect for a different moment in his typical day and emblematic of the taste and style of 1960s American man. Every garment and accessory made for his wardrobe is accompanied by a small booklet, a valuable reference for precisely identifying the year of production and every sartorial and stylistic detail of the outfits.

Campus Hero

As campus hero, Ken proudly wears the sweater Barbie knitted for him, paired with white trousers, red socks, and white sneakers. He escorts Barbie to the pep rally and pregame dance, waving the pennant bearing his university's monogram. The outfit is reissued in 1964 with the letter "M" instead of "U."

In Training

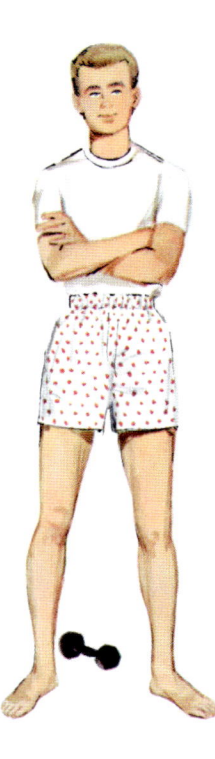

Ken's training gear includes a knit T-shirt, elastic-waist briefs or boxers, a workout manual, and a set of dumbbells.

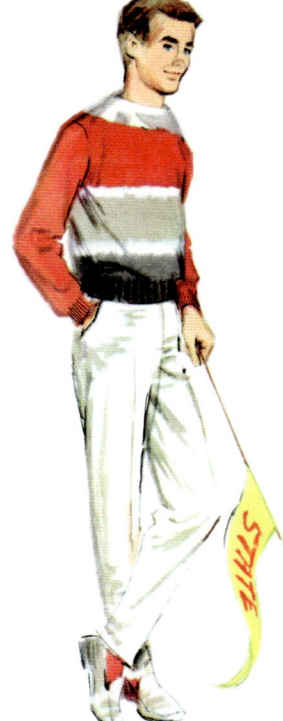

Sleeper Set

Ken sleeps in a chic striped pajama set with a solid-colored collar, available in long or short sleeves. Before bed, he has a late-night snack of a sugar bun with a glass of milk and then sets his alarm for the next morning.

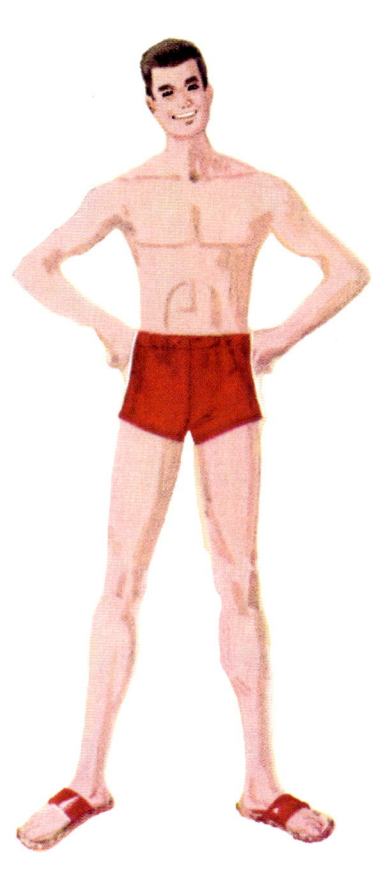

Basic Ken Doll
(also known as Flock Hair Ken)

Tall and sporting a fresh crew cut, Ken is the ideal companion for Barbie. He stands on a special display base included in the box, wears swim trunks and sandals, and comes with a towel. Made of sturdy flesh-colored vinyl with movable arms, legs, and head, Ken is easy and fun to dress in his stylish wardrobe.

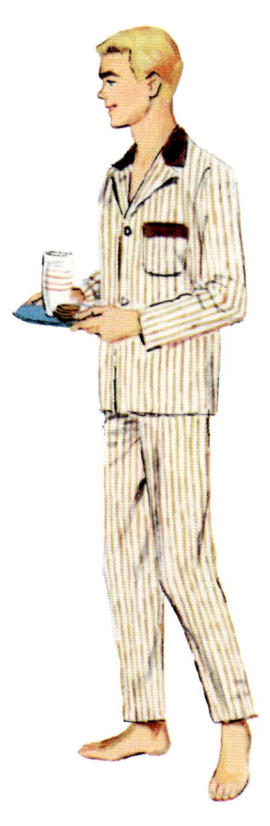

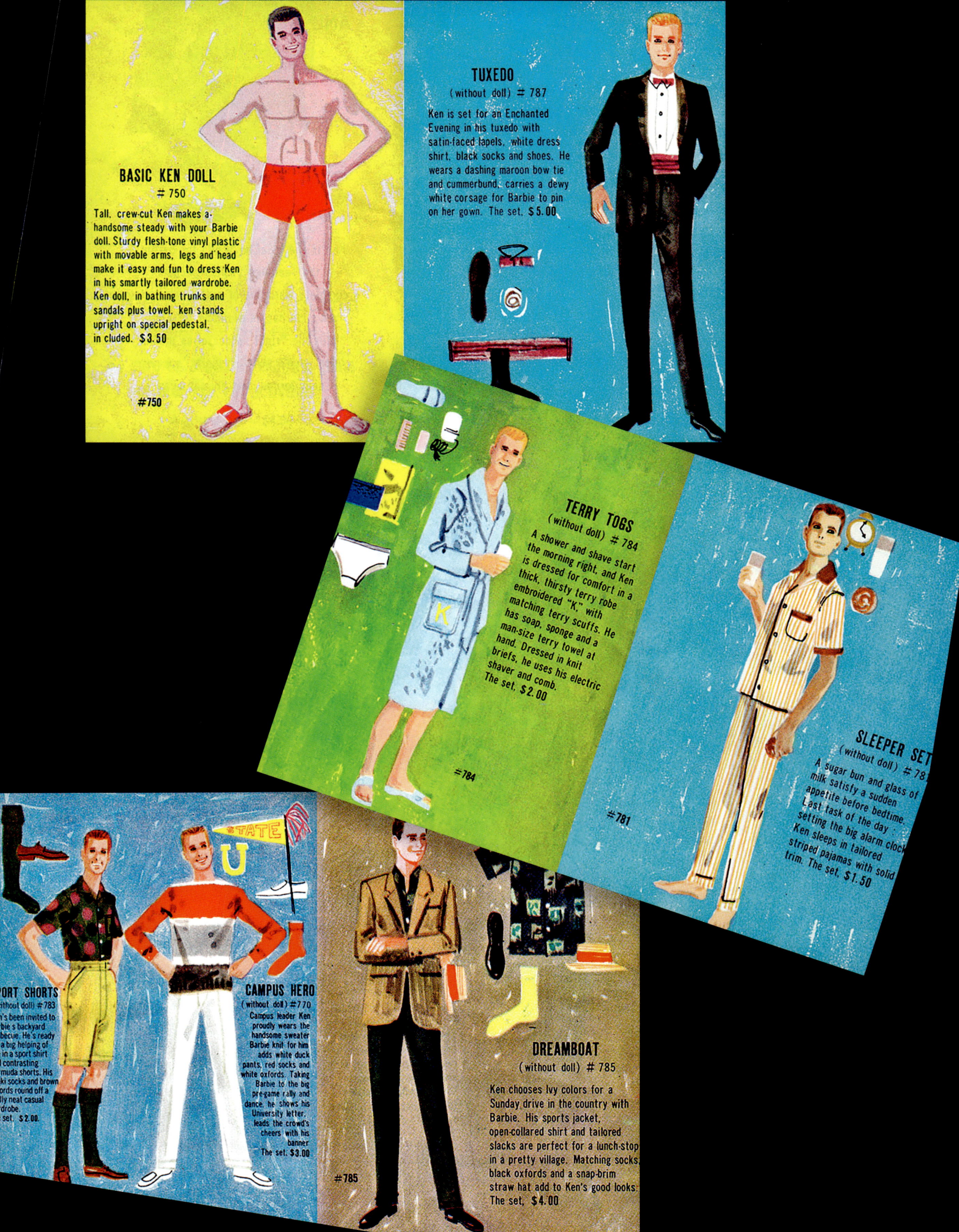

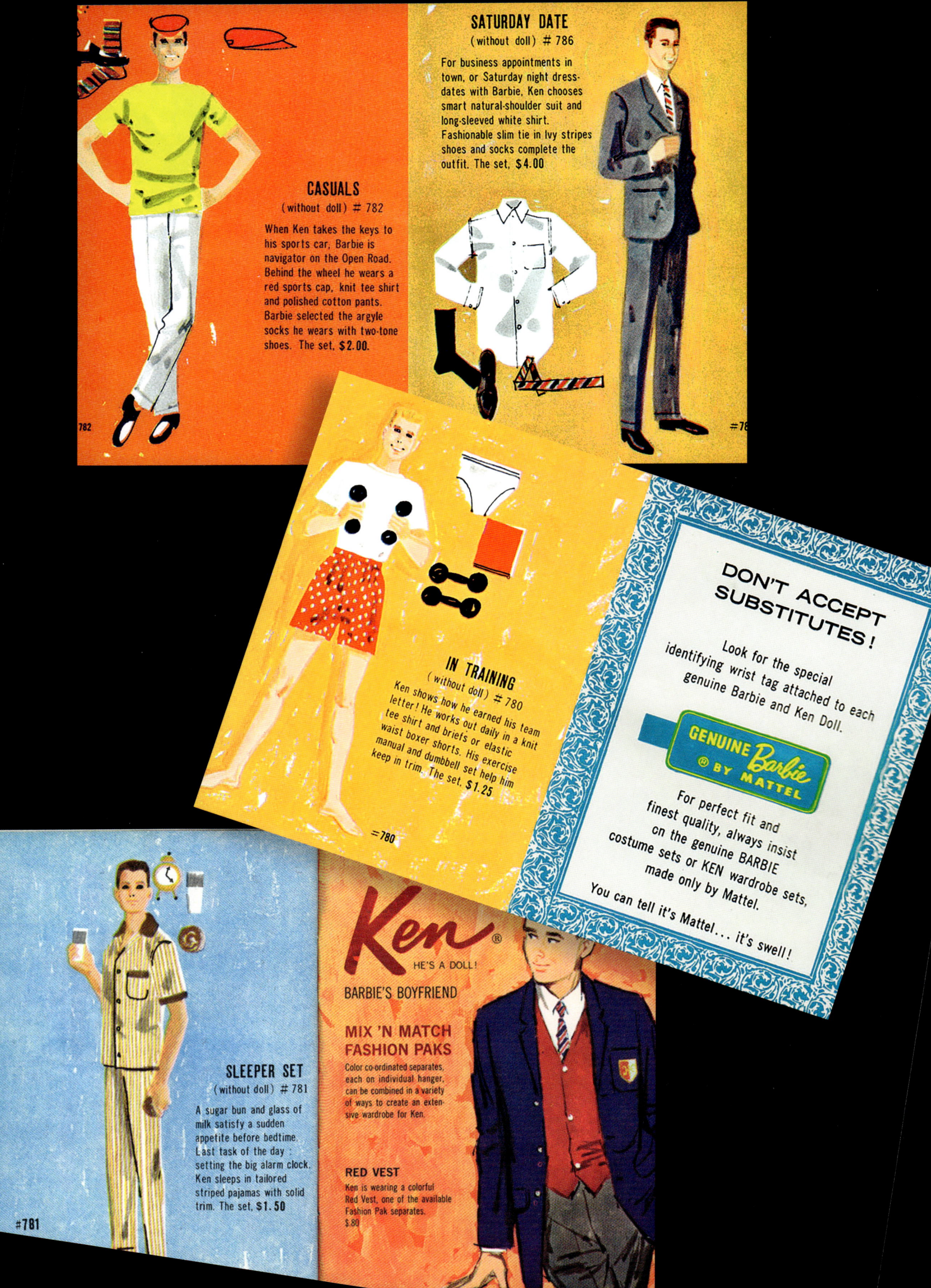

Casual

When he hops into his sports car, Ken wears a red newsboy cap, a knit T-shirt, and shiny cotton trousers.

Dreamboat

As an outfit for a weekend getaway with Barbie, Ken wears a sports jacket, a shirt, and tailored trousers in earth tones. The set includes matching socks, black Oxfords, and a straw hat.

Saturday Night Date

Whether for a business meeting in the city or a Saturday night out with Barbie, Ken goes for a sleek suit with natural shoulders, a white shirt, a narrow tie, striped socks, and polished shoes.

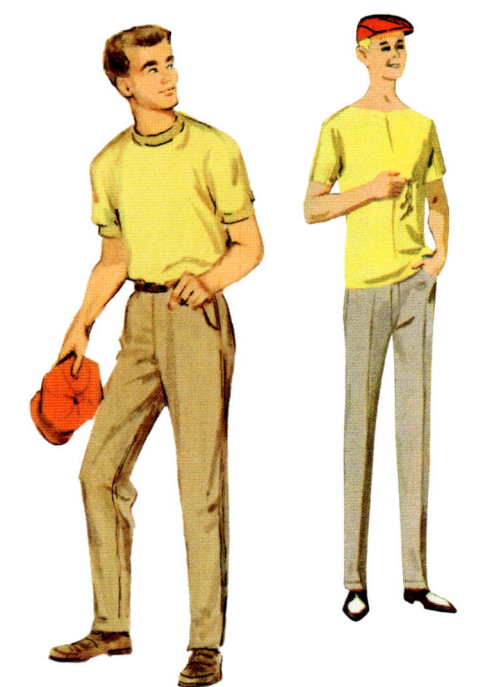
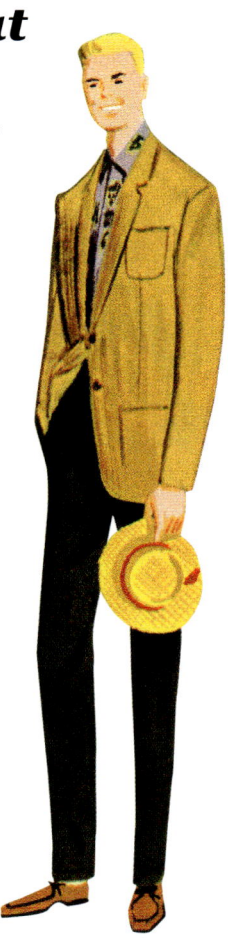
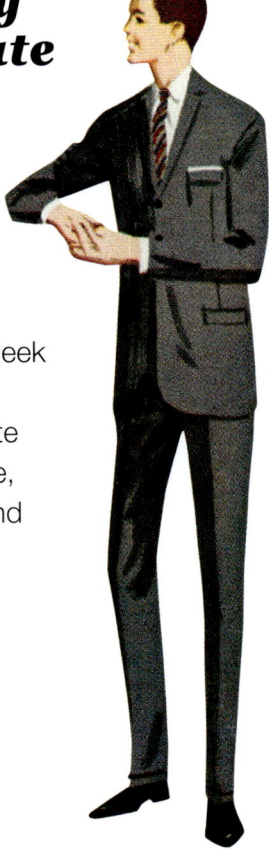

Tuxedo

On special nights out, Ken wears a classic tuxedo with satin lapels, a white shirt, burgundy cummerbund and bow tie, and black shoes and socks. A white boutonniere adds the perfect touch of class.

Sport Shorts

For a backyard barbecue at Barbie's, Ken opts for a sporty shirt with contrasting Bermuda shorts, khaki socks, and brown Oxfords—a relaxed yet carefully curated look.

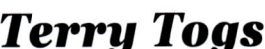
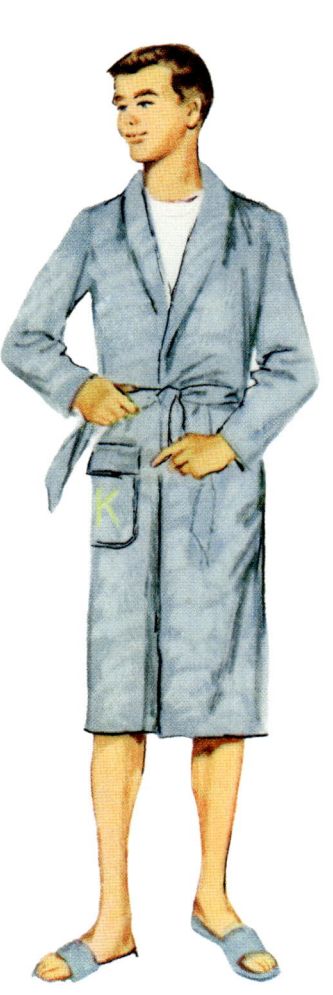
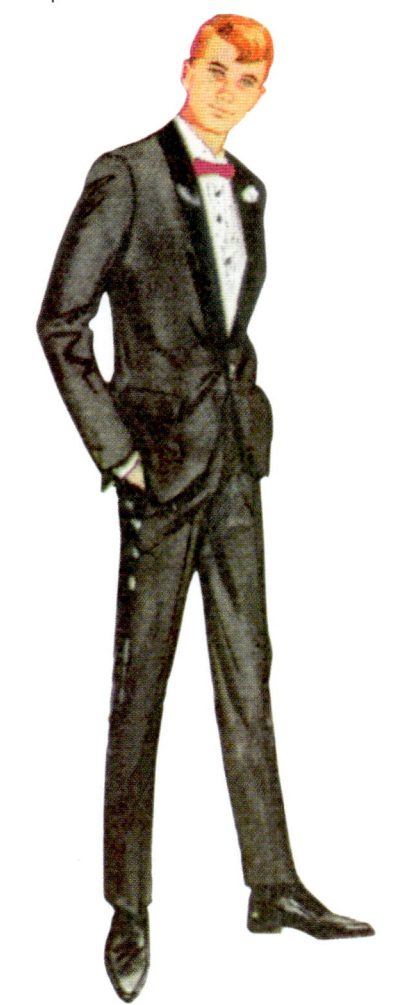

Terry Togs

What better way to start the day than with a shower and a perfect shave? For his morning routine, Ken wears a terry cloth robe embroidered with the letter "K" and matching terry slippers. The kit includes underwear, soap, a shower sponge, towel, electric razor, and comb.

When Barbie made her debut as a Teenage Fashion Model Doll in 1959, she was immediately provided with an extraordinary wardrobe: nineteen outfits and a four-piece lingerie set that perfectly captured the fashion culture of the time—a refined blend of Italian, French, and American styles which, in that historical moment, were shaping the rules of a new Western elegance. Charlotte Johnson, Mattel's fashion designer, created a true masterpiece with Barbie's wardrobe. It was a collection of garments that reflected the era's prevailing aesthetic codes and the silhouettes and cuts that had long been standard on fashion runways and in couture houses, with seasonal wardrobes including day wear, evening wear, cocktail attire, travel clothes, cruise outfits, and formal evening gowns.

For men, this kind of fashion structure was not yet common. It wouldn't be until the 1970s that a major shift occurred. In 1972, after Brioni's first men's runway show at the Sala Bianca of Palazzo Pitti in Florence (1952), the first all-male fashion event officially launched—Pitti Uomo—bringing together styles from casual to chic. A historic milestone!

When Johnson set out to design Ken's first wardrobe, she drew on the experience gained with Barbie and succeeded in creating a set of distinctly original menswear pieces. The nine different outfits celebrated a perfectly balanced elegance, combining American casual and athletic styles with more classic and tailored European ones.

This is clearly reflected in Ken's wardrobe, which from its very first collection in 1961, stood out for its remarkable completeness—a true rarity for the time—driven by his role as Barbie's boyfriend. That role demanded a variety of looks for every occasion, and the wardrobe evolved and adapted to international trends over the decades.

Ken's debut wardrobe set the standards and range of styles that would be reissued and expanded every year throughout the 1960s, from beachwear to casual outfits, cruise attire to sportswear, lounge and sleepwear to campus clothes, and, of course, formal looks like the tuxedo—the most celebrated piece in his wardrobe, reimagined in countless ways across Ken's more than sixty-year history.

Since 1961, the tuxedo has been the most frequently reissued garment in Ken's collections, even recreated as a collector's item for adult fans. Among the most iconic tuxedo designs are those from the Ken brand's thirtieth anniversary in 1991, the Wedding Day Gift Set of 2009, and a super-stylish 2013 version by Robert Best for a limited-edition Silkstone Ken.

The design process behind Ken's earliest collections matched the technical and sartorial excellence of the most prestigious fashion houses—particularly between 1961 and 1971. Just like their counterparts in Paris, Milan, and New York, Mattel's designers began with concept sketches, which were then turned into prototypes by patternmakers.

In Ken's case, one accessory received special attention: his shoes. From 1961 to 1967, they were marked

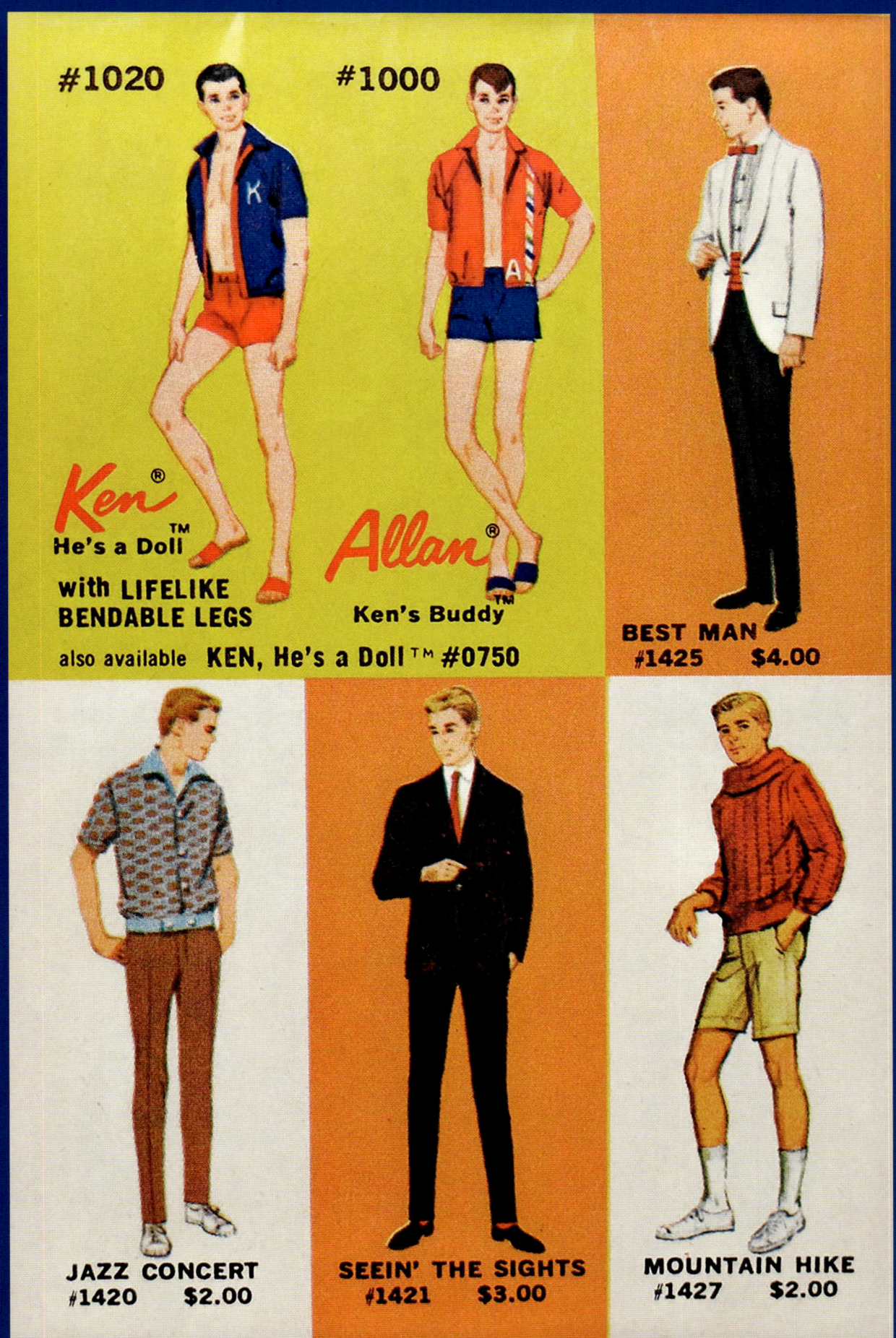

Promotional illustrations of sought-after Ken and Allan outfits, including the standout Best Man look from 1966.

Barbie® and Ken®

"Japan" on the soles and made of soft, flexible plastic. Between 1961 and 1963, most of Ken's outfits came with matching shoes and small accessories mounted on cardboard inside the box. Between 1963 and 1964, these began to be packaged separately in small cellophane bags.

Each of Ken's garments bore a fabric tag reading "Fashions for Ken / Ken / © by Mattel," ensuring the utmost attention to finishing, hems, linings, zippers, and buttons. Because it was difficult to source miniature zippers and buttons, Mattel established a company in Japan, YKK, managed by Yoshida Kogyo, specializing in scaled-down fasteners.

The clothing sewn for Ken in 1961 featured some unique tailoring elements. All trousers, for example, had visible zippers and no snap buttons; the pants in the Campus Hero, Dreamboat, and Saturday Date outfits had cuffs. In 1962, the trousers were redesigned with hidden zippers and press-stud closures—a technical improvement better suited to large-scale production.

Once completed, Ken's outfits were sold in four types of packaging: square, large square, rectangle, and large rectangle—the last of which was rare and used only until 1964 for the tuxedo.

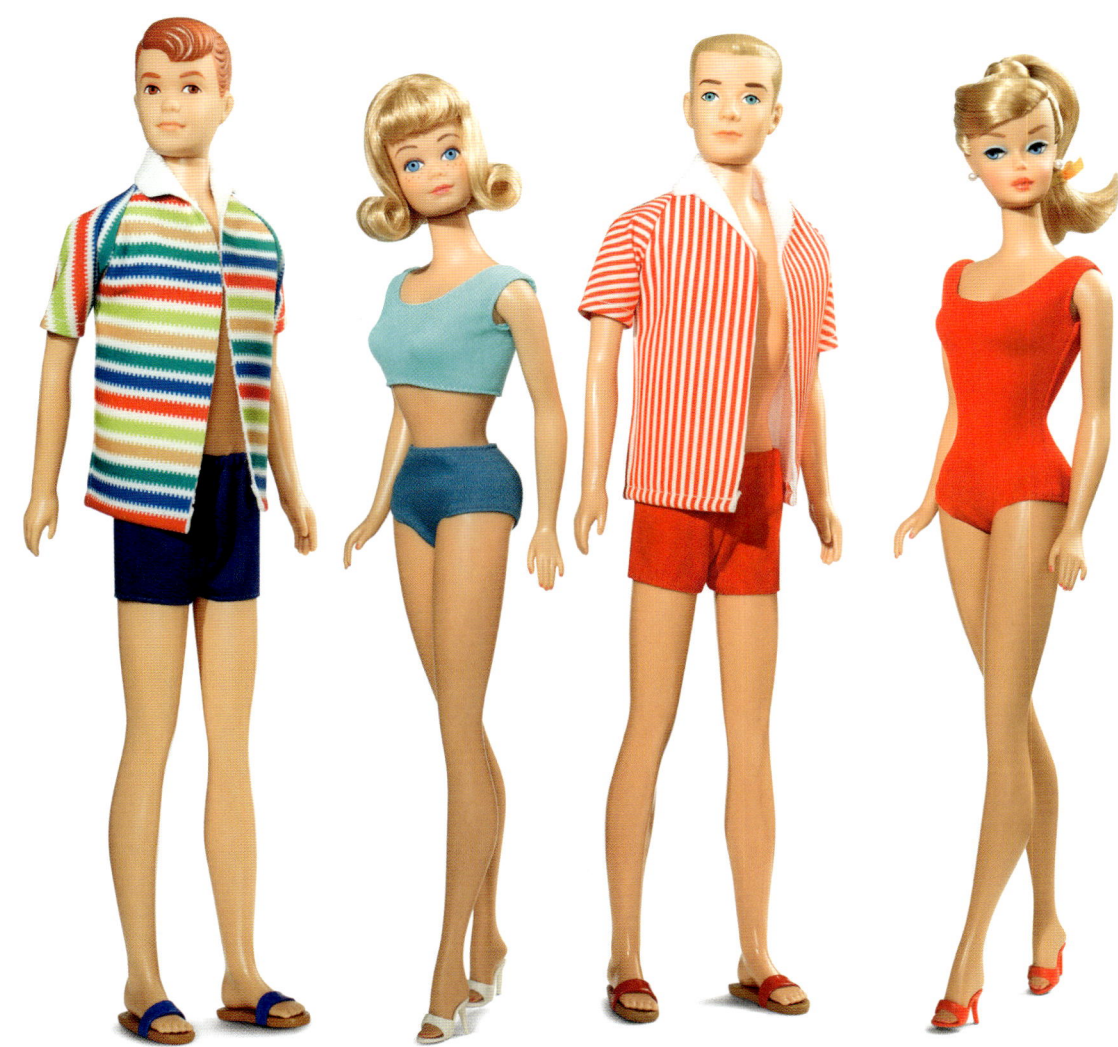

Double couples: Barbie and Ken with their best friends, Allan and Midge, 1964.

Opposite:
Barbie and Ken in a graphic from 1963.

The 1960s

Just as with women's fashion, men's fashion was upended in the 1960s by the rise of *prêt-à-porter* (ready-to-wear), which—especially among young people—began to replace haute couture. As was already the case in Europe, stores and department chains in the United States began offering standardized sizing, with tailored garments reserved for a smaller and smaller circle of clients.

Ken emerged at the beginning of this decade, a time when fashion was entering a phase of intense experimentation with styles, silhouettes, and tailoring techniques—marking the first real emergence of trends dictated by the young for the young, born more in the streets than in the *maisons* (fashion houses). By the end of the decade, the Paris runways were featuring collections by up-and-coming Japanese designers like Hanae Mori (1926–2022), Issey Miyake (1938–2022), Kenzo Takada (1939–2020), and Kansai Yamamoto (1944–2020). Meanwhile in London, amid the miniskirt revolution and student protests, the rebellious spirit of Swinging London had already been claimed by two new icons: the lithe model Twiggy (b. 1949) and the Beatles, whose relaxed, offbeat style found its epicenter in the boutique I Was Lord Kitchener's Valet, opened by fashion entrepreneur John Paul.

British youth split into Rockers and Mods, while in the United States, the rise of hippie culture introduced a look that stood in direct contrast to the orderly, codified world of traditional fashion—a clear rejection of the rules imposed by politics and society. In the US, meanwhile, a new kind of casual elegance began to take hold, shaped by the demands of a more active lifestyle and championed by figures like Ralph Lauren (b. 1939) and Calvin Klein (b. 1942).

The production of Ken's clothing in the 1960s—with over fifty different outfits, theatrical costumes, and travel ensembles—undoubtedly came closest to a creative process that mirrored haute couture techniques, featuring designs rich in details, refined tailoring, and first-rate accessories. Following the first 1961 collection of nine different ensembles (which were reissued the following year), 1962 marked the debut of three new outfits, accompanied by eleven additional "fashion packs"—smaller cardboard sets sold with individual garments or accessories.

In 1963, Ken's wardrobe expanded with nine more pieces, and in 1964 with twelve new outfits, four travel suits, three theatrical costumes, and another eleven fashion packs. That same year, Ken also met his best friend, Allan. Since their body proportions were identical, the two shared clothes and even ad campaigns.

Like Midge and Barbie, Ken and Allan were launched with a shared campaign featuring their trendiest pieces labeled Fashion for Ken & Allan, using the slogan: "The Ken and Allan tailored wardrobe is of finest quality materials for perfect fit and finish."

In 1965, Ken and Allan were given six new outfits designed to be comfortably worn thanks to the new bendable-leg models. By 1966, this first haute couture era reached its peak, with ten new outfits that are still among the most sought-after by collectors today. Yet this rich early wardrobe was already being surpassed by 1969, when the New Good-Lookin' Talking Ken debuted. This new version had a more muscular physique and came with four new outfits, from breakfast attire to rally gear, including styles with Edwardian flair (#1430, Town Turtle) and Eastern-inspired elegance (#1431, Guruvy Formal). The designs featured more generous fits and a wide variety of colors and patterns—ushering Ken firmly into the 1970s.

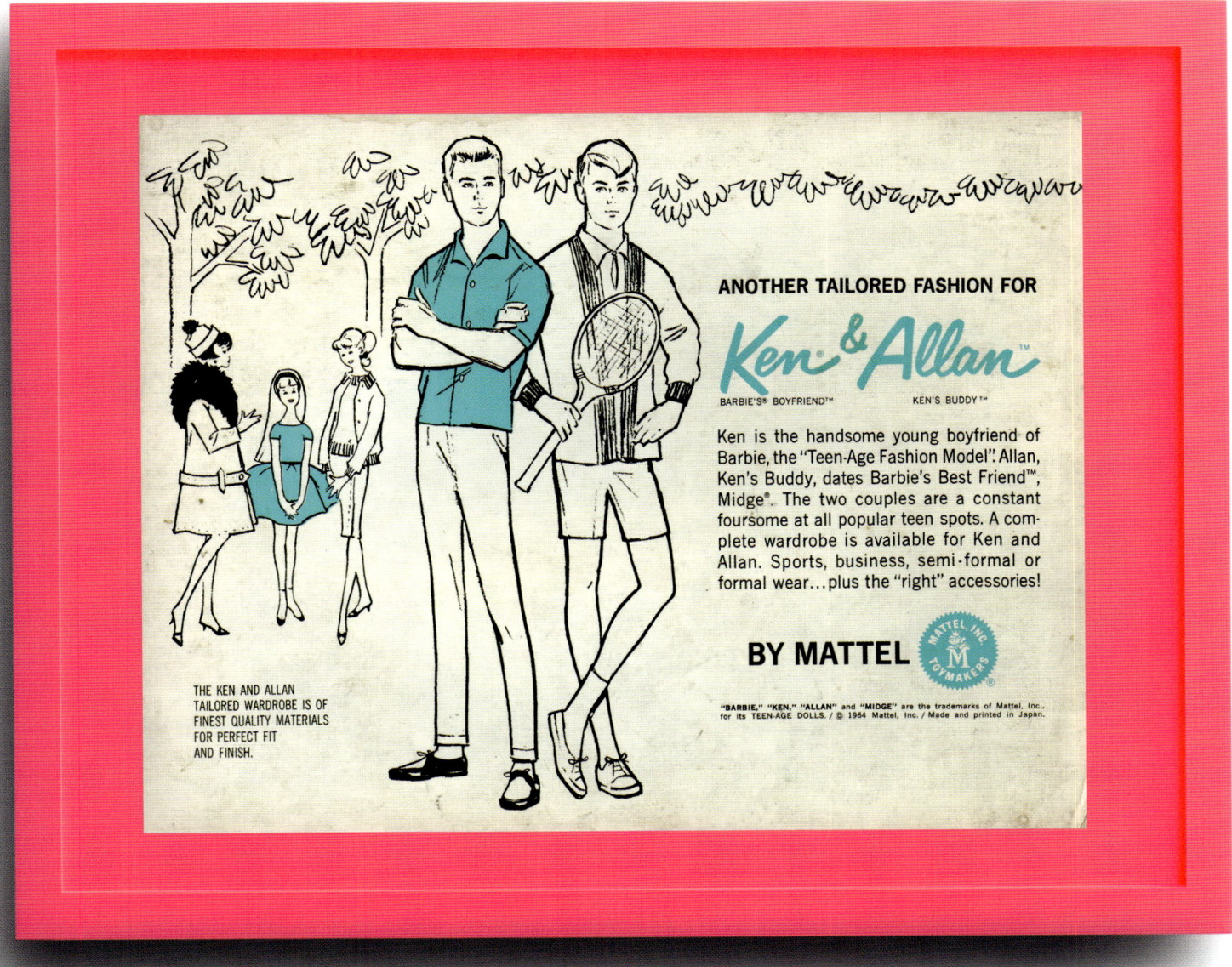

Illustration from 1964 promoting the tailored quality of Ken's and Allan's wardrobes.

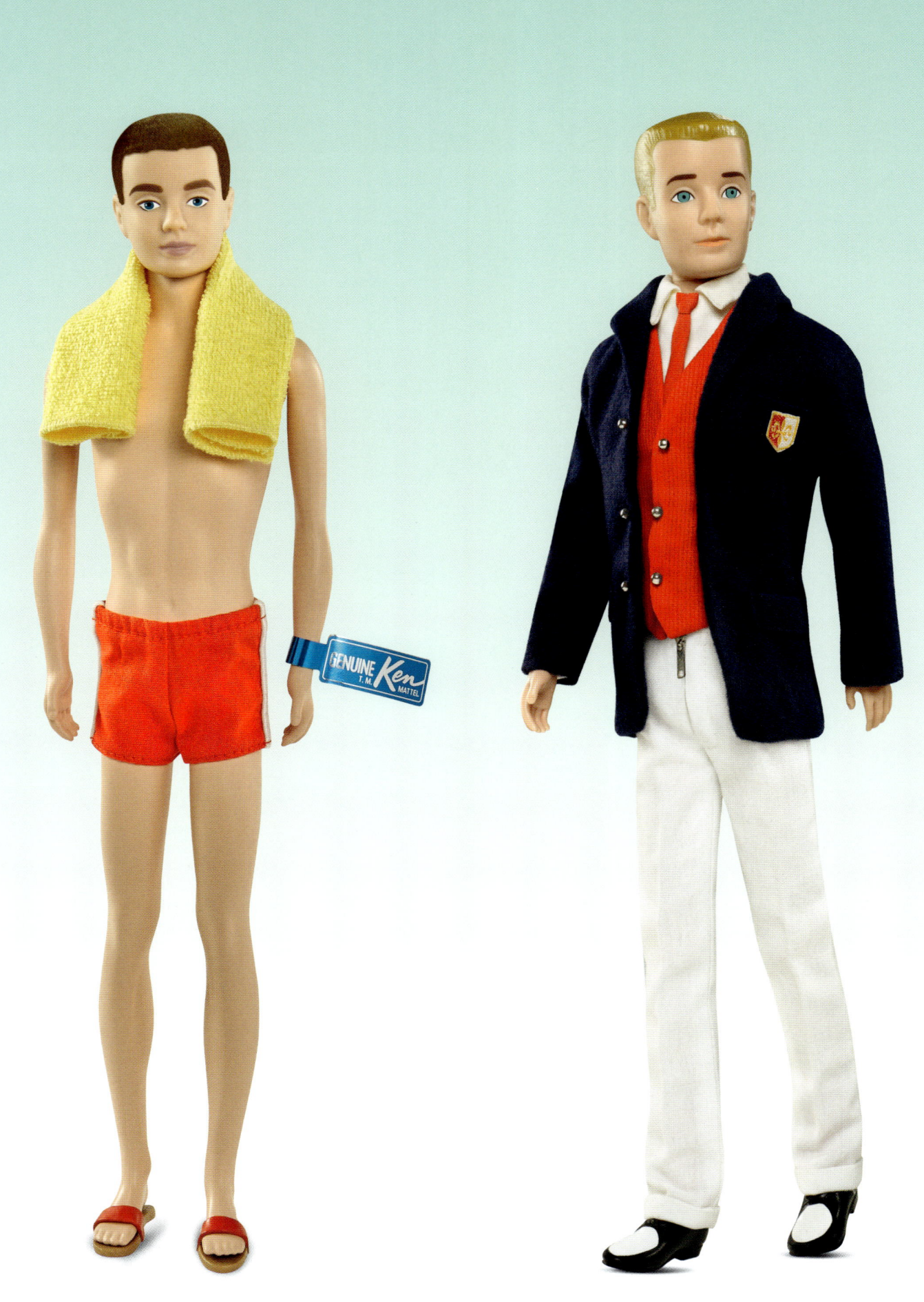

Ken as Flock Hair, Victory Dance, and Tuxedo, 1961, together with Allan, 1964.

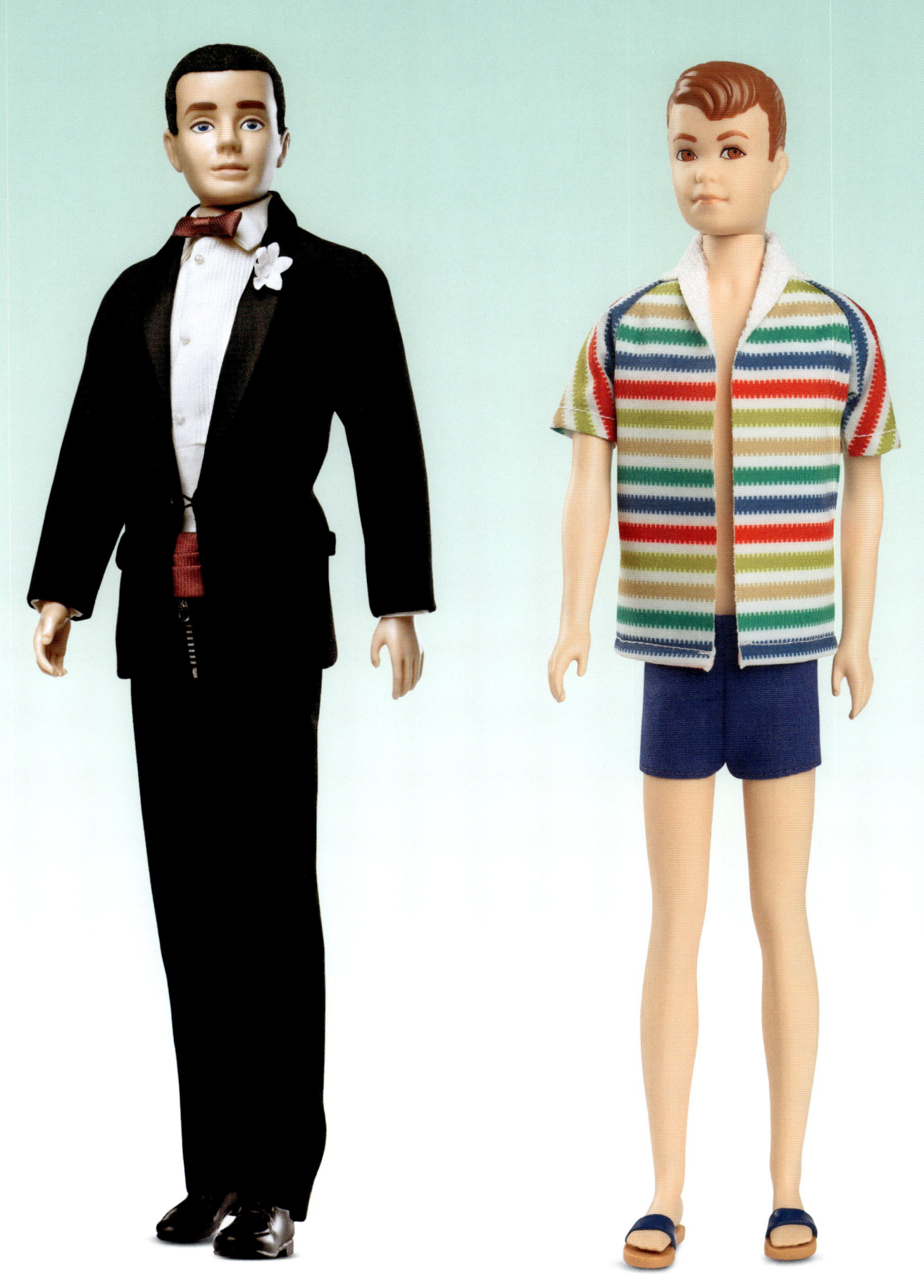

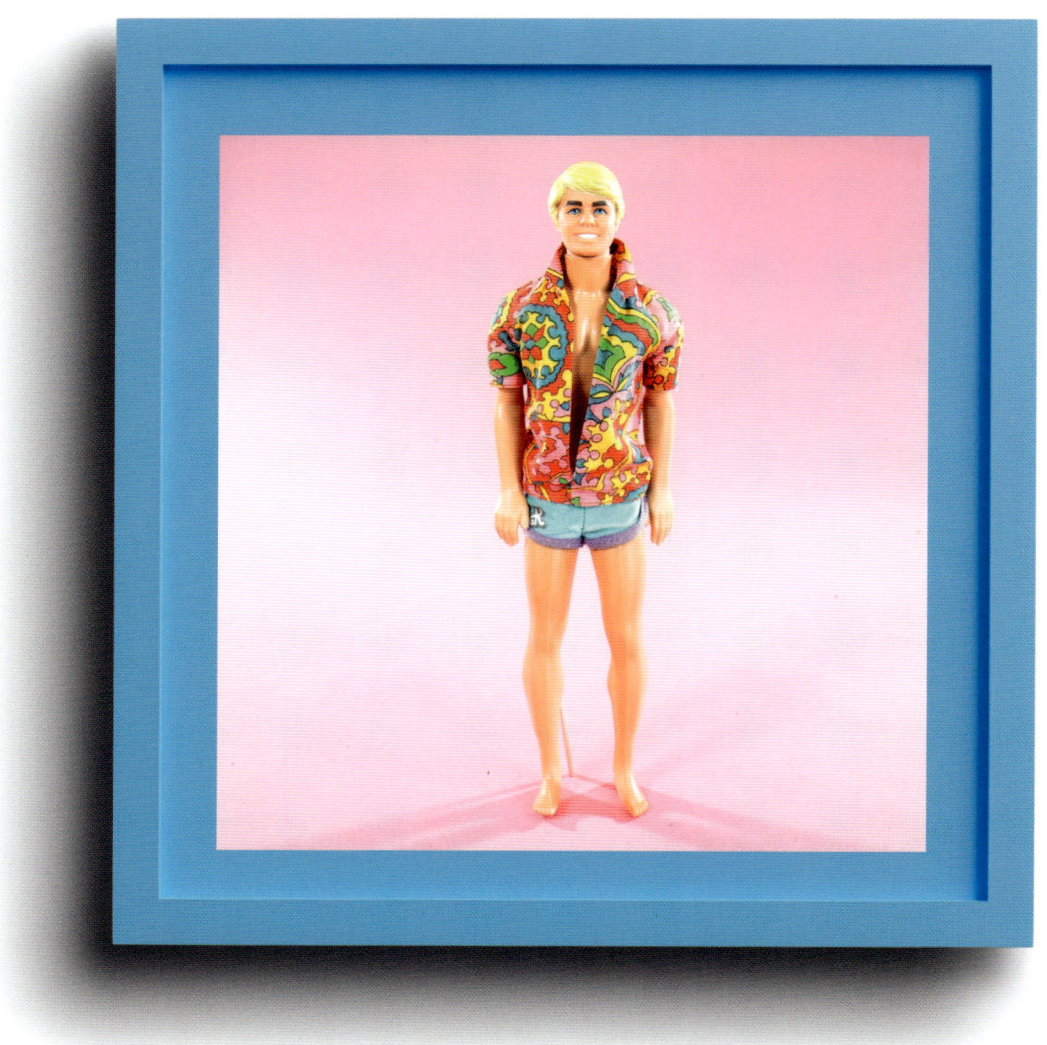

The 1970s

The global rise of a distinctly American fashion style came just a few years later, in the 1970s, with the disco phenomenon. It was in this context that a new king of fashion emerged: Halston (Roy Halston Frowick, 1932–1990). SuperStar Ken perfectly captured this new aesthetic, which spread from America to the rest of the world. He wore a dazzling cobalt-blue jumpsuit, a belt with a raised star buckle, oversized silver sunglasses with red lenses, a bracelet, a watch, and a red neck scarf.

While America leaned into sequins and glitter, London and much of Europe embraced punk—a youth-driven movement whose secular priestess was none other than Vivienne Westwood (1941–2022). The informal jeans-and-tee look for young men now alternated with a sharply defined classic code: a simple single-breasted jacket with a center vent, straight-leg trousers, a shirt, and a hat as the essential accessory.

The true turning point in Ken's clothing production—the shift from haute couture to fast fashion—came in 1972 with the launch of the Fashion Originals and Best Buy Fashions lines, followed in 1973 by Get-Ups 'N Go Fashions. The detailed tailoring of earlier years was now a thing of the past. With the exception of the 1972 Fashion Originals, these new clothes no longer carried the vintage fashion for the Ken label.

After the sensational launch of the very popular SuperStar Ken, three more fashion lines were introduced: Fashion Collectibles, Fashion Favorites, and Designer Originals. These were produced with more standardized tailoring, but were highly desirable for their bold graphics—thanks to the disco trend and the strong influence of what was then taking shape in men's fashion, such as Fashion Collectibles #2794 from 1979, which looks straight out of a Missoni collection.

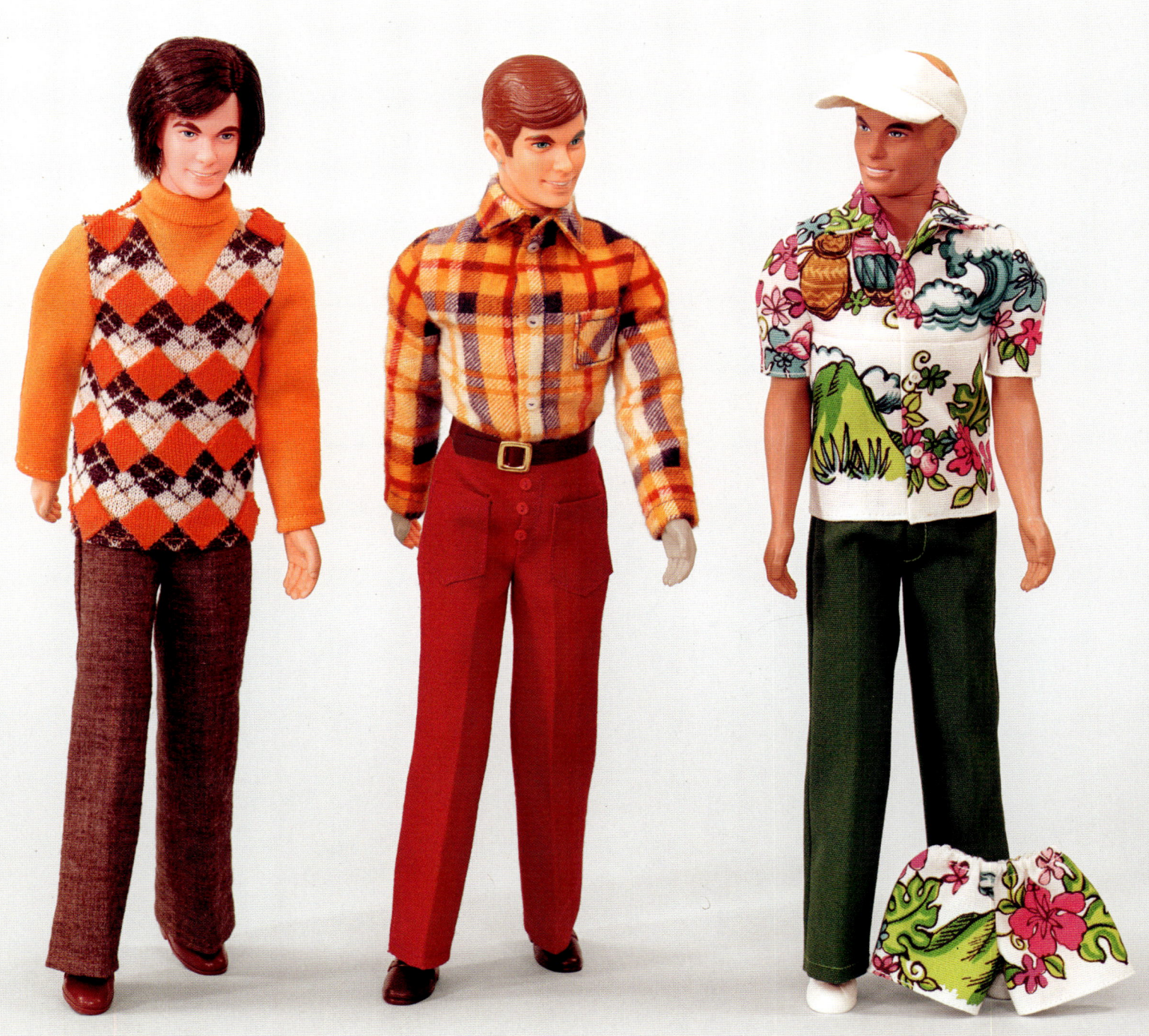

Opposite:
Psychedelic shirt and running shorts for Ken Fashion, 1970.

Above:
Some outfits from the Best Buy Fashion line, 1975.

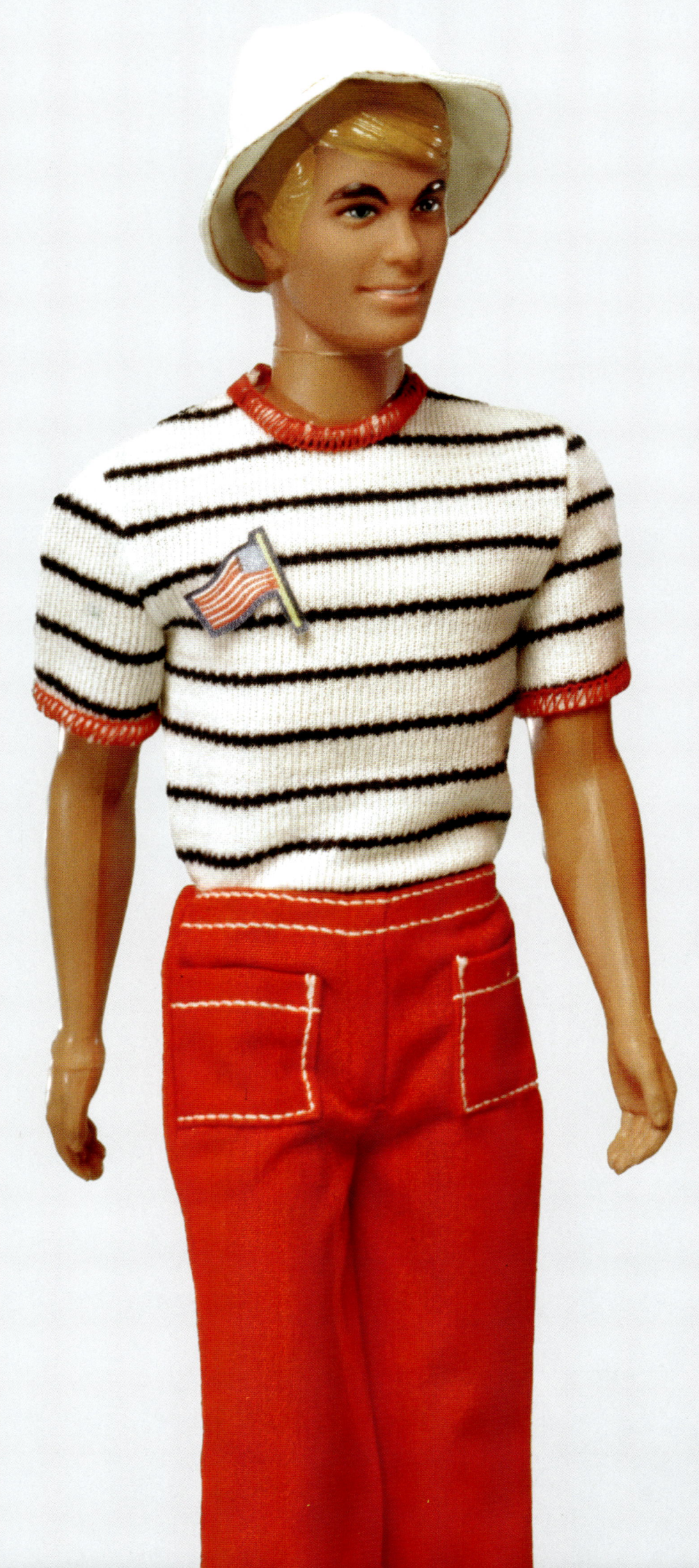

Ken wearing select outfits from
Best Buy Fashion, 1976.

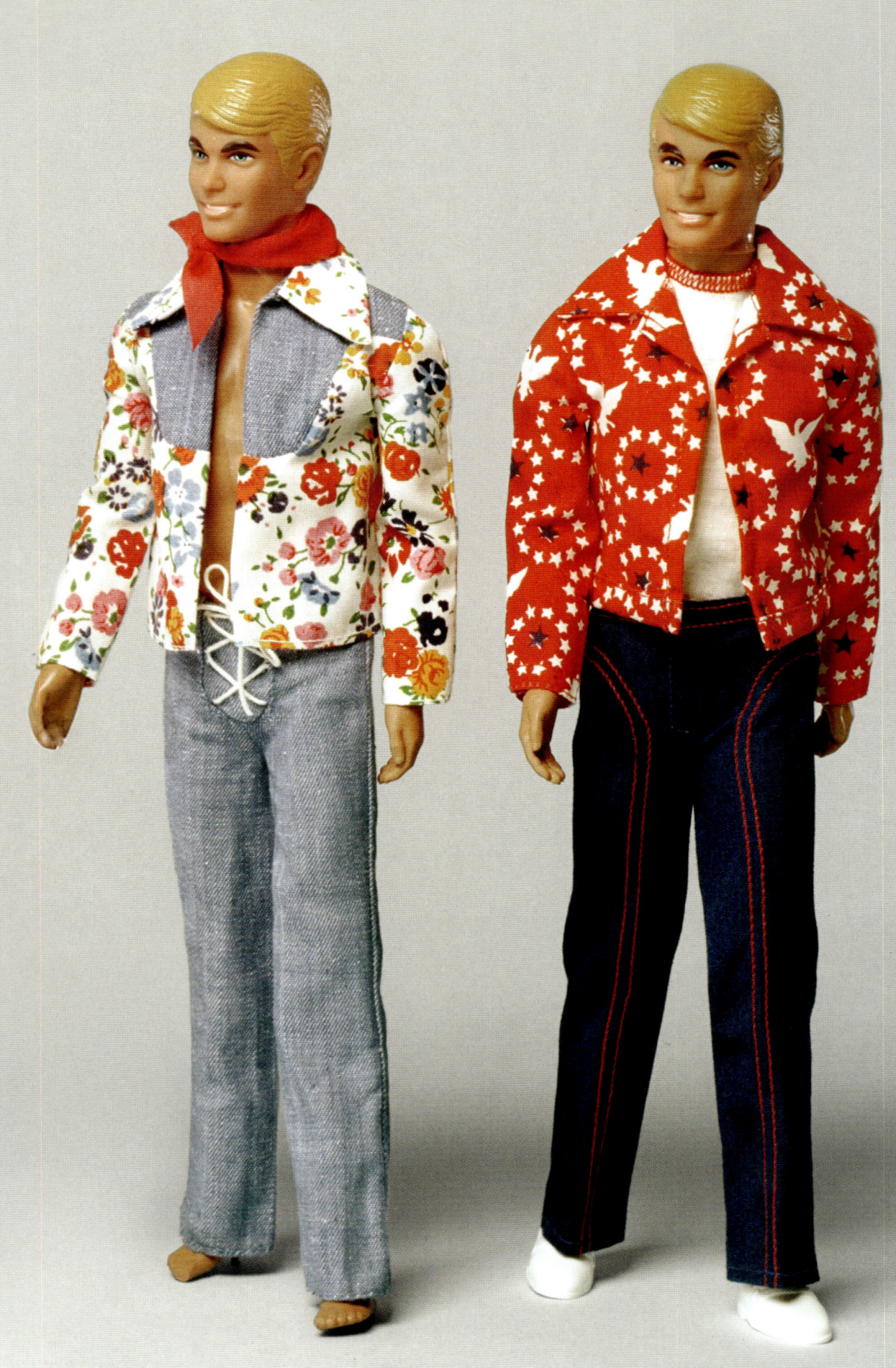

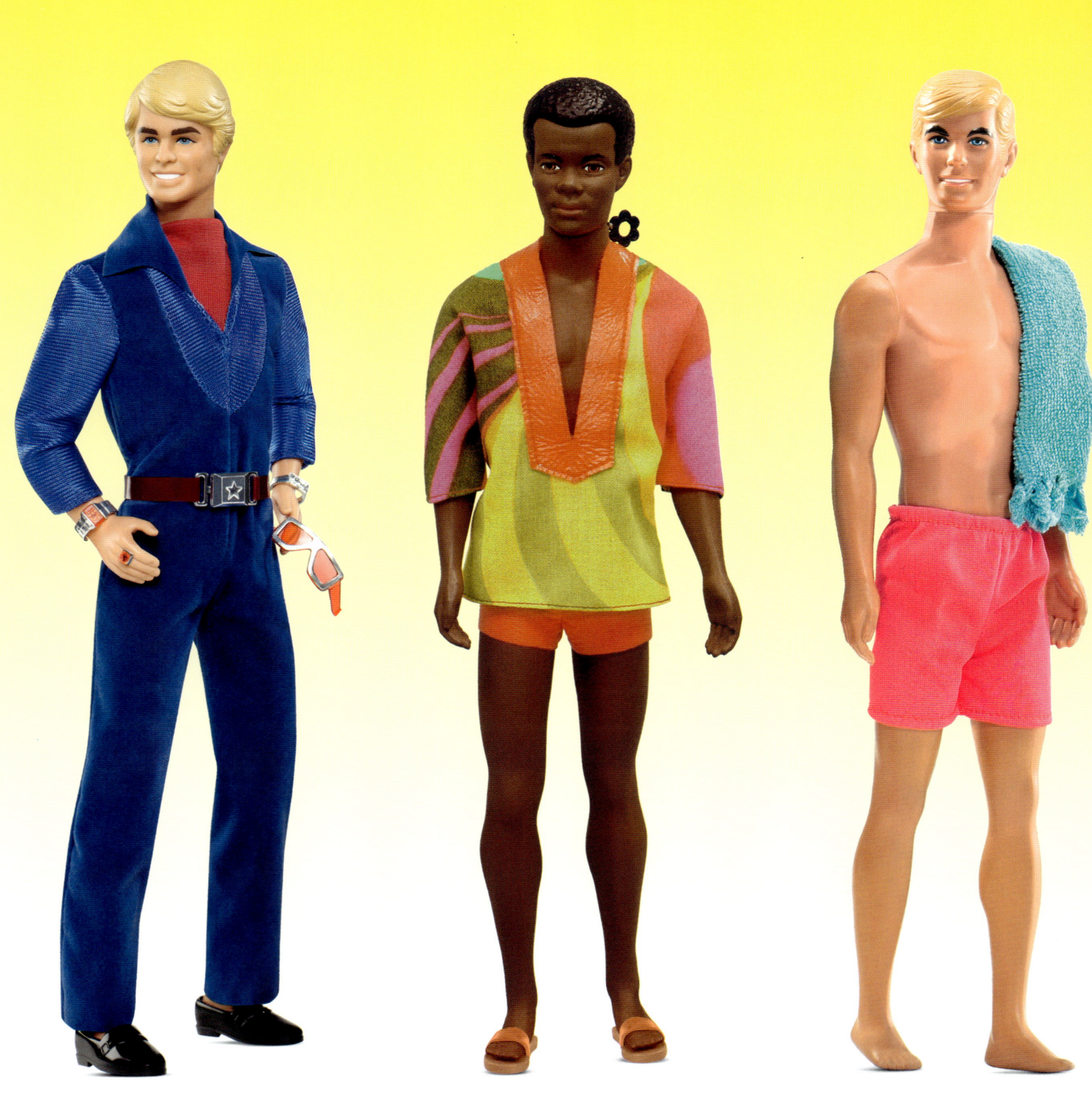

Ken and friend Brad wearing iconic outfits released between 1970 and 1978.

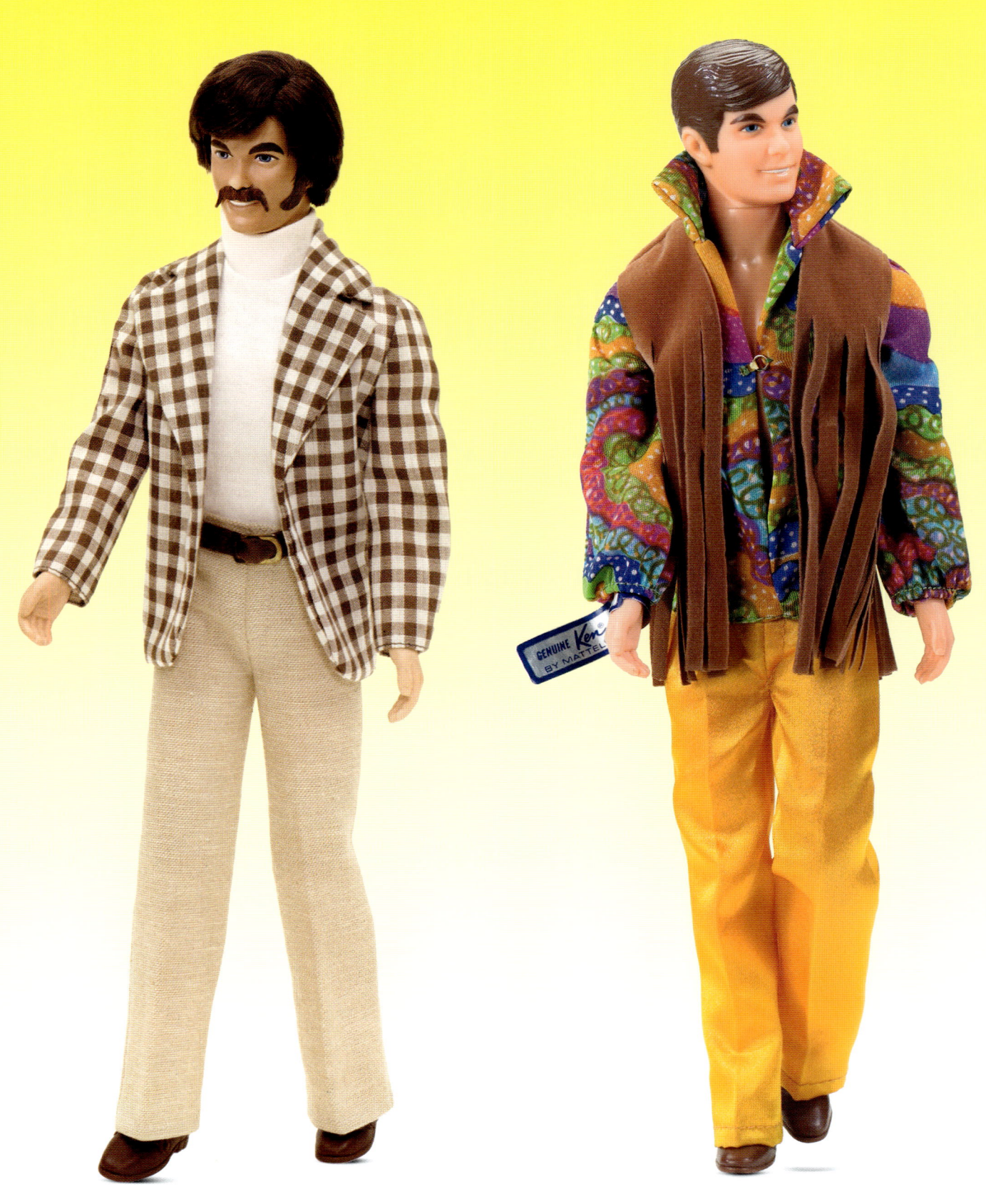

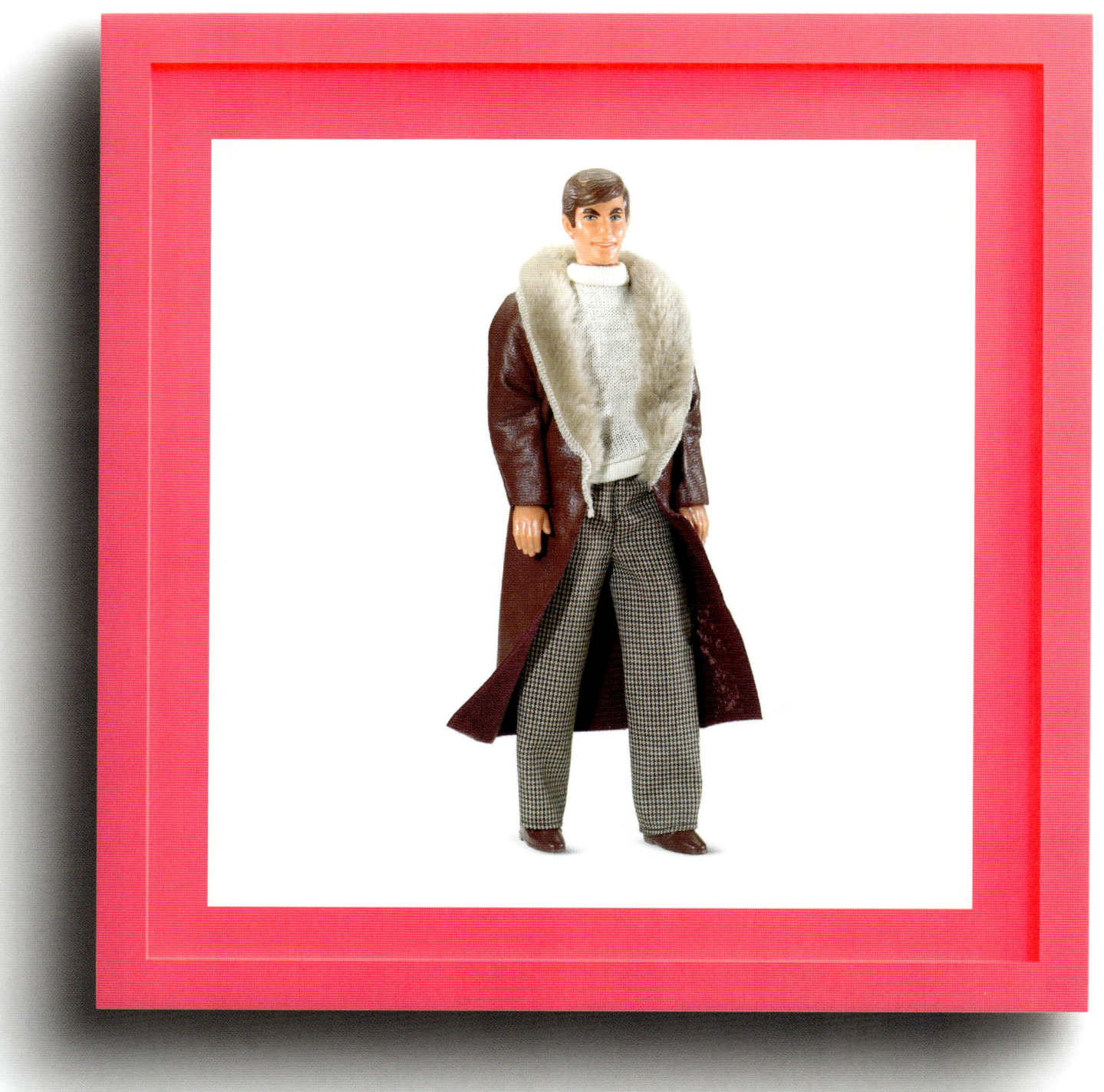

The 1980s

The 1980s brought yet more fashion lines for Ken, such as Fashion Classics and Designer Originals, which featured more refined details and even reversible designs (like Twice As Nice). The rise of the metropolitan elegance of young, ambitious, and bold New York yuppies—dressed in Giorgio Armani or Versace—took form in the most iconic Ken of the decade: Day-to-Night Ken (1985), released in both white and Black versions. With a dual look for work and nightlife, he wore an impeccably tailored pinstripe suit during the day and something flashier for a night out at the fabled Studio 54 in Manhattan.

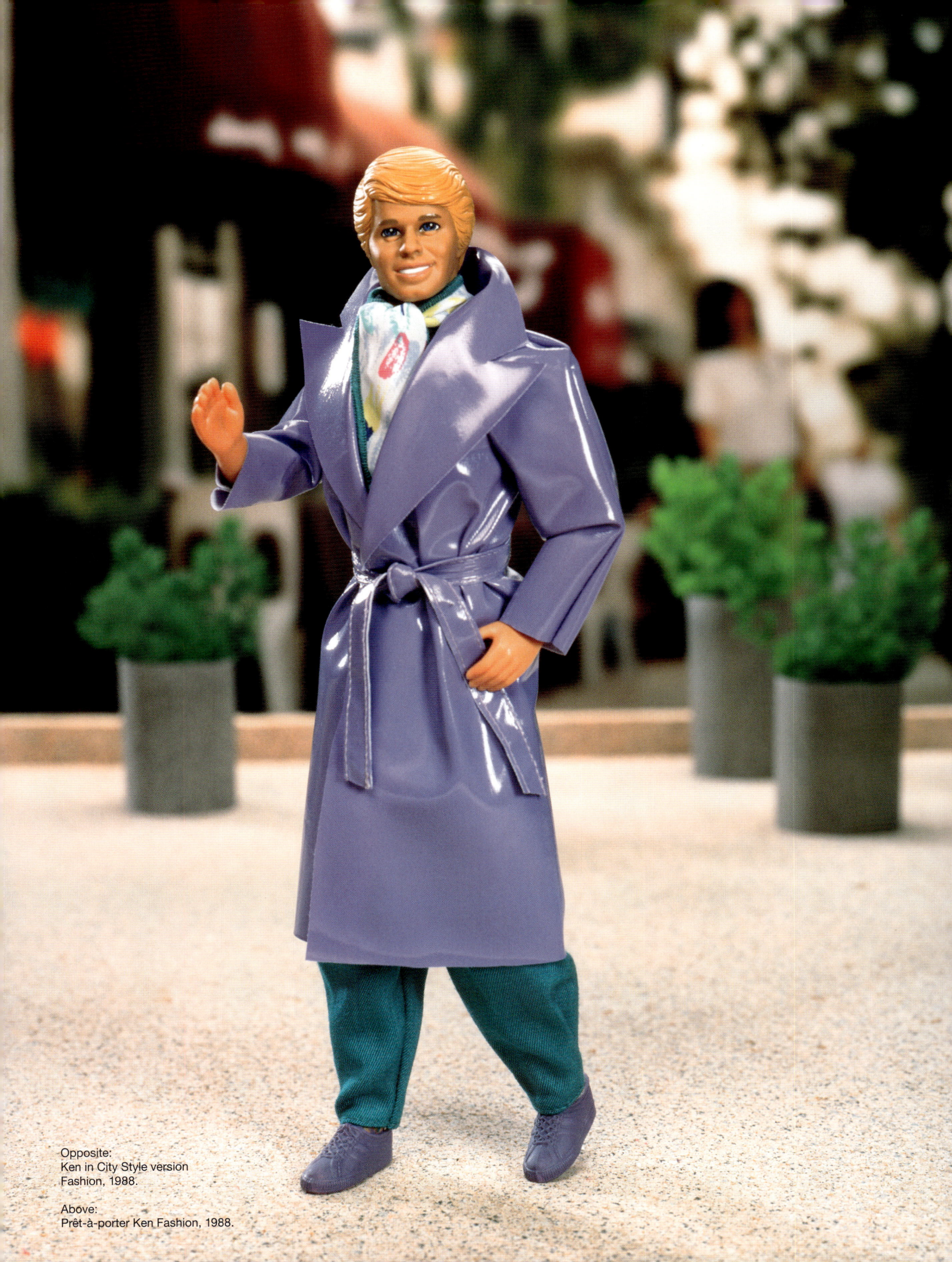

Opposite:
Ken in City Style version
Fashion, 1988.

Above:
Prêt-à-porter Ken Fashion, 1988.

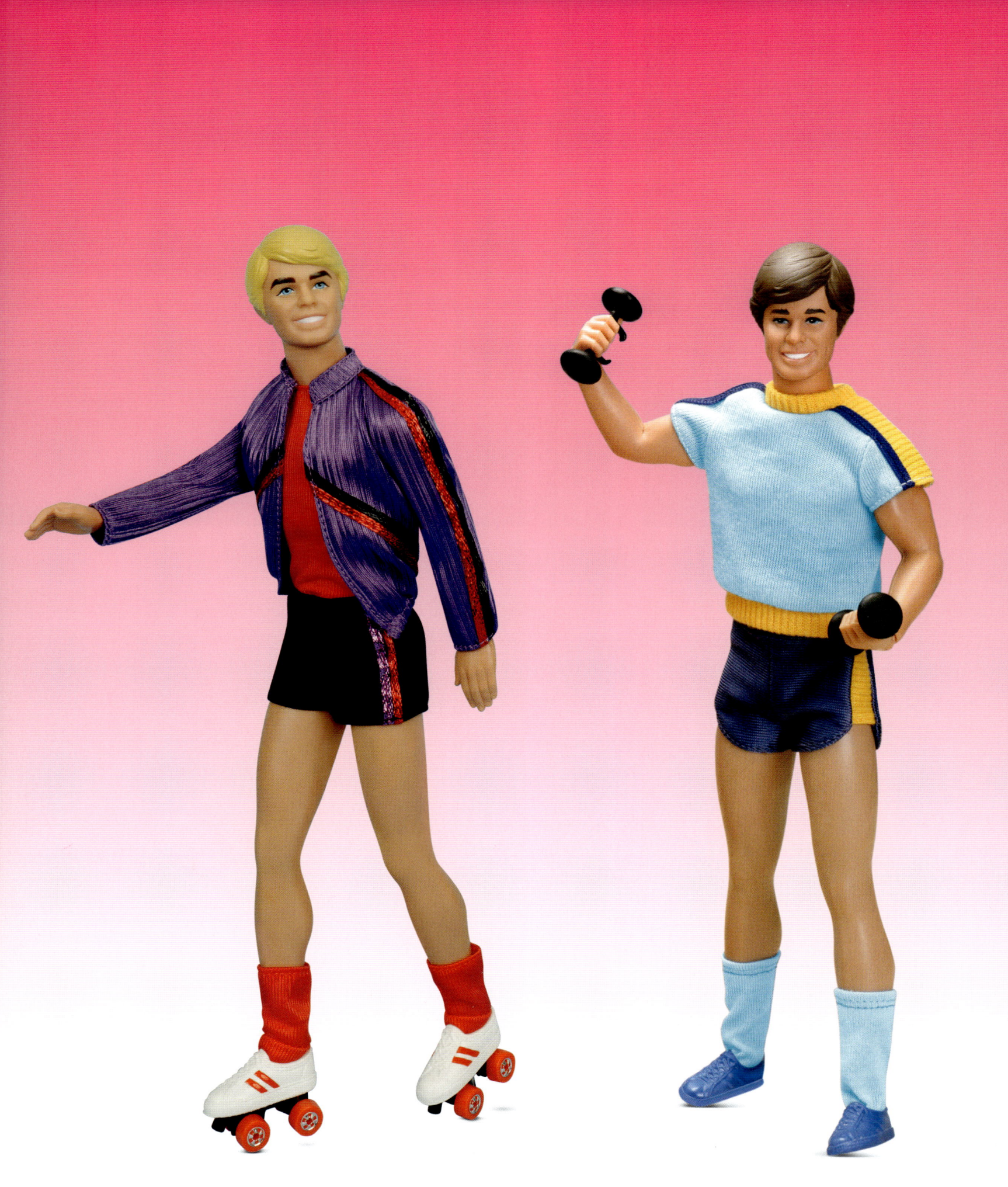

Ken and friend Steven wearing iconic outfits released between 1980 and 1985.

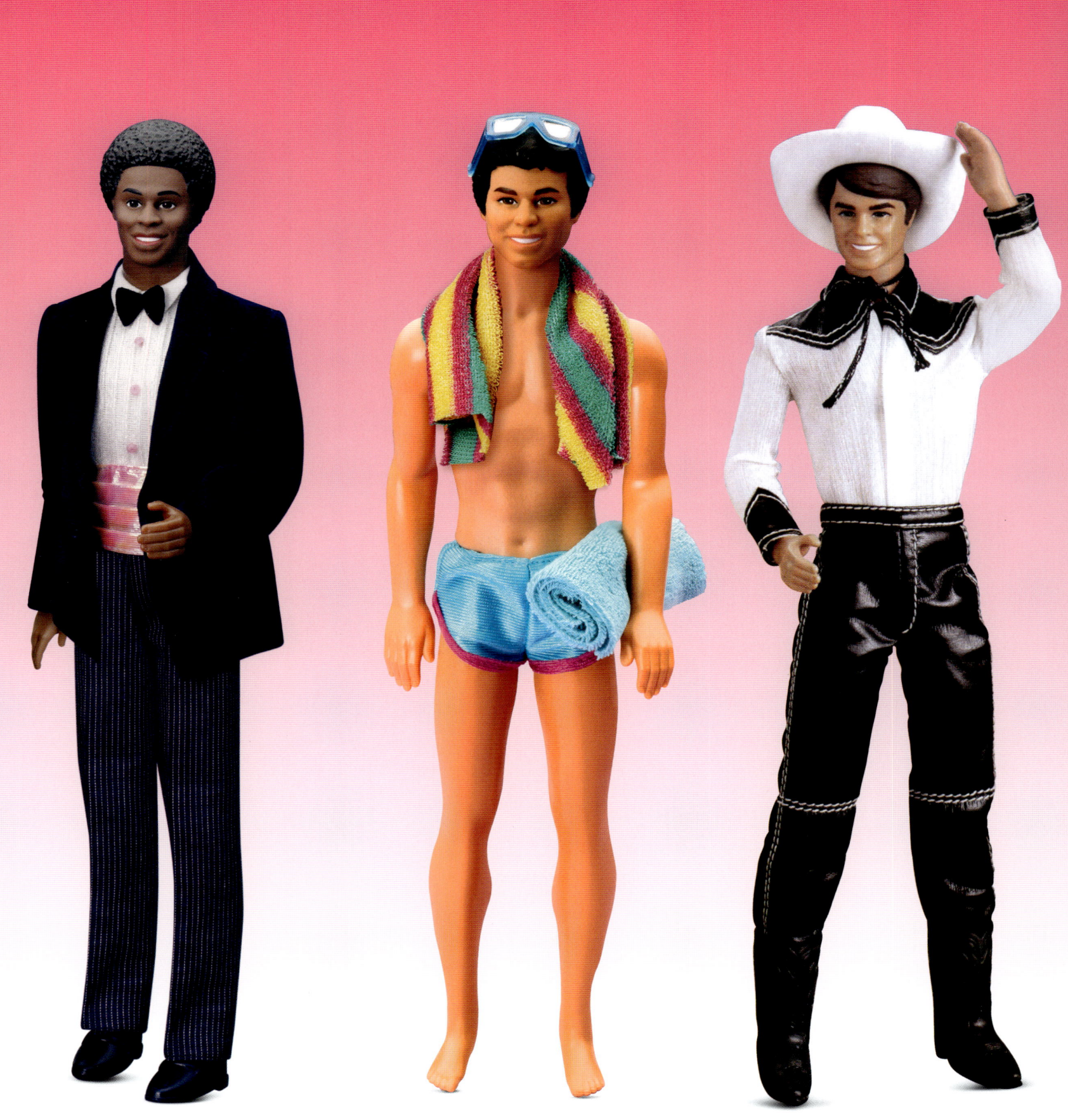

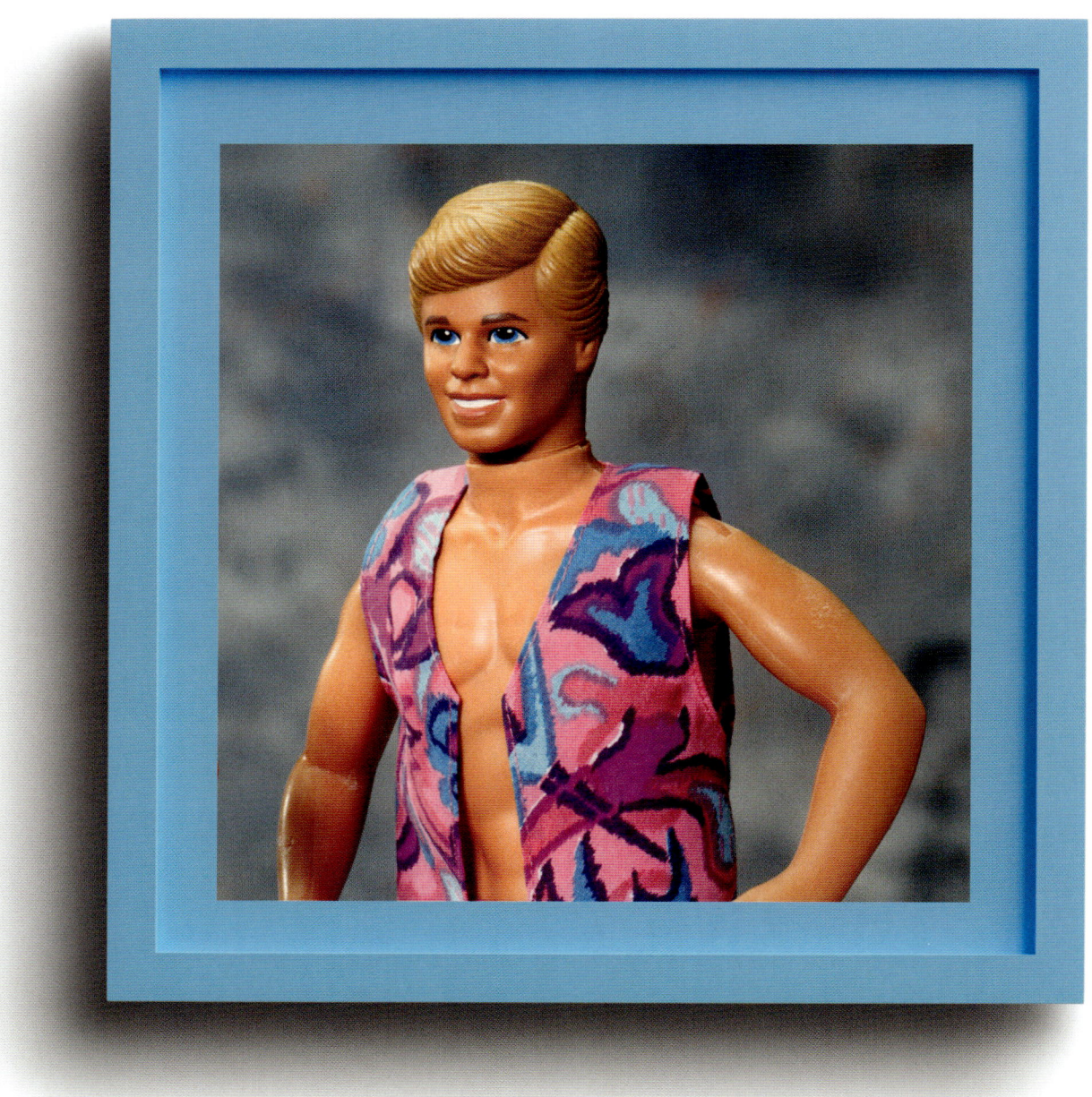

The 1990s / 2000s

After so much attention to haute couture fashion trends, Ken's wardrobe evolved again. Starting in the 1990s, he began wearing explicitly labeled *prêt-à-porter* looks. At the same time, his aesthetic became the subject of attention from established fashion houses, which began to create exclusive designs for him.

After two very colorful collections by Benetton (United Colors of Benetton Ken, 1990–1991), Ken was reimagined by three more fashion designers over the years, transforming into an experienced model of streetwear (2005), punk (2009), and pop (2016).

In 2005, following his 2004 breakup with Barbie, Ken returned with an updated look, styled by fashion designer Phillip Bloch. This new aesthetic took inspiration from contemporary male icons.

In 2009, at Colette in Paris, British designer Gareth Pugh offered his personal tribute to Ken with fifty handmade models and a full punk makeover. The design was inspired by Pugh's own menswear debut (F/W 2009/2010), marked by bold contrasts of glossy and matte black patent leather with a distinctively dark edge.

Then, in 2016, it was Jeremy Scott's turn: He created a personalized Moschino Ken, this time paired with Barbie, replicating the look he and model Stella Maxwell had worn to the 2015 MTV VMAs. It was a psychedelic triumph of explosions of color!

Opposite:
My First Ken Fashion, 1990.

Below:
Ken Fashionistas, 2018.

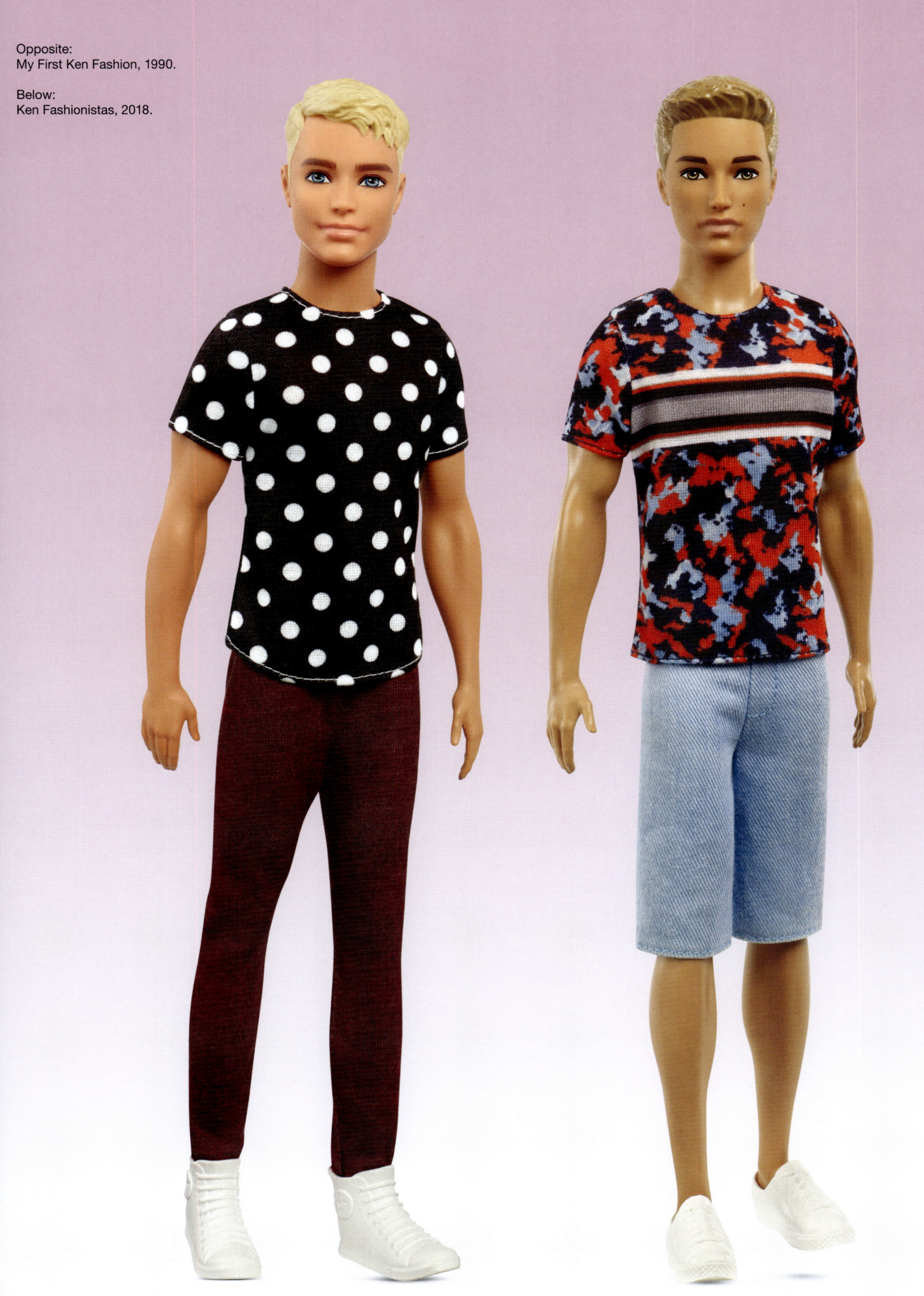

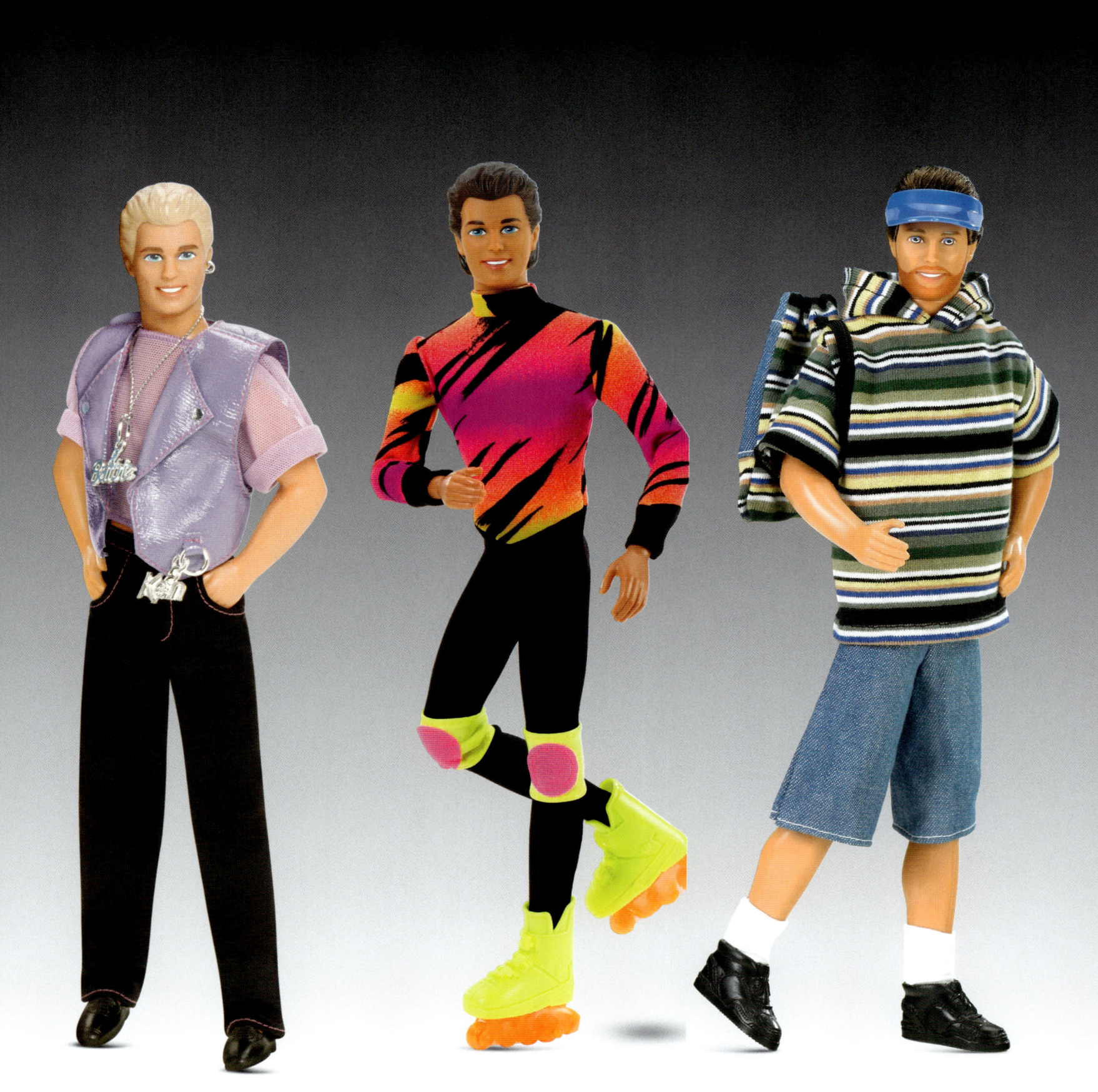

Ken with some of the most iconic looks of the 1990s, from Totally Hair Ken and Earring Magic Ken to Shaving Fun Ken and Motorcycle Ken, 1992–1994.

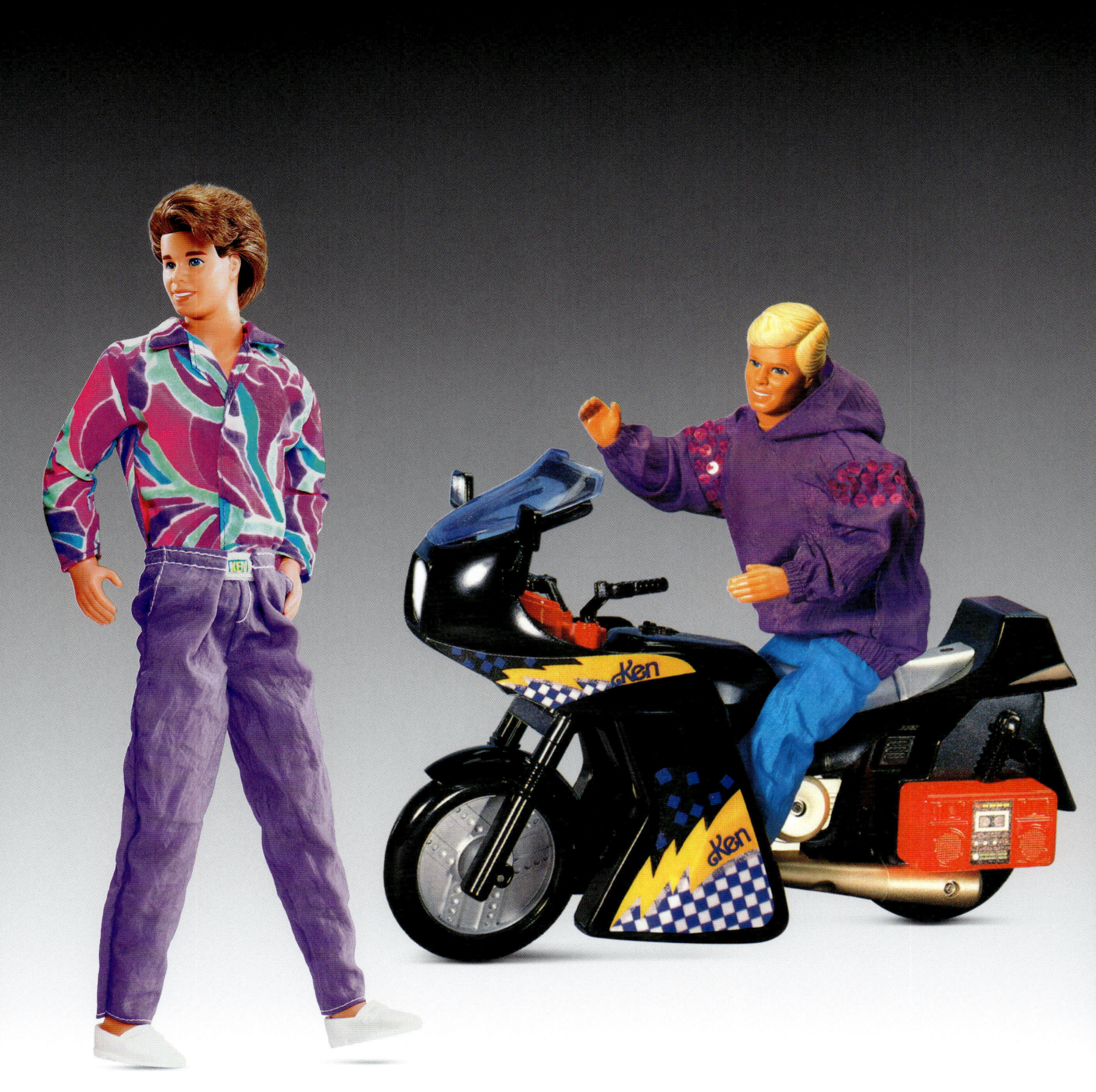

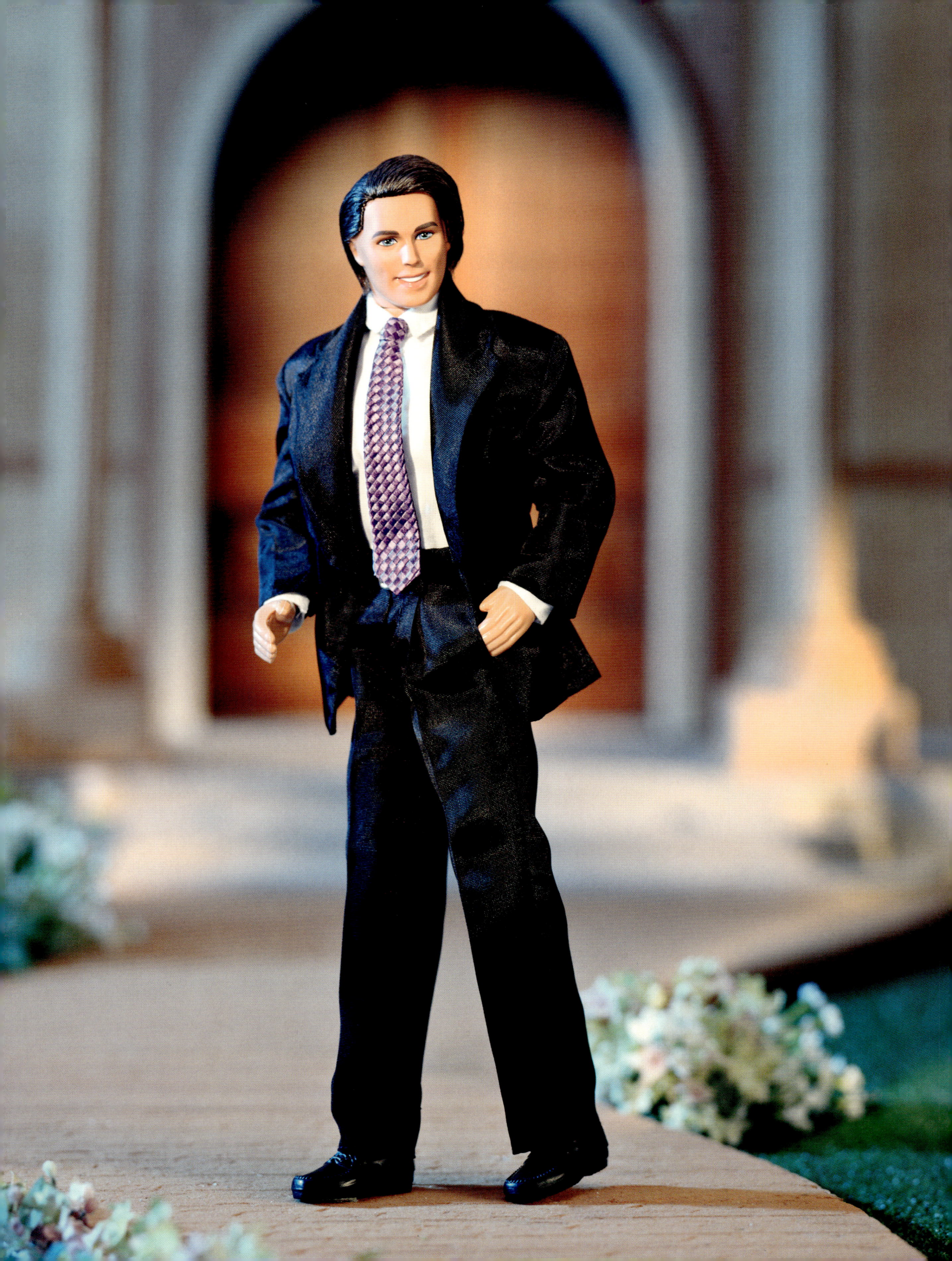

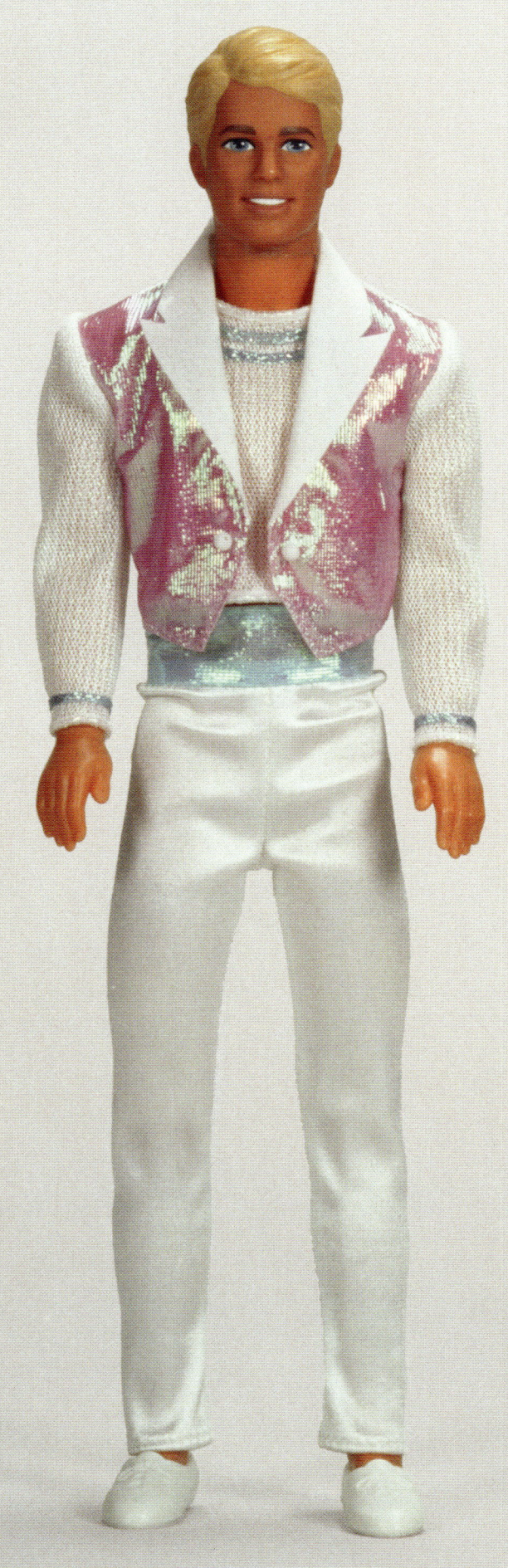

Opposite:
Totally Cool Ken, 1997.

Above:
My First Ken Doll, 1992.

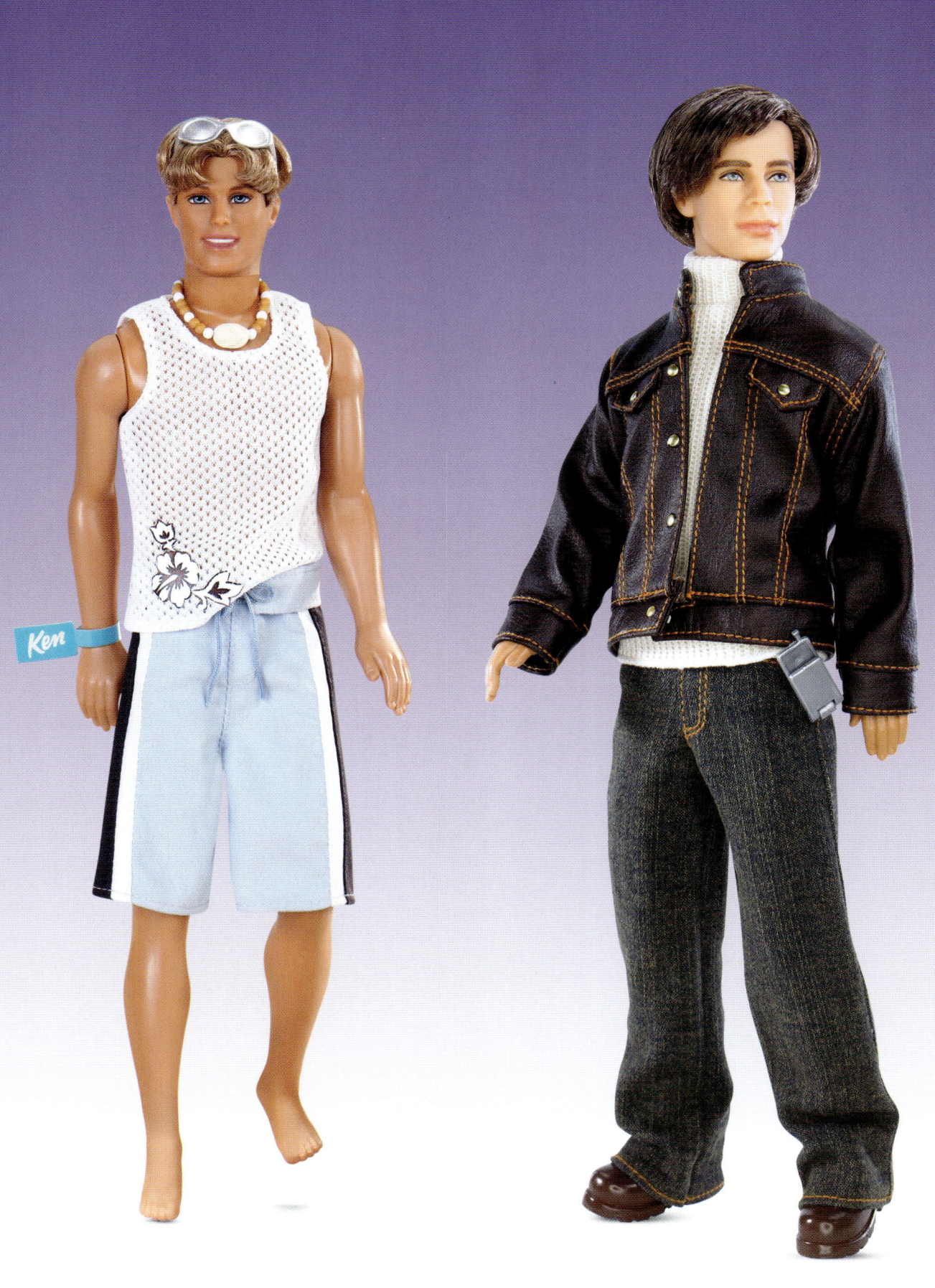

Cali Girl Ken (2003), Kurt Fashion Fever (2005), Cali Guy Blaine Doll (2004), Steven Beach Party (2008), Fashion Fever Ken (2006).

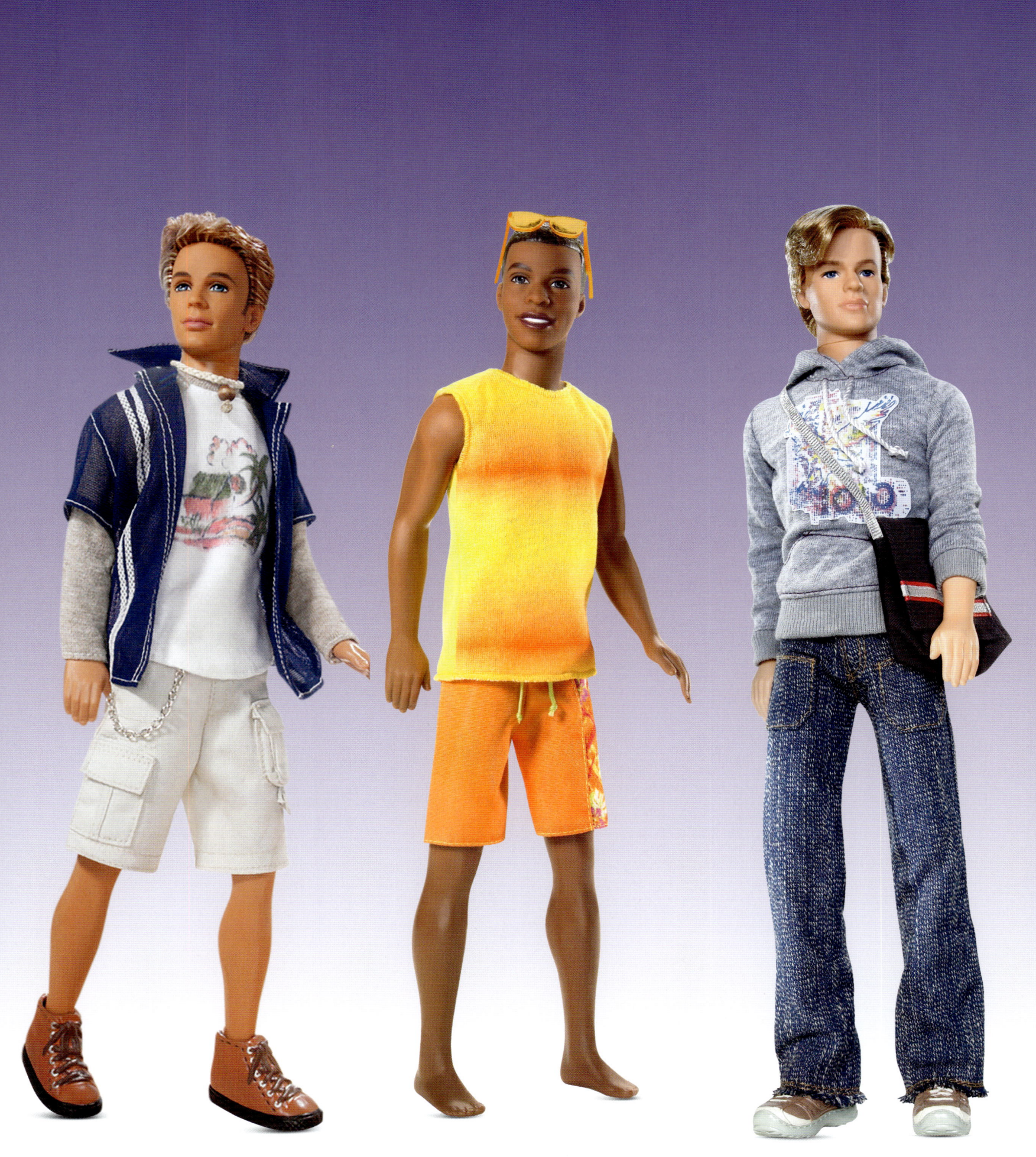

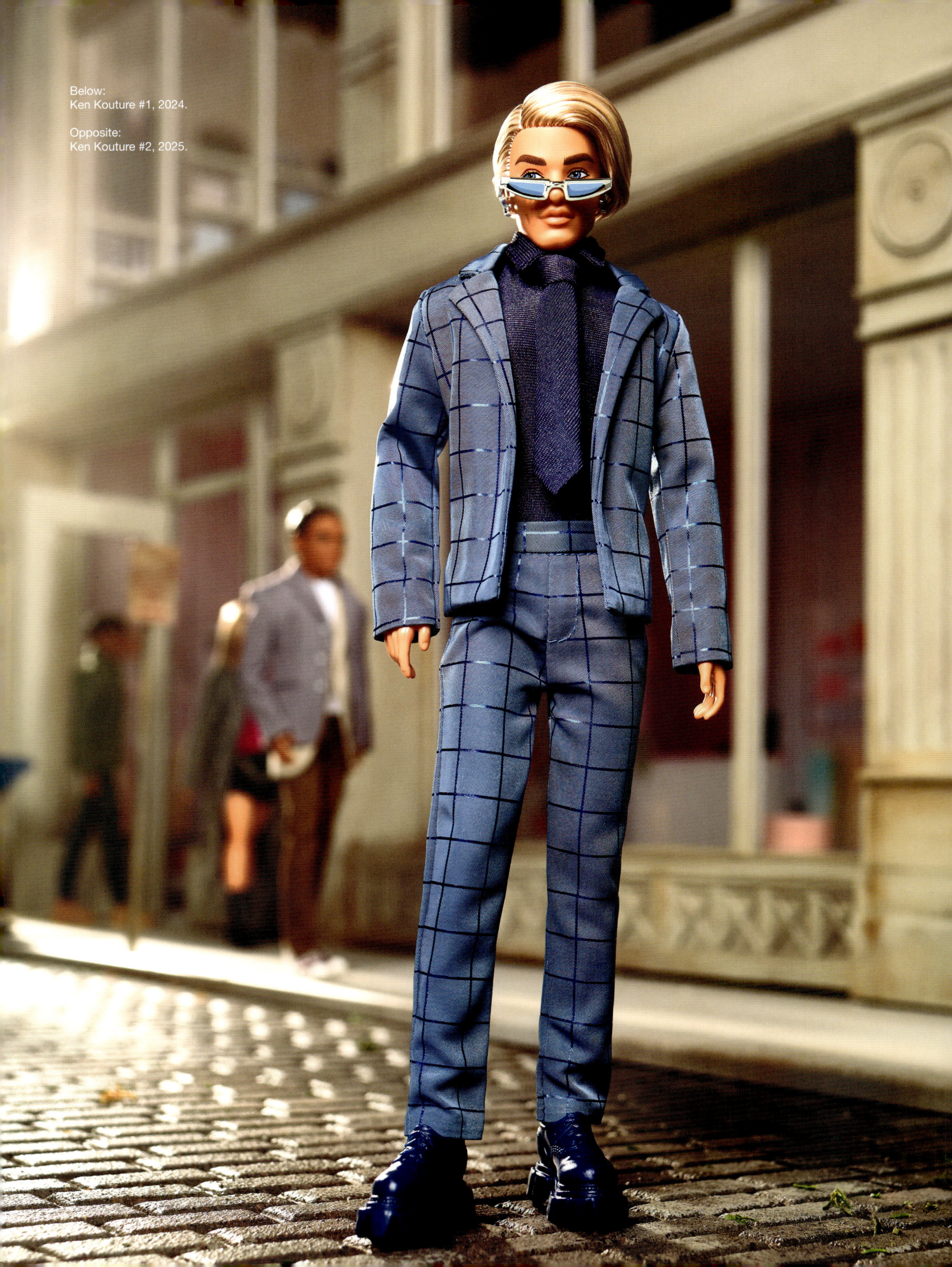

Below:
Ken Kouture #1, 2024.

Opposite:
Ken Kouture #2, 2025.

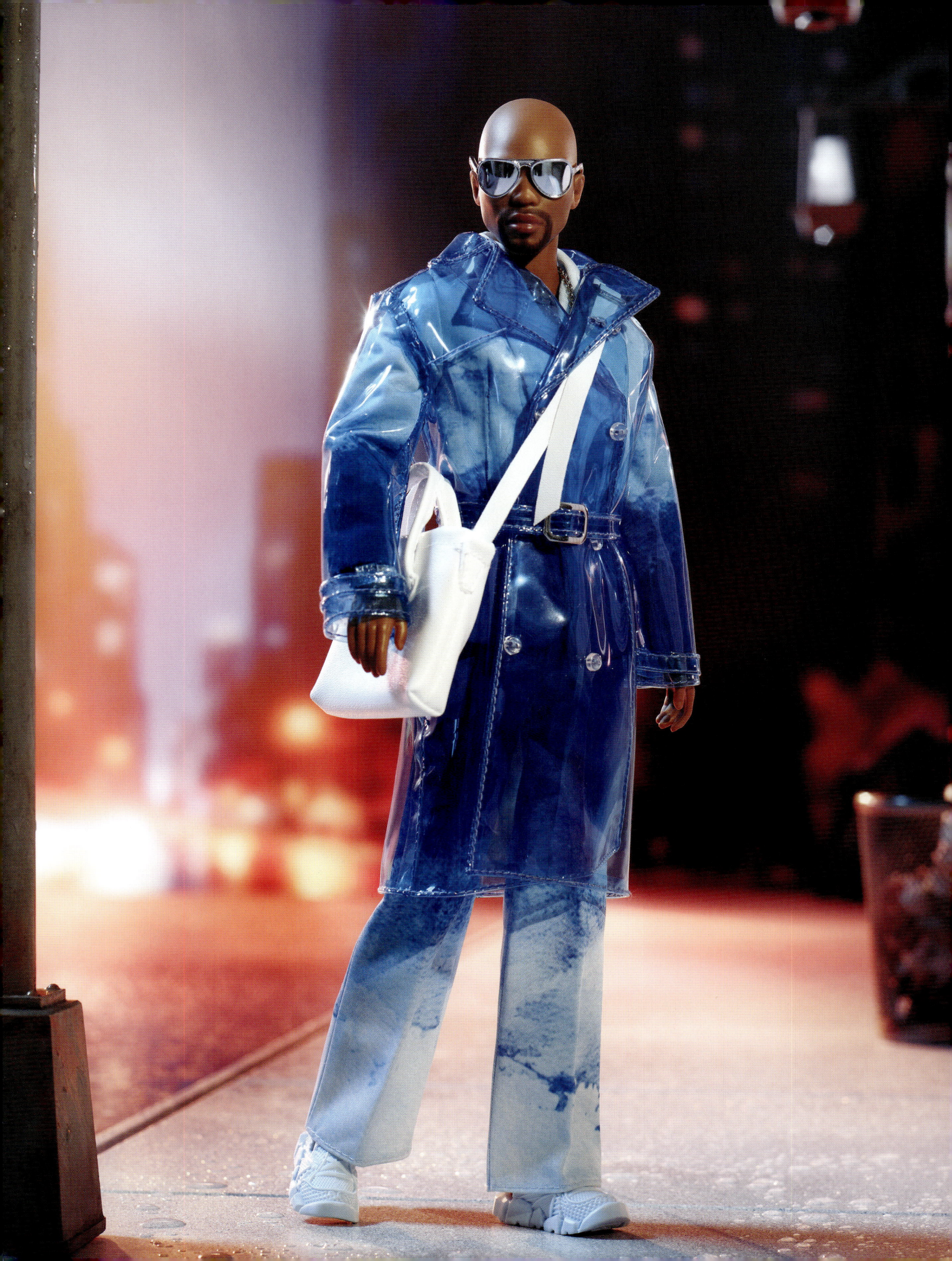

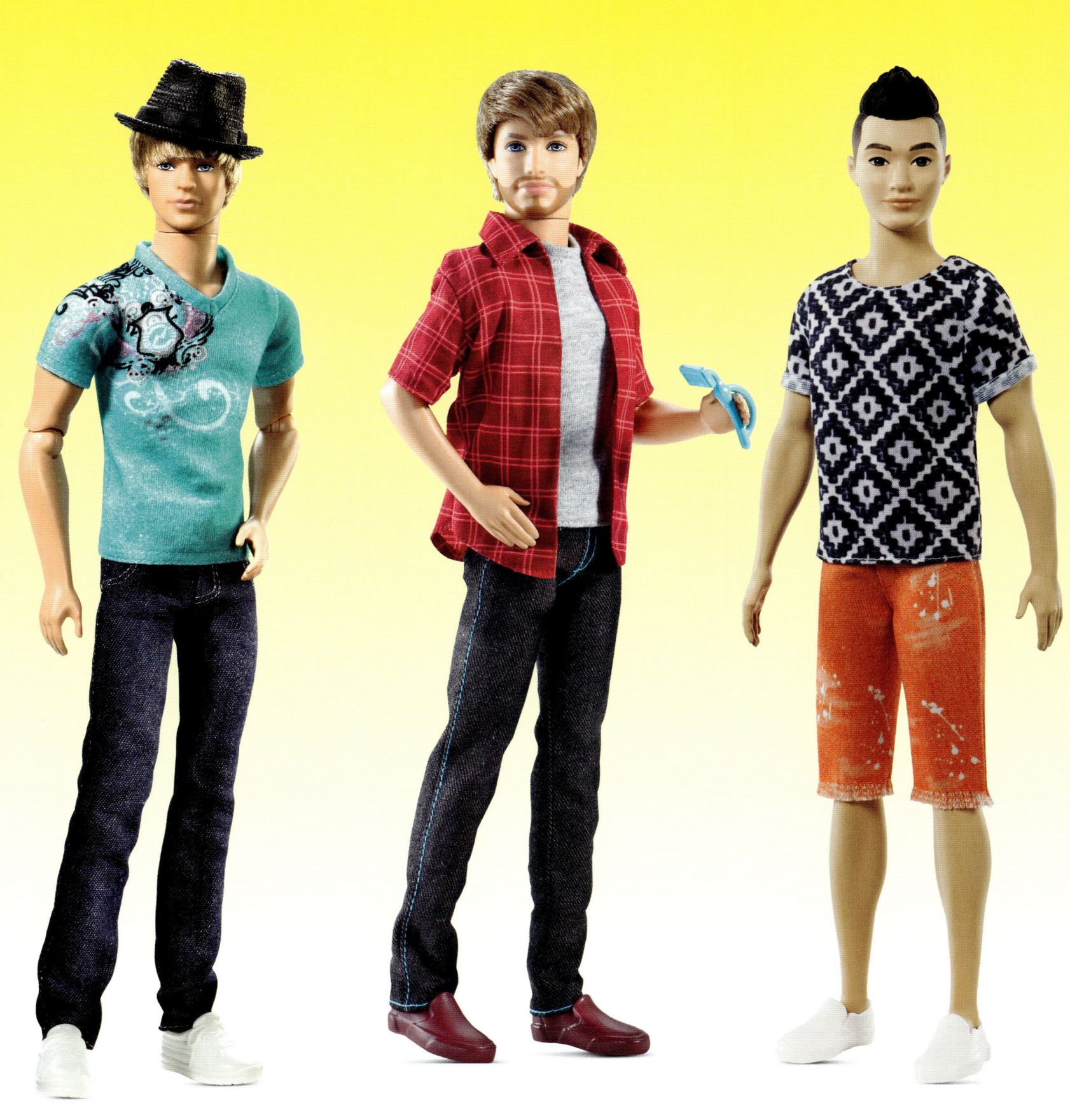

Ken Fashionistas released between 2011 and 2021, including Shaving Fun Ken (2011, second from left).

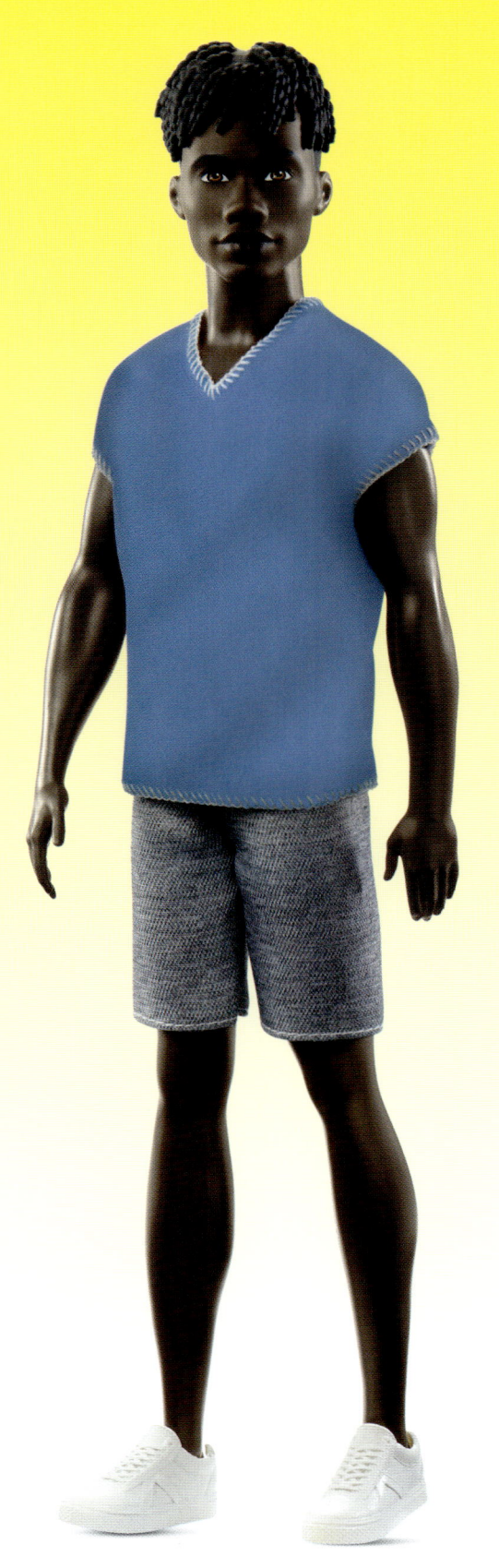
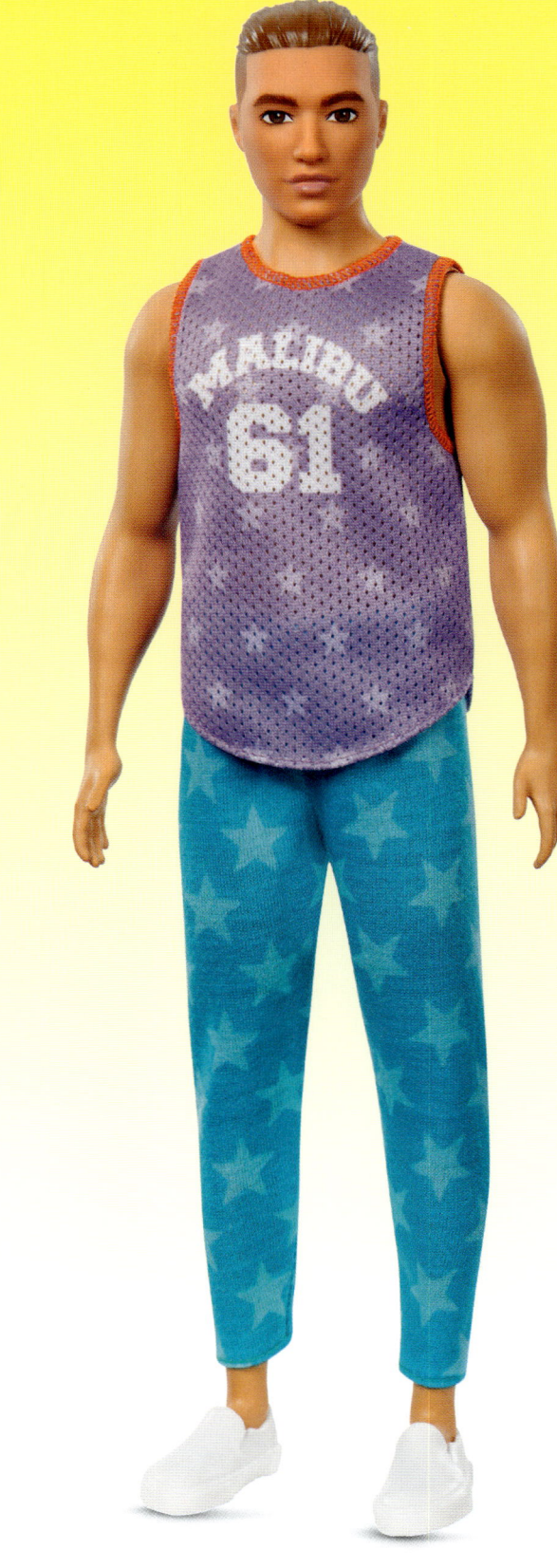

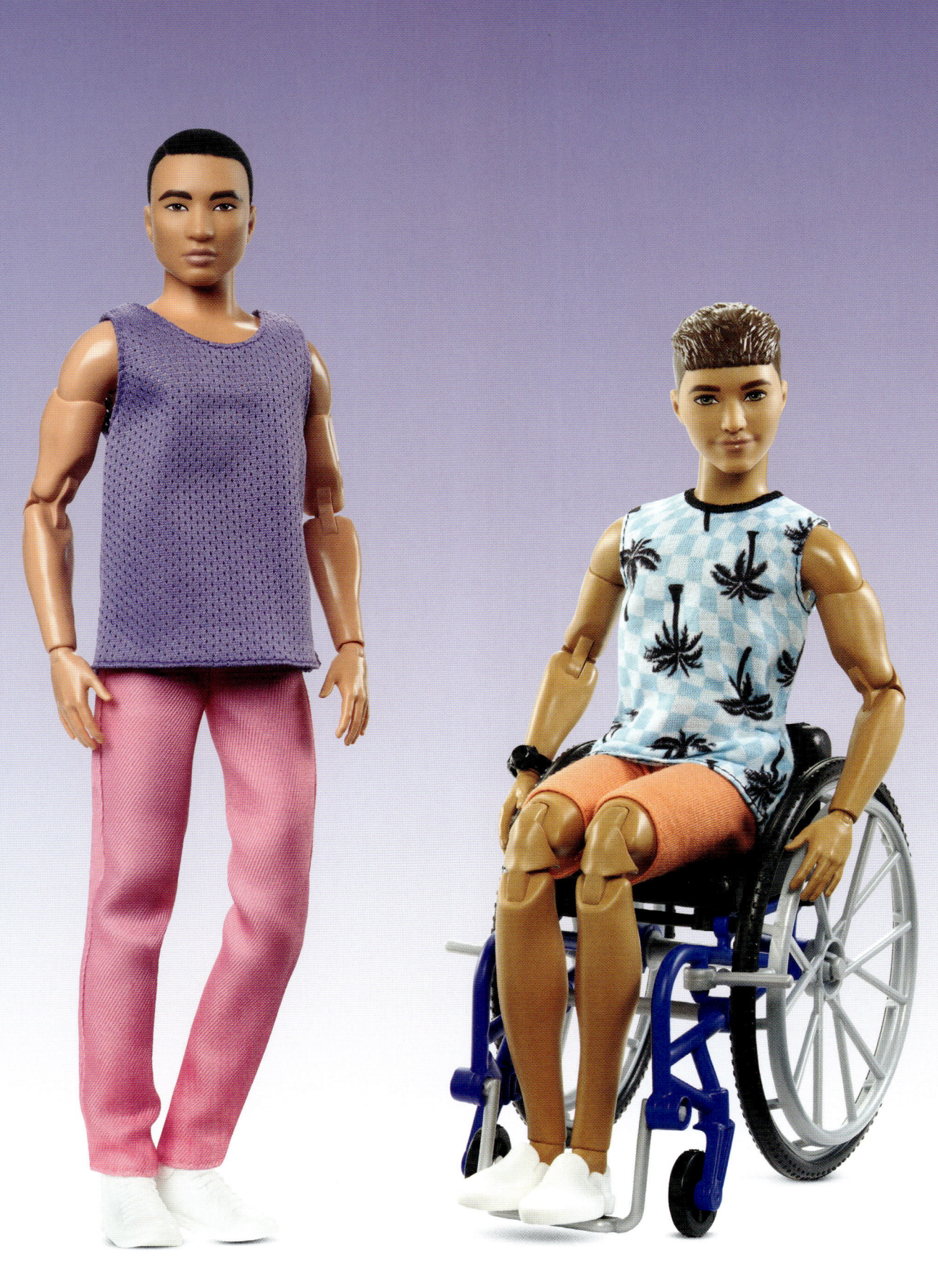

Ken and his new looks for
the Fashionistas (since 2011),
Resort Style (2023), BMR (2019),
and Looks (2021) lines.

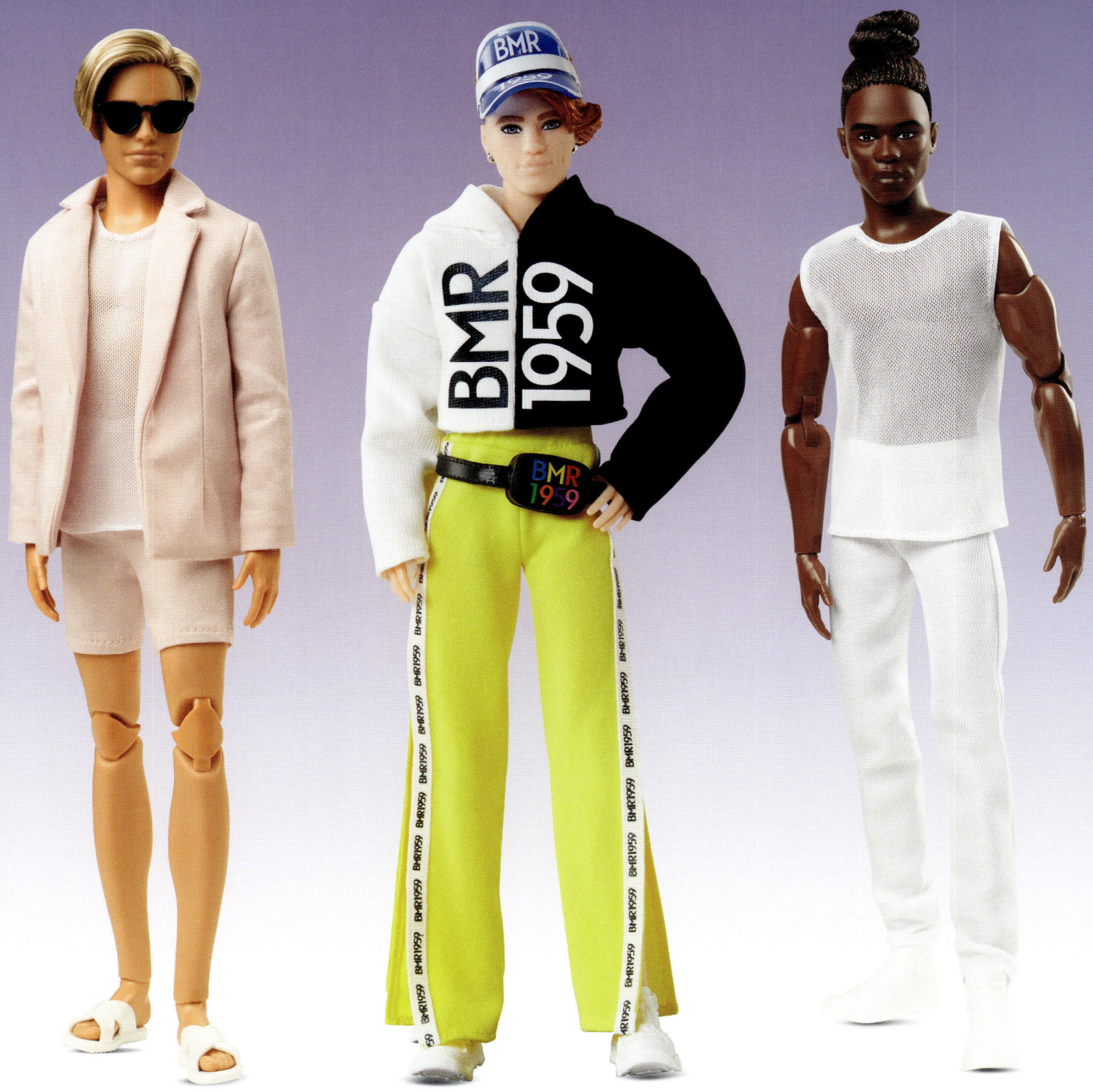

KEN'S ICONIC SPORT OUTFITS
1962–2025

While Ken's wardrobe has evolved with the times—moving from 1961 into the hippie and disco styles of the 1970s, to the pop look of the '80s, to the streetwear and hip-hop vibes of the '90s and 2000s—one thing has remained constant: Ken has always complemented his workouts with an extensive sportswear wardrobe.

1961
Barbie and Ken Tennis Set

1962
Time for Tennis

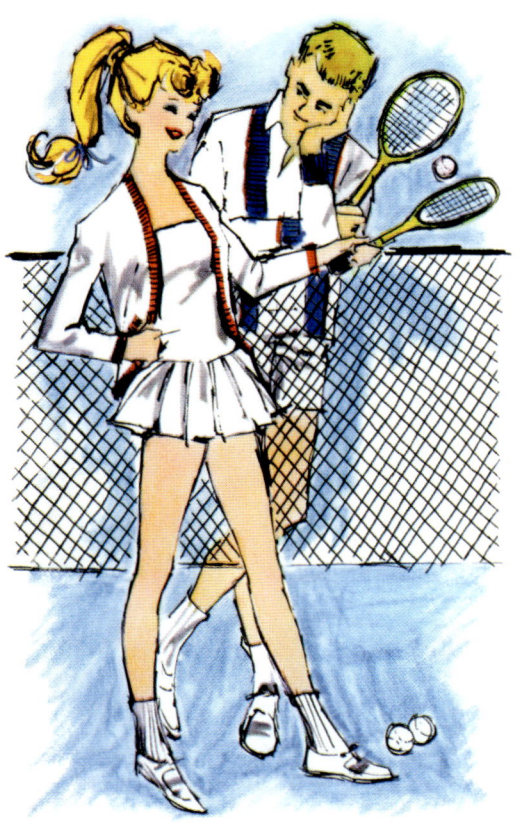

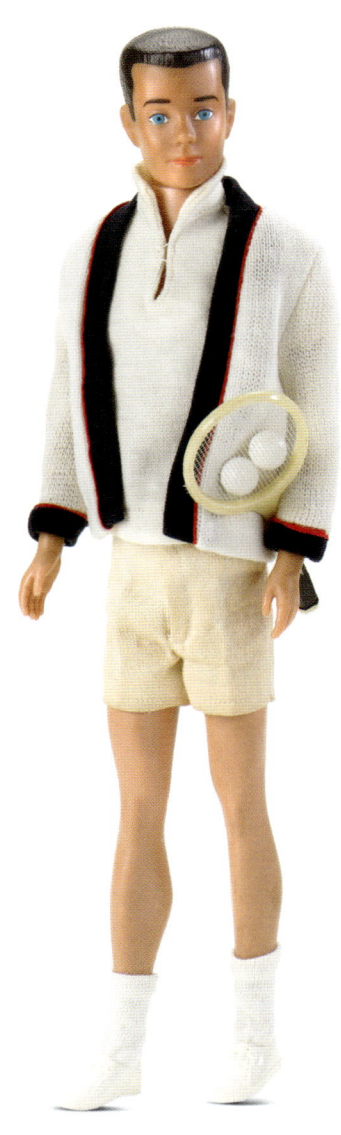

1963
*Fun on Ice
Ski Champion*

1964
*Ice Skate Date
Sportsman*

(Fashion for Ken and Allan)

1971
*Skiing Scene
Golf Gear*

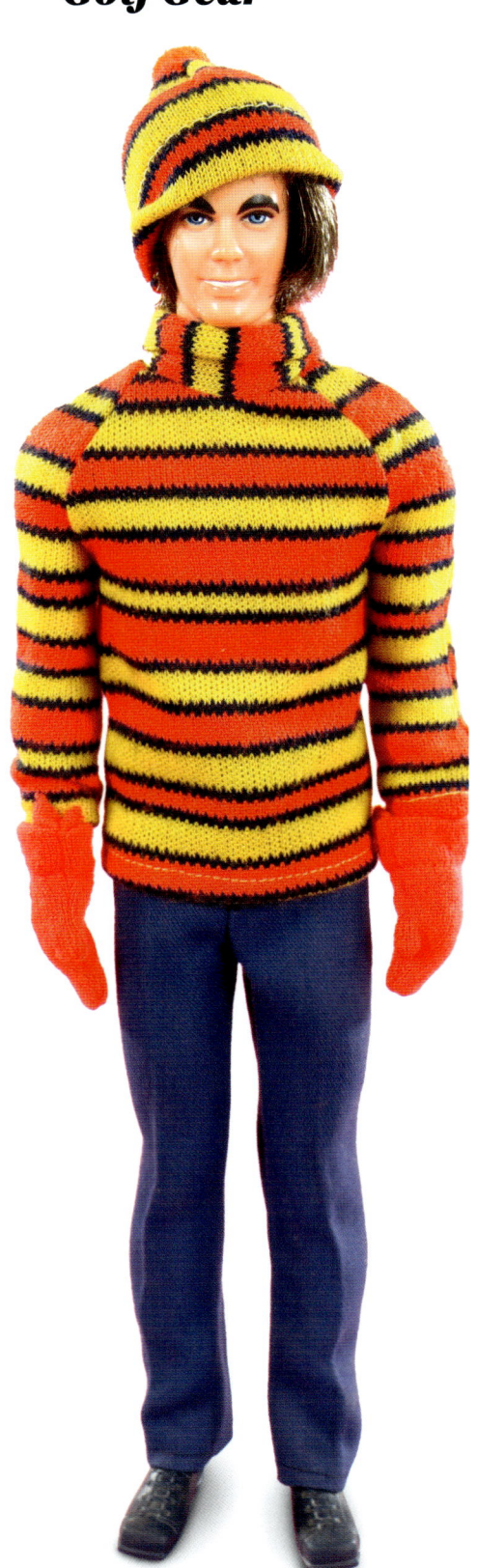

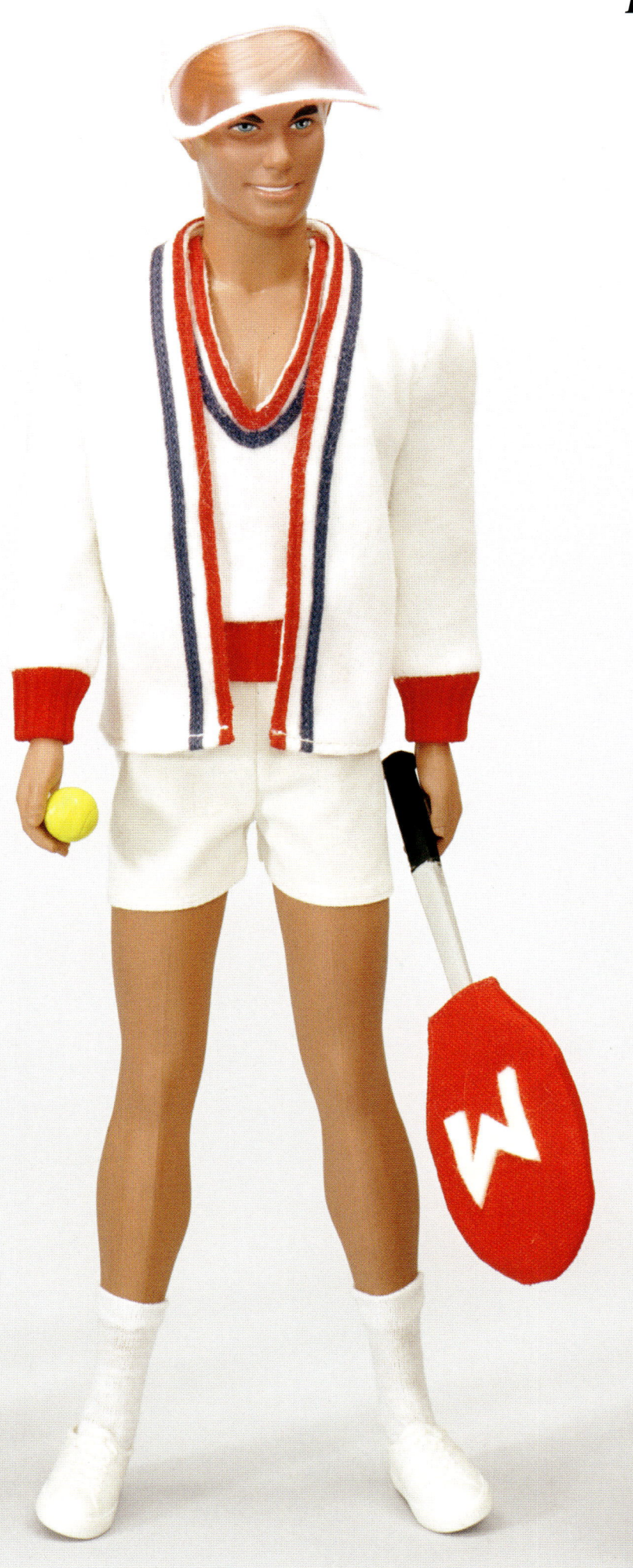

1974
Tennis

1975
Gold Medal Ken

Ken and Barbie celebrate the upcoming 1976 Winter Olympics in Canada together. In the hockey player mold (see image on the right), Ken wears a red uniform with blue and white accents; in the skier mold, a suit in the same colors, complete with a belt, yellow vest with race bib #9, red hat, goggles, boots, blue skis, and poles. In both outfits, he proudly wears a gold medal around his neck.
In other words, "The world's winningest Olympic athlete!"

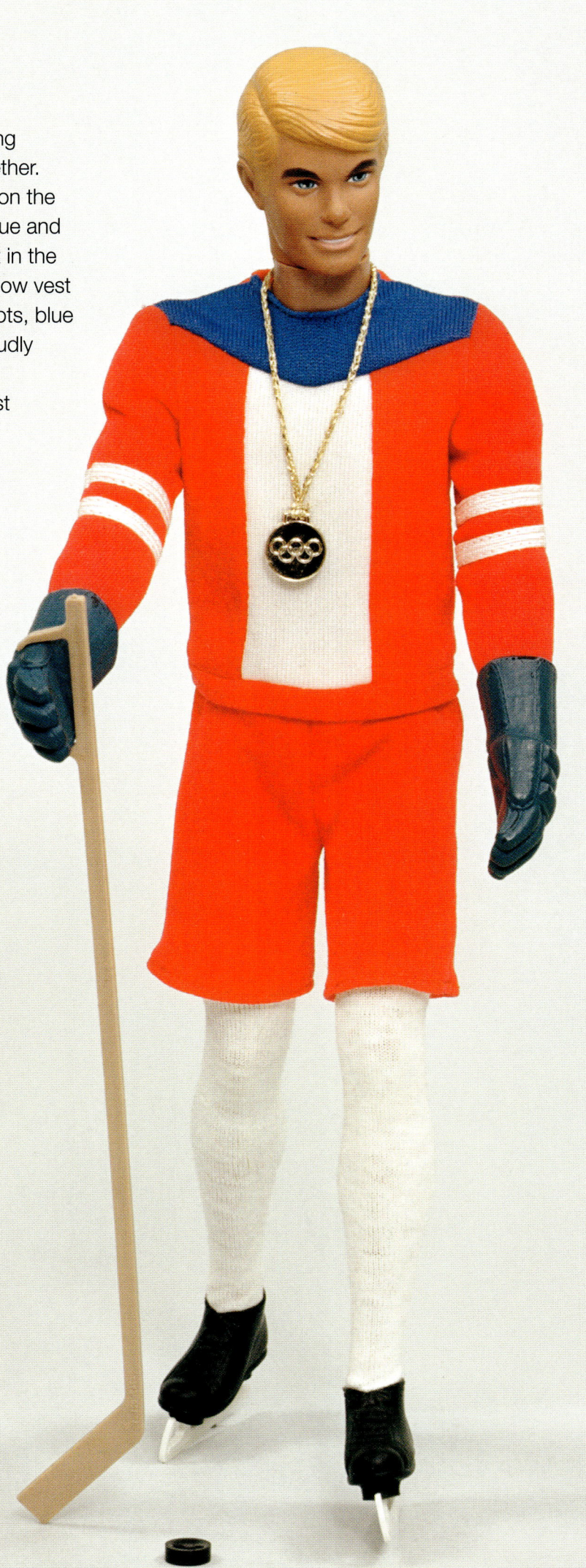

1976
Gold Medal Ken Swimmer

This Olympic swimming champion Ken was produced by Mattel Europe to mark the 1976 Olympics in Canada. Wearing a red, white, and blue swim brief like those of American athletes, Ken also wears a gold medal.

1979
Sun Lovin' Malibu Ken

By now an icon of surf culture, Ken sports a golden tan, molded blond hair, and turquoise swim trunks.

1980
Roller Skating Ken

"He's king of the roller scene!"

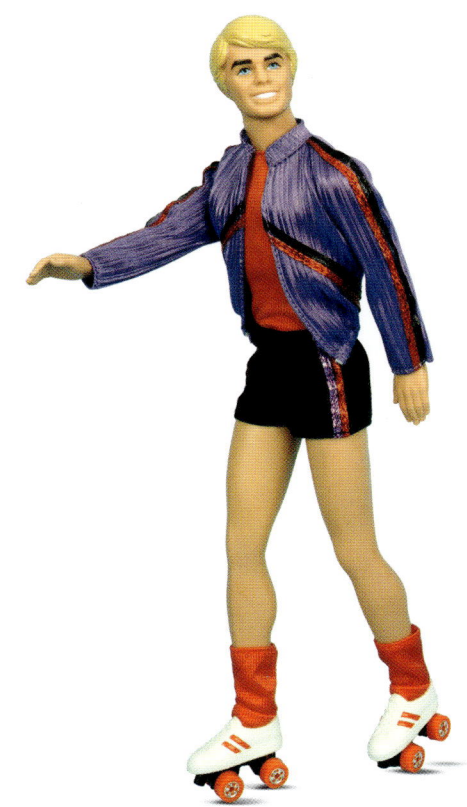

1979
Sport & Shave Ken
(Tennis)

This model features yellow shorts with a white and blue waistband, white T-shirt with navy trim, and a yellow "ALL STAR MARATHON" sticker. On his feet: blue and white tennis shoes. Ken also comes with a razor accessory, for shaving.

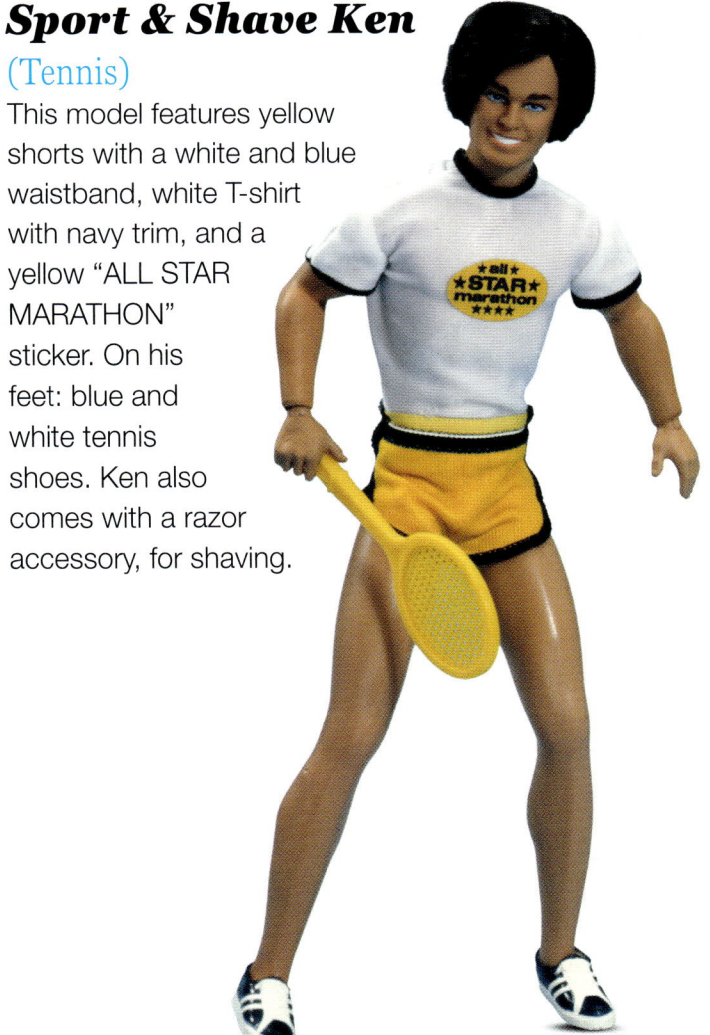

1982
Super Sport Ken

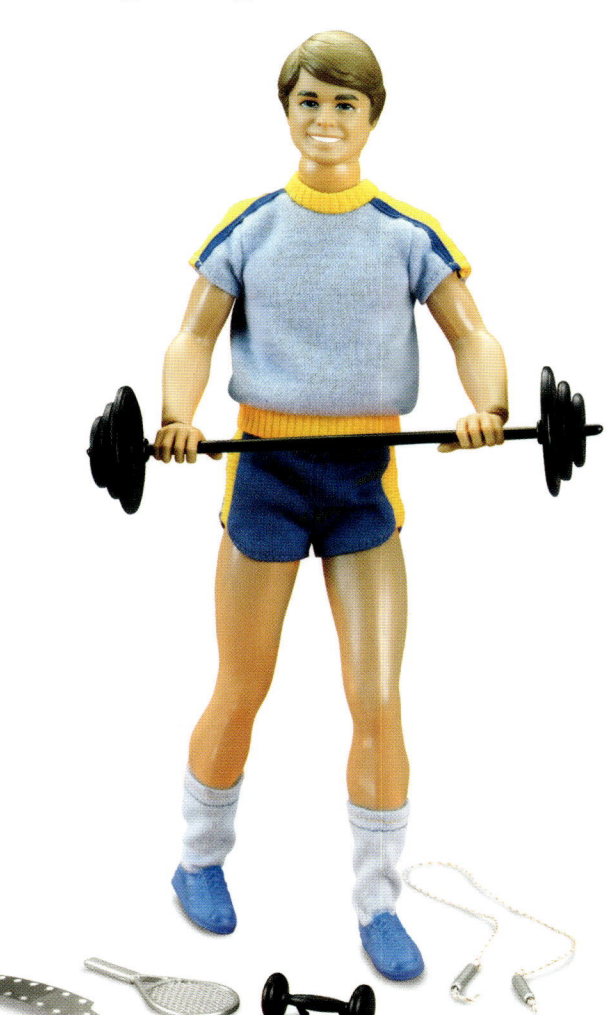

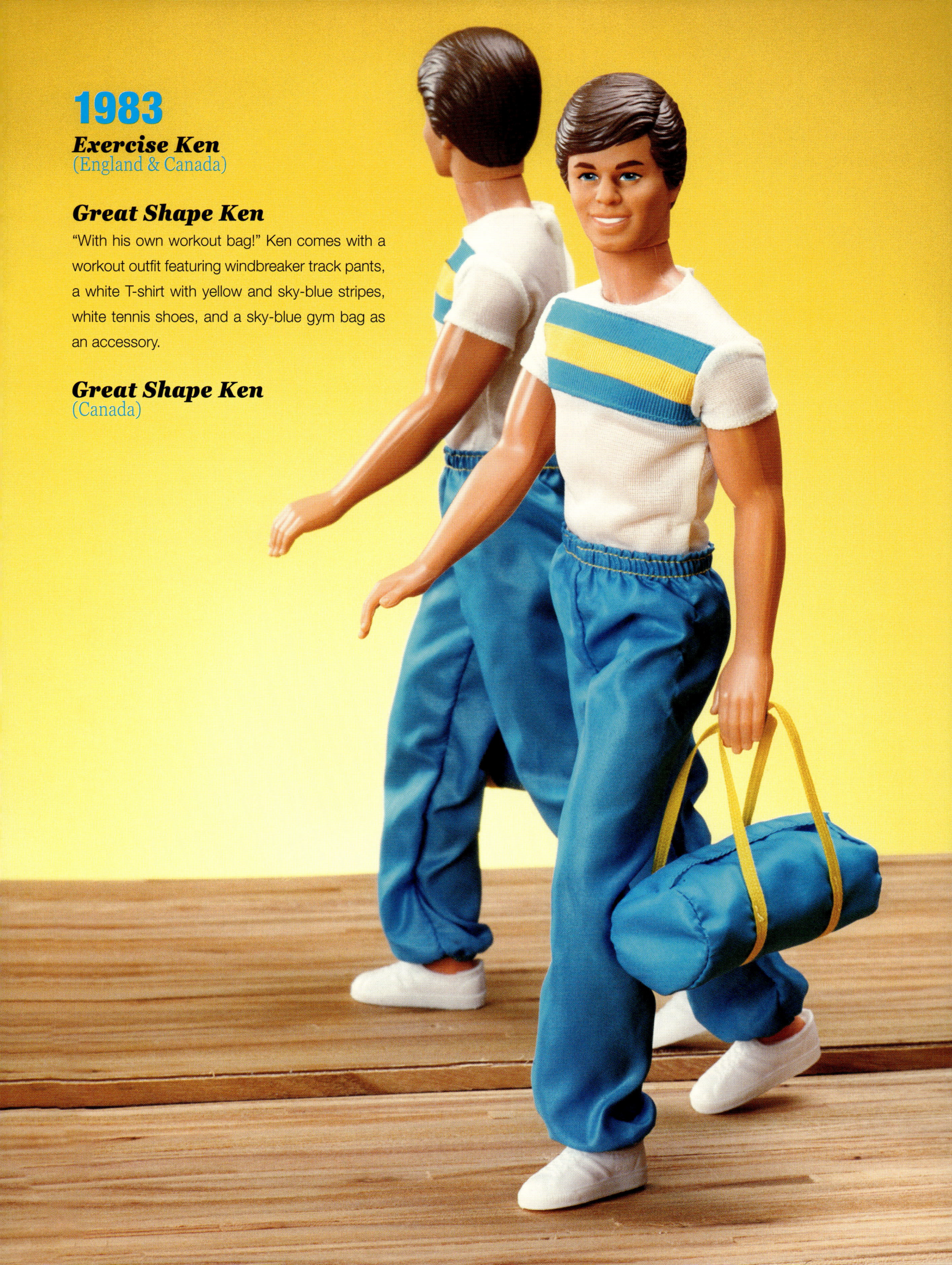

1983
Exercise Ken
(England & Canada)

Great Shape Ken
"With his own workout bag!" Ken comes with a workout outfit featuring windbreaker track pants, a white T-shirt with yellow and sky-blue stripes, white tennis shoes, and a sky-blue gym bag as an accessory.

Great Shape Ken
(Canada)

1985–1986
Sport Music Ken
(Mexico)

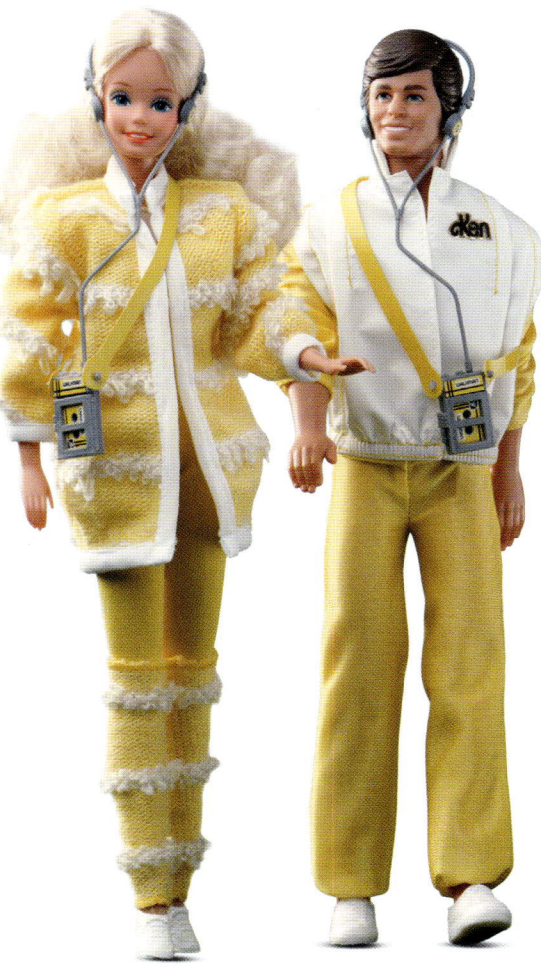

Tennis Ken (Europe)

1988
Olympic Ken
Created to celebrate the 1988 Olympics, Ken wears white pants, a white jacket with Olympic rings, pink sleeves, and a Nehru collar.

1989
Work Out Ken (Peru)
Sports Club Ken
A new outfit dedicated to golf.
Ken and the All Stars
(All Stars Ken)

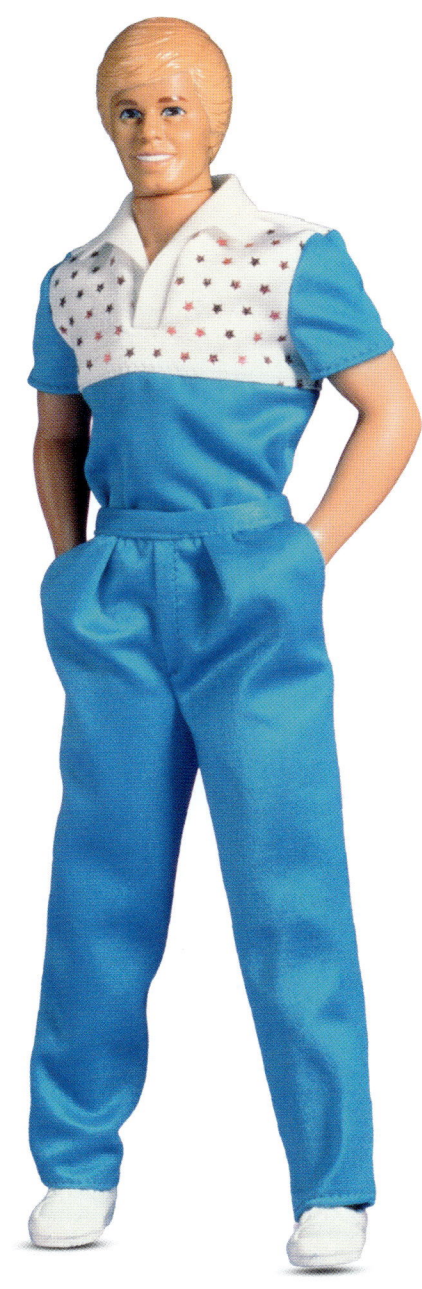

"Basketball star to party hit!"
Ken sports a basketball outfit with shorts, tank top, white socks, and a sky-blue gym bag that transforms into pants.

1990
Team All Stars!
In line with the fashion trends of the moment, Ken joins Barbie and friends in the enthusiastic pursuit of fitness. The "All Stars" bags include a surprise: They transform into party outfits—pants for Kenand a skirt for Barbie.

Sports Club European Exclusives!
Abroad, the "All Star Team" becomes "Sports Club," with Ken appearing as an accomplished golfer.

"Snowboarding!"
"Au traineau!"
Ski Fun Ken

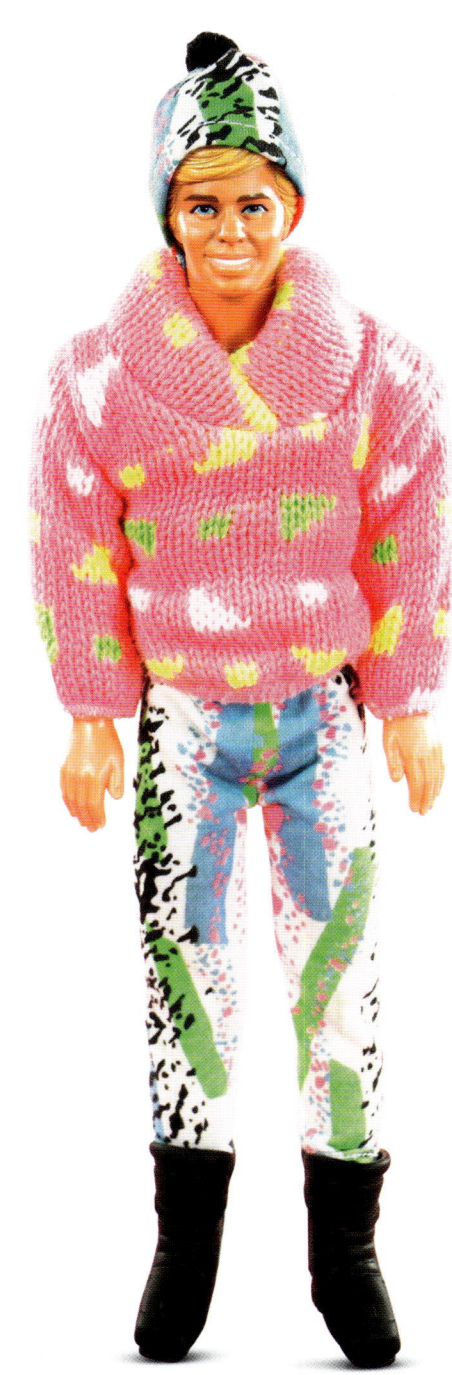

157

1991
Rollerblade Ken
"Skates flicker 'n flash!"

1994
"Lifeguard Ken races to the rescue on his WaveRunner!"
Ken celebrates the legend of the *Baywatch* lifeguards, stars of the TV series that aired from 1989 to 2001: white T-shirt, red nylon windbreaker with "Lifeguard" logo, red swim trunks, and a *Baywatch* rescue float.

Winter Sport Ken

1995
In-Line Skating Ken
(Canada)
Cool and speedy! They skate, dash, catch some air, and perform amazing stunts with their ultra-flexible bodies and light-up skates.

1996
Ocean Friends Ken
The wetsuit magically disappears in warm water and reappears in cold water. Ready to dive into ocean depths, Ken wears a painted black wetsuit, mask and snorkel, flippers, an oxygen tank strapped to his back.

1997
Olympic USA Skater Ken

1999
Swim Ken & Tommy
"Floating kickboard! Tommy really kicks!" Ken and his little brother Tommy get ready for a sunny beach day.

2000
Surf City Ken
Surf City Ken Beach Play Set

2002
Skate Date Ken

2010
Barbie and Ken Harley Davidson Set
In full Harley style, Barbie and Ken show off their motorcycle helmets, piercings, and tattoos.

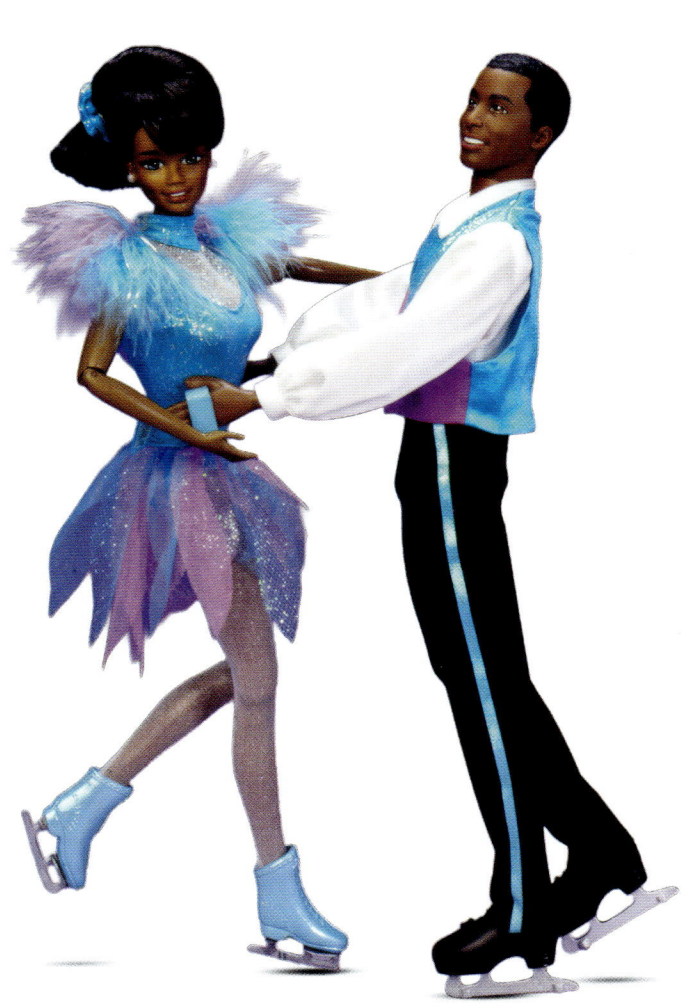
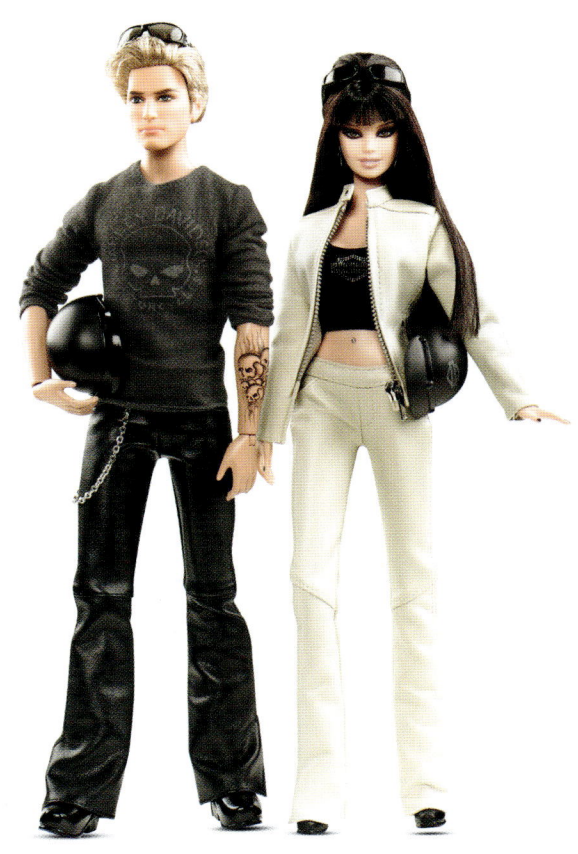

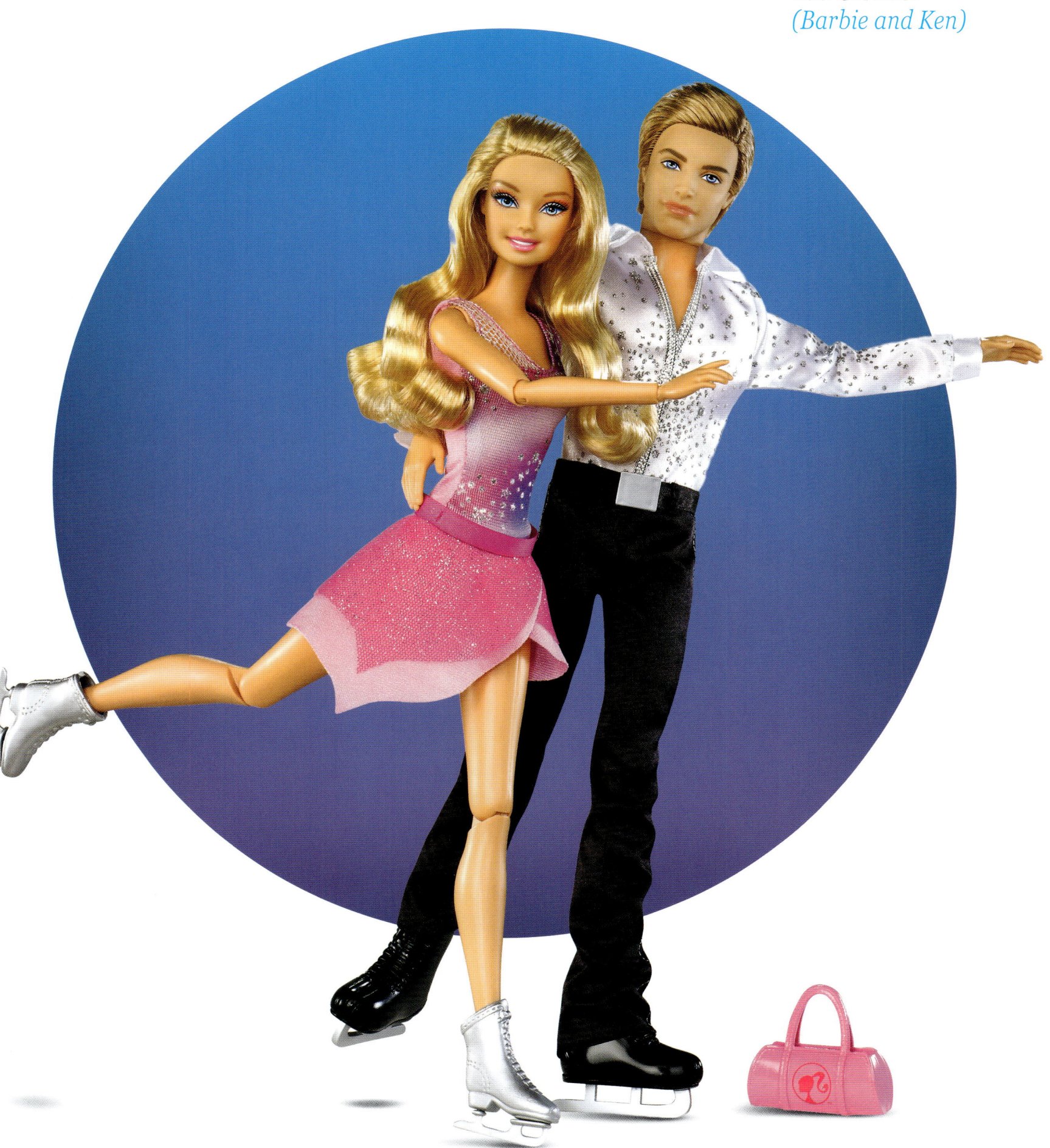

2011
Barbie I Can Be... Ice Skater
(Barbie and Ken)

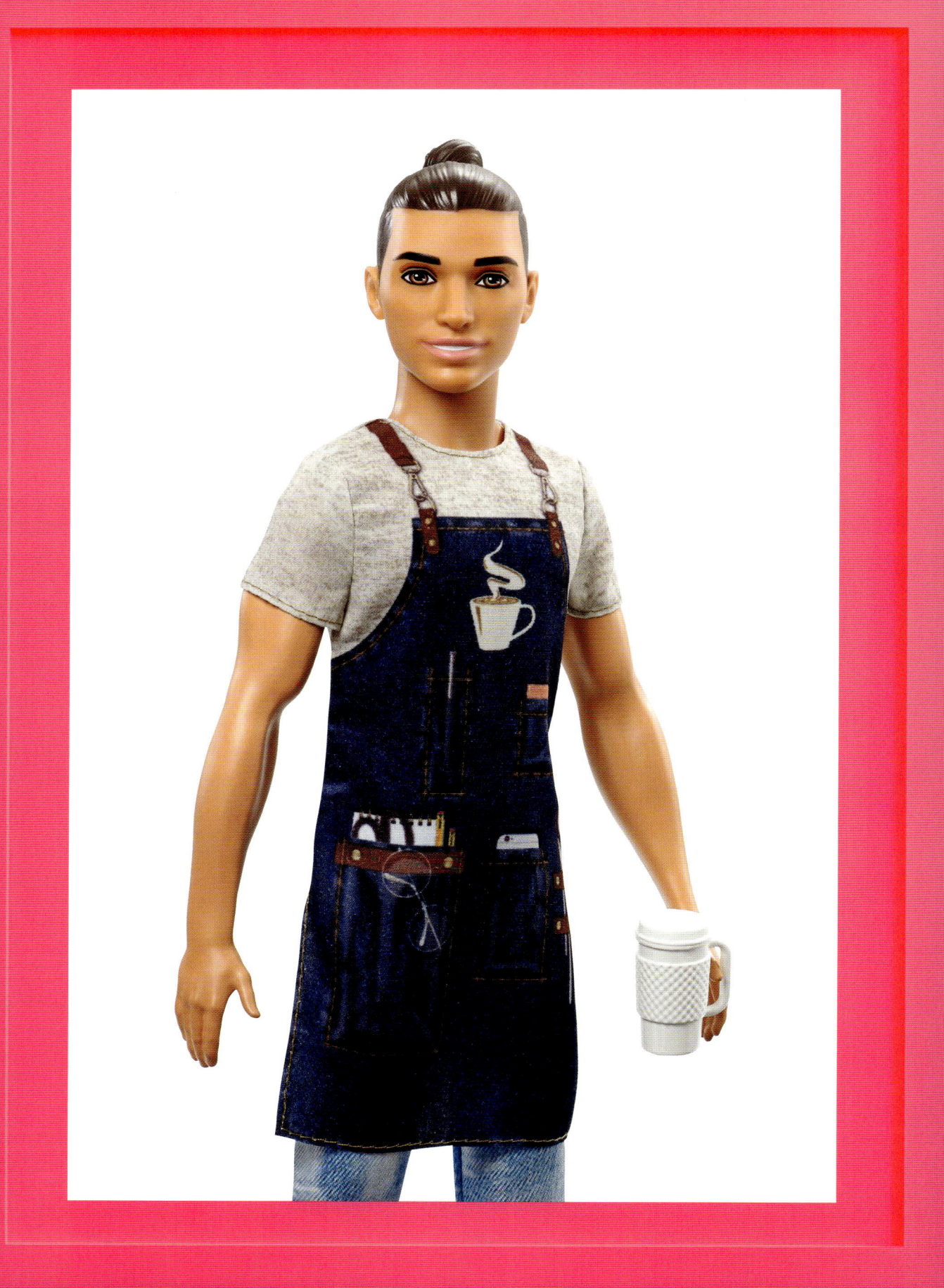

Ken as a barista, 2019.

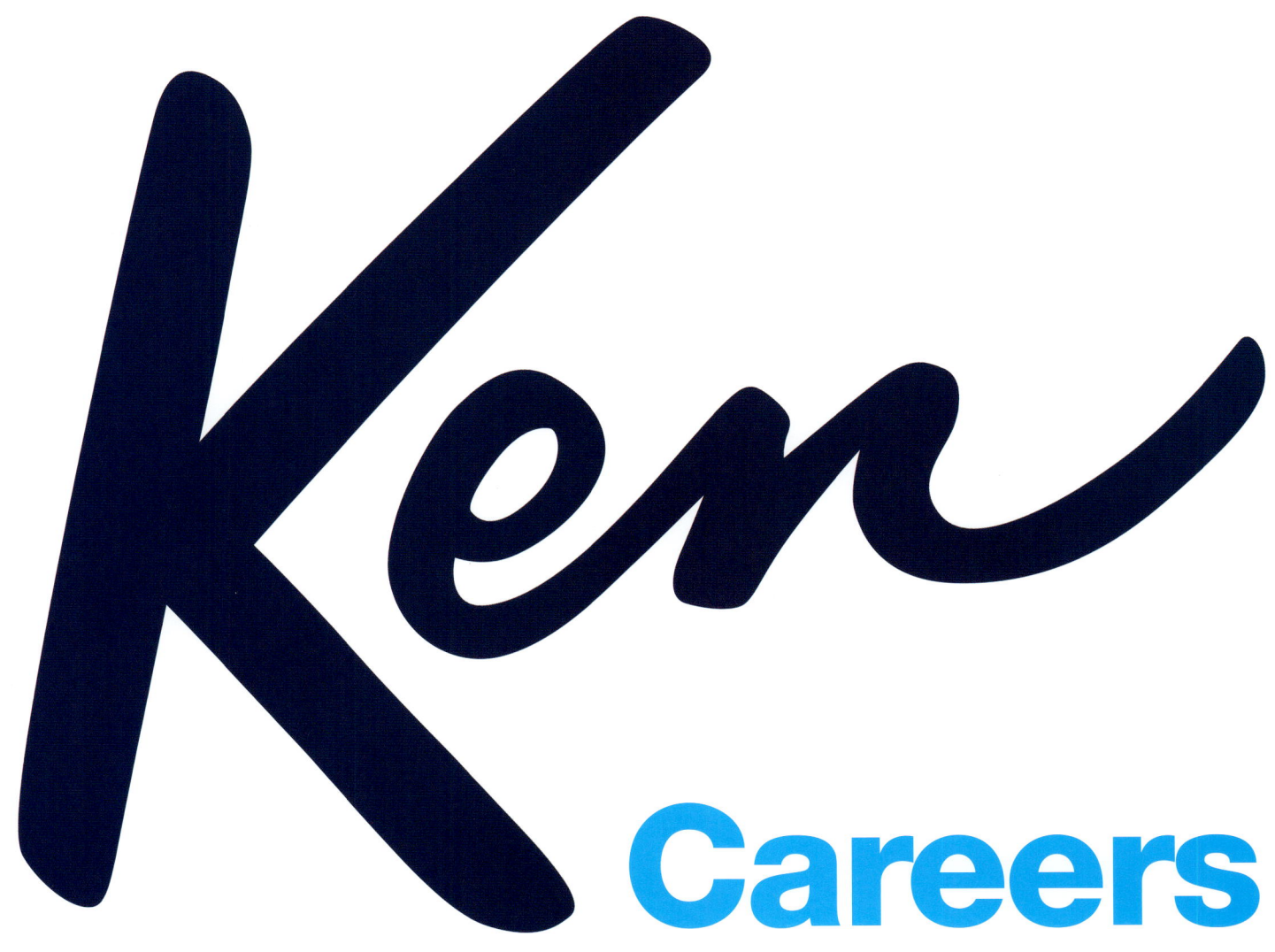

Ken Careers

Wearing his red poplin swimsuit, Flock Hair Ken #750 immediately brings to mind the beach, the ocean, and the world of young Californians riding the waves on their surfboards. Over the course of his sixty-five-year history, however, Ken has taken on dozens of careers, stepping into roles ranging from doctor, astronaut, chef, and country singer to actor—and of course, lifeguard. In fact, that was his very first job, followed closely by tennis player and football player. Sports have been a great passion of his, which he's also turned into a profession—as a coach and much more.

1962 Beach Guy

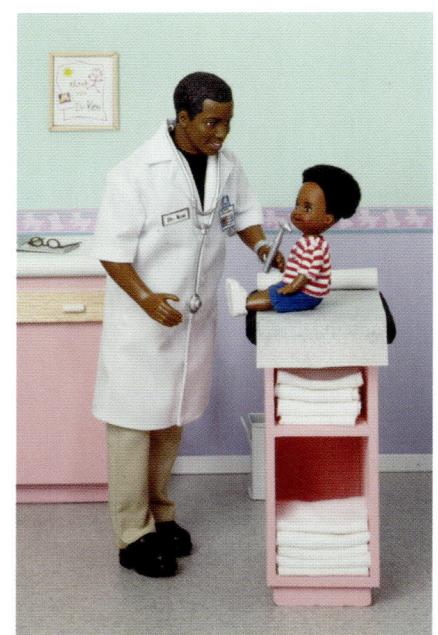

1963
Actor
Boxer
(clothing pack)
Campus Hero
Doctor
(clothing pack)
Football Player
(clothing pack)
Sailor
Skier

1964
Drum Major
(clothing pack)
Pilot
(clothing pack)
Soda Jerk

1965
Astronaut
(clothing pack)
Reporter
(clothing pack)

1966 Best Man

1970 Rock Star

1974 Olympic Gold Medalist

1975
Olympic Hockey Player
(clothing pack)
Olympic Skier
Olympic Swimmer

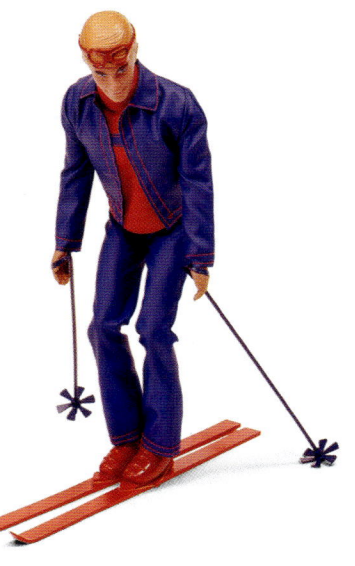

1978 TOURIST

1977 *Movie Star*

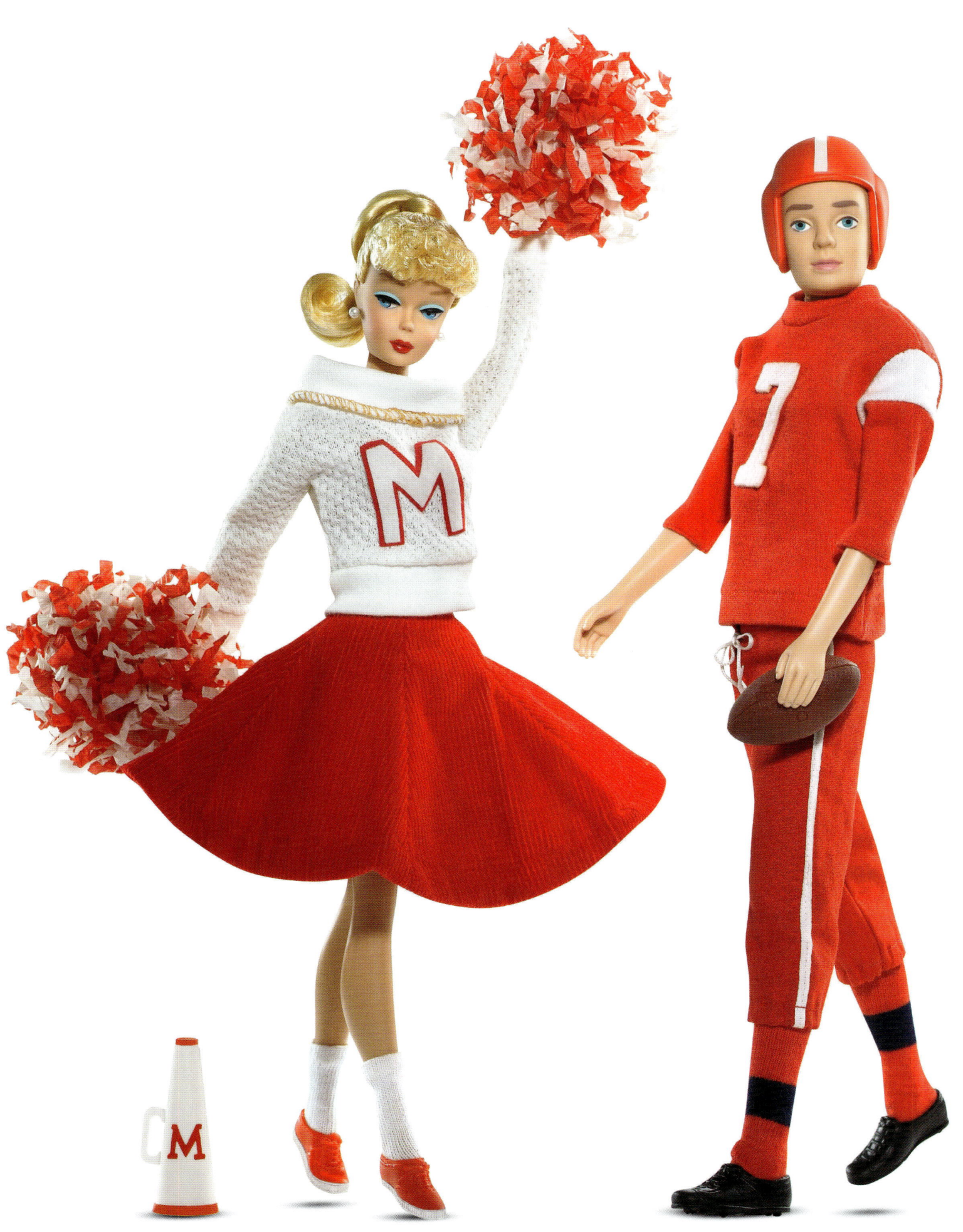

Ken as football player with Barbie as cheerleader, 1963.

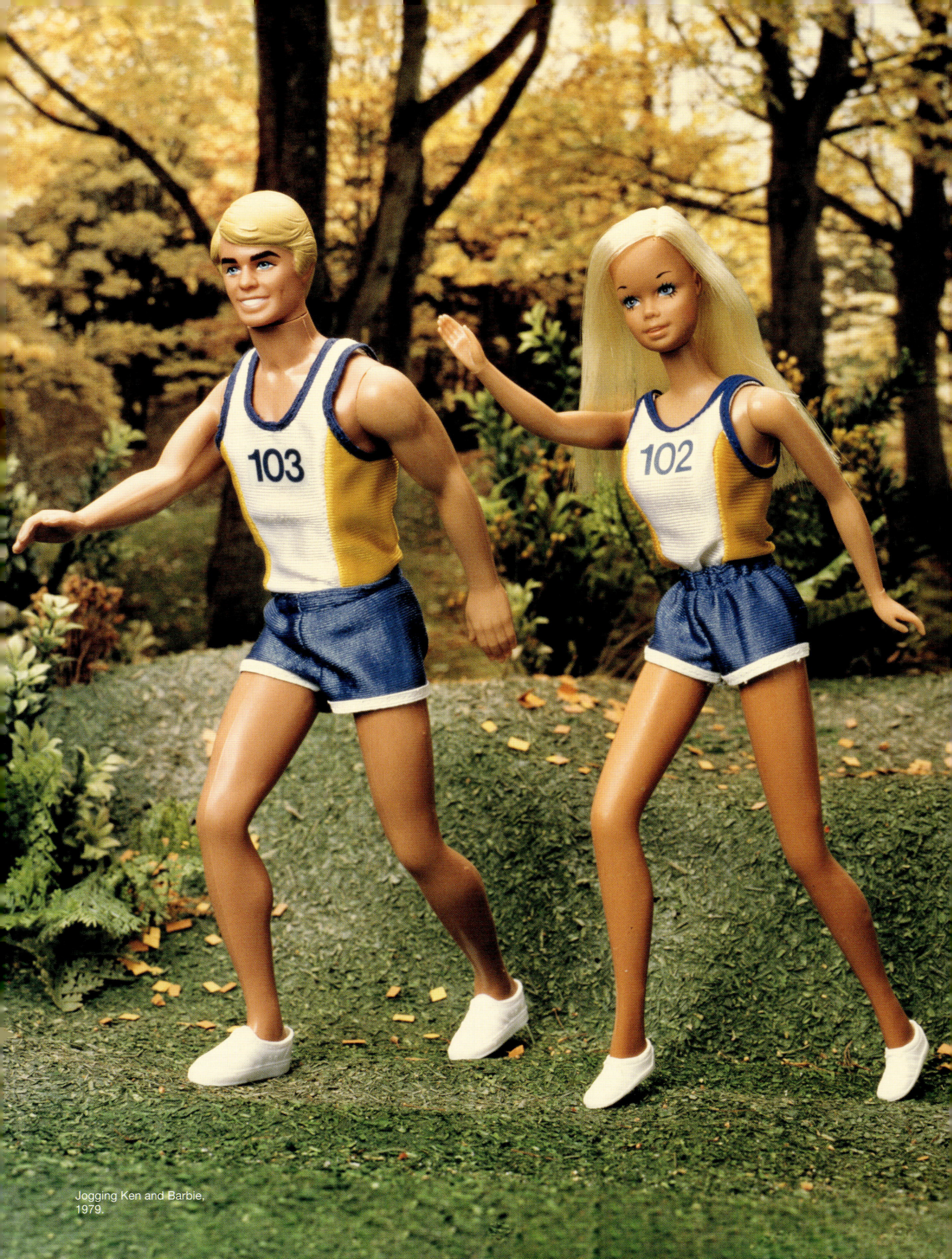
Jogging Ken and Barbie, 1979.

1979 Jogger/Runner

1980
Cowboy
Dancer
Roller Skater

1981 Bodybuilder

1982 Companion

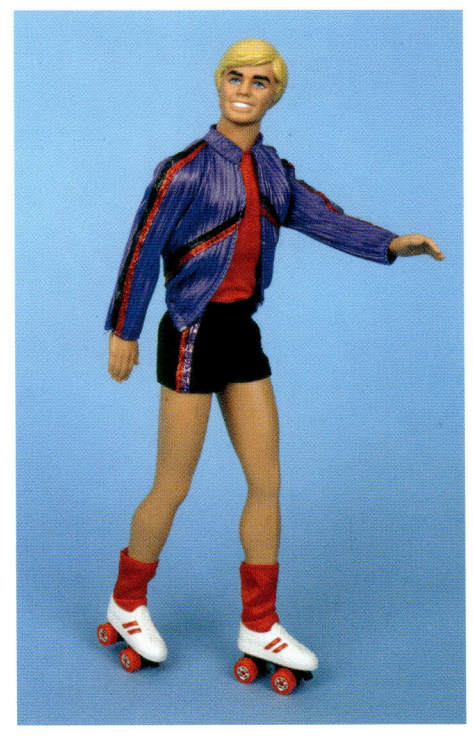

1986 Birthday Boy

1983 GYMNAST

1987 Cameraman *(playset)*

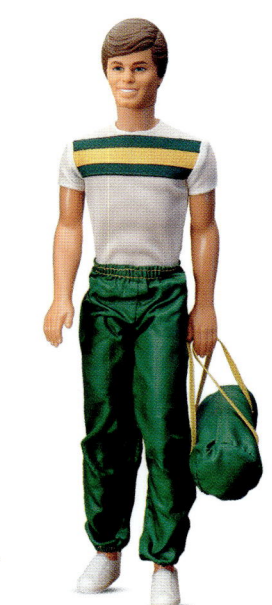

1988
OLYMPIC ATHLETE
(exclusive for Venezuela)
PIZZA DELIVERY GUY

1989 BASEBALL PLAYER *(clothing pack)*

1994 Bodyguard

1995 BANKER *(playset)*

1991
Hairdresser
Rollerblade Skater

1992
BUSINESSMAN
COACH *(clothing pack)*
RAPPER

1996 STARFLEET COMMANDER

165

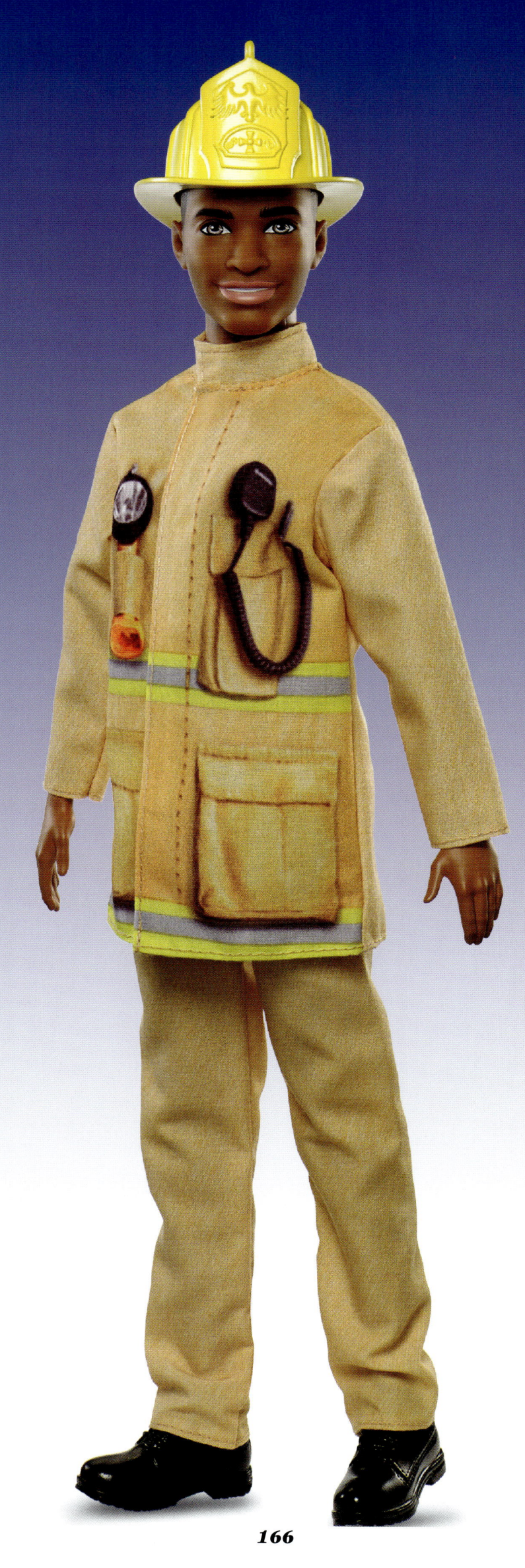

Ken as a firefighter, 2018.

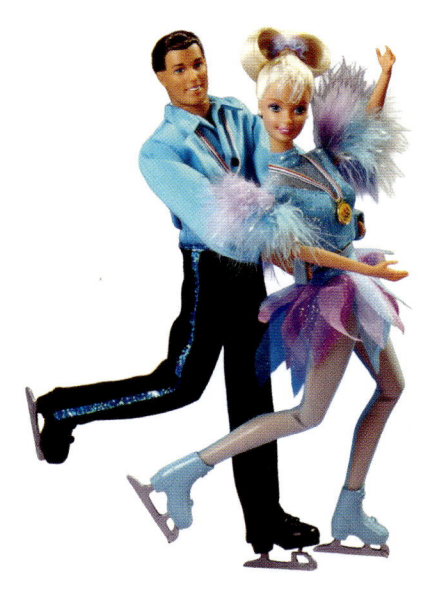

1997
Olympic Figure Skater

1998 *Motorcyclist*

1999
**STUDENT
COUNTRY SINGER**

2003
Film Director
Model

2010
Fireman

2000 Photographer

2012 SNOWBOARDER

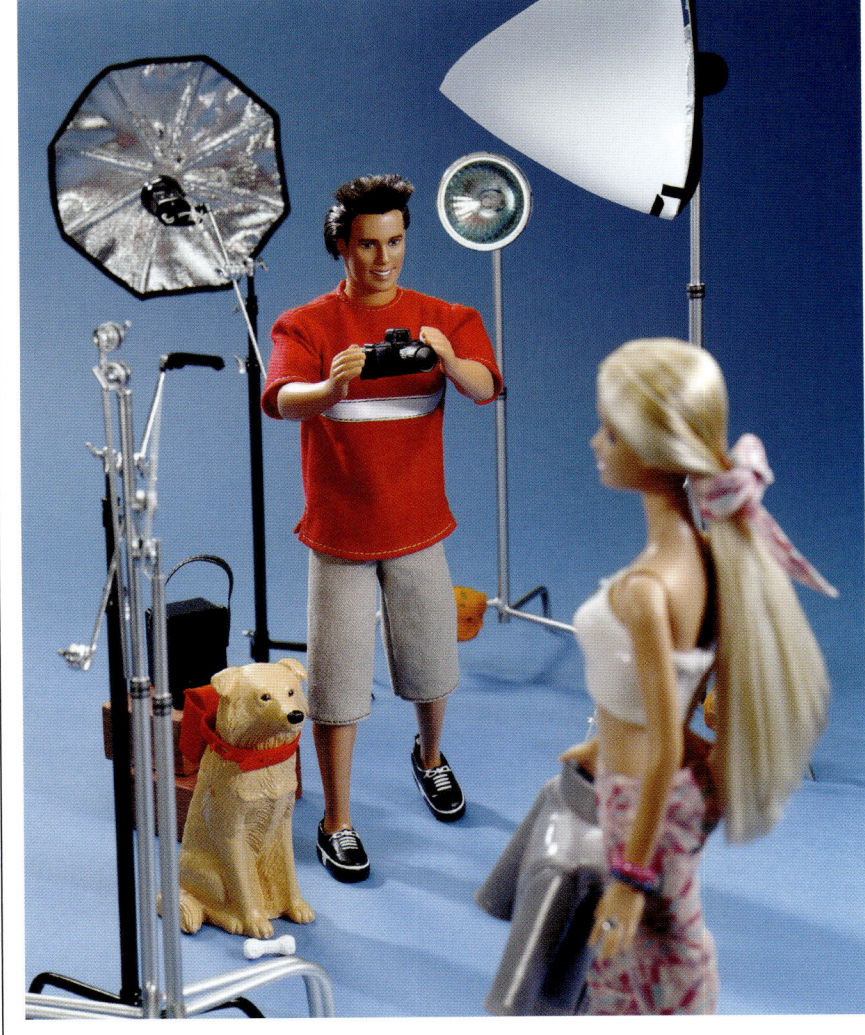

2015 SPY

2019

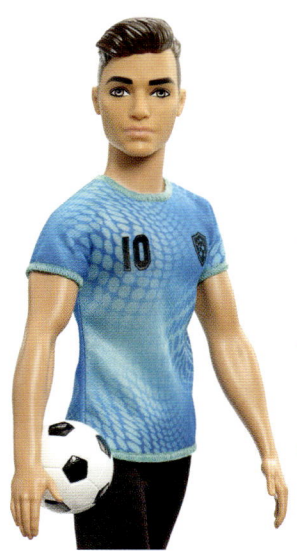

Barista
Farmer
Golfer *(clothing pack)*
Pizza Maker *(clothing pack)*
Referee *(clothing pack)*
Soccer Player

2020

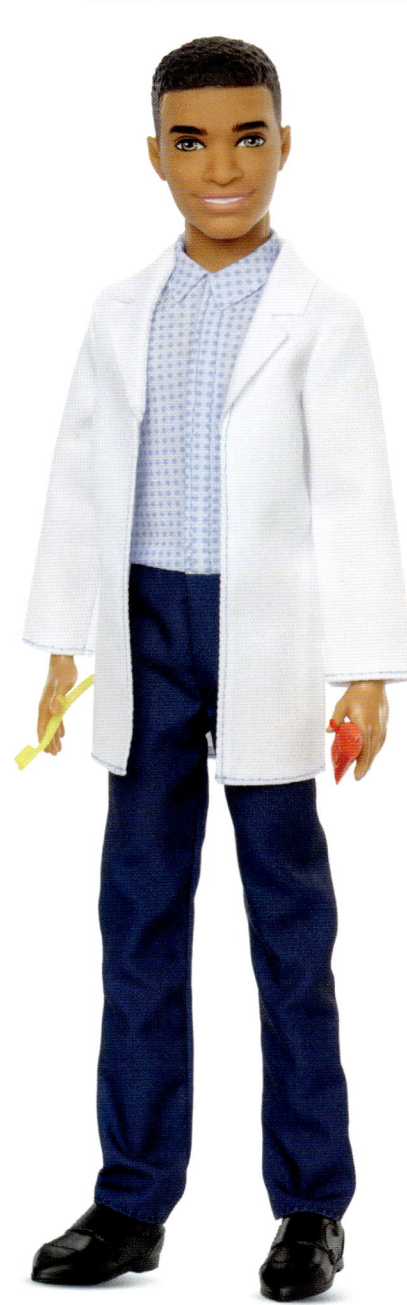

Dentist

Dog Trainer

Hamburger Cook *(clothing pack)*

Saxophonist *(clothing pack)*

Science Teacher *(clothing pack)*

Wildlife Veterinarian

2021 Nurse

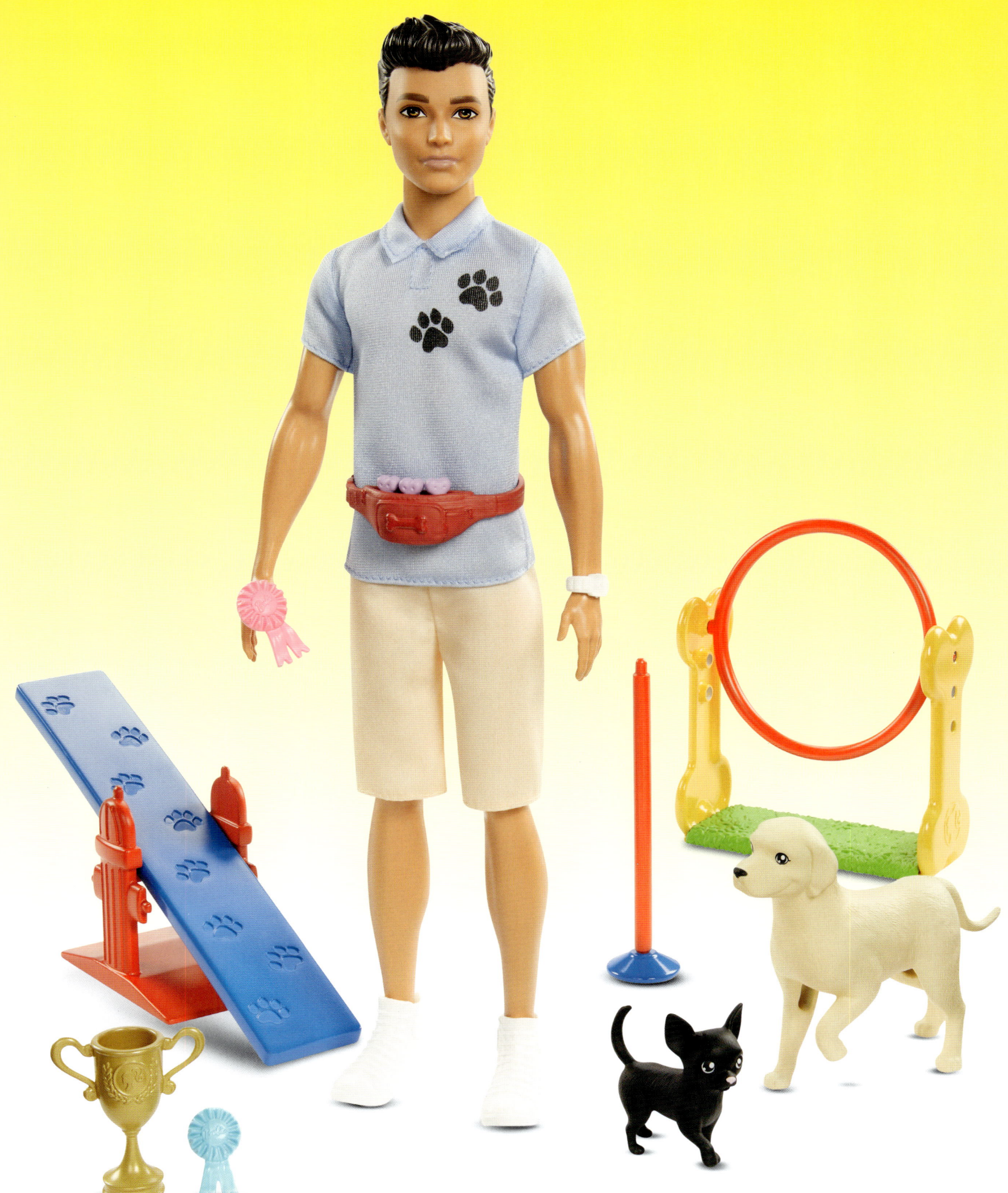

Ken as Dog Trainer, 2020.

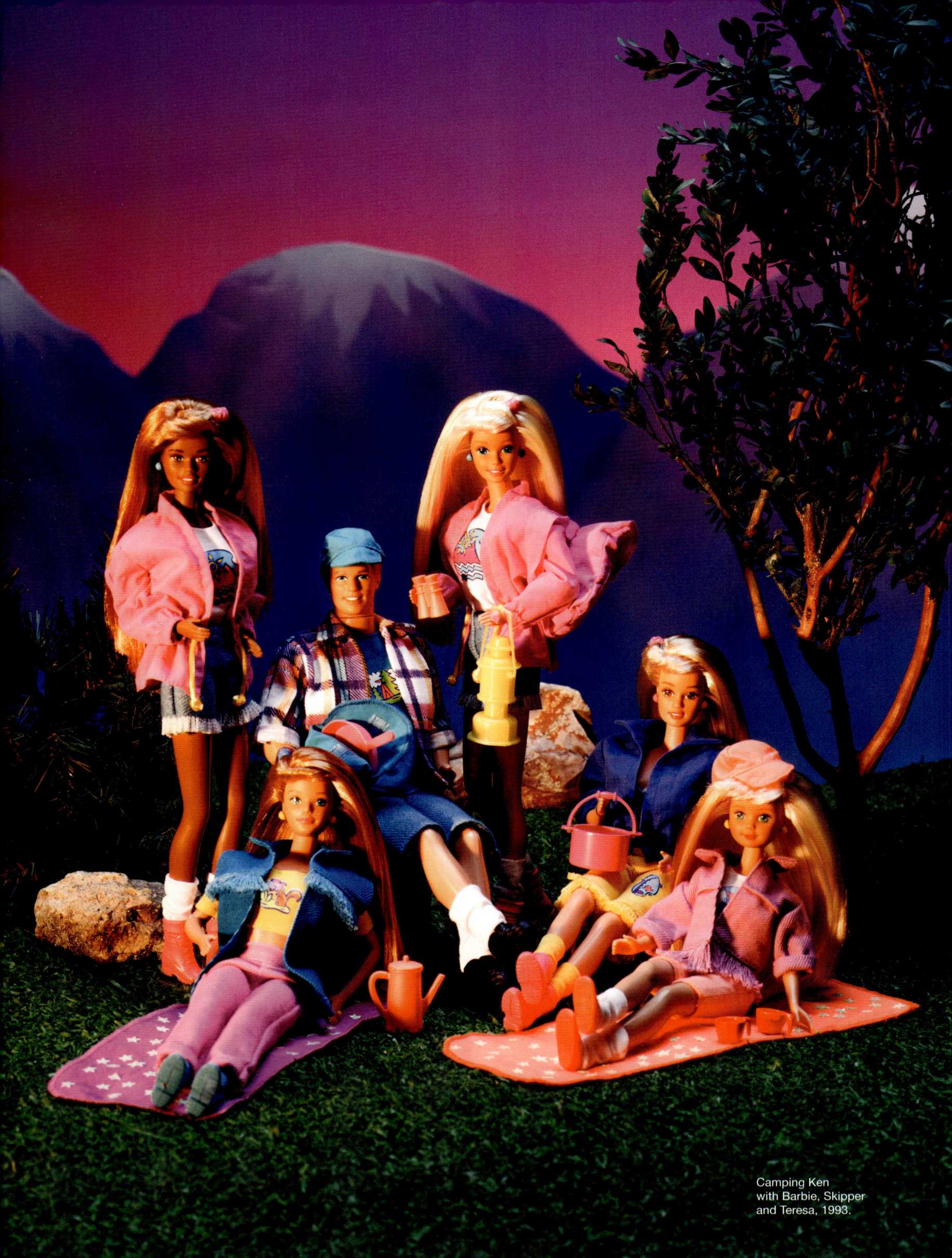

Camping Ken with Barbie, Skipper and Teresa, 1993.

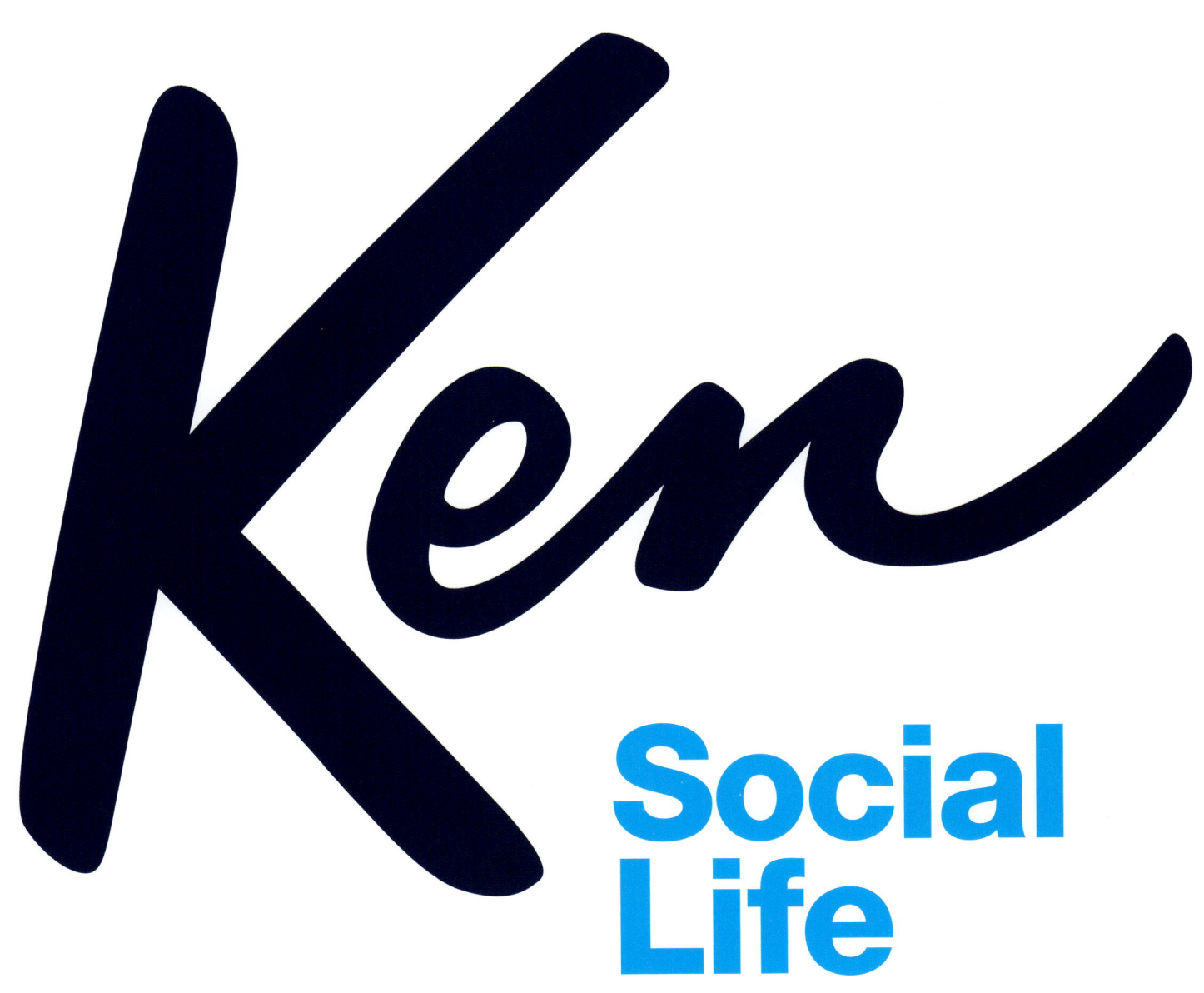

After his first appearance, **Ken's** personality and many details of his background were revealed, through books published by Random House in the early 1960s. From those books, we learn that his father is a lawyer and that his surname, **Carson**, directly references the Carson/Roberts advertising agency, which collaborated with Mattel on Barbie brand's first promotional campaigns. Barbie, likewise, was given a surname—Roberts (Barbie Millicent Roberts).

Very little is known about Ken's family tree: his parents are Edna and Kenneth Carson. His grandparents and his sister, Izzy Carson, appear briefly between the late 1980s and early 1990s, though the only consistent family presence in Ken's life has been his younger brother, **Tommy**—who, over time, becomes close to Barbie's younger sister, **Kelly** (later **Chelsea**).

Ken's family, therefore, consists primarily of his friends—starting, of course, with Barbie. As early as 1963 we meet Midge, Barbie's best friend; the following year, in 1964, **Allan** appears. In fact, the new friends emerge as foils and complements to Ken and Barbie. Together, during the 1960s, they share clothing, shoes, and accessories.

Allan Sherwood, whose name comes from Allan Segal, husband of Barbara Handler (who married at just nineteen), is undoubtedly Ken's true best friend, introduced by Mattel in the same year **Skipper**, **Barbie's** sister, also makes her first appearance. Allan remains a legendary figure—appearing and reappearing over more than sixty years of history—and is Ken's only friend with a last name.

When Allan first appeared, he wore, like Ken, a beach outfit consisting of blue shorts, a multicolor striped shirt, and blue sandals. Since his physical proportions were identical to Ken's, Allan always shared Ken's wardrobe, and as a result, no clothing was ever made exclusively for him. He reappeared in 1991 under the name "Alan," and again in December 2002 in the Mattel **Happy Family** line—an offshoot from the main Barbie line that focused on Alan and Midge's family. His true comeback occurred in the realm of fashion, when he became a "fashionisto" in his own right. In Greta Gerwig's film *Barbie* (2023), Allan, played by Michael Cera, is Ken's eccentric friend, but one who stands out for his distinctly contemporary outfits: a multicolor button-up shirt, shorts, and sandals—a perfect mix that looks like it came straight off the runways of Gucci or Prada.

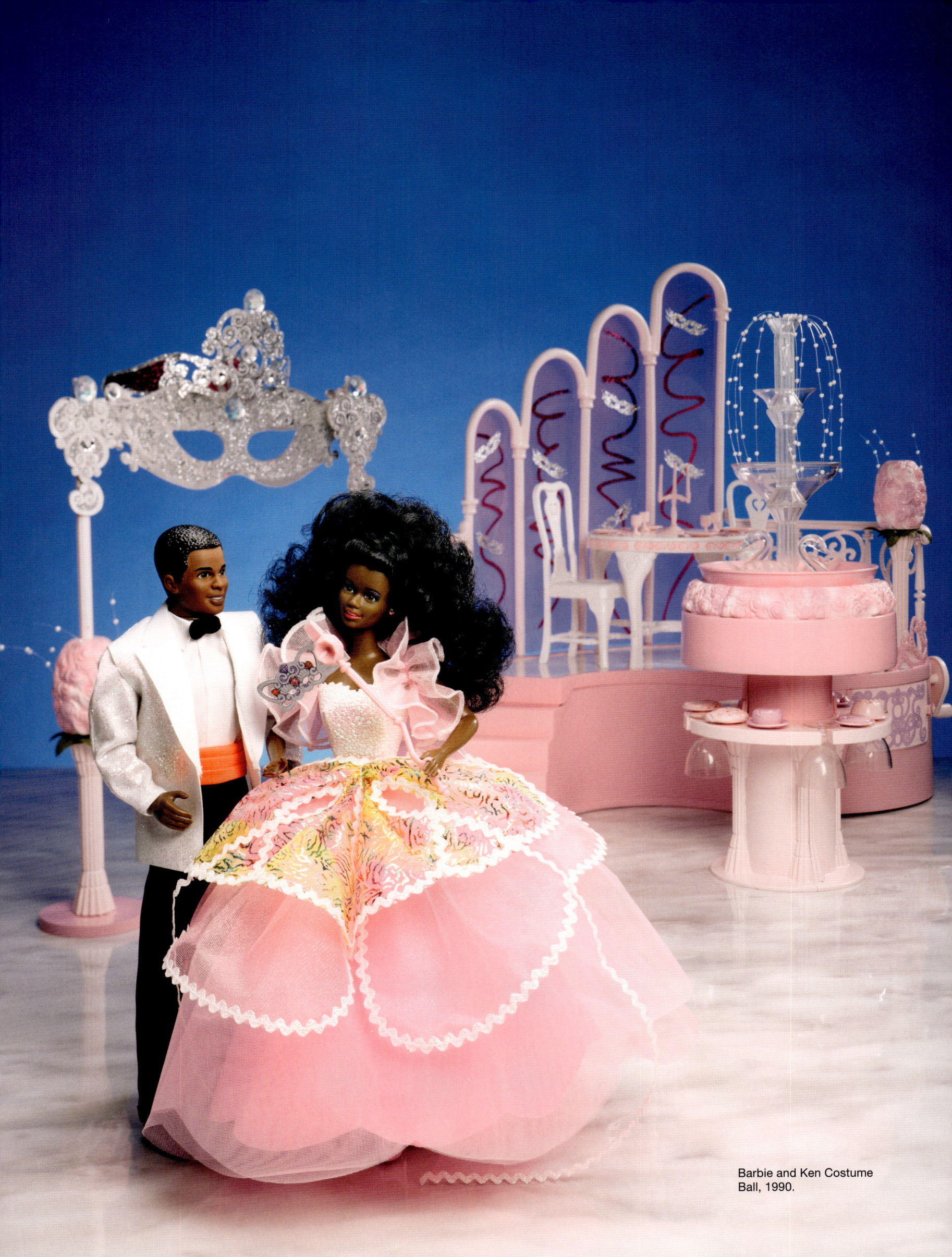

Barbie and Ken Costume Ball, 1990.

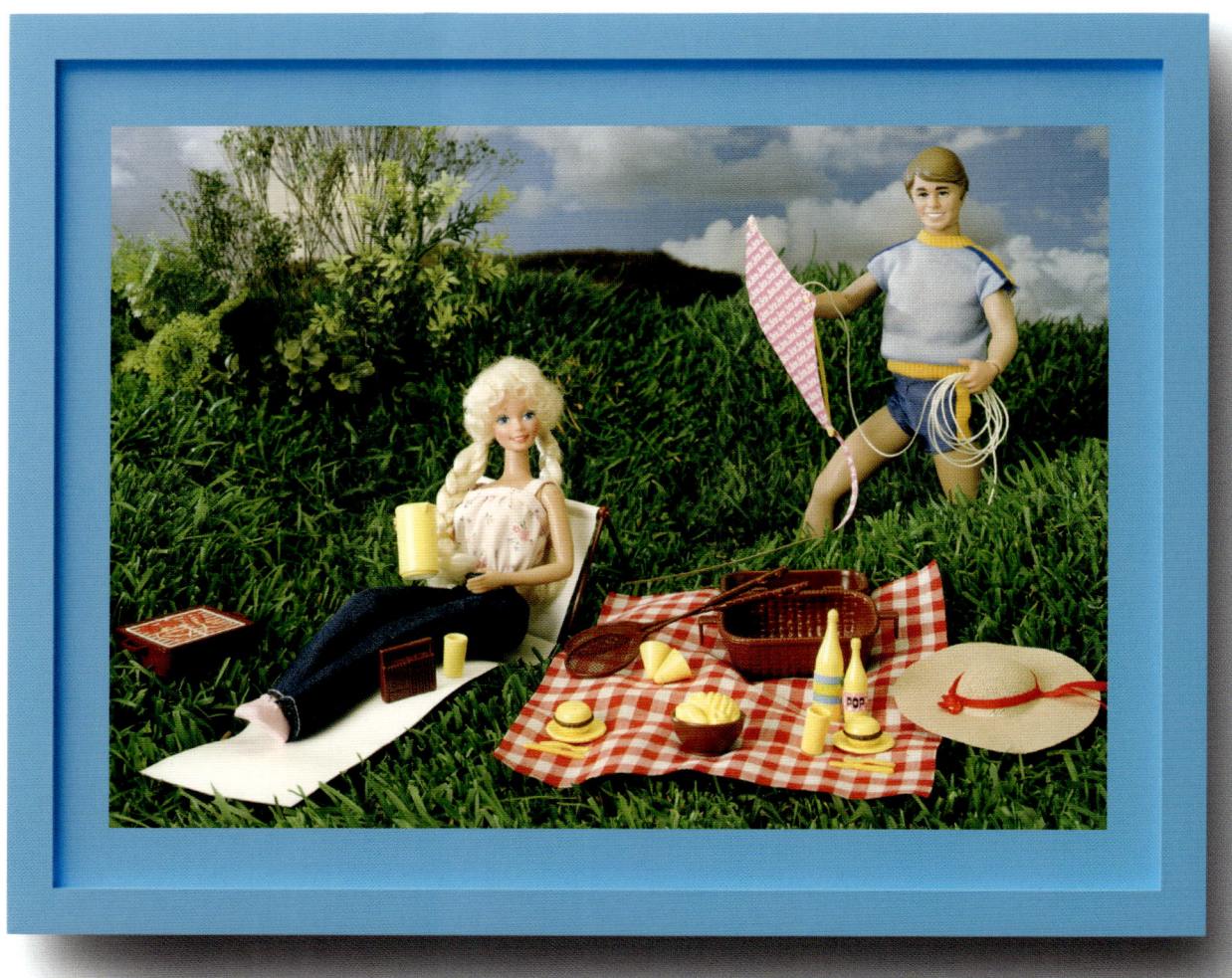

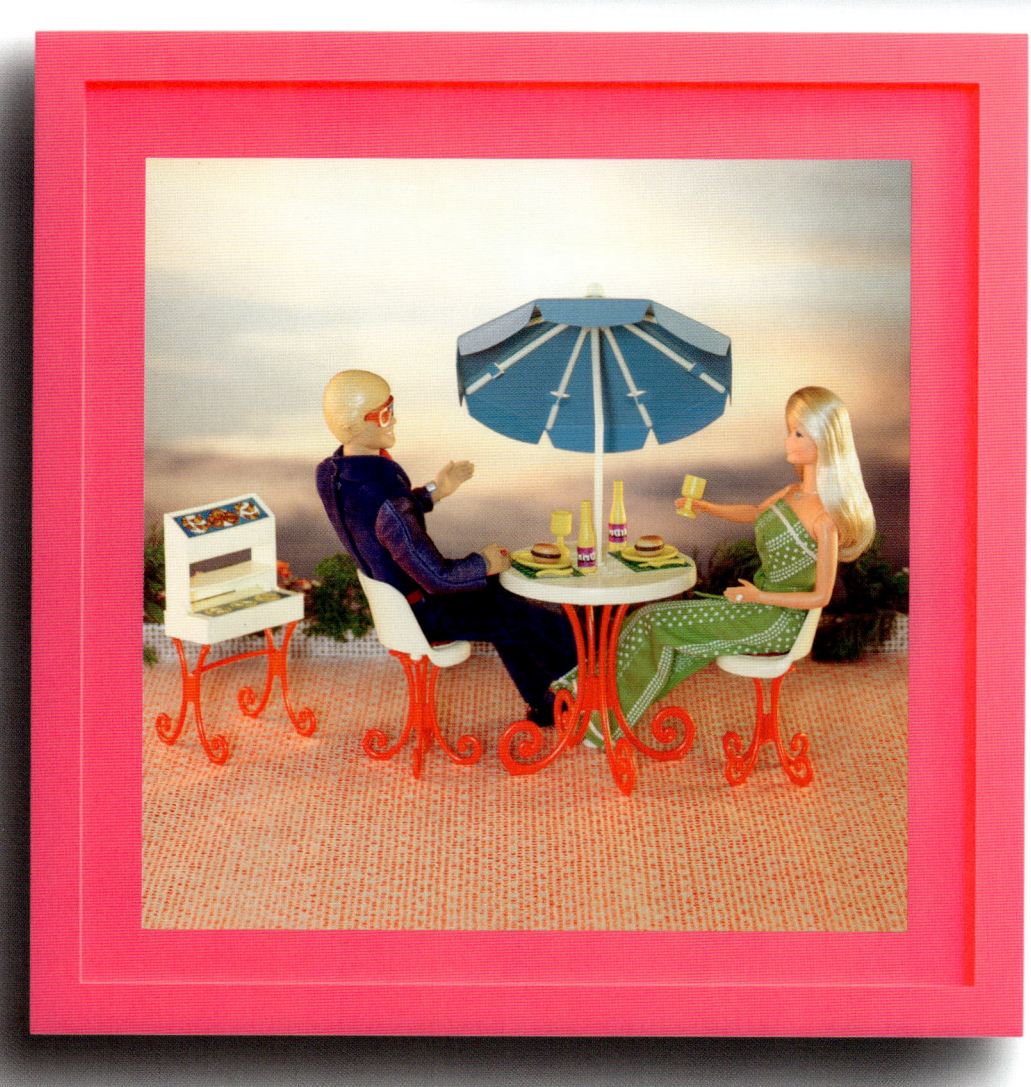

Above:
Ken and Barbie Play
Paks Picnic set, 1982.

Left:
Ken and Barbie
Garden Party, 1982.

Opposite:
The Waltz Barbie
and Ken gift set, 2003.

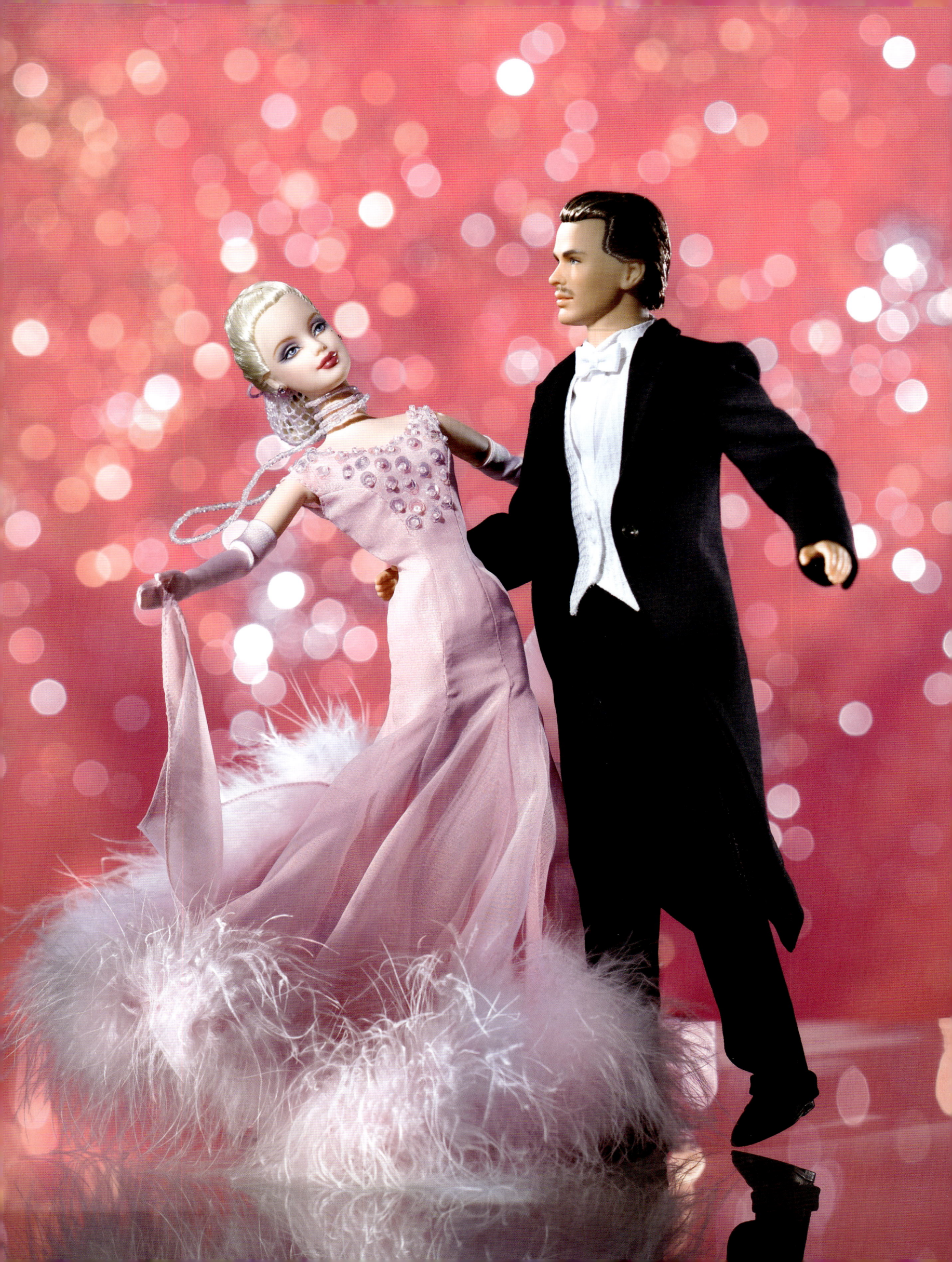

Ken's friends

The colorful world of Ken and Barbie is the result of countless chance meetings, adventures, and travels set against a backdrop of period-appropriate houses, cars, airplanes, shops, and design objects. Some of the major players in Ken's ever-expanding world are:

Skipper, Barbie's sister (1964)
Christie (1968)
Teresa (1968)
Brad (1969)
Curtis (1974)
Cara (1975)
Derek (1985)
Steven (1987)
Stacie, Barbie's sister (1992)
Kelly/Chelsea, Barbie's sister (1995/2011)
Nikki (2006)
Grace (2009)

In Ken and Barbie's world, there's also room for pets: he's had just one horse and a dog, while she's had seven horses and five dogs, along with three ponies and two cats.

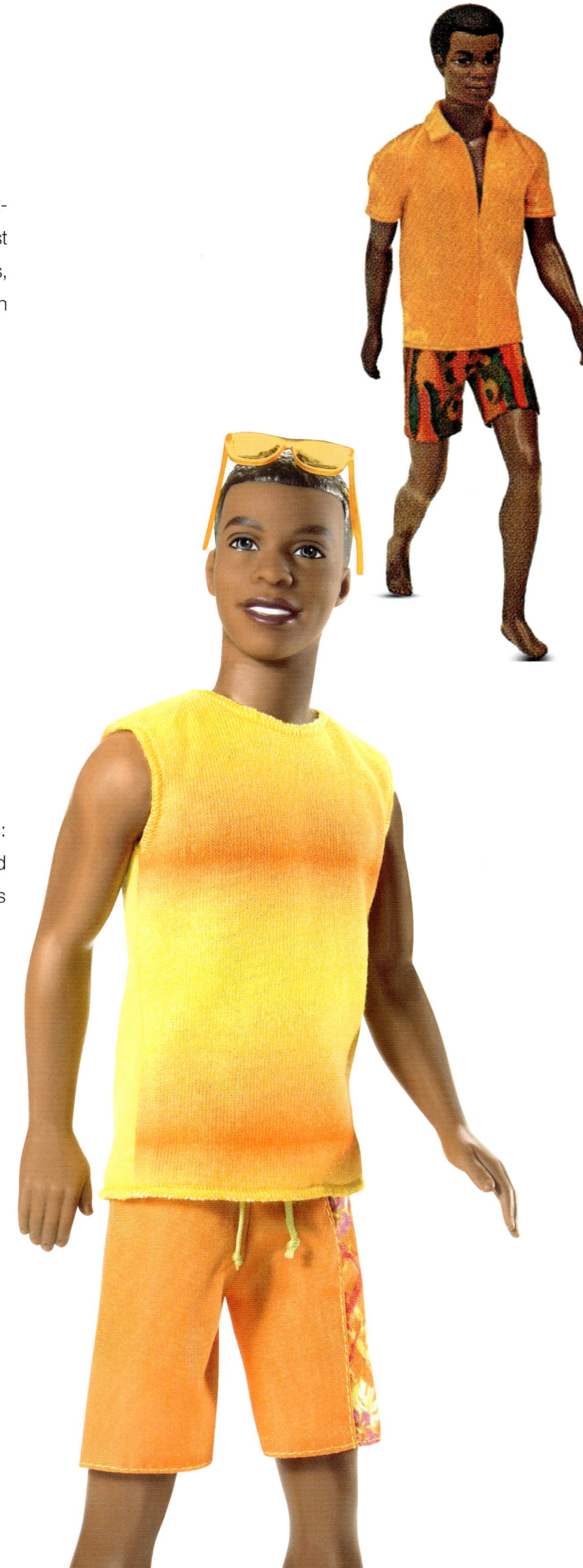

Ken's friends, Brad (1969), Steven (2008) and, opposite, Allan (1964).

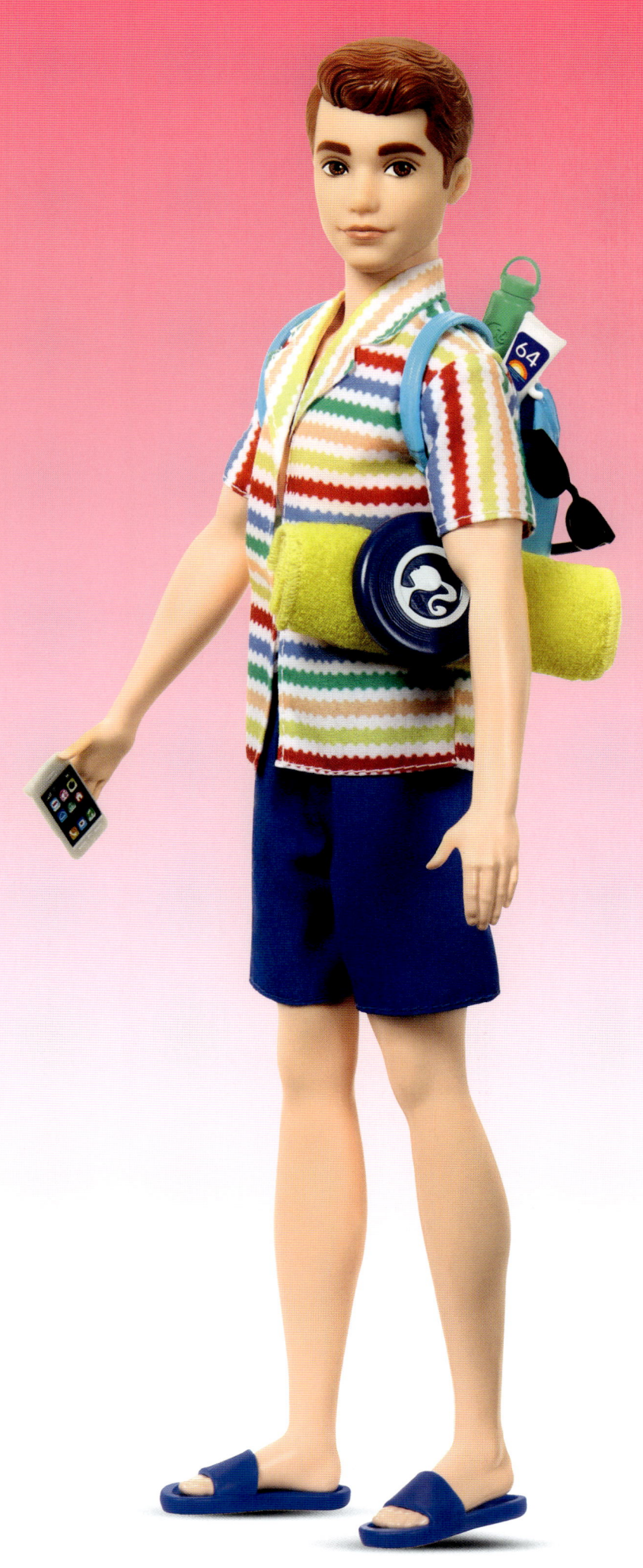

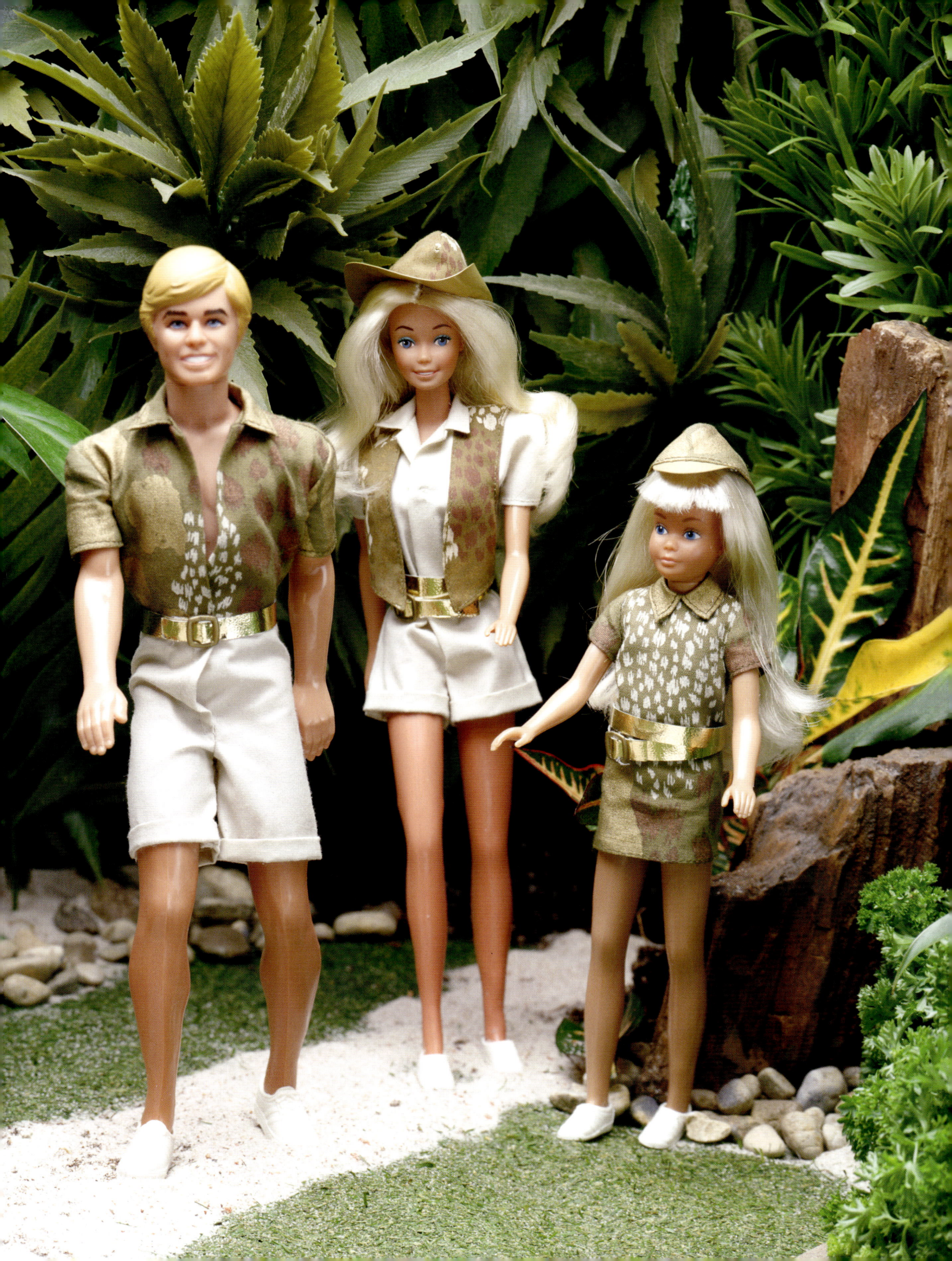

Lifestyle

After the DreamHouse of 1962, Barbie's city life changes as she moves to a smaller town and into the Town House (1974), complete with elevator. Ken is right by her side: the two travel in the Country Camper (1971) and the Beach Bus (1974), and aboard the iconic catamaran (1976) and the Speed Boat (1990).

For her travels, Barbie also has a plane (1990). Her passion for cars has put her behind the wheel of the legendary Star 'Vette (1977) and also a Ferrari (1989), Porsche (1992), Lamborghini (1993), Fiat 500 (2009), and of course the classic Volkswagen Beetle (1978).

Ken, on the other hand, gets his own car in 1984, the Dream'Vette, followed in 2012 by a red Mini Cooper with a personalized license plate that reads "Ken."

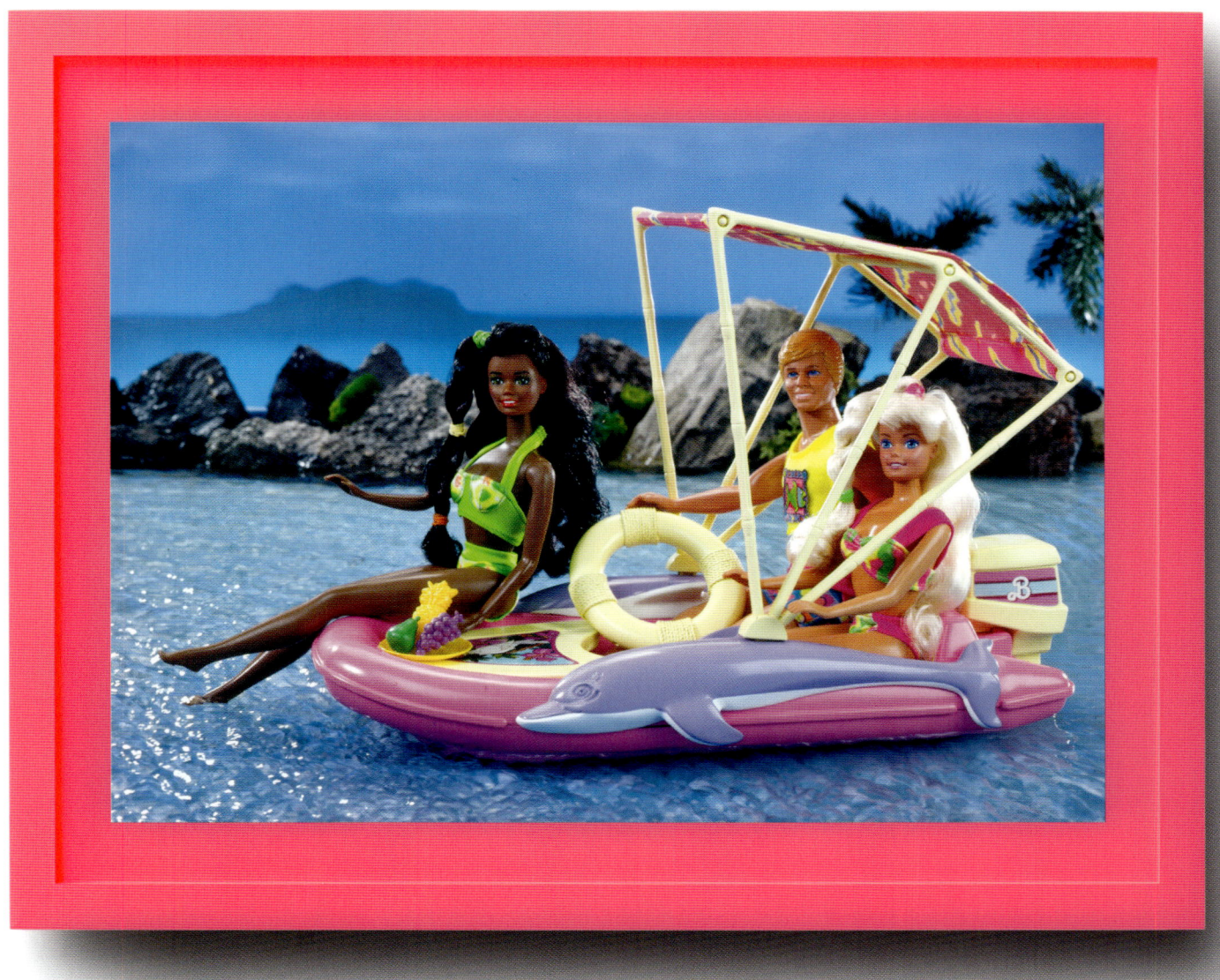

Opposite:
Ken on safari with Barbie and Tutti, 1983.

Above:
Ken with Barbie and Christie on the
Hawaiian Fun Island Hopper Boat, 1990.

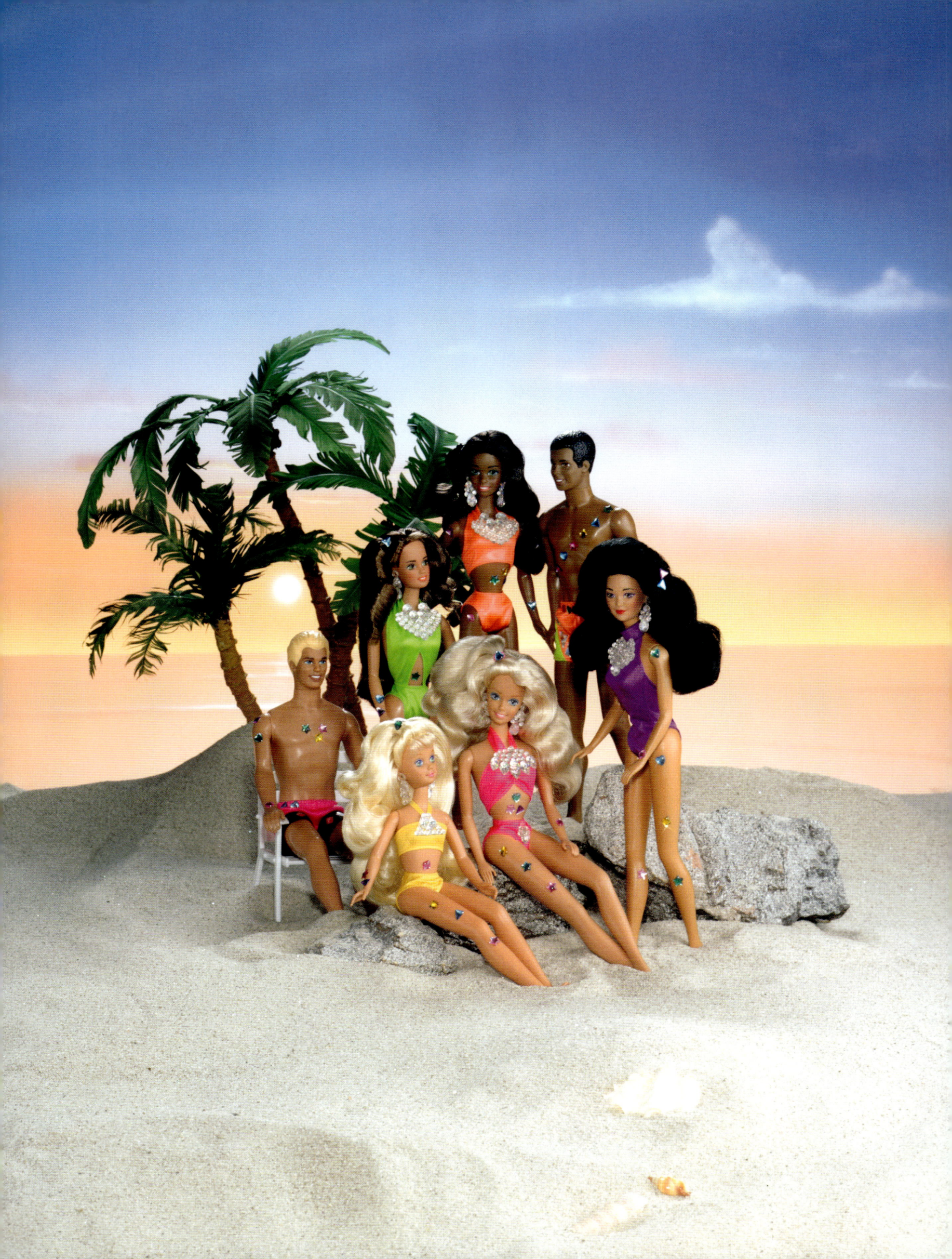

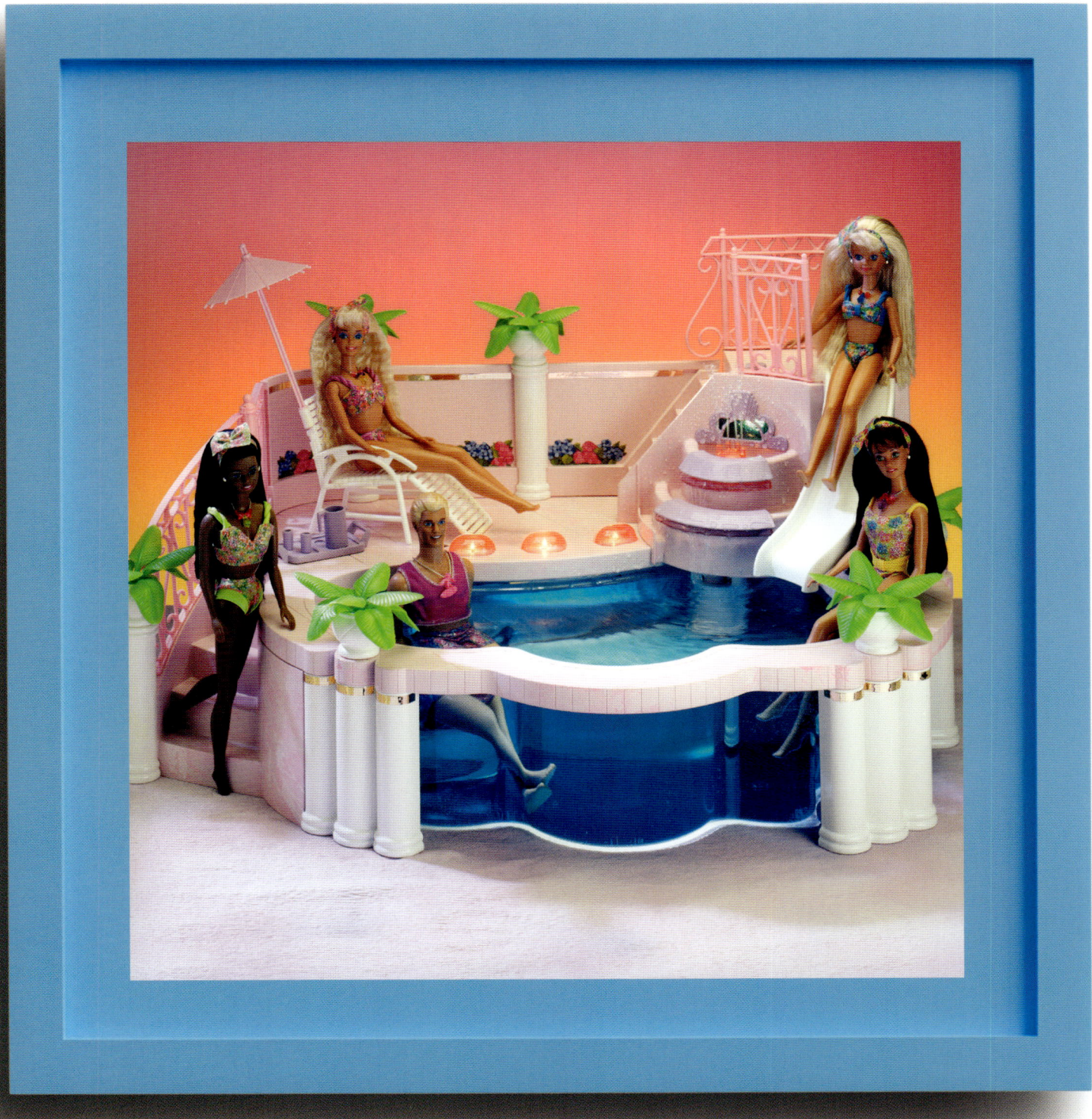

Opposite:
Sun Jewel Barbie, Ken, Kira, Teresa, Steven, Christie, and Skipper, 1993.

Above:
Ken together with Barbie and her friends in the Fountain Pool, 1993.

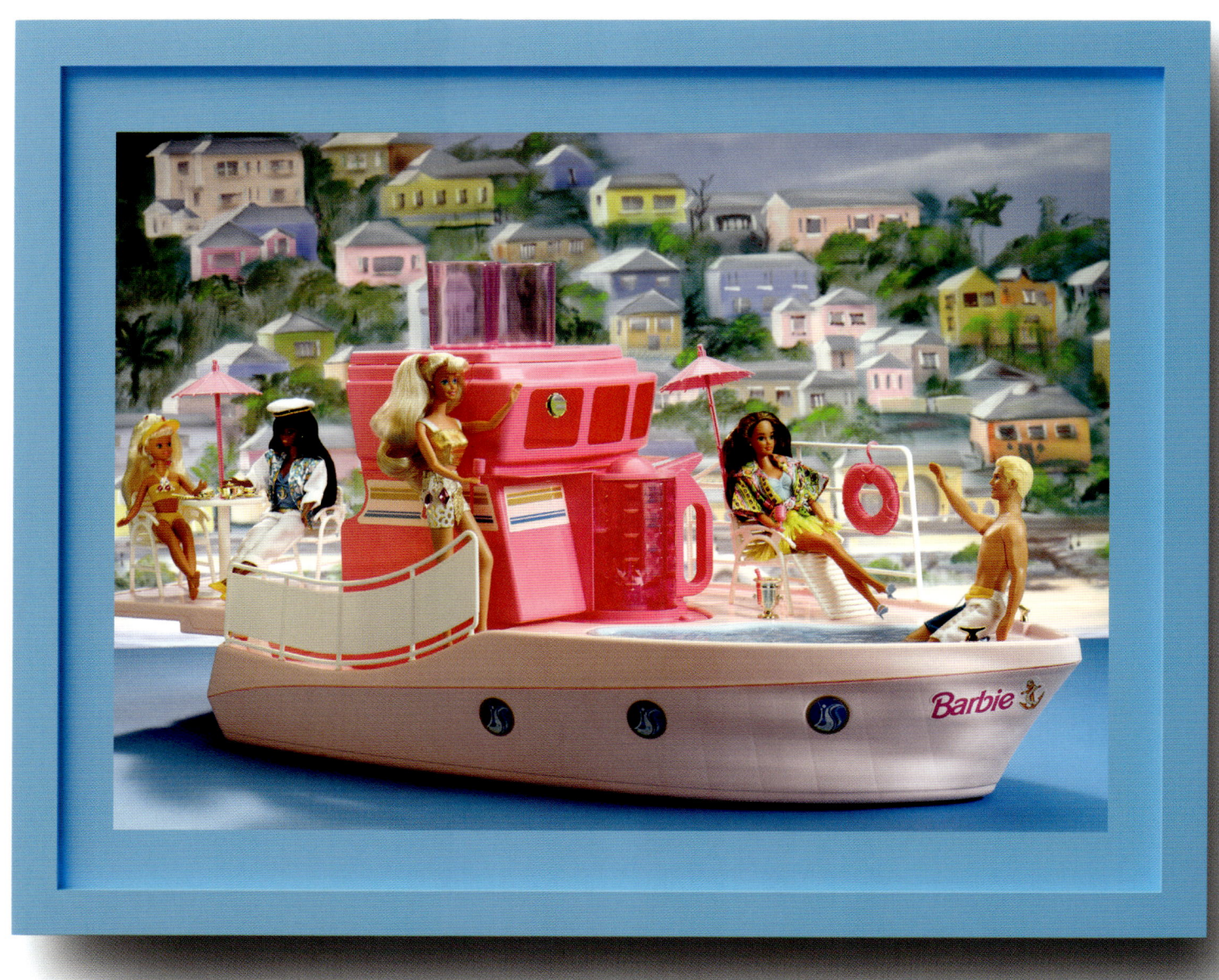

Above:
Ken, Barbie, and friends on the Dream Boat, 1994.

Opposite:
So Much To Do Picnic Set, 1995.

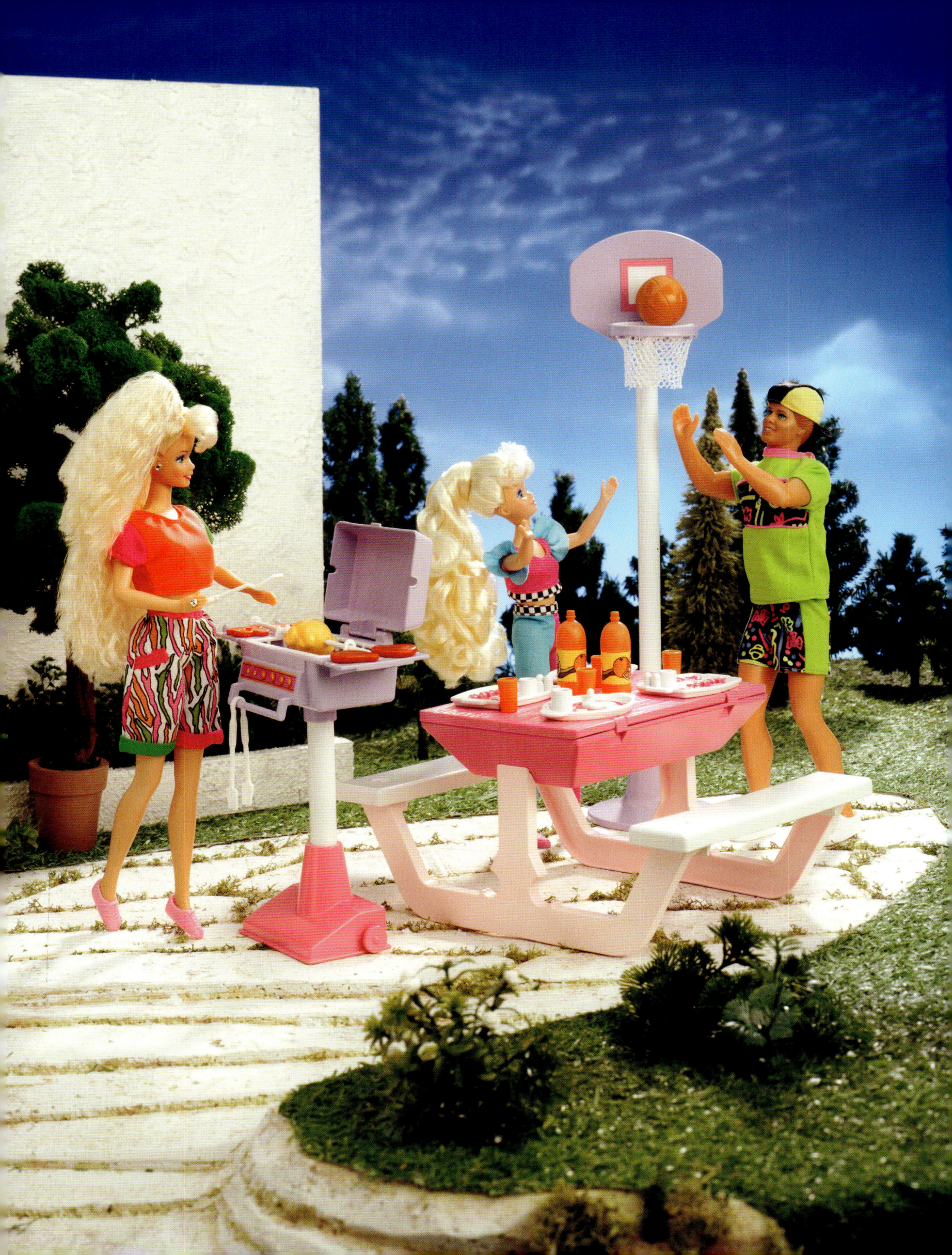

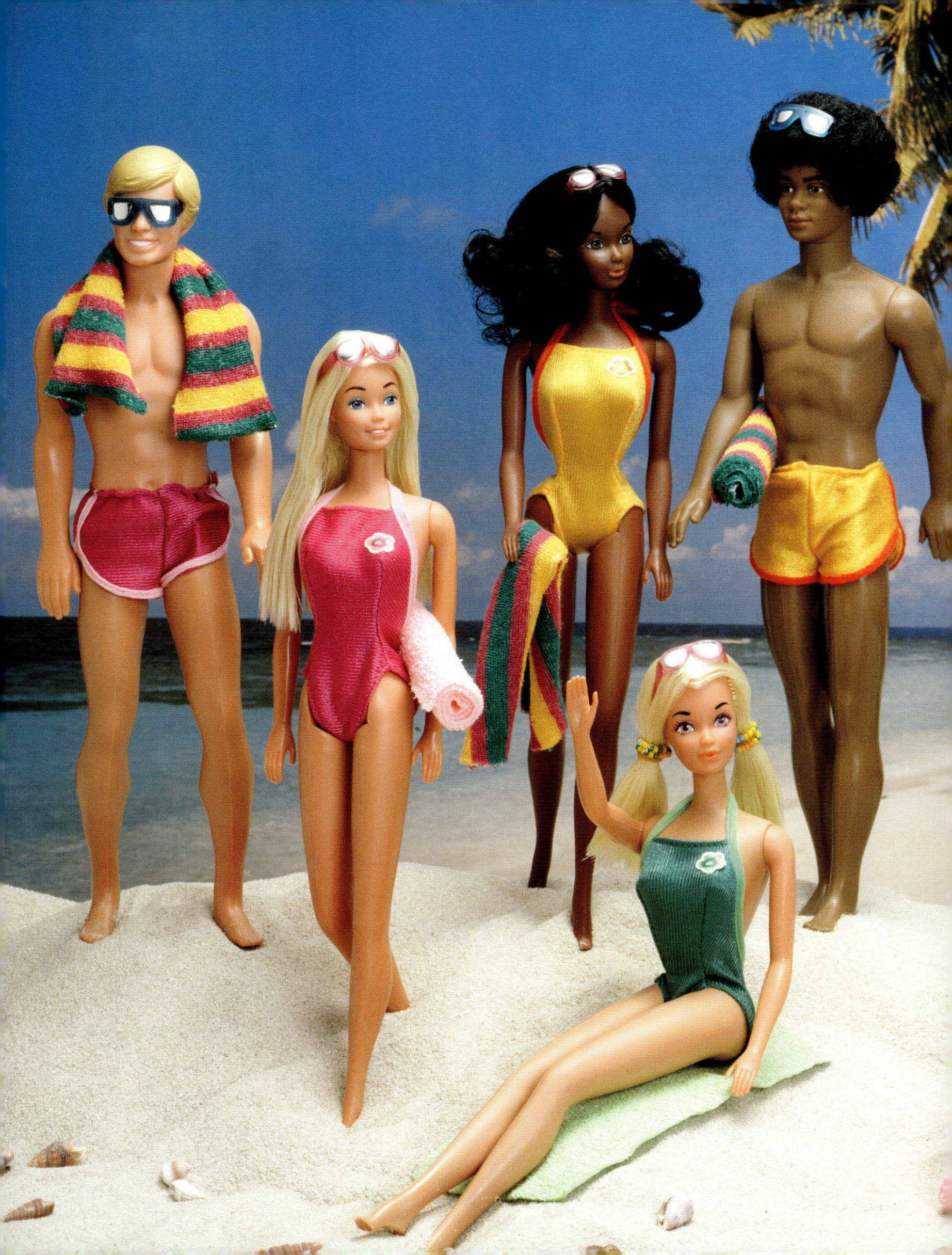

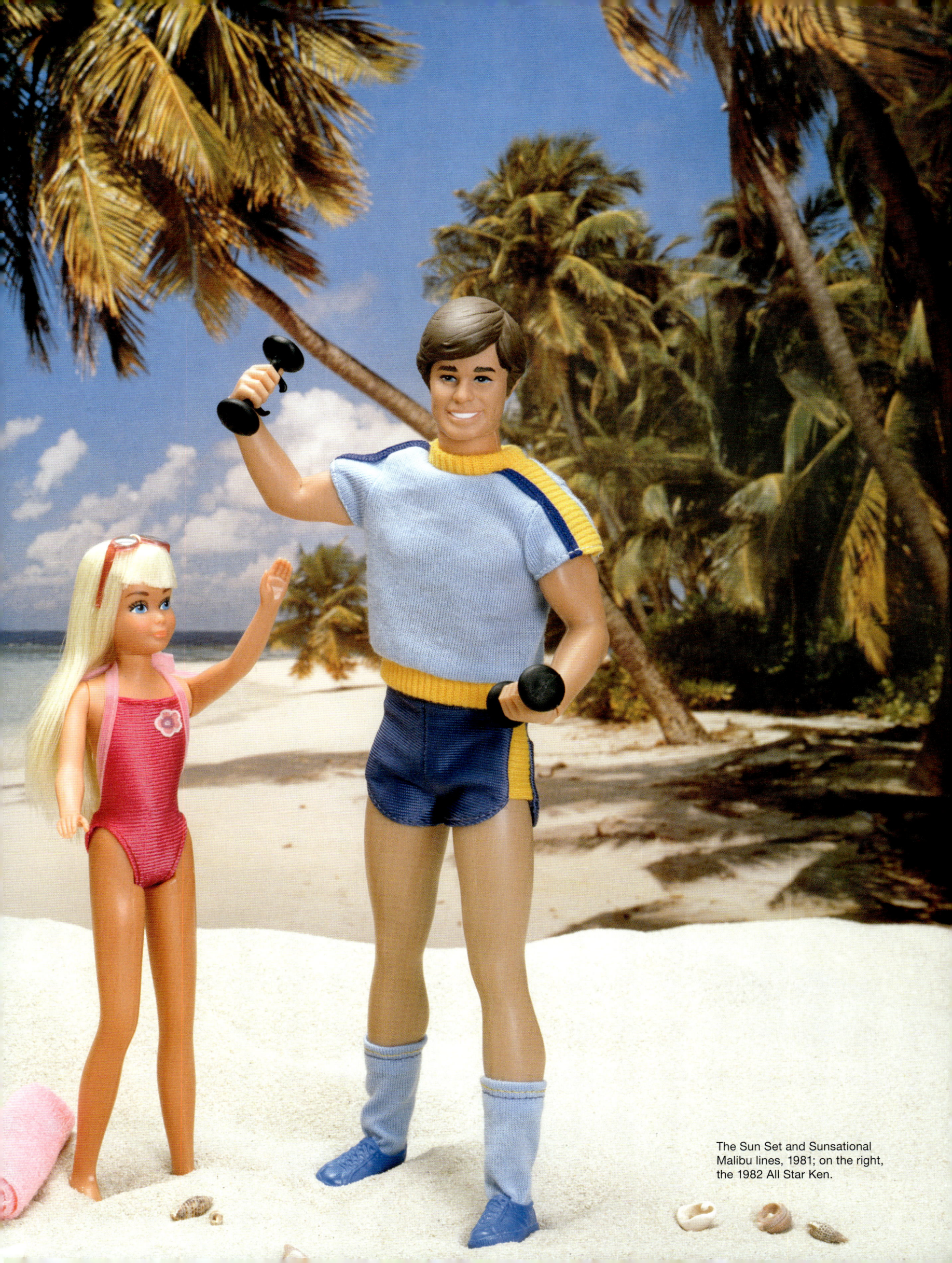

The Sun Set and Sunsational Malibu lines, 1981; on the right, the 1982 All Star Ken.

Ken + Barbie
in sports, fashion, and film

The bond between Ken and Barbie has been commemorated through numerous gift sets, created to celebrate the couple's limitless possibilities—whether in everyday life, sports, fashion, or cinema. On these pages, we showcase some of the most iconic examples.

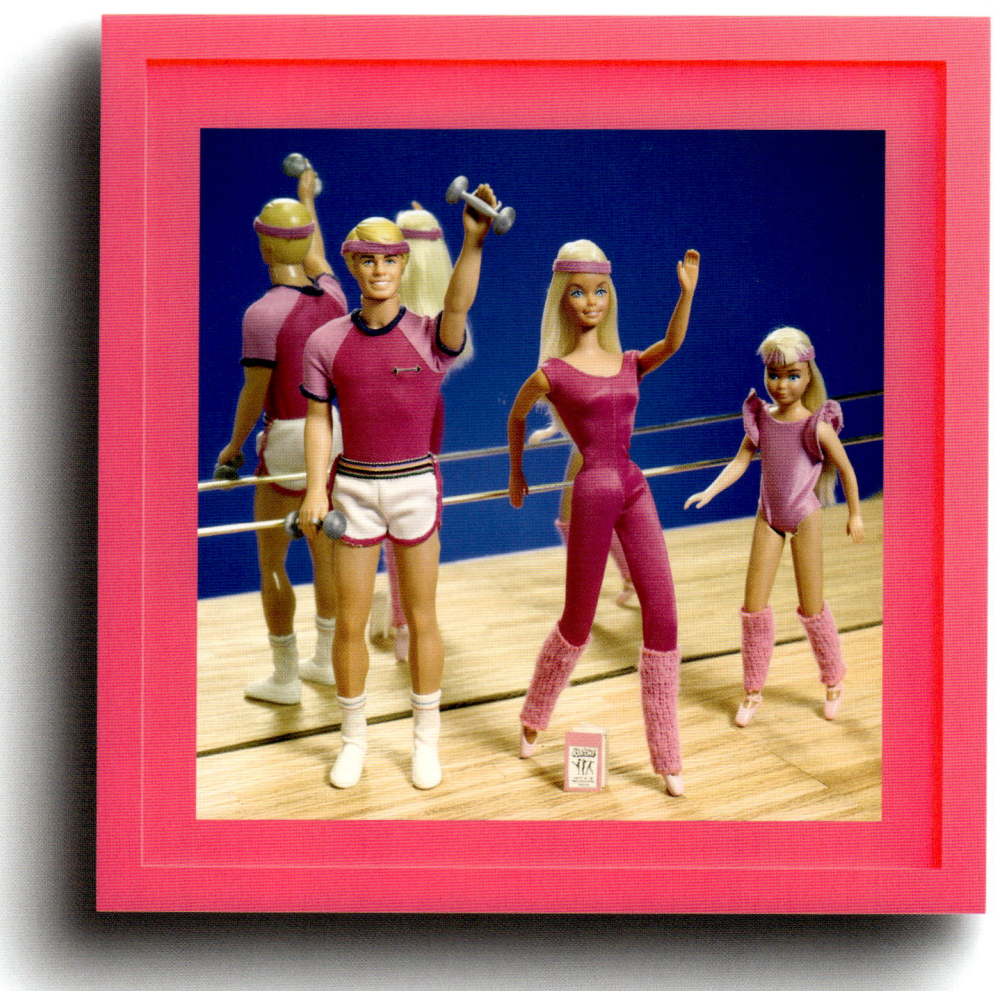

1961
Barbie and Ken Tennis Set
Barbie and Ken Mix n' Match Set

1962
Fashion Queen Barbie
(Barbie, Ken, and Midge)

1963
Fashion Queen Barbie & Ken Trousseau
Barbie, Ken and Midge on Parade
Barbie & Ken Little Theatre Gift Set
Barbie, Ken and Midge Pep Rally Set
Wedding Party (Barbie, Ken, Midge, and Skipper)

1968
Barbie & Ken Fabulous Formal Set

1969
Red, White N' Wild Ken

1972
Barbie et Ken et leurs nouveaux habillages (France)

1978
SuperStar

1982
Barbie & Friends (Barbie, P.J., and Ken)
"They have fun doing things together!"
Great Shape (Barbie, Ken, and Skipper)

186

1983
Campin' Out Set (Barbie and Ken)

1988
Tennis Stars (Barbie and Ken)

1989
Cool City Blues (Barbie, Ken, and Skipper)

1990
Dance Magic (Barbie & Ken)

1991
Barbie & Friends (Barbie, Ken, and Skipper)
"Dressin' up with Mickey, Minnie & Donald!"
Wedding Party Midge (Barbie, Ken, Midge, Alan, Todd, and Kelly)

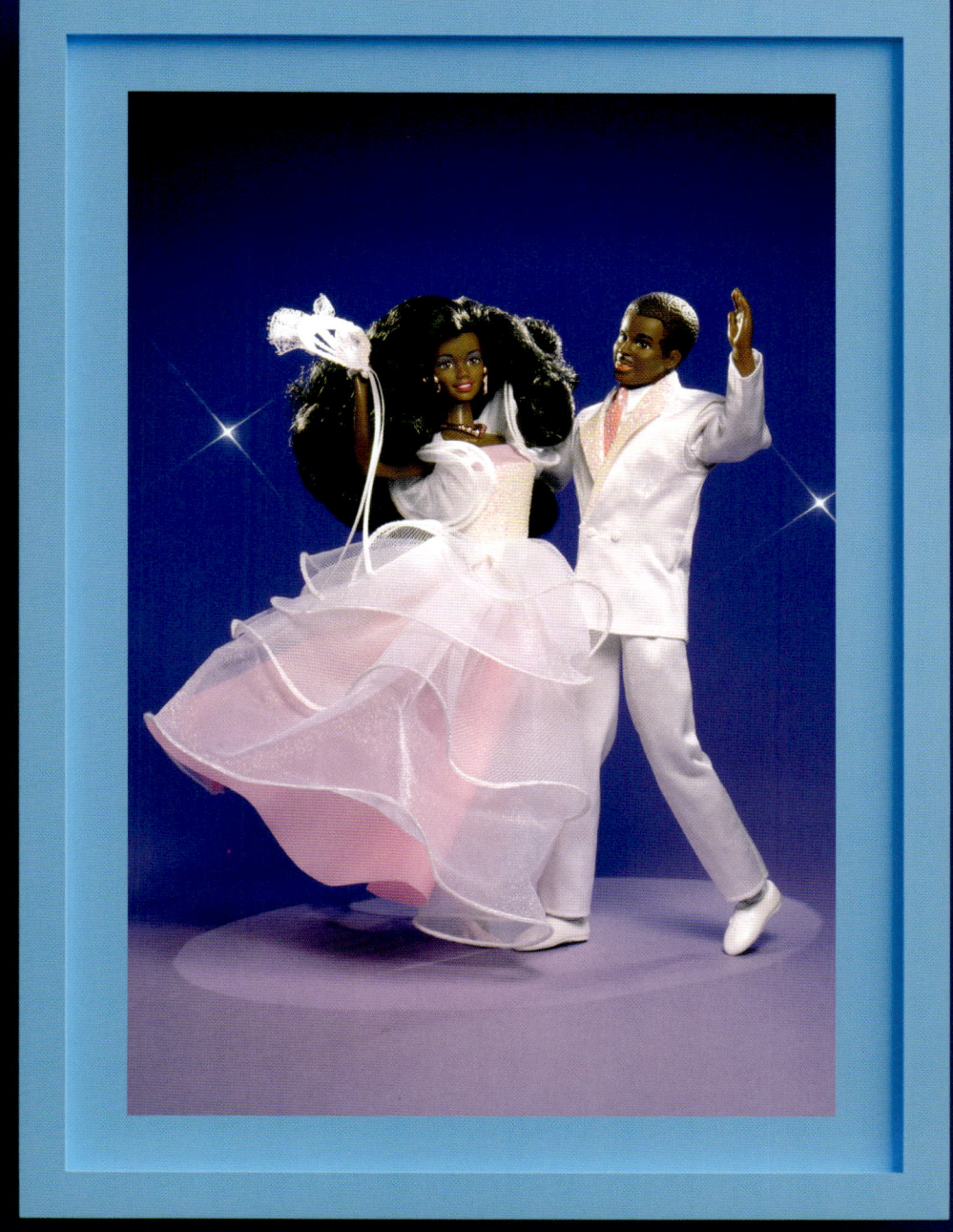

Opposite:
Super Dance gift set, 1982.

Right:
Dance Magic, 1990.

1993

Beach Fun
"Party on the sand in style!"
Disney Weekend Vacation Deluxe
 Island Fun
Secret Hearts
Wedding Fantasy
 "Oh well, for now it's just a dream!"
Stars & Stripes Army (Barbie and Ken)

1996

Star Trek
Wedding Fantasy

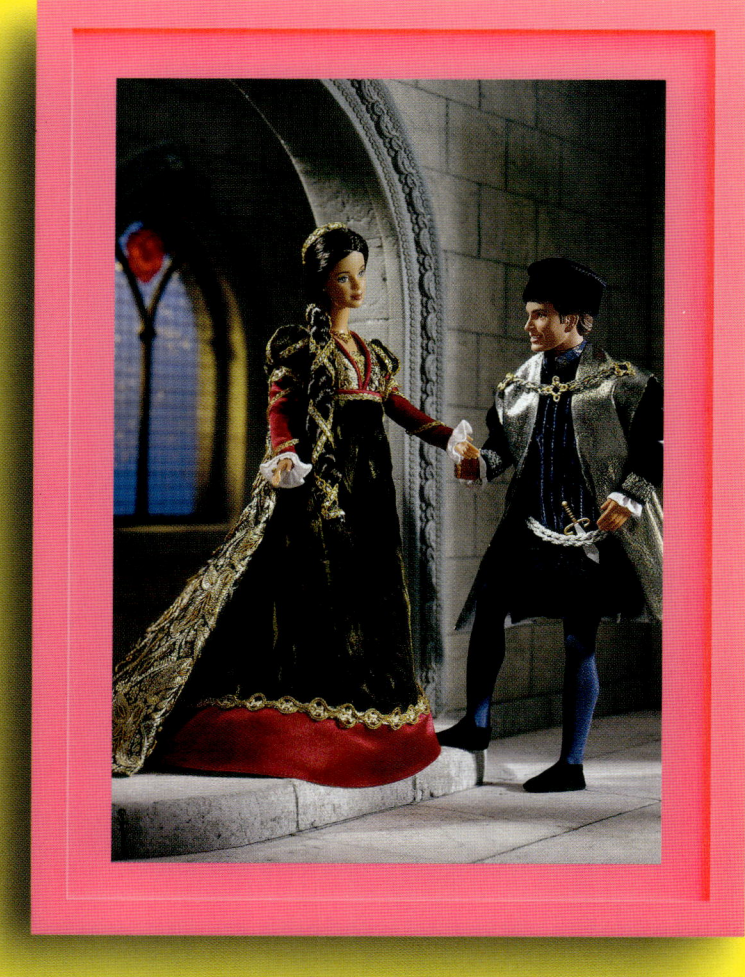

Romeo and Juliet, 1998.
X-Files, 1998.

1997

Halloween Party

1998

Barbie & Kenny Country Duet
Olympic Skater
Phantom of the Opera
Romeo and Juliet
Walt Disney World Resort Vacation
 (Barbie, Ken, Kelly e Tommy)
X-Files

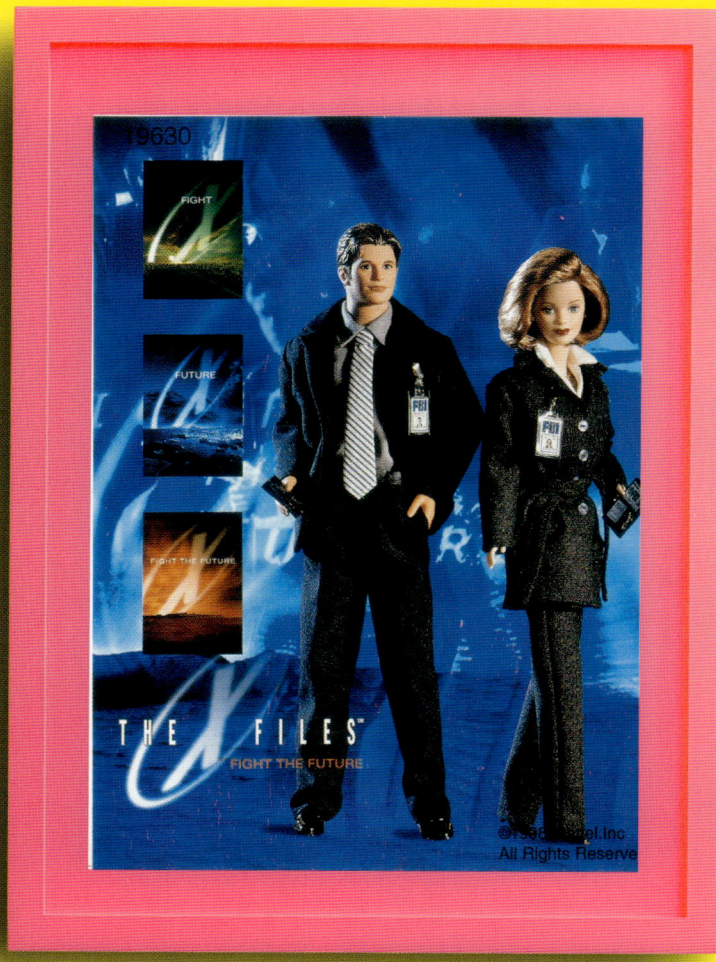

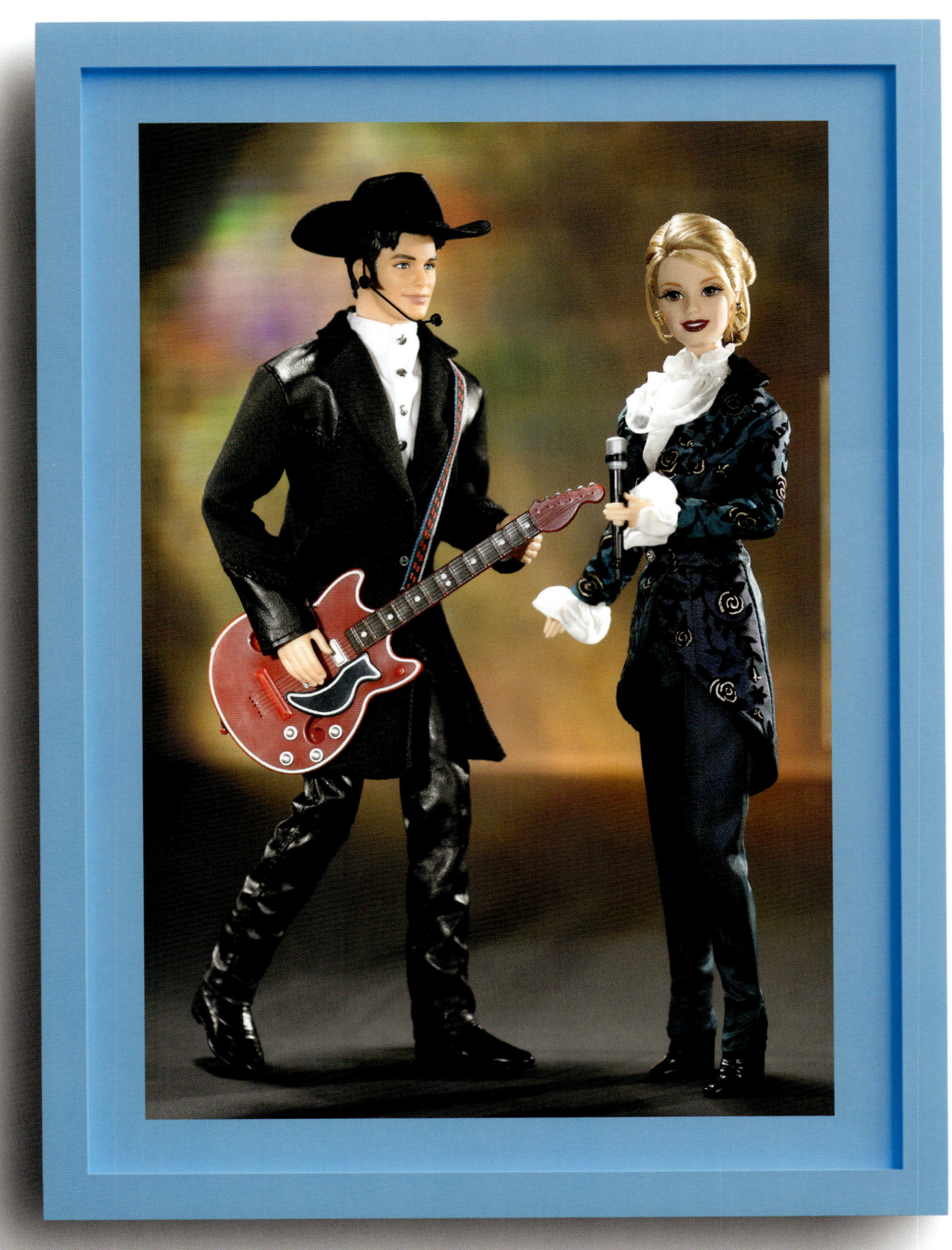

Barbie & Ken Country Duet, 1998.

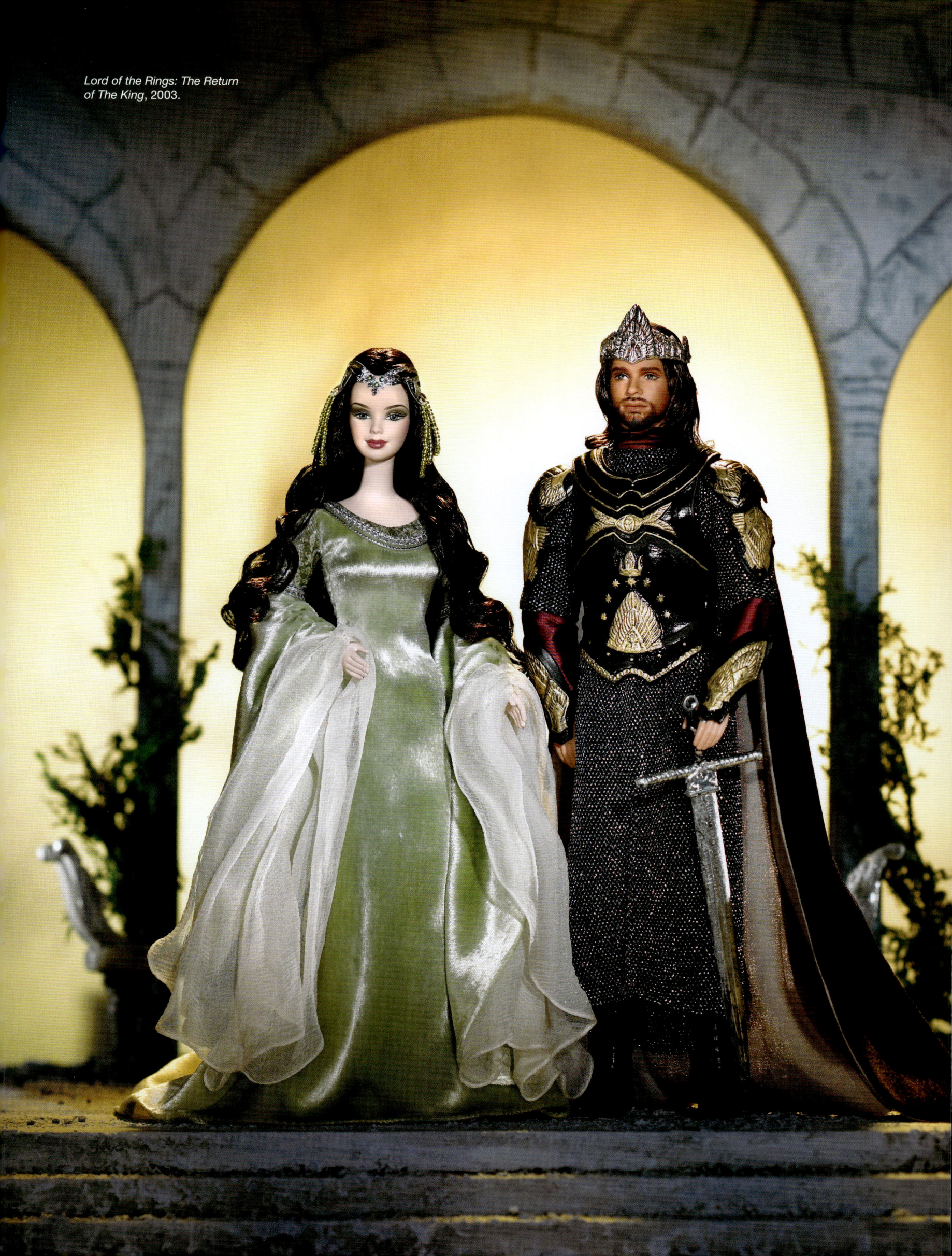
Lord of the Rings: The Return of The King, 2003.

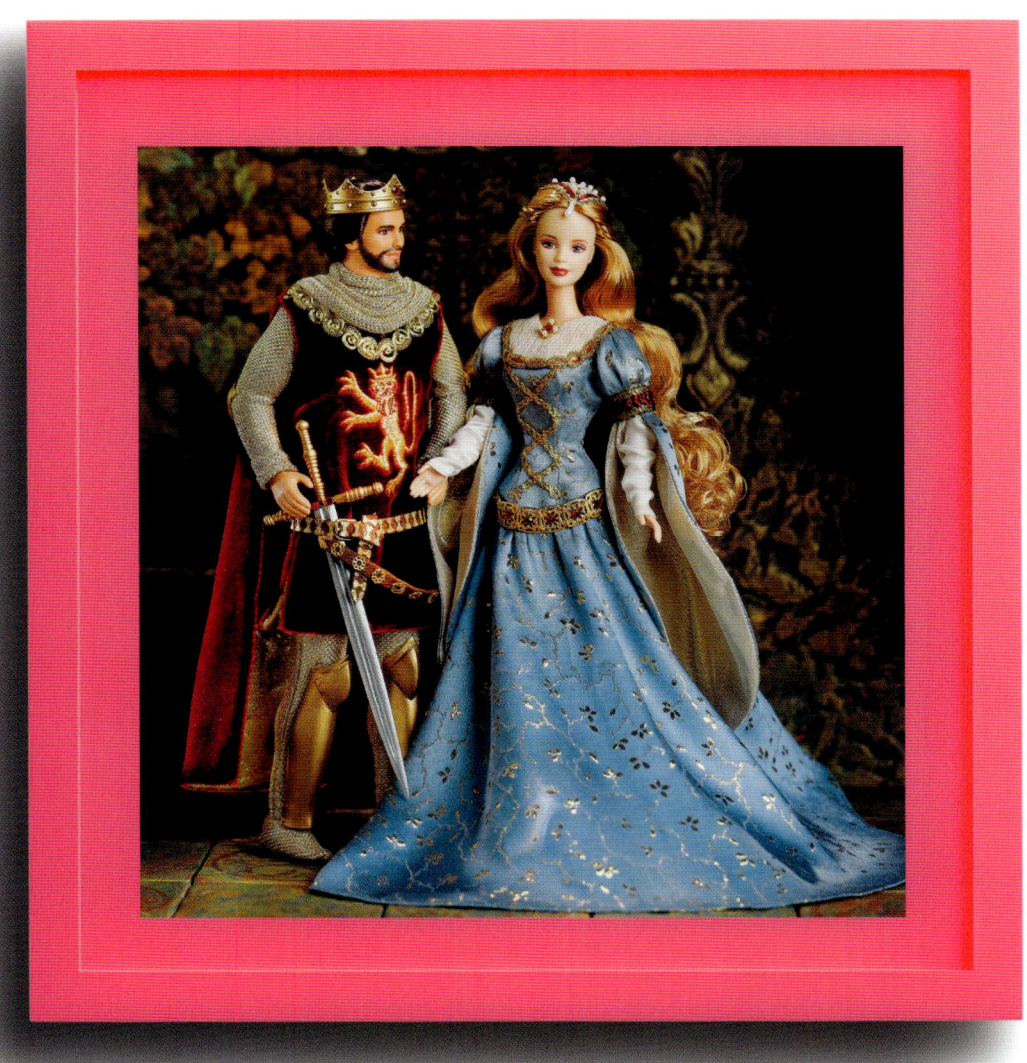

1999
Happy Holidays Indian Special Edition
King Arthur and Queen Guinevere

2000
Addams Family
Merlin & Morgan le Fay

2001
Tales of the Arabian Nights
The Munsters

King Arthur and Queen Guinevere, *1999 and* Merlin & Morgan le Fay, 2000.

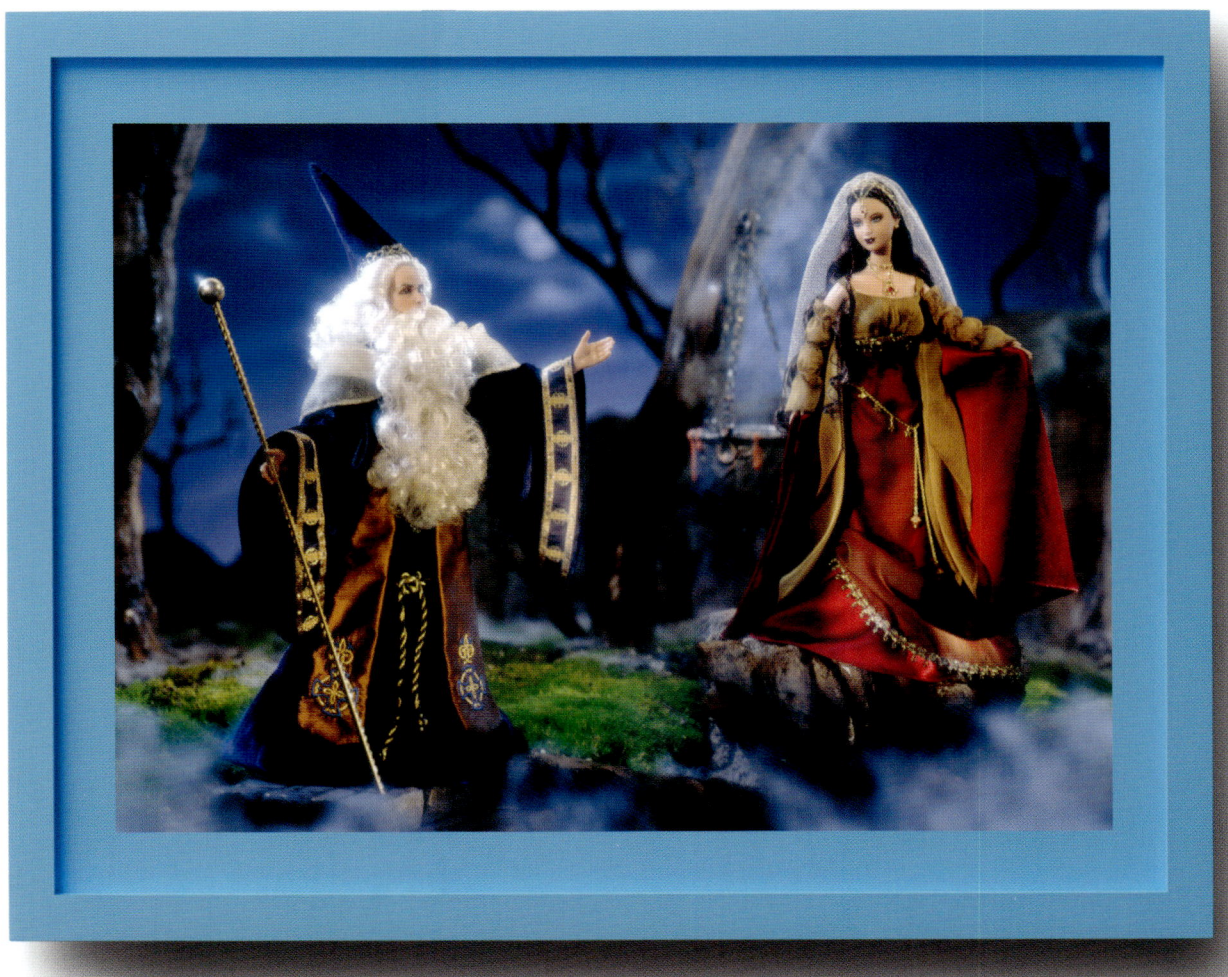

2002
James Bond 007
Tango

2003
Barbie Fashion Model Collection/45th
 Anniversary Gift Set
Jude Deveraux "The Raider"
 The Waltz
Lord of the Rings: The Return
of the King (Barbie and Ken
 as Arwen and Aragorn)

2004
Barbie as The Princess and the Pauper/
 Princess Anneliese and Julian Wedding
 Gift Set (Barbie, Ken, and Kelly)

2006
Barbie as Sleeping Beauty Gift Set
 (Barbie, Ken, and Kelly)
Friday Night Dream Date Gift Set
 Zac Posen Gift Set

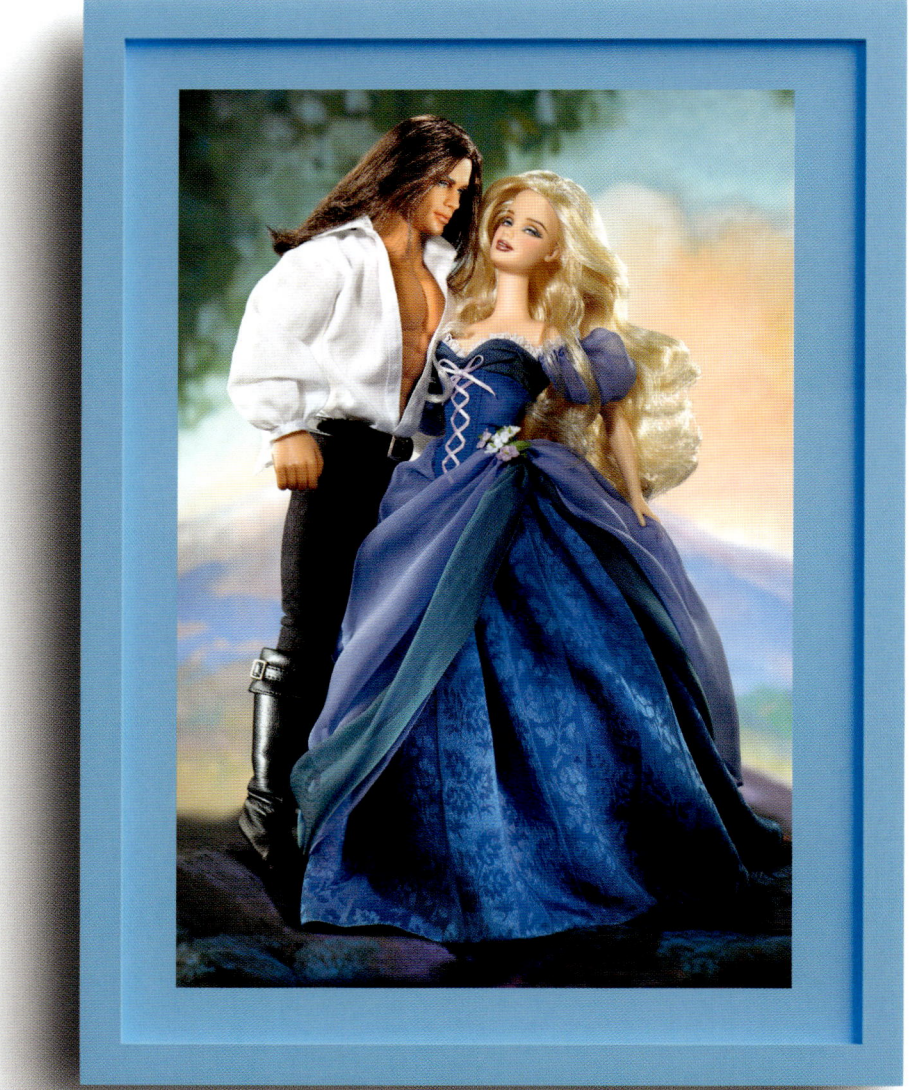

Jude Deveraux "The Raider,"
2003 and Dream Date,
1961 and 2006.

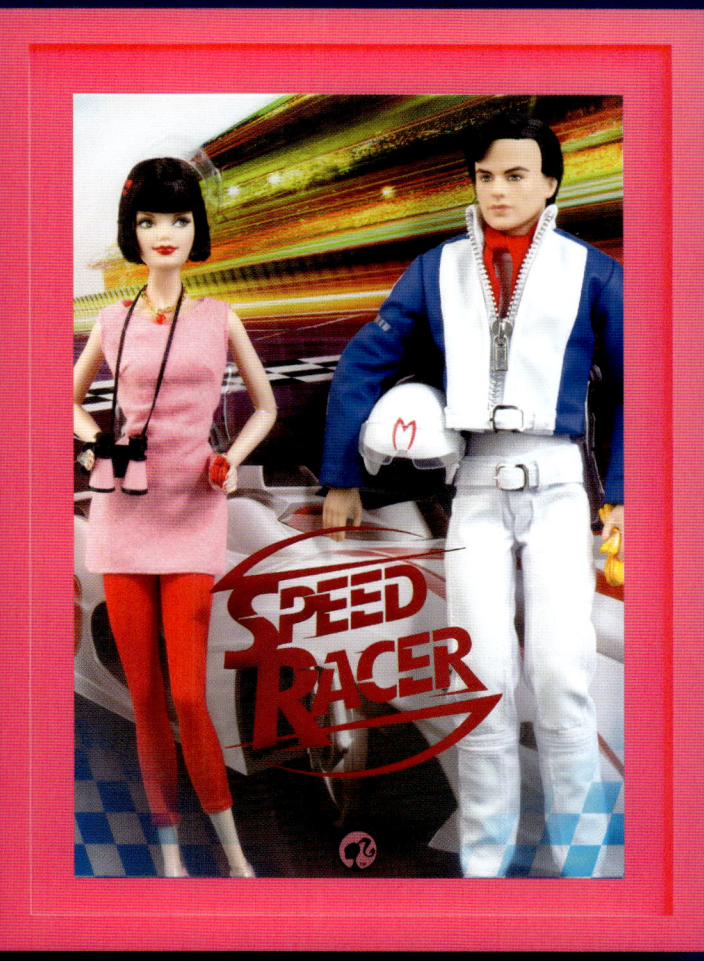

2007
Speed Racer Gift Set

2008
Barbie In India (Barbie and Ken)
(India, European Edition)
Campus Spirit Gift Set

2009
*Barbie Princess & Prince
Picture Harley-Davidson
Wedding Day Gift Set*

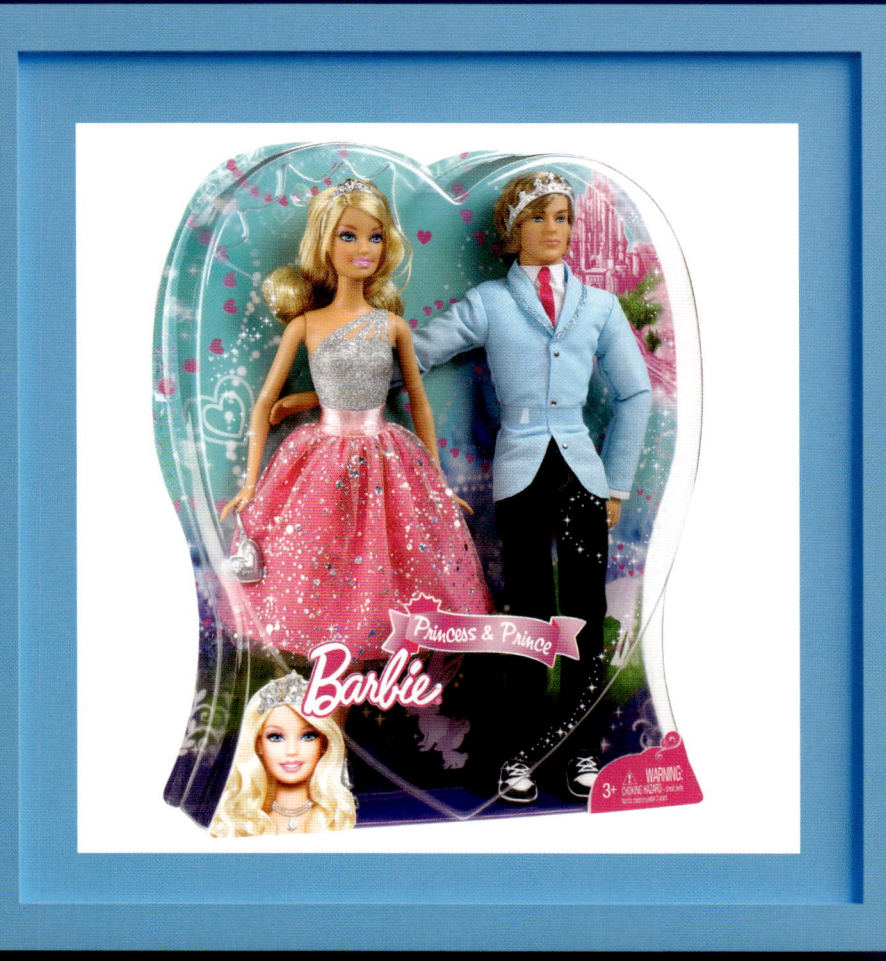

Speed Racer, 2007 and
Princess and Prince, 2009.

2010
Picture Toy Story 3: Made For Each Other
Police Officer and Firefighter

2011
In the Swim
She Said Yes!

2016
Moschino Gift set

2020
Wonder Woman 1984 Gift set

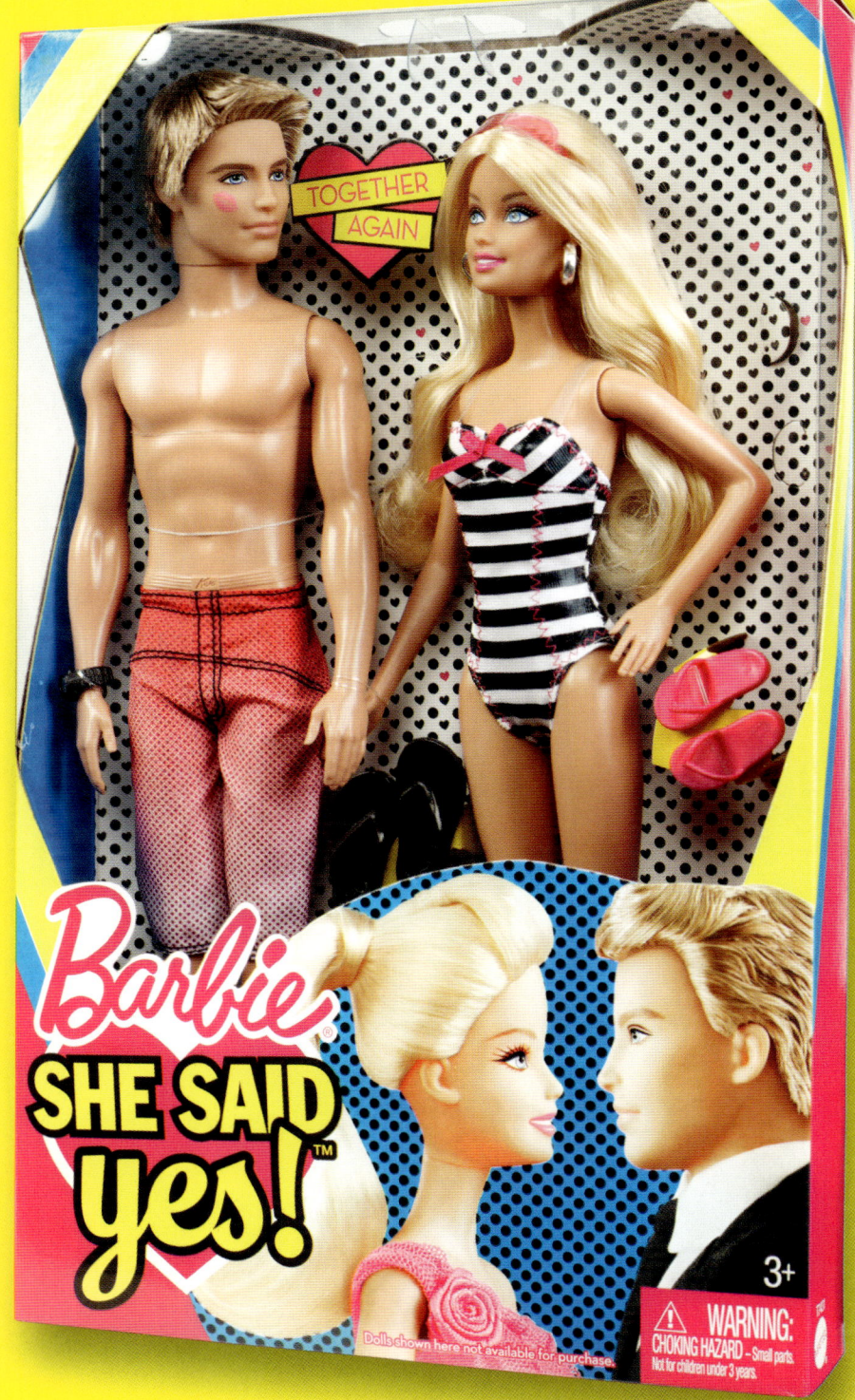

She Said Yes, 2011.

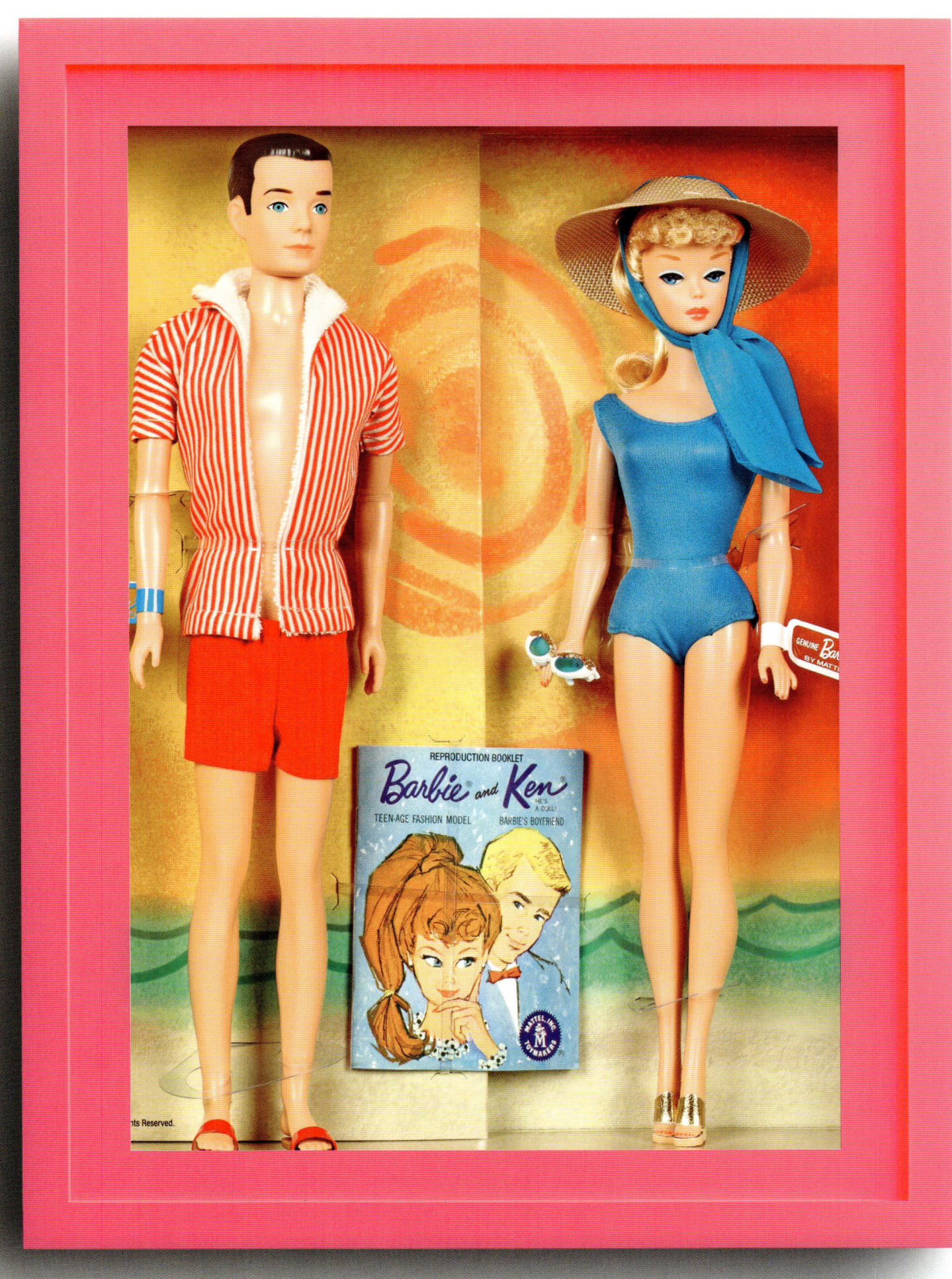

In the Swim, 2011.

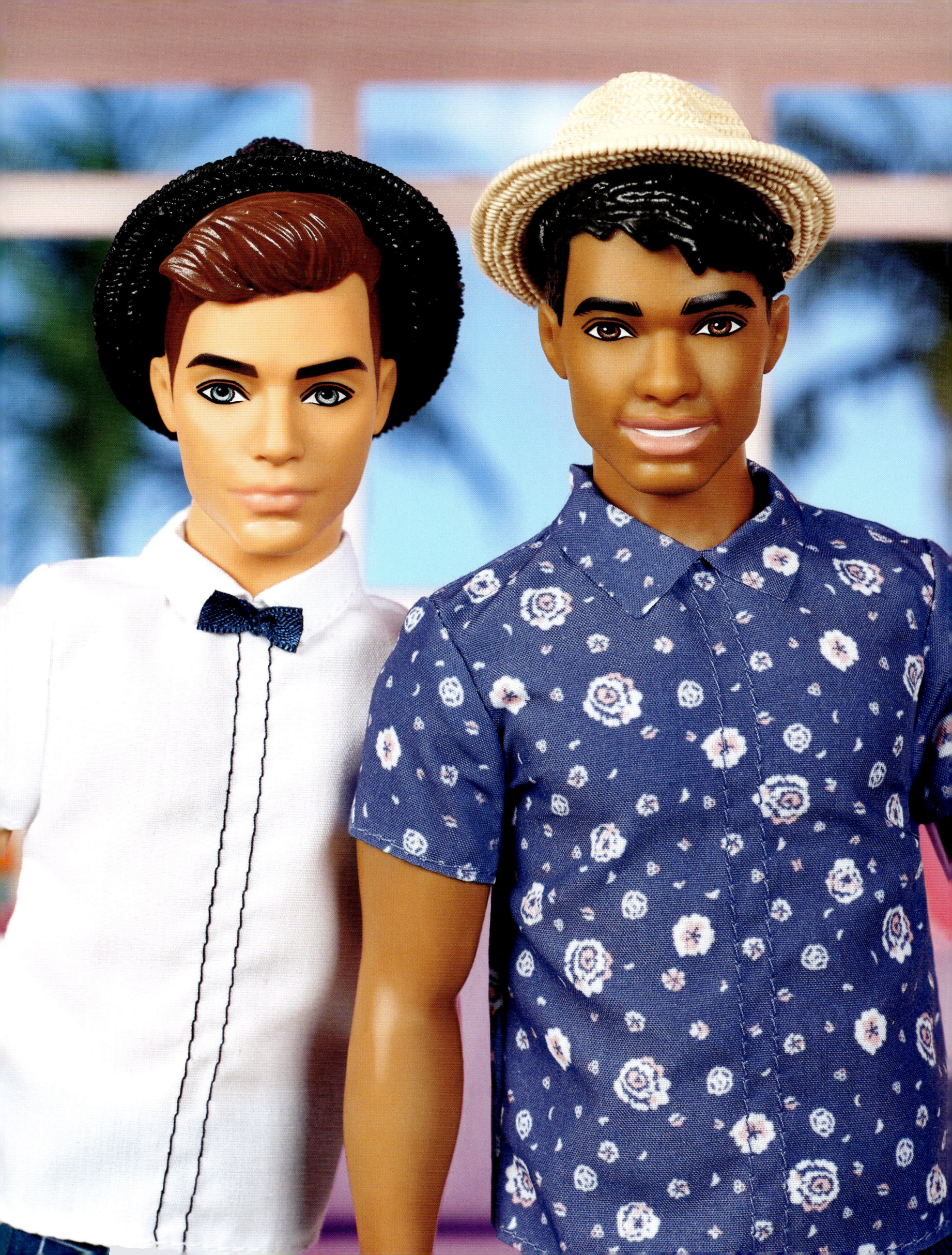

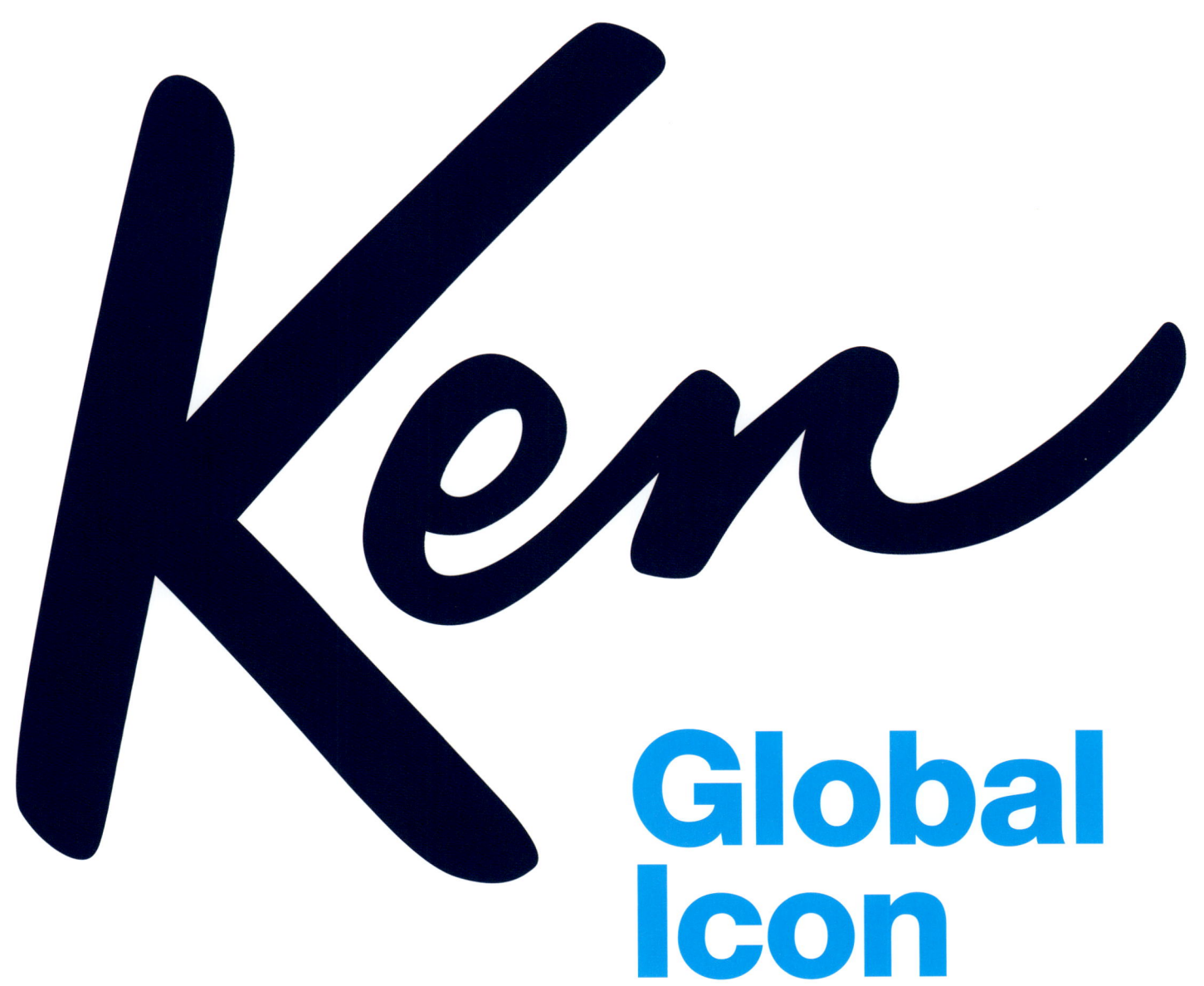

Ken

Global Icon

Everyone needs a Ken!

Previous page:
Ken Fashionistas dolls, 2025.

From his very first appearance in 1961, Ken has mostly played two roles: Barbie's companion and boyfriend. At first, no further detail was provided about him—allowing children to use their imaginations to create his backstory, careers, and adventures. From a certain point of view, this creative freedom was a strength because it left so many possibilities for this new character. If we study Ken's arc, we see that his character made the most notable transformation in terms of behavior and identity within the Barbie universe. In the early years, he was devoted to being Barbie's supportive, sports-loving partner, but he gradually came into his own—so much so that in 2004, after forty-three years, the couple broke up when Ken decided not to marry Barbie. At the time, Mattel's VP of marketing, Russell Arons, stated that Barbie had grown tired of Ken's indecisiveness and decided it was time to spend some time apart. "Like other celebrity couples, their Hollywood romance has come to an end." But it was Ken's great tenacity that won her back in 2011, with a spectacular advertising campaign launched between New York and Los Angeles, built around a slogan that left no room for doubt: "Barbie, I want you!"

And it's not just in love that we see Ken's change of course—we can see it in his looks too. After transforming into SuperStar Ken in 1978—complete with a new face mold, a dazzling smile, dimples, blue eyes, and platinum-blond hair parted to the side—Ken's evolution continued in 1981 when Sunsational Malibu Ken marked the debut of the first Black Ken, with a stylish Afro hairstyle and a bright yellow swimsuit.

From the 1990s on, more attuned to streetwear and pop and punk cultures, Ken began to take on the role of fashion icon as well, becoming a model for four different brands that redefined his image: colorful Benetton editions in 1990 and 1991 (United Colors of Benetton Ken), a distinctly street-style version in 2005

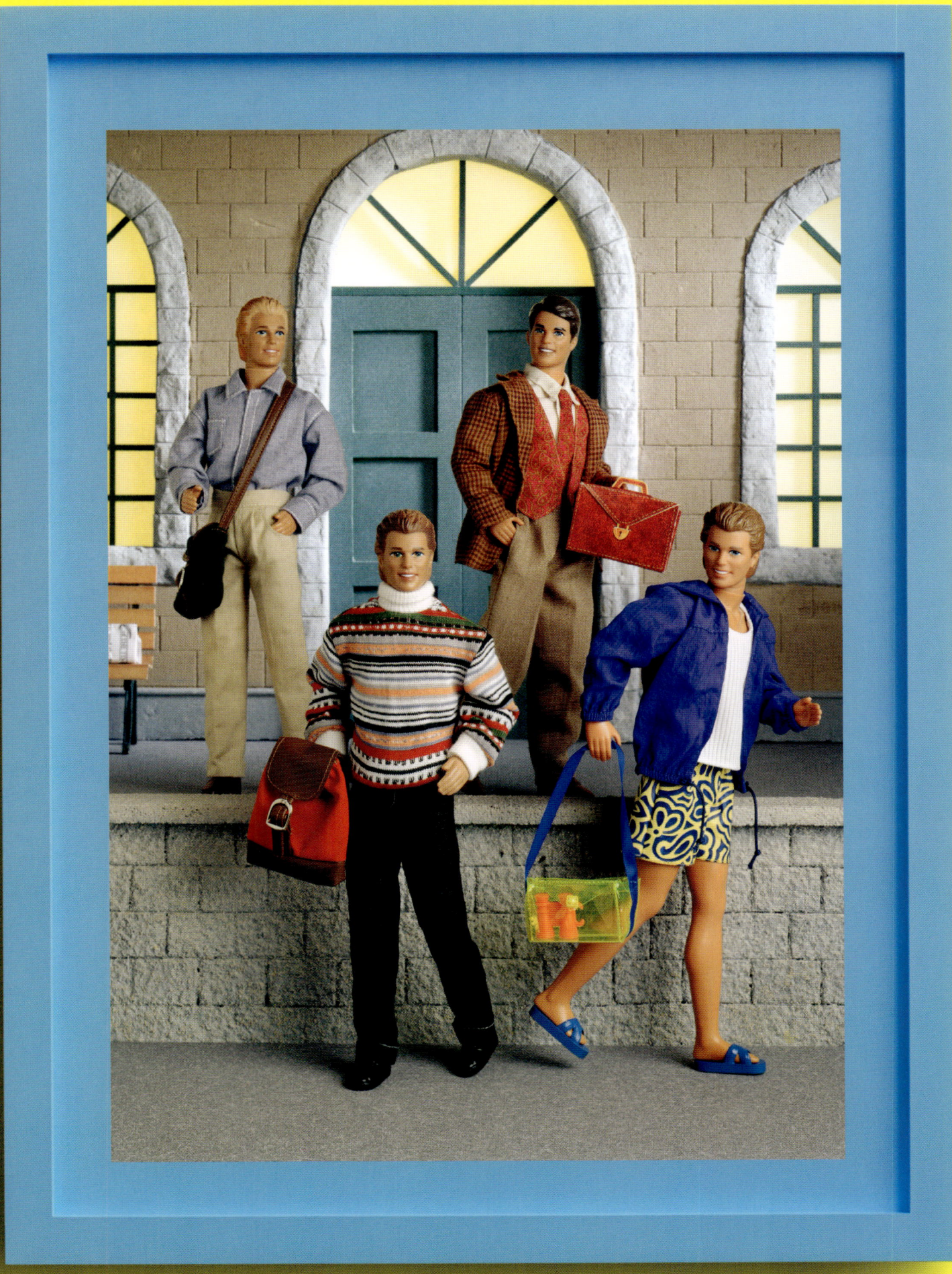

Selected outfits from the
On The Go Fashions, 1994.

(by Phillip Bloch), a darker, edgier reinterpretation in 2008 (by Gareth Pugh), and an unmistakably pop vision in 2016 thanks to Jeremy Scott for Moschino. But the real revolution came in 2011 with the launch of the Ken Fashionistas line. Fifteen new Ken dolls were introduced in 2017, with three different body types (original, slim, and broad), seven skin tones, nine face shapes, eight hair colors, and nine different hairstyles, all dressed in looks that reflected a distinctly contemporary style, from sporty to professional. This was a turning point, which catapulted Ken into a new generation defined by a global outlook—one that, like Barbie's world, now better reflected the world around us. The message Ken now embodies is crystal clear: There's no single "normal," no one standard of beauty.

Ken has, in short, radically transformed. The image of "Barbie's Boyfriend," as he appeared in 1961, is long outdated. In its place stands a fully realized character. And beginning in 2023, with the release of the Barbie movie, we witnessed a true "Kenaissance"—a rebirth that turned Ken into a full-fledged star, ready to write a new story where everyone can see themselves reflected. Because today, Ken belongs to everyone. And everyone wants to be Ken.

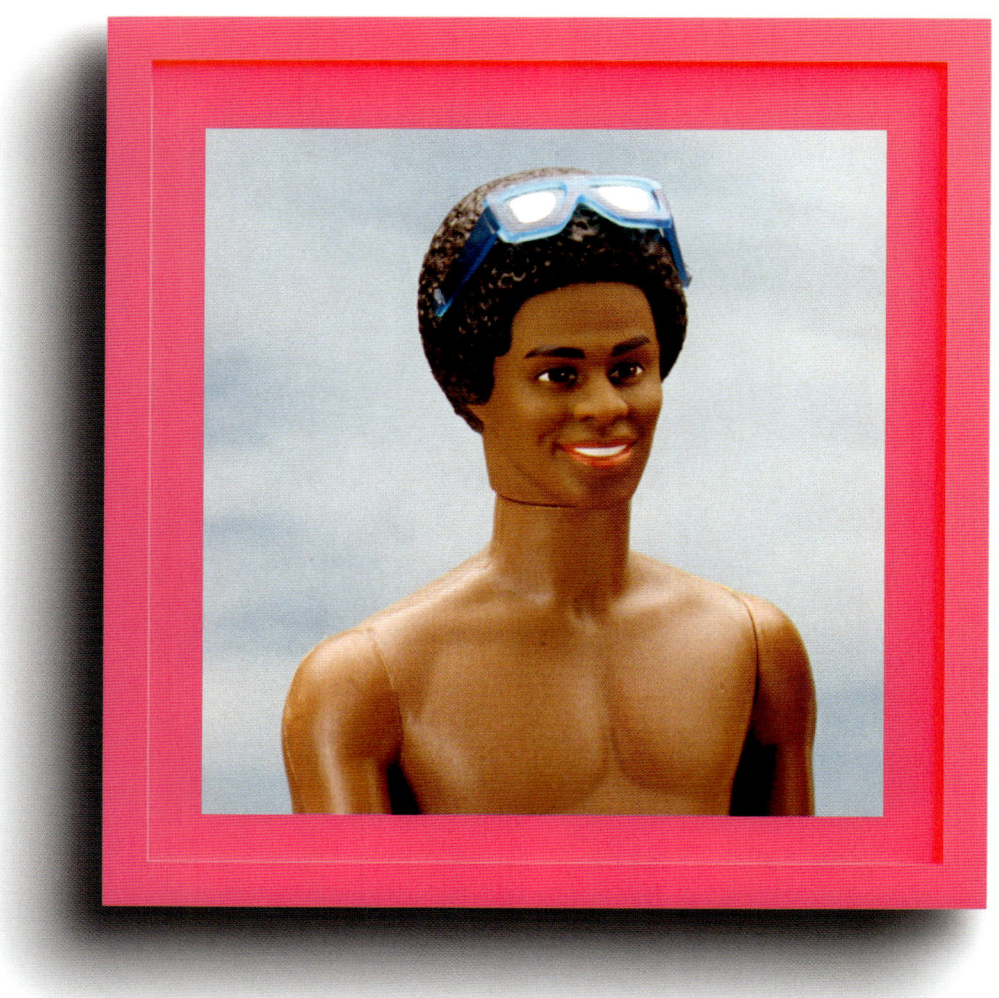

Sunsational Malibu Ken, 1983.

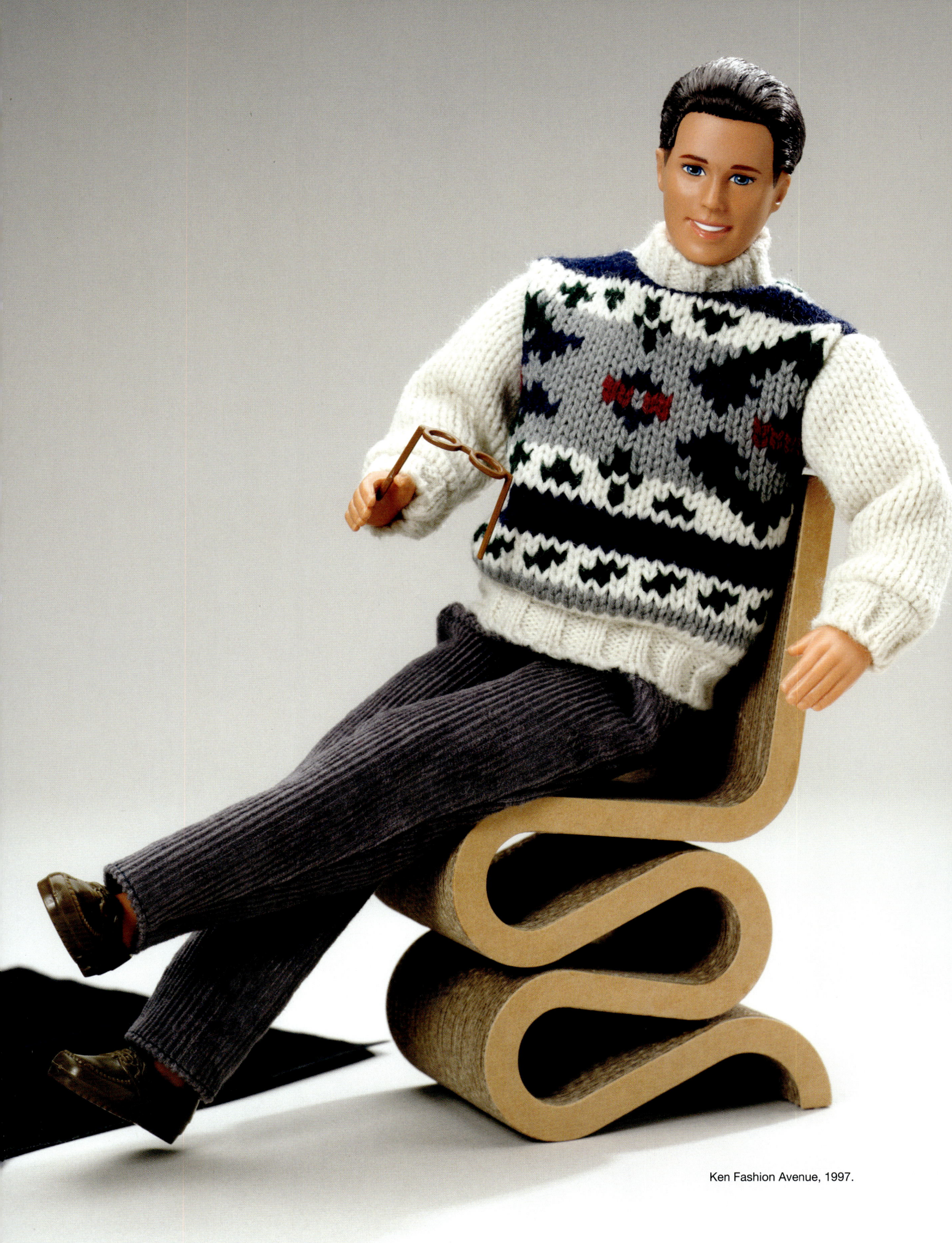
Ken Fashion Avenue, 1997.

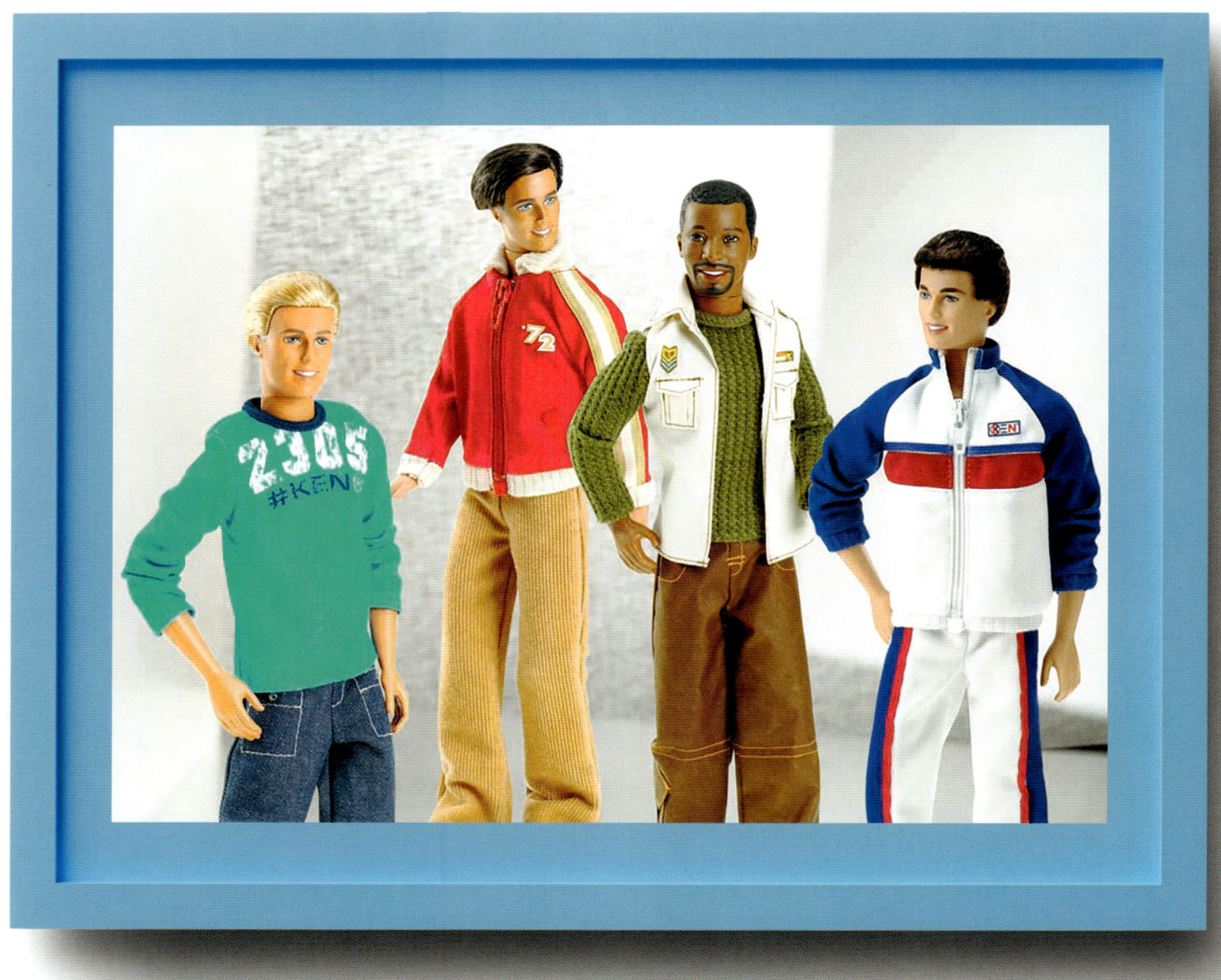

Fashion Ken, 2004.

Opposite and pages 203-6:
Barbie the Movie Ken, 2023.

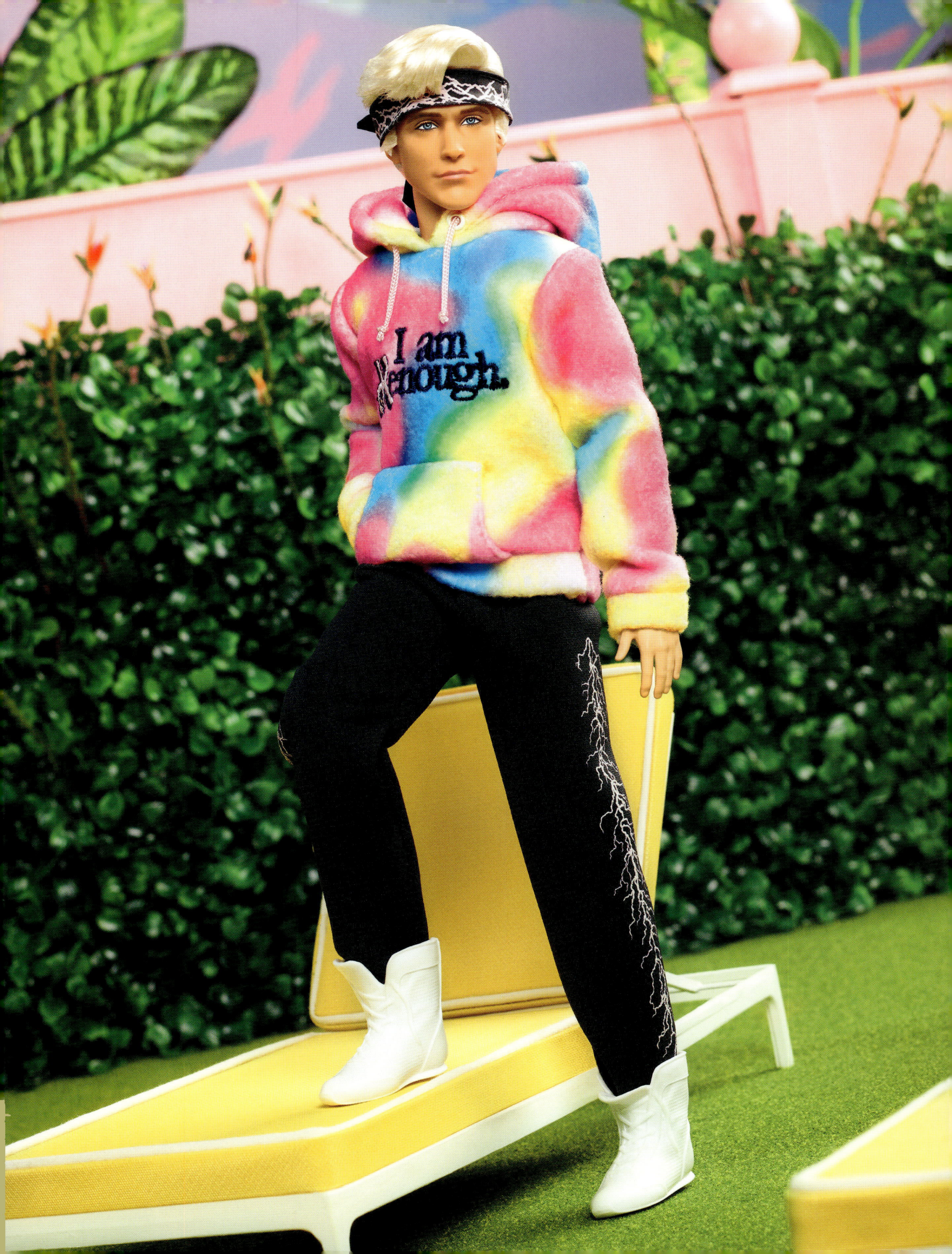

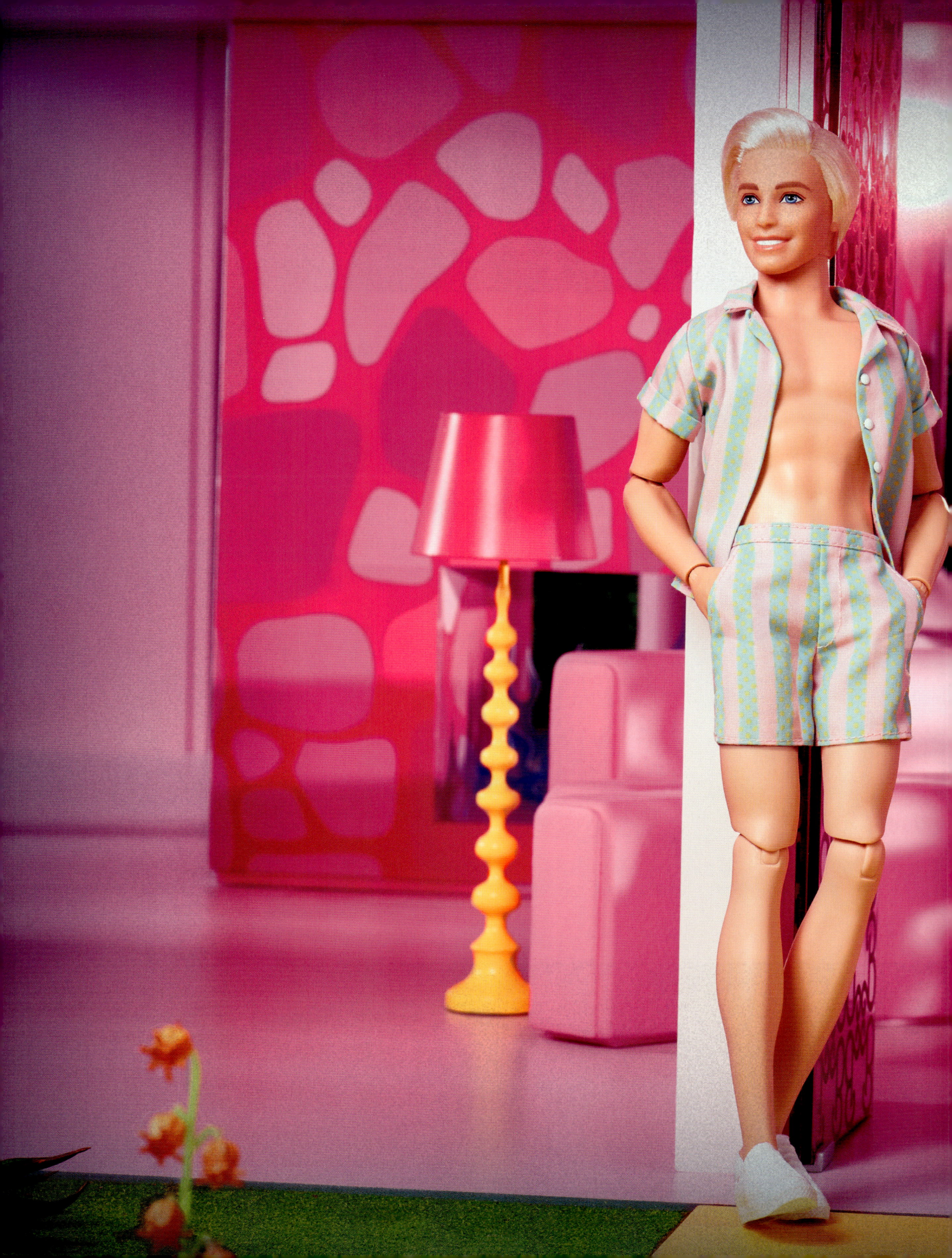

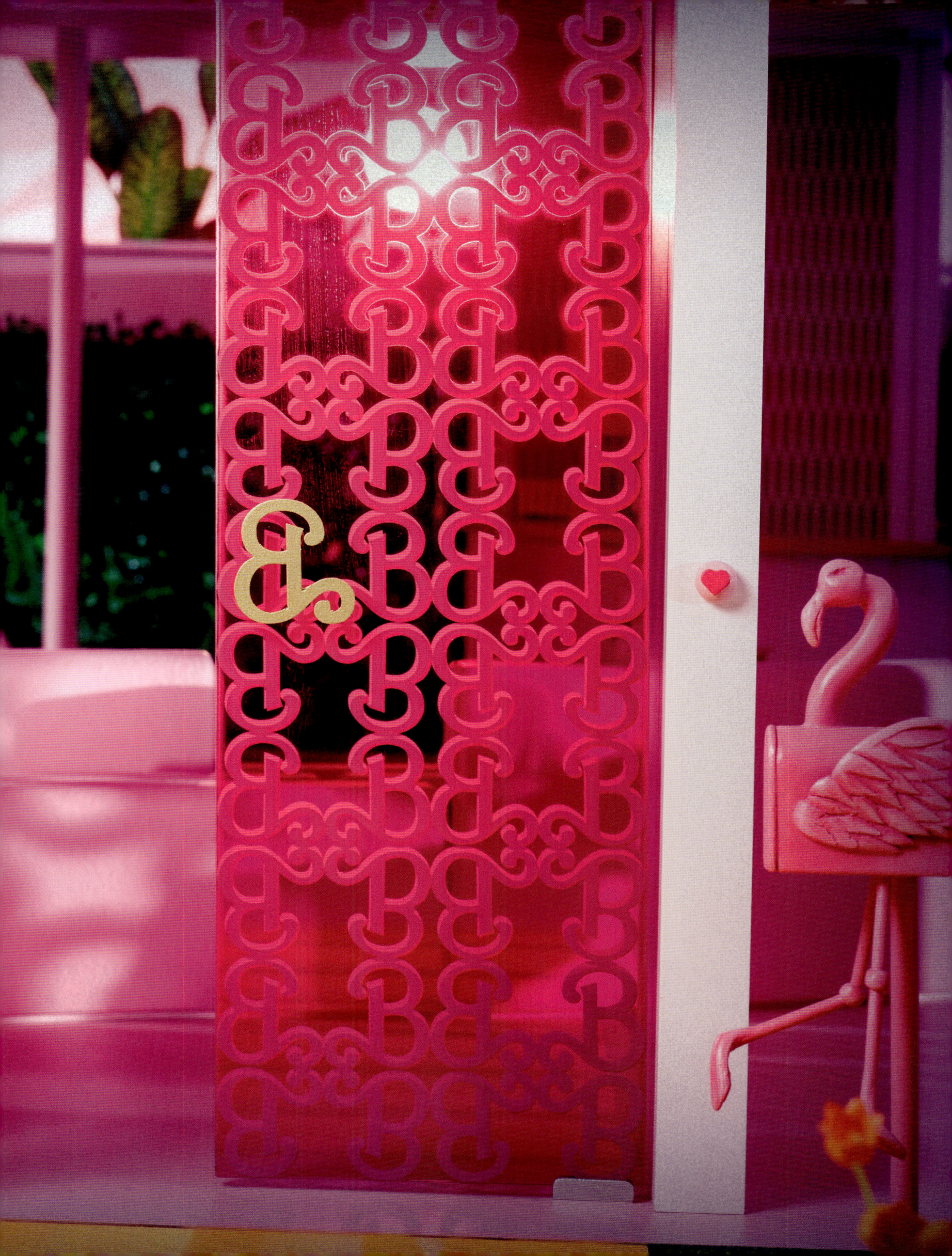

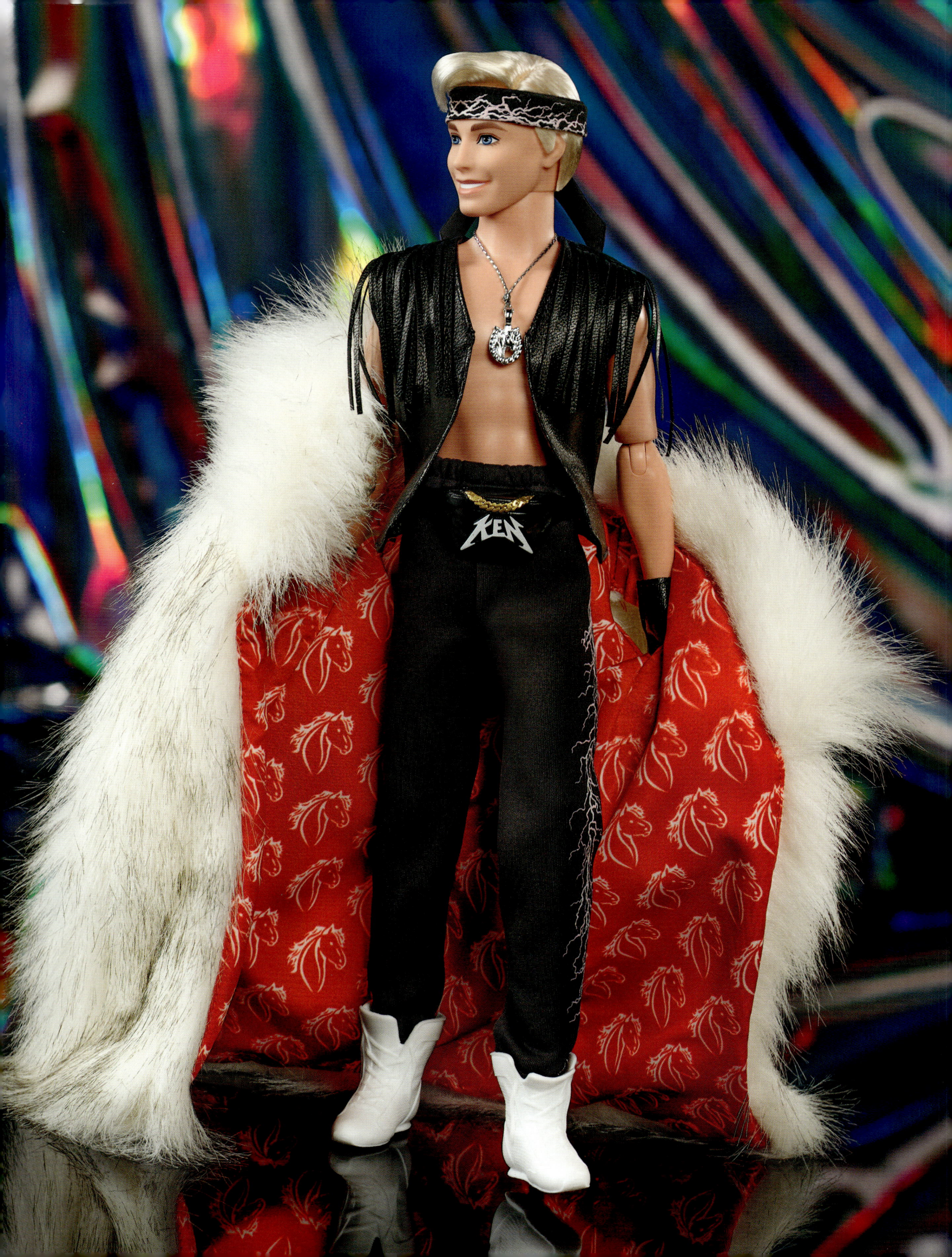

Bibliography

Mattel Catalogue of Toys, 1961–2025

Augustyniak, J. Michael. *The Barbie Doll Boom: Identification & Values*. Collector, 1996.

Barbie: Guida completa fashion. Fabbri, 2000.

Barbie: Künstler und Designer gestalten für und um Barbie. Wunderlich, 1994.

Barbie Bazaar: Mattel & Christmas Catalog Reprints of Barbie Doll 1959–1965. Murat Caviale, 1994.

Bazzano, Nicoletta. *La donna perfetta: Storia di Barbie*. Editori Laterza, 2008.

BillyBoy*. *Barbie: Her Life & Times*. Crown, 1987.

Blitman, Joe. *Barbie Doll & Her Mod, Mod, Mod World of Fashion: 1967–1972*. Hobby House, 1996.

Capella, Massimiliano. *Barbie: The Icon*. 1st ed. G Editions, 2016.

Capella, Massimiliano. *Barbie: The Icon Celebration*. 2nd ed. 24 ORE Cultura, 2024.

Cianfanelli, Elisabetta, James H. Dickson, Gabriele Goretti, and Emilio Petrone. *Barbie sogna Caterina de' Medici*. Polistampa, 2008.

Coleman, Dorothy S., Elisabeth A. Coleman, and Evelyn J. Coleman. *The Collector's Book of Dolls' Clothes: Costumes in Miniature: 1700–1929*. Crown, 1975.

Deutsch, Stefanie. *Barbie: The First 30 Years: 1959 through 1989: An Identification and Value Guide*. Collector, 1996.

DeWein, Sibyl and Joan Ashabraner. *The Collector's Encyclopedia of Barbie Dolls and Collectibles*. 1st ed. Collector, 1977.

DeWein, Sibyl and Joan Ashabraner. *The Collector's Encyclopedia of Barbie Dolls and Collectibles*. 2nd ed. Collector, 1988.

DeWein, Sibyl St. John. *Collectible Barbie Dolls: 1977–1979*. Published by the author, 1980.

Doreen Carvajal. "With Museum Shows in Europe, Barbie Gets Her Moment with the Masters." *The New York Times*, March 11, 2016.

Eames, Sarah Sink. *Barbie Fashion: The Complete History of the Wardrobes of Barbie Doll, Her Friends and Her Family: Vol. 1, 1959–1967*. Collector, 1990.

Fagnola, Daniela. "Una Barbie oggi per salvare una donna domani." *Vogue Italia*, November 1997.

Farago, Stephanie. *The Magic & Romance of Art Dolls*. Farago, 1986.

Fennick, Janine. *The Collectible Barbie Doll: An Illustrated Guide to Her Dreamy World*. Courage Books, 1996.

Fox, Carl. *Le bambole*. Garzanti, 1973.

Gayton, Anthony. *The original Ken® Book: Ken® & Allan Dolls and Their Clothing 1961–1967*. 7th ed. Published by the author, 2025.

Gellene, Denise. "Fame Dogs 'Real' Barbie, Ken." *Los Angeles Times*, January 29, 1989.

Handler, Ruth and Jacqueline Shannon. *Dream Doll: The Ruth Handler Story*. Longmeadow Press, 1994.

Gerber, Robin. *Barbie and Ruth: The Story of the World's Most Famous Doll and the Woman Who Created Her*. Collins Business, 2009.

Germano, Ivo. *Barbie: Il fascino irresistibile di una bambola legendaria*. Castelvecchi, 2000.

Hanquez-Maincent, Marie-Françoise. *Barbie poupée totem: Entre mère et fille, lien ou rupture?* Autrement, 1998.

"It's splitsville for Barbie and Ken." *CBS News*, February 12, 2004.

Jacobs, Laura. *Barbie: What a Doll!* Artabras, 1994.

Jacobs, Laura. *Barbie: In Fashion*. Abbeville, 1994.

La casa di Barbie. Giunti, 1976.

Lawrence, Cynthia and Bette Lou Maybee. *Here's Barbie: Stories About the Fabulous Barbie and Her Boyfriend Ken*. Random House, 1962.

Le Dan, Dominique. *Barbie, Midge, Ken et les autres*. Éditions de l'amateur, 1998.

Levinthal, David. *Barbara Millicent Roberts: An Original*. Pantheon, 1998.

Lord, M. G. *Forever Barbie: The Unauthorized Biography of a Real Doll*. Avon, 1995.

Mandeville, Glenn A. *5th Doll Fashion Anthology: Price Guide*. Hobby House, 1996.

Manos, Paris and Susan Manos. *The World of Barbie Dolls*. Collector, 1983.

Massimo Arcangeli and Sandro Mariani. "Ken, lo storico fidanzato di Barbie, compie (anche lui) 60 anni." *Il Fatto Quotidiano*, May 2, 2021.

Melillo, Marco. *The Ultimate Barbie Doll Book*. Krause, 1996.

Miranda Collinge. "The Hollow Man: What Do You Mean 'Just' Ken?" *Esquire*, June 22, 2023.

Monier, Anne. *Barbie*. Musée des Arts Décoratifs, 2016. Published following the exhibition *Barbie* at the Musée des Arts Décoratifs, Paris.

Noel Ceballos. "La vera storia di Ken, il fidanzato ufficiale di Barbie." *GQ Italia*, July 25 2023.

Olds, Patrick C. *The Barbie Doll: Years 1959–1996*. Collector, 1996.

Parija Kavilanz. "Barbie's boyfriend Ken gets diverse makeover." *CNN Money*, June 20, 2017.

Rand, Erica. *Barbie's Queer Accessories*. Duke University Press, 1995.

Rogers, Mary F. *Barbie Culture*. Sage, 1999.

Royer, Marie. *My Vintage Barbies: A Comprehensive Reference Guide of Barbie Through the Vintage Years 1959–1979 and Beyond*. MVB Circle, 2021.

Sarasohn-Kahn, Jane. *Contemporary Barbie Dolls: 1980 and Beyond*. Antique Trader, 1997.

Scacchi, Anna. "Barbie da fidanzata d'America a icona pop." In *Miti americani oggi*, edited by Caterina Ricciardi and Sabrina Vellucci. Diabasis, 2005.

Scottie Andrew. "Who is Ken, really? The history of the world's most misunderstood doll." *CNN Style*, July 22, 2023.

Shibano, Keiko Kimura. *Barbie in Japan*. Murat Caviale, 1994.

Spencer, Carol. *Dressing Barbie: A Celebration of the Clothes That Made America's Favorite Doll and the Incredible Woman Behind Them*. Harper, 2023.

Steele, Valerie. *Art, Design, and Barbie: The Evolution of a Cultural Icon*. Exhibitions International, 1995.

Tarnowska, Maree. *Poupées de mode*. Éditions d'art Monelle Hayot, 1986.

Thiemer, François. *Barbie: Poupée de collection*. Polichinelle, 1985.

Thomas, Jeannie Banks. *Naked Barbies, Warrior Jones, and Other Forms of Visible Gender*. University of Illinois, 2003.

Toffoletti, Kim. *Cyborgs and Barbie Dolls: Feminism, Popular Culture and the Posthuman Body*. I. B. Tauris, 2007.

Tosa, Marco. *Barbie: I mille volti di un mito*. Mondadori, 1997.

Tosa, Marco. *Effetto Bambola: Storia, Tecnica, Collezionismo*. Idealibri, 1987.

Tosa, Marco. *Le bambole*. 1st ed. Idealibri, 1989.

Tosa, Marco. *Le bambole*. 2nd ed. Fabbri Editori, 1991.

Westenhouser, Kitturah B. *The Story of Barbie*. 1st ed. Collector, 1994.

Westenhouser, Kitturah B. *The Story of Barbie Doll*. 2nd ed. Collector, 1999.

Zak Maoui. "*Barbie* rende (finalmente) giustizia ad Allan, l'amico dimenticato e meglio vestito di Ken." *GQ Italia*, April 6, 2023.

WEBSITES

www.BarbieDB.com
http://www.manbehindthedoll.com
https://somethingabouttheboy.com

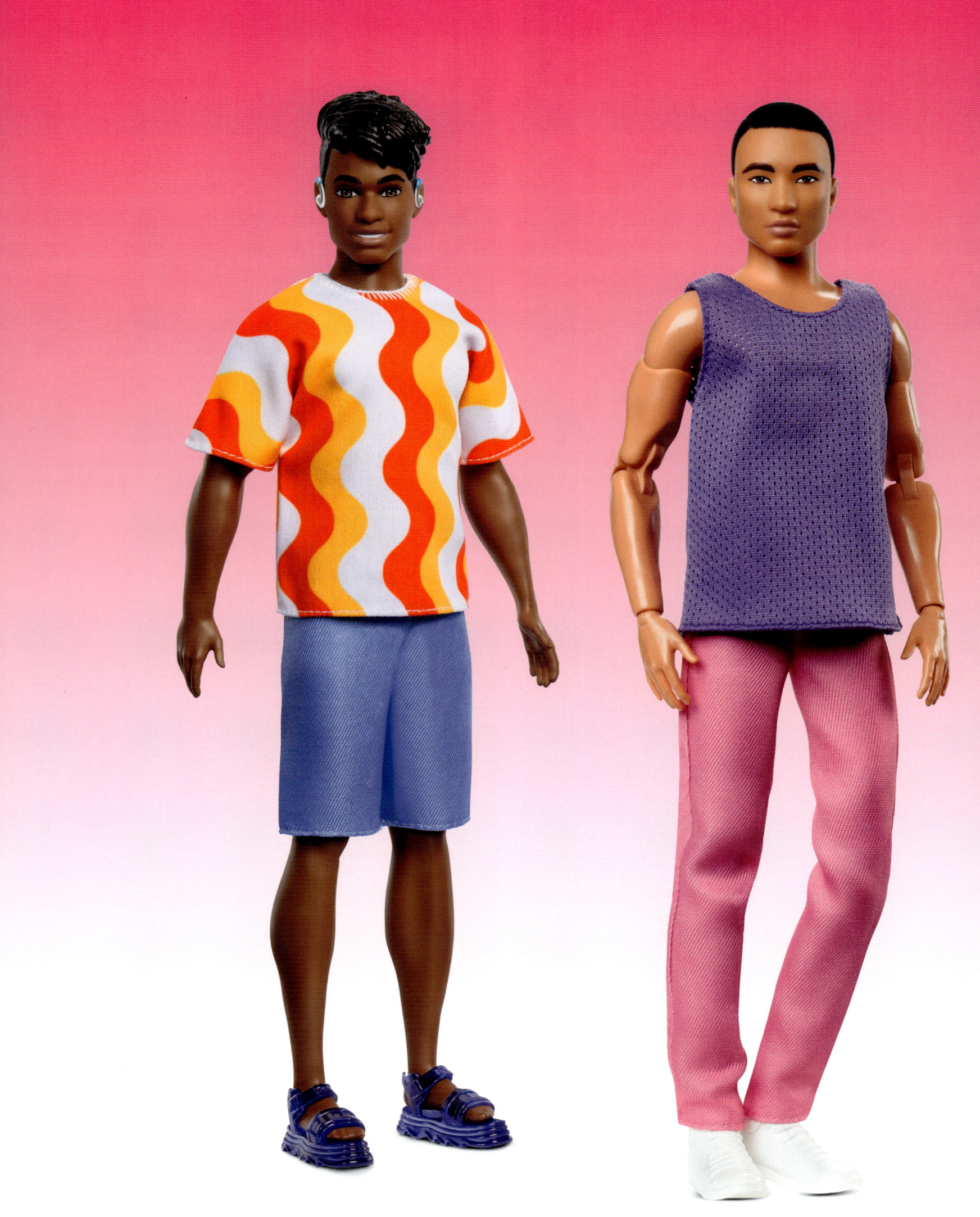

Ken Fashionistas released between 2019 and 2023, including Looks Ken (2022, second from left) and Camping Ken (2022, far right).

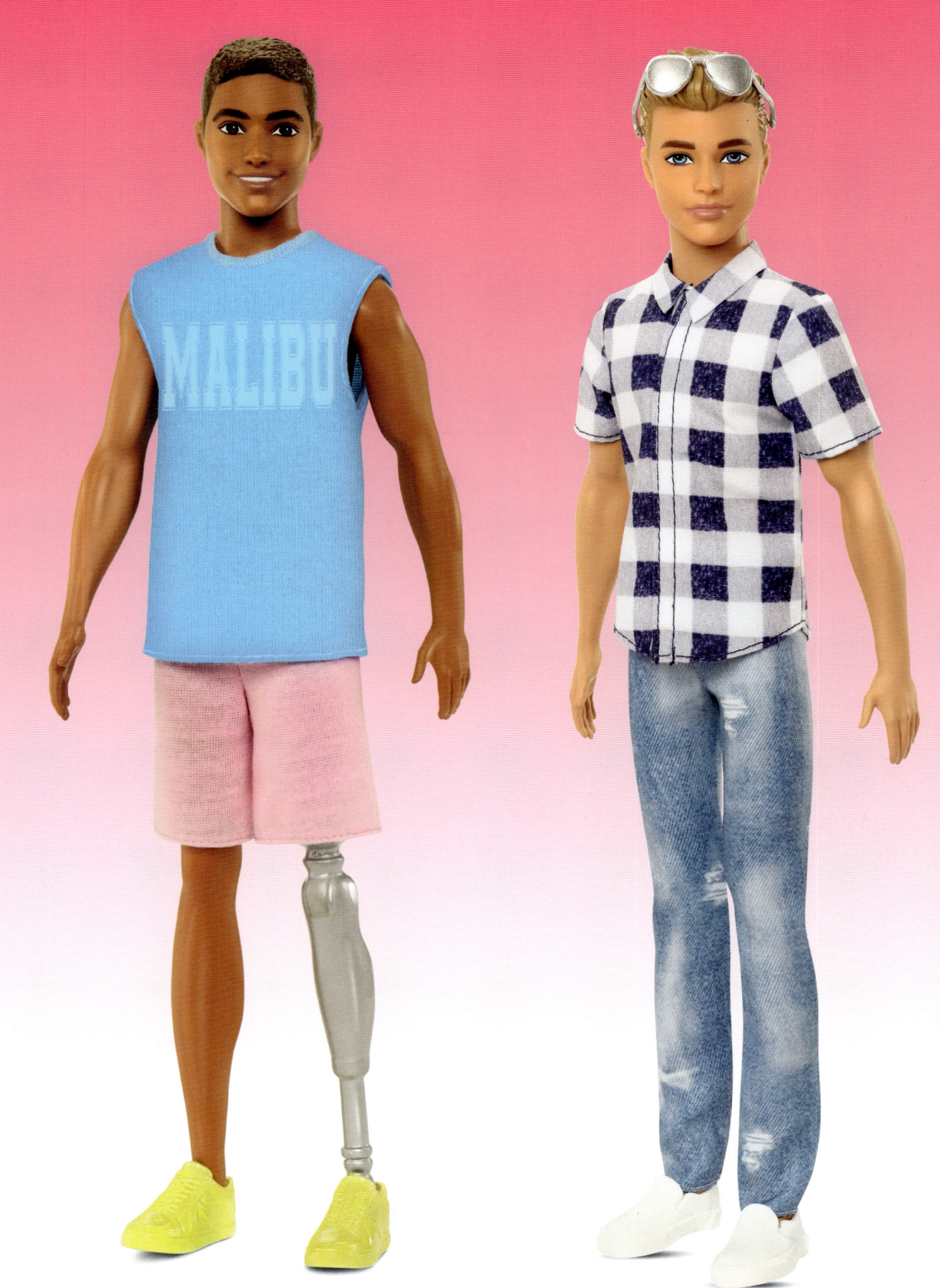

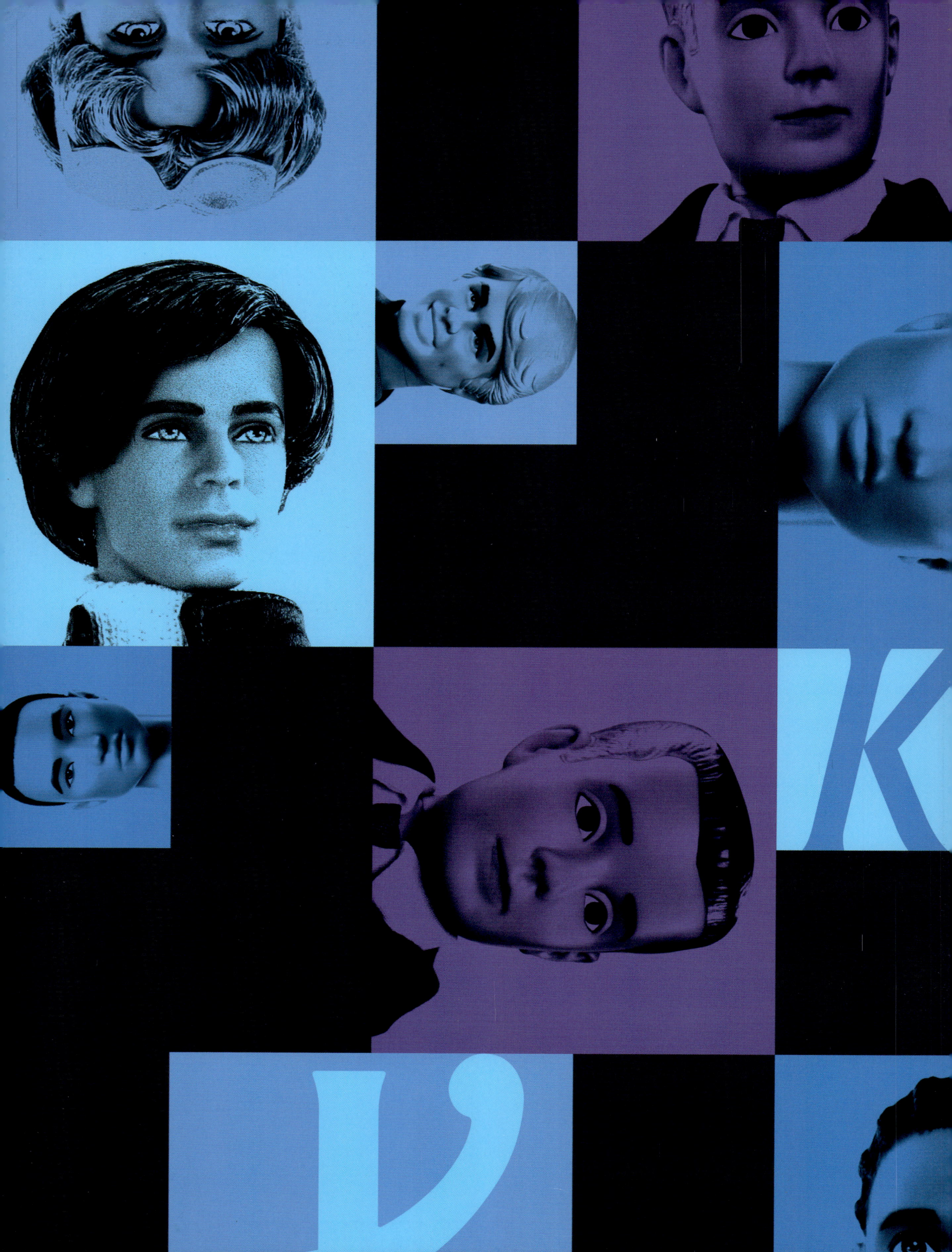